ICELAND

JENNA GOTTLIEB

ICELAND
GREENLAN
SEA
Denmark Strait
Bolungarvík
Ísafjörður
Ísafjarðardjúp
Drangajökull
Húnaflói
Skagafjörður
Arnarfjörður
West Fjords
Patreksfjörður
Breiðavík
Drangsnes
Skagaströnd
Blönduós
Sauðárkrókur
Varmahlíð
Hóp
Reykhólar
Hvammstangi
Laugarbakki
Breiðafjörður
Stykkishólmur
Búðardalur
Hellissandur
Ólafsvík
Grundarfjörður
Snæfellsnes Peninsula
Bifröst
Reykholt
Langjökull
Borgarnes
Hvanneyri
Faxafloí
Akranes
REYKJAVÍK
Laugarvatn
Þingvallavatn
Mosfellsbær
Reykholt
Flúðir
Sandgerði
Hafnarfjörður
Reykjanesbær
Njarðvík
Reykjanes Peninsula
Hveragerði
Selfoss
Grindavík
Stokkseyri
Hella
Hvolsvöllur
NORTH
ATLANTIC
OCEAN
Vestmannaeyjar
Heimaey

NORWEGIAN SEA
Grímsey
Raufarhöfn
Þistilfjörður
Kópasker
85
Bakkafjörður
Bakkaflói
Siglufjörður
Skjálfandi
Ólafsfjörður
Húsavík
Dalvík
Grenivík
Eyjafjörður
87
864
Vopnafjörður
82
North Iceland
Jökulsárgljúfur
Laugar
Akureyri
Reykjahlíð
Mývatn
1
917
Bakkagerði
East Fjords
94
Seyðisfjörður
Egilsstaðir
93
Neskaupstaður
F26
96
Hallormsstaður
Eskifjörður
Reyðarfjörður
The Highlands
Fáskrúðsfjörður
Hálslón
Hofsjökull
Djúpivogur
Kvíslavatn
Vatnajökull
Þórisvatn
Höfn
Langisjór
Öraefajökull
Kirkjubæjarklaustur
204
0
25 mi
25 km
© AVALON TRAVEL

Contents

DISCOVER

Iceland

Scale soaring mountaintops. Dive into some of the clearest water in the world. Explore crystalline ice caves and mineral-rich lava tubes. Hike the rim of a remote volcano that rises from an arctic desert. Witness a rainbow materialize over a thundering waterfall. Iceland is a place not just to see, but to experience.

Iceland is revered for its breathtaking landscapes, unrivaled trekking, and arctic wildlife. Three national parks and a dozen smaller reserves protect these resources. Vatnajökull National Park makes up 13 percent of the country and contains the largest glacier in the world outside the poles. Geothermal pools, like the famous milky waters of the Blue Lagoon, bubble up from beneath the earth and provide a place to soak away your worries.

If city life is more your speed, Reykjavík is waiting for you. Stroll the capital's streets and explore the galleries, coffeehouses, intimate concert venues, and music shops—you can't help but feel the city's creative energy. Handcrafted local beers replace specialty coffees as the drink of choice come evening time, when low-key daytime hangouts morph into pulsing parties that fuel a thriving nightlife scene.

Clockwise from top left: Icelandic horses; Snorralaug (Snorri's Pool) in Reykholt; Dettifoss waterfall; Reykjavík's Parliament House; whale near Húsavík; fireworks over Akranes.

In summer, the days seem endless—the sun shines for nearly 24 hours around the solstice. And winter tourism is increasing, with visitors lured by the chance to hunt the northern lights, yet another of Iceland's spectacular natural wonders. Watching the lights flicker in the sky, changing colors, disappearing and popping up again stronger and brighter, makes braving the wind and rain worth it.

For scenery and adventure, Iceland is unmatched.

Clockwise from top left: northern lights appearing in the west; Jökulsárlón, the Glacier Lagoon; annual Viking Festival in Hafnarfjörður; Siglufjörður.

10 TOP EXPERIENCES

1 **Northern Lights:** Watching the green and white lights dance and flicker in the sky is a magical experience (page 19).

2 **Blue Lagoon:** Bathe in the famous milky blue waters (page 86) of the lagoon, and then seek out some of the island's other **hot springs** and **swimming pools** (page 27).

3 **Hiking:** Iceland is a hiker's paradise with mountains, volcanoes, lava fields, and valleys begging to be explored (page 29).

4 Wildlife-Watching: From reindeer to puffins to whales, Iceland is rich with wildlife (page 25).

<<<

5 Road-Tripping the Ring Road: Explore the country's highlights via this loop road around the island (page 22).

>>>

6 The Golden Circle: Touring this classic route provides a perfect introduction to Iceland's natural wonders (page 90).

<<<

7 **Waterfalls:** Take in wondrous waterfalls like **Goðafoss** (page 188) and **Dettifoss** (page 200).

8 National Parks: Iceland's three majestic national parks are free to enter and explore (pages 90, 130, 199, and 232).

9 Jökulsárlón: You won't be able to stop taking photos at the Glacier Lagoon, where icebergs that calve from the glacier's edge drift by (page 231).

10 Reykjavík Nightlife: The capital city may be small, but its nightlife is legendary (page 47).

Planning Your Trip

Where to Go

Reykjavík

Home to two-thirds of Iceland's population, the capital city is the **cultural and social hub** of the country, with an energy distinct from the rest of the island. Here you'll find chic hotels, eclectic restaurants, and top-notch shopping on the main street, **Laugavegur**—not to mention a thriving **art scene** and vibrant **nightlife.** Pay a visit to the distinctive church **Hallgrímskirkja,** the placid pond **Tjörnin** near city hall, and, for a taste of history, the **National Museum of Iceland.** A trip to the **old harbor** is also a must—take in a concert at the striking glass hall **Harpa,** or head out on a **whale-watching** tour.

Reykjanes Peninsula and the South

Outside of Reykjavík, the **Reykjanes Peninsula** and the natural sights in South Iceland get the most traffic on the island. The Reykjanes Peninsula is home to charming fishing villages, **Keflavík** airport, and the **Blue Lagoon,** where you can take a healing dip in the heated water. The **Golden Circle** route encompasses three key

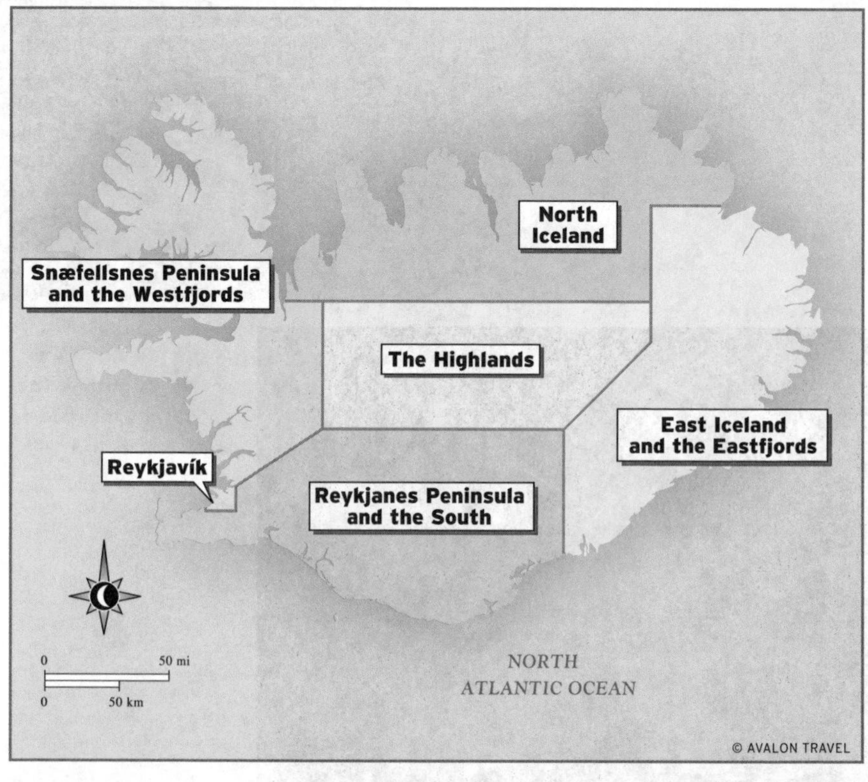

sights: the powerful waterfall **Gullfoss,** bubbling geothermal phenomenon **Geysir,** and history-steeped national park **Þingvellir.** Some of the best **hiking** trails in the country are in the south. A favorite is the **Laugavegurinn Trail,** where you'll see towering mountains, vast glaciers, hot springs, roaring rivers, and stunning waterfalls.

Snæfellsnes Peninsula and the Westfjords

Called "Iceland in miniature" by locals, the **Snæfellsnes Peninsula** has a bit of everything: quaint fishing towns, spectacular mountains, hiking, whale-watching, and even a glacier you can walk on—**Snæfellsjökull,** world famous as the starting point of Jules Verne's *A Journey to the Center of the Earth.* Endless coastlines, offbeat museums, and beautiful rocky landscapes await in the **Westfjords.** For outstanding bird-watching, visit the **Látrabjarg cliffs** in summer to check out thousands of nesting puffins.

North Iceland

Iceland's "second city," low-key **Akureyri** offers beautiful botanical gardens, first-rate hotels and restaurants, and a booming art scene. It's the perfect place to base yourself for a visit to the north. The **Mývatn region** lures visitors with its birdlife-rich lake, gorgeous hiking trails, vast lava fields, enormous craters, soaring mountains, and soothing **Mývatn Nature Baths. Jökulsárgljúfur,** part of **Vatnajökull National Park,** offers a number of treasures, including the gigantic canyon **Ásbyrgi** and **Dettifoss,** the largest waterfall in Iceland. **Húsavík** has some of the best **whale-watching** opportunities on the island, with a chance to see as many as 12 species of whales.

East Iceland and the Eastfjords

Looking for the "ice" in Iceland? Head to East Iceland, where the giant white **Vatnajökull glacier** will take your breath away. Drive or hike right up into the glacier's edge in **Skaftafell,** home to snowcapped mountains, green fields, and black-sand beaches. Hikers can scale **Mount Snæfell,** the highest mountain (excluding glaciers) in Iceland, with spectacular views spanning the highlands to the sea. Weave through the unspoiled **Eastfjords,**

a whale in Húsavík

where each fjord has its own charm. The east is the most remote part of the island, and summer is the only practical time to tour this region.

The Highlands

The uninhabited interior draws adventure seekers and avid hikers with its unique and unforgiving landscape. Iceland's **largest glaciers** (Vatnajökull, Langjökull, and Hofskjökull) are the backdrop to the highlands, with dramatic scenery cut by wind and ice. Hike the rim of **Mount Askja,** a volcano with a lake-filled crater and sensational views. Askja emerges from the eerie, desolate **Ódáðahraun lava field,** the largest desert in Europe. You have to stay abreast of the weather forecast in the highlands—it can snow any day of the year here.

When to Go

Iceland is a **year-round destination,** but when to visit depends on what you want to do and what you'd like to see. For instance, winter is not the time to go hiking, but the lower airfare and hotel prices during the off-season, as well as the lure of northern lights, draw many people over this season.

Summer (June-August)

The summer is the **high season** and offers the **best weather** to explore all of Iceland's **outdoor activities** such as hiking, diving, whale-watching, glacier-walking, bird-watching, and swimming. Average temperatures in the summer range 10-25°C (50-76°F). The landscape is green and lush and the days long. The **midnight sun** has to be seen to be believed. June-August is also the best time to embark on a **Ring Road trip,** as the roads are the best this time of year, and the weather is not likely to cause many problems. That said, it's important to closely monitor the weather forecast for wind or heavy rain.

While the summer offers the best weather and the freedom to explore the island, it comes at a price. Airfare and hotel rates are highest during these months, and there is a rush of tourists.

Autumn (September)

Autumn attracts travelers who want to **avoid the tourist crush** of summer but still explore some of the countryside and enjoy outdoor activities. There remains plenty of daylight, and **hiking** is viable in the fall, but you must monitor the weather because storms can pop up. It's also possible to see **northern lights** this time of year; check the forecast at www.vedur.is.

Fall is perfect for a long weekend in **Reykjavík.** This time of year is also known for local festivals in the capital city, such as the Reykjavík International Film Festival in September and music festival Iceland Airwaves at the end of October. Average temperatures in September and October range 2-10°C (36-50°F). The winds can make it feel colder.

Winter (October-April)

Iceland's **low season,** winter isn't a bad time to visit if you're willing to go with the flow, as the weather can be unpredictable at best and punishing at worst. Pluses are that airfare and hotel prices are the lowest of the year, you won't battle crowds anywhere, and this is the best time to catch a glimpse of the **northern lights.** Popular outdoor activities during the winter include **riding snowmobiles and horses** and **skiing** in the north. Temperatures tend to hover around freezing with averages of minus-3 to 3°C (26-38°F). The winds make it feel colder.

The downside to winter travel is, unsurprisingly, the **changeable, challenging weather.** You will likely encounter wind, rain, snow, sleet, and everything in between.

Chasing the Northern Lights

northern lights

The biggest winter attraction in Iceland is the northern lights. People travel from around the world to catch a glimpse of the green, white, blue, and red lights dancing in the night sky. The phenomenon is caused by solar winds, which push electronic particles to collide with molecules of atmospheric gases, causing an emission of bright light.

There's something very special about bundling up in your warmest winter gear, trekking outside the main towns to avoid bright lights, and hunting for the aurora borealis. The best time to see northern lights is **October-February.** Forecasts predict visibility at www.vedur.is, the national weather website. When the forecast is strong, it's best to drive (or take a tour bus) to a dark area and look up. It doesn't have to be far—just outside city center where the lights are low. Northern lights tours are offered by **Reykjavík Excursions** (www.re.is).

Travel to the countryside is limited in the winter as **many roads are closed,** and even open roads can have tough conditions. Also, **many establishments outside Reykjavík close** for the winter.

Spring (May)

April and May fall in between the low winter season and high summer season and are good options for **budget-conscious** travelers. You have a crack at **decent weather** without paying the extraordinary summertime prices. That said, the weather is unpredictable, so a visit in April can feel like winter—it's **hit or miss.** But if the weather is pleasant enough, you can enjoy hikes, horse riding, whale-watching, and all that Reykjavík has to offer. The temperatures for April and May range 0-8°C (32-47°F).

horses in winter

Before You Go

Visas and Officialdom

Visitors to Iceland must arrive with a valid **passport** that expires no sooner than three months after your intended departure date. Travelers from the United States, Canada, Australia, New Zealand, the United Kingdom, and Ireland do not require a visa for trips shorter than 90 days. However, if you would like to stay longer, you need to procure a permit from the Directorate of Immigration (www.utl.is), which is very difficult to get. There are different, more lenient rules for residents of European Union and European Economic Area countries.

Reservations

The **Blue Lagoon** must be booked in advance through its website, www.bluelagoon.is. Be sure to reserve as soon as possible because time slots frequently sell out, even in the winter. If you're considering any **private or small-group tours,** be sure to book those in advance. It's also recommended to make **dinner reservations during the Christmas season** because there are limited options, and it's necessary to book **New Year's Eve dinner reservations** far in advance (think August). As Iceland is a sparsely populated island with limited accommodations, it's strongly recommended you **book accommodations in advance.** For summer trips, plan to book hotels and guesthouses at least six months in advance to get the best choices at the most favorable prices. For the rest of the year, plan to book rooms at least three months in advance. Campervans and motorhomes, which should only be rented during the summer months for safety reasons, should be booked far in advance as well, at least five months before your arrival date.

West Iceland

Transportation

GETTING THERE

Flying into Iceland is a pretty seamless experience. The country's main carrier, **Icelandair** (www.icelandair.com), serves more than 30 destinations in the United States, Canada, and Europe. **WOW air** (www.wowair.com) also offers cheap flights from the United States, Canada, and Europe. Iceland's accessibility has been the island's main selling point as a travel destination, as the country is just five hours from New York City and about three hours from London.

For those traveling from mainland Europe, a **ferry** can be a great option, especially if you want to bring a car, camper, or bicycle for the trip. **Smyril Line** (www.smyril-line.fo) runs a ferry to Iceland from Denmark, Norway, and the Faroe Islands. The ferry drops you off in Seyðisfjörður in East Iceland, which is convenient if you're traveling with a car and want to spend time in the countryside. But if you want to stay in the south, where Reykjavík and the Golden Circle attractions are, a ferry may not be the best option.

GETTING AROUND

Having access to a **car** gives you the ultimate freedom in seeing the island on your own schedule (but expect to pay dearly, especially in summer). If you plan to stay in Reykjavík for most of your trip, or want to do short day trips in the southern or western parts of the country, it's not necessary to rent a car. You can book **tours** and travel by **bus.**

Road Tripping the Ring Road

TOP EXPERIENCE

This recommended itinerary takes you clockwise around Iceland. The **Ring Road (Route 1)** encircles the island, connecting many of the most popular attractions. Paved for most of its 1,332-kilometer length, it's the most accessible route around the country.

Keep in mind that it's always necessary to check road conditions before you head out in your car. Because the weather can be so challenging, it's ideal to plan a trip around the Ring Road in the **summer.** Despite snow removal during the winter, snowfall can close parts of the route in the east and north.

Day 1: Soak in the Blue Lagoon

After landing at **Keflavík International Airport,** take the Fly Bus or pick up your rental car and drive east on Route 41 to **Reykjavík.** If you are arriving in the morning or afternoon, head south on Route 43 and make a stop at the **Blue Lagoon** (book in advance) near Grindavík to soak in the soothing, geothermally heated water. Revived from jet lag, you're ready to experience the capital city's epic nightlife.

Day 2: Head North to Akureyri

From Reykjavík, drive north on the Ring Road to **Borgarnes** and visit the **Settlement Center** to get a taste of Iceland's rich history. Head north again on the Ring Road and then east on Route 518 to **Húsafell** to check out the gorgeous waterfalls of **Hraunfossar,** where the water flows out of lava formations tumbling to the river below. Circle back to the Ring Road and continue driving north to **Akureyri,** where you'll spend the next two nights. As time allows, explore the city's botanical gardens, shops, and restaurants.

Day 3: Hike and Bird-Watch in Mývatn

From Akureyri, head east on the Ring Road to the **Mývatn region** with its mighty lake, vast lava fields, gigantic craters, and unique rock

relaxing in the Blue Lagoon

Winter Wonders

Sure, Iceland's winter weather can be challenging. But you'll be rewarded with truly unique experiences that make it all worthwhile.

- **Hunt for northern lights:** The main season to see northern lights is October-February. Book a guided tour or venture out on your own.
- **Soak in the Blue Lagoon:** This is the most popular tourist attraction in Iceland for a reason, and is just as special in the winter. It's soothing and beautiful to soak during light snowfalls or while watching northern lights dance above on clear nights.
- **Tour the Golden Circle:** Iceland's number one tour is available year-round. Book a bus tour or drive the attraction-heavy route yourself. The frozen **Gullfoss** falls and rocky landscape are gorgeous when mantled in winter white.
- **Take a glacier walk:** Tour operators offer the unique opportunity to hike on a glacier. They supply all the necessary equipment and provide pickups at your hotel or guesthouse. **Icelandic Mountain Guides** (www.mountainguides.is) offers a year-round guided tour walking on a glacier in Skaftafell.
- **Ride majestic Icelandic horses:** Icelandic horses are hardy creatures that are beautiful to ride along the snowy landscape. Akureyri-based tour company **Saga Travel** (www.sagatravel.is) offers horse-riding day tours from Akureyri and Mývatn.
- **Go cross-country skiing up north:** Iceland isn't known for its skiing, but it does have a well-maintained ski area in its north, not too far from Akureyri. The **Hlíðarfjall** ski area (www.hlidarfjall.is) has more than a dozen well-kept trails.

a glacier walk tour

- **Ride snowmobiles:** It's spectacular to glide atop the pristine white snow on crisp and clear winter days. **Vatnajökull Travel** (www.vatnajokull.is) features a year-round tour that includes snowmobile rides on Vatnajökull glacier, the biggest glacier in Europe.
- **Embark on an art museum crawl in Reykjavík:** If the weather outside is frightful, head indoors to explore Iceland's modern artists, like Erró, and old masters such as Jóhannes Kjarval at the **Reykjavík Art Museum.**

formations. Go hiking, watch the rich birdlife, and soak in the decadent **Mývatn Nature Baths.** On the way back from Mývatn to Akureyri, be sure to stop at the glorious waterfall **Goðafoss.** Spend the night in Akureyri.

Day 4: Whale-Watch in Húsavík

Head northeast via Route 85 to **Húsavík,** a placid seaside town known for its spectacular **whale-watching** and comprehensive **Húsavík Whale Museum.** From Húsavík, head south on Route 85 to **Ásbyrgi,** a horseshoe-shaped gorge with

Skógafoss falls

towering rock walls and raw nature. Next head to the tremendous waterfall **Dettifoss,** where you'll feel the crushing force of the glacial water tumbling below. Continue south on Route 85 to link back up with the Ring Road and drive on to the eastern town **Egilsstaðir,** where you'll spend the night.

Day 5: Explore the Glacial East

Today, you'll get to enjoy some actual ice in Iceland. From Egilsstaðir, drive south on the Ring Road to **Vatnajökull glacier,** Europe's largest ice cap. Continue to **Jökulsárlón,** a glacier lagoon, and **Skaftafell,** the southern portion of **Vatnajökull National Park,** to take in the black sands and glacial landscape. If you're feeling adventurous and the weather is pleasant, consider a glacier walk tour. Continue west on the Ring Road to **Vík,** where you'll spend the night.

Day 6: Tour the Golden Circle

From Vík, continue west on the Ring Road, starting with a visit to the fishing village of **Skógar,** where you can see the waterfall **Skógafoss,** one of the tallest in Iceland. Then tour the **Golden Circle,** comprising a trio of must-see sights. Head west on the Ring Road and north on Route 35 to visit the geothermal area of **Geysir,** where the hot spring Strokkur erupts every 5-7 minutes. Next visit nearby **Gullfoss,** Iceland's most famous and most photographed waterfall. Head west on Routes 35, 37, 365, and 36 to **Þingvellir National Park,** a geological wonder that is also the birthplace of democracy in Iceland. Drive southwest on Route 36 to **Reykjavík** to spend the night.

Day 7: Hang Out in Reykjavík

Spend as much time in Reykjavík as possible before heading back to Keflavík for your flight. For suggestions for a longer stay in the city, see page 26. If you only have time for a quick coffee, check out Reykjavík's oldest coffeehouse, **Mokka,** or pick up one of the city's famous hot dogs at **Bæjarins Beztu Pylsur.** Drive back to Keflavík.

Best Wildlife-Watching

WHALES

Several whale-watching tour companies operate around the island. Some head out year-round, while others are restricted to the summer. The main whale-watching destinations are in the south (Reykjavík), west (Grundarfjörður), and north (Dalvík and Húsavík).

- **Reykjavík:** Operating from Reykjavík's harbor, whale-watching tours offer opportunities to see minke, blue, and fin whales as well as dolphins and porpoises (year-round).
- **Grundarfjörður:** This western town is your best shot at catching a glimpse of orcas (it's possible to see orcas year-round, but is more likely during the winter months).
- **Dalvík:** You may see humpback whales, minke whales, blue whales, harbor porpoises, and dolphins on tours leaving from the harbor of this small northern fishing town (year-round).
- **Húsavík:** The unofficial whale-watching capital of the island has several species off its shores, including minke, humpback, pilot, northern bottlenose, sperm, sei, fin, orca, and blue whales (mid-May-late Oct.).

PUFFINS

From April through August, it's possible to see puffins in several parts of the country.

- **Heimaey:** Thousands of visitors flock to this island off the south coast to walk along the sea cliffs and spend time with its puffin population (June-Aug.).
- **Flatey:** This western island is a good place to spot migrating puffins in the summer (June-Aug.).
- **Látrabjarg:** In West Iceland, trails allow you to access the colossal Látrabjarg cliffs, where puffins gather to nest in intricate crevices (May-Aug.).
- **Borgarfjörður Eystri:** Get a close-up view of puffins at this fjord in East Iceland, which has an observation platform connected to a small islet that the birds love (mid-Apr.-mid-Aug.).

reindeer in East Iceland

SEALS

Six species of seals have been spotted off the coast of Iceland. Most commonly sighted are **gray seals** and **harbor seals.** The remaining four species (hooded, harp, bearded, and ringed seals) are hit or miss. In the summer, you have a good chance of spotting gray seals and harbor seals around the **Vatnsnes Peninsula** in the north. The peninsula is also home to the **Icelandic Seal Center,** which contains wonderful exhibits about these creatures. The center's staff has information on the best sites for seal-watching opportunities.

REINDEER

Iceland's reindeer herds live only in **East Iceland.** The best places to view them during the summer are the areas around **Mount Snæfell.**

The Best of Reykjavík

With quaint museums, cool music venues, and top-notch restaurants, small Reykjavík makes a big impression.

Day 1

Explore downtown Reykjavík and all the shops, galleries, restaurants, and coffeehouses the city has to offer. Walk down the street **Skólavörðustígur** to the landmark church **Hallgrímskirkja** to check out the amazing interior, beautiful organ, and view from the top. Grab coffee or lunch on Skólavörðustígur at **Café Babalu,** which makes tasty lattes and light meals like crepes and panini. The street is also where you can pick up a traditional Icelandic sweater at the **Handknitting Association of Iceland.**

Walk down the main street, **Laugavegur,** and pop into the **Hrim** stores for Icelandic design and **Mál og Menning** for books, T-shirts, and other tourist wares. Walk toward city hall and stroll around the man-made pond **Tjörnin,** where you can check out swans, ducks, and other birds.

For dinner, consider one of the city's trendy restaurants, like **Fiskfelagid** for the freshest catch of the day or **Bambus** for Asian fusion. Reykjavík nightlife is epic, and venues like **Húrra** and **Kex Hostel** are perfect for checking out local DJs or live bands and dancing the night away.

Day 2

Reykjavík's harbor has a lot to see. Have breakfast at **Café Haiti** and watch boats enter the harbor. Sign up for a **whale-watching** or **bird-watching** excursion for a chance to spot minke whales, dolphins, fin whales, blue whales, and seabirds (depending on the season). Once back on land, walk to the **Saga Museum** to learn about Iceland's history and enjoy a coffee and snack or light meal at the in-house restaurant, **Matur og Drykkur.** Walk over to **Harpa** concert hall to take in a concert or just check out the amazing interior and architecturally striking exterior.

Walk back downtown and explore the **Reykjavík Art Museum,** then have dinner at

Reykjavík

Get Yourself in Hot Water

From waterfalls to boat trips to hot springs, water is a constant tourist attraction in Iceland.

A trip to Iceland would not be complete without visiting the **Blue Lagoon** just outside of Grindavík. Against a backdrop of lava fields, the man-made hot spring soothes and exhilarates at the same time. And that goes for any weather conditions—rain, snow, or sunshine. Soaking within the deep mist is a unique and slightly eerie experience, one you will remember—and talk about—for ages.

Up north, the **Mývatn Nature Baths** feel secluded in comparison to the Blue Lagoon, with fewer people and more room to wade. The water comes from the National Power Company's borehole in Bjarnaflag, scorching when it arrives at the basin next to the man-made bathing lagoon but cooling significantly before filtering into it. The bottom of the lagoon contains minerals beneficial to the skin. The bathing experience is divine, relaxing every inch of your body.

Tourists who visit **local swimming pools** will quickly see how integral they are to Icelandic culture. It's common to see families, friends, and coworkers relaxing in a hot tub and talking about politics, music, or the latest movies. The pools are also a great alternative to outdoor activities when the weather is particularly bad—which can happen in Iceland at any time, in any season.

Mývatn Nature Baths

An important note: You must shower before entering pools or hot tubs. Icelanders shower, sans bathing suit, in gender-divided locker rooms prior to taking a dip, and you're expected to do the same. Just go with the flow.

wildly popular sushi restaurant **Osushi.** Stop by **Bar 11** to hear some local live music.

Day 3

Go to **Mokka** café on Skólavörðustígur for breakfast—the waffles with homemade jam and fresh cream are delightful. Then visit Reykjavík's best record shops: Head to **12 Tónar,** a few doors up from Mokka, and **Lucky Records** near Hlemmur bus station.

Instead of going directly to the airport, sign up for a bus transfer to the **Blue Lagoon** to enjoy the glorious waters. Then head to Keflavík for your flight.

Iceland Getaway

If you don't have a lot of time, it's possible to see some of the country's highlights in four short days.

Day 1

After landing at **Keflavík International Airport,** either pick up your rental car or take the Fly Bus into **Reykjavík.** If you are arriving in the morning or afternoon, make a stop at the **Blue Lagoon** near Grindavík for a soothing soak. Head to Reykjavík and check into your accommodation. Explore some of Iceland's **nightlife** by taking in a concert at **Harpa** concert hall or having a couple of drinks at **Kex Hostel,** a favorite among locals and tourists alike.

Day 2

Spend the day exploring Reykjavík, including the landmark church **Hallgrímskirkja,** the **Reykjavík Art Museum,** and the **National Gallery of Iceland.** Have a delicious dinner at **Fish Market.**

Day 3

Spend a day in the **Snæfellsnes Peninsula** exploring charming fishing villages and the mighty **Snæfellsjökull glacier,** which appeared in Jules Verne's classic tale *A Journey to the Center of the Earth.* Visitors will see interesting rock formations, black-sand beaches, and thriving birdlife.

Day 4

Before your flight, wander Reykjavík's numerous **cafés, galleries,** and **shops.** You can pick up gifts and quality clothing at top-notch stores like **66 North** and **Geysir** and take a break at **Mokka** or **Café Babalu.**

Harpa concert hall

Best Day Hikes

Iceland is undeniably a hiker's paradise. The mountainous landscape begs to be climbed, lava fields invite you to explore, and the highlands offer the adventurous a place to conquer.

- **Mount Esja** is the picture-perfect backdrop to Reykjavík and a favorite hiking destination for locals and tourists. The hike is eight kilometers round-trip and relatively easy, but it does get steeper toward the top. Along the way, you'll see a placid stream and gorgeous scenery. The vista from the top is breathtaking, with views of Reykjavík across the bay (page 72).

- Hike to the summit of **Mount Hekla** via a moderately challenging seven-kilometer trail crossing lava fields and you'll be rewarded with gorgeous views which, on clear days, include Vatnajökull glacier (page 104).

- Looking for a challenging day hike? Consider the **Fimmvörðuháls Trail,** which some tackle over two days but which can also be done in a long day hike of around 8-10 hours. Along the way you see gorgeous lava fields, glaciers, and waterfalls (page 110).

- In the west, **Mount Akrafjall** offers moderate hiking, with two paths from which to choose. The shorter climb (about two hours) gains 555 meters in elevation and offers a lovely view of the outskirts of Akranes. If you're up for a longer climb (about five hours), the more strenuous path climbs 643 meters, and on clear days you can see Snæfellsjökull glacier (page 121).

- For those who make it to the highlands, hiking the rim of **Mount Askja** is a must. The approximately two-hour trek is moderate, and the trail is well maintained and sees a bit of traffic from hikers. It offers special views of looming mountains, lava fields, and the spectacular Víti crater (page 241).

Mount Akrafjall

- Hiking in **Hveradalir,** a geothermal area, is a popular option. For those seeking a taste of the highlands without committing to an all- or multi-day hike, a three-kilometer loop trail near Neðri-Hveradalir (Lower Hveradalir) takes you through the glacial landscape, juxtaposed with bubbling hot springs and the muted hues of the desert-like earth (page 246).

Reykjavík

Reykjavík is having a moment. Relatively affordable airfares are drawing weekenders from both sides of the Atlantic, giving Iceland's capital city a chance to show off its urban appeal and individualistic style.

Reykjavík's history dates back to AD 874, when Ingólfur Arnarson from Norway established the first settlement in Iceland. The city slowly grew over the centuries, and in 1786, Reykjavík was established as an official trading town.

Today, Reykjavík has a lot of people, cars, and trees, in stark contrast to the rest of the country. Roughly 220,000 of Iceland's 340,000 residents live in the capital city. Though it's small, its energy mimics that of bigger cities like Berlin. Reykjavík residents are known to have two lives: They work by day, and by night become musicians, artists, novelists, or poets. While strolling on Reykjavík's main street, Laugavegur, you'll see street art among the high-end shops, musicians playing impromptu concerts outside coffeehouses, and small art galleries boasting original "Icelandic Design." It's undeniably a creative city.

While Reykjavík can seem quite urban with its galleries and restaurants, nature is never too far away. The air is unbelievably clean, and whales can be seen passing by the harbor during the summer.

PLANNING YOUR TIME

Given its small size, Reykjavík can be "done" in 1-2 days depending on your level of interest. Some travelers treat Reykjavík as their starting point before heading out on the Ring Road or booking day trips into the countryside, while others travel to Reykjavík specifically for the nightlife and art scene.

ORIENTATION

Reykjavík is the most compact capital city in all of Europe. Its downtown and the old harbor are situated in the northern half of the city, and the main bus station (BSÍ) is in the south. Most of the hotels, museums, shops, and restaurants are also in the northern half. The main street in central Reykjavík is

Previous: downtown Reykjavík; a park near the Alþingishúsið. **Above:** Hallgrímskirkja.

Look for ★ to find recommended sights, activities, dining, and lodging.

Highlights

★ **Reykjavík Art Museum (Listasafn Reykjavíkur):** It's three museums in one, showcasing sculpture, contemporary art, and the works of beloved Icelandic artist Jóhannes Kjarval (page 33).

★ **Hallgrímskirkja:** The "Church of Hallgrímur" is a striking national monument dedicated to one of Iceland's most cherished and celebrated poets. Its tower boasts spectacular views (page 37).

★ **National Gallery of Iceland (Listasafn Íslands):** The largest collection of Icelandic art on the island has everything from classic portraits to gorgeous landscapes (page 41).

★ **Tjörnin:** Close to Reykjavík City Hall, this pond is a lovely place to take a stroll and enjoy the birdlife (page 41).

★ **Harpa:** This striking concert hall features individual glass panels that light up during the darkness of winter (page 42).

★ ***Sólfar:*** The large boat sculpture by the sea has been delighting photographers and tourists for decades (page 43).

★ **Perlan:** This unique dome-shaped building has one of the best views of Reykjavík from its outdoor deck (page 44).

★ **Hiking Mount Esja:** An easy climb on basalt rock climaxes with gorgeous views out to sea (page 72).

Laugavegur, which starts in the east. As you move west, it eventually becomes Bankastræti, which ends as Austurstræti. The streets tend to have long names, and there isn't a grid system in place, but the city is small enough that you won't get too lost. Hlemmur bus station on the east end of Laugavegur is Strætó's main depot downtown. It can connect you to just about anywhere in central and greater Reykjavík.

Sights

CENTRAL REYKJAVÍK

★ Reykjavík Art Museum (Listasafn Reykjavíkur)

The **Reykjavík Art Museum** is actually three museums (Hafnarhús, Kjarvalsstaðir, and Ásmundarsafn) in three different locations. Admission is 1,600ISK, and children under 18 and seniors are free. Each museum is open 10am-5pm daily, and if you purchase a ticket to any one of the three museums, you also gain access to the other two—although entry is only available on the same day your ticket was purchased. Each museum is fairly small, and you can hit all three in one day; an hour at each is sufficient.

HAFNARHÚS

Hafnarhús (Tryggvagata 17, tel. 354/590-1200, www.artmuseum.is), which focuses on contemporary art and has three floors of exhibitions, is the crown jewel of the three museums, in part because of its permanent collection of paintings and prints by Erró, one of the most celebrated modern Icelandic artists. His pieces displayed here range from light pop art with bright colors and interesting characters to samples of line sketches from his earlier work. While the art can be playful, Erró also tackles political and social issues. Hafnarhús also houses works by other Icelandic artists, as well as rotating exhibitions of foreign painters, designers, and visual artists.

KJARVALSSTAÐIR

Kjarvalsstaðir (Flókagata 24, tel. 354/517-1290, www.artmuseum.is) explores the works of Icelandic painter Jóhannes Kjarval

Reykjavík's stunning setting

Central Reykjavík

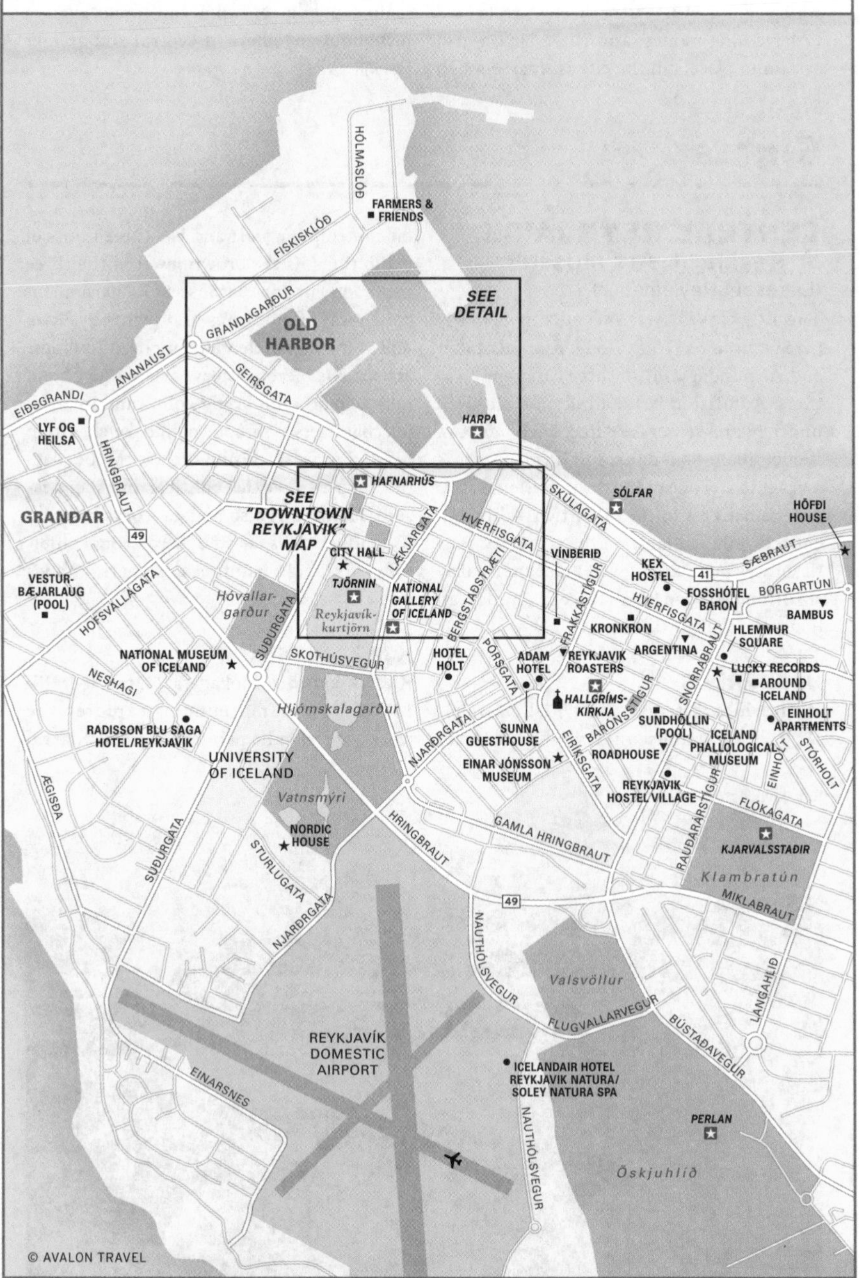
HÓLMASLÓÐ
FARMERS & FRIENDS
FISKISLÓÐ
GRANDAGARÐUR
OLD HARBOR
SEE DETAIL
ÁNANAUST
GEIRSGATA
EIÐSGRANDI
LYF OG HEILSA
HARPA
HRINGBRAUT
HAFNARHÚS
SEE "DOWNTOWN REYKJAVÍK" MAP
SÓLFAR
HÖFÐI HOUSE
GRANDAR
49
LÆKJARGATA
HVERFISGATA
SKÚLAGATA
SÆBRAUT
CITY HALL
VÍNBERIÐ
KEX HOSTEL
41
VESTUR-BÆJARLAUG (POOL)
HOFSVALLAGATA
TJÖRNIN
NATIONAL GALLERY OF ICELAND
BERGSTAÐASTRÆTI
FRAKKASTÍGUR
FOSSHÓTEL BARON
BORGARTÚN
BAMBUS
Hóvallargarður
Reykjavíkurtjörn
SUÐURGATA
KRONKRON
HLEMMUR SQUARE
ARGENTINA
NATIONAL MUSEUM OF ICELAND
SKOTHÚSVEGUR
HOTEL HOLT
ÞÓRSGATA
ADAM HOTEL
REYKJAVIK ROASTERS
LUCKY RECORDS
AROUND ICELAND
NESHAGI
HALLGRÍMSKIRKJA
SNORRABRAUT
Hljómskalagarður
BARÓNSSTÍGUR
SUNDHÖLLIN (POOL)
EINHOLT APARTMENTS
RADISSON BLU SAGA HOTEL/REYKJAVIK
NJARÐARGATA
SUNNA GUESTHOUSE
ICELAND PHALLOLOGICAL MUSEUM
STÓRHOLT
ROADHOUSE
UNIVERSITY OF ICELAND
EINAR JÓNSSON MUSEUM
EIRÍKSGATA
EINHOLT
ÆGISÍÐA
Vatnsmýri
REYKJAVIK HOSTEL VILLAGE
FLÓKAGATA
RAUÐARÁRSTÍGUR
GAMLA HRINGBRAUT
HRINGBRAUT
NORDIC HOUSE
KJARVALSSTAÐIR
SUÐURGATA
STURLUGATA
Klambratún
MIKLABRAUT
49
NJARÐARGATA
NAUTHÓLSVEGUR
LANGAHLÍÐ
Valsvöllur
FLUGVALLARVEGUR
BÚSTAÐAVEGUR
REYKJAVÍK DOMESTIC AIRPORT
ICELANDAIR HOTEL REYKJAVIK NATURA/ SOLEY NATURA SPA
EINARSNES
NAUTHÓLSVEGUR
PERLAN
Öskjuhlíð
© AVALON TRAVEL

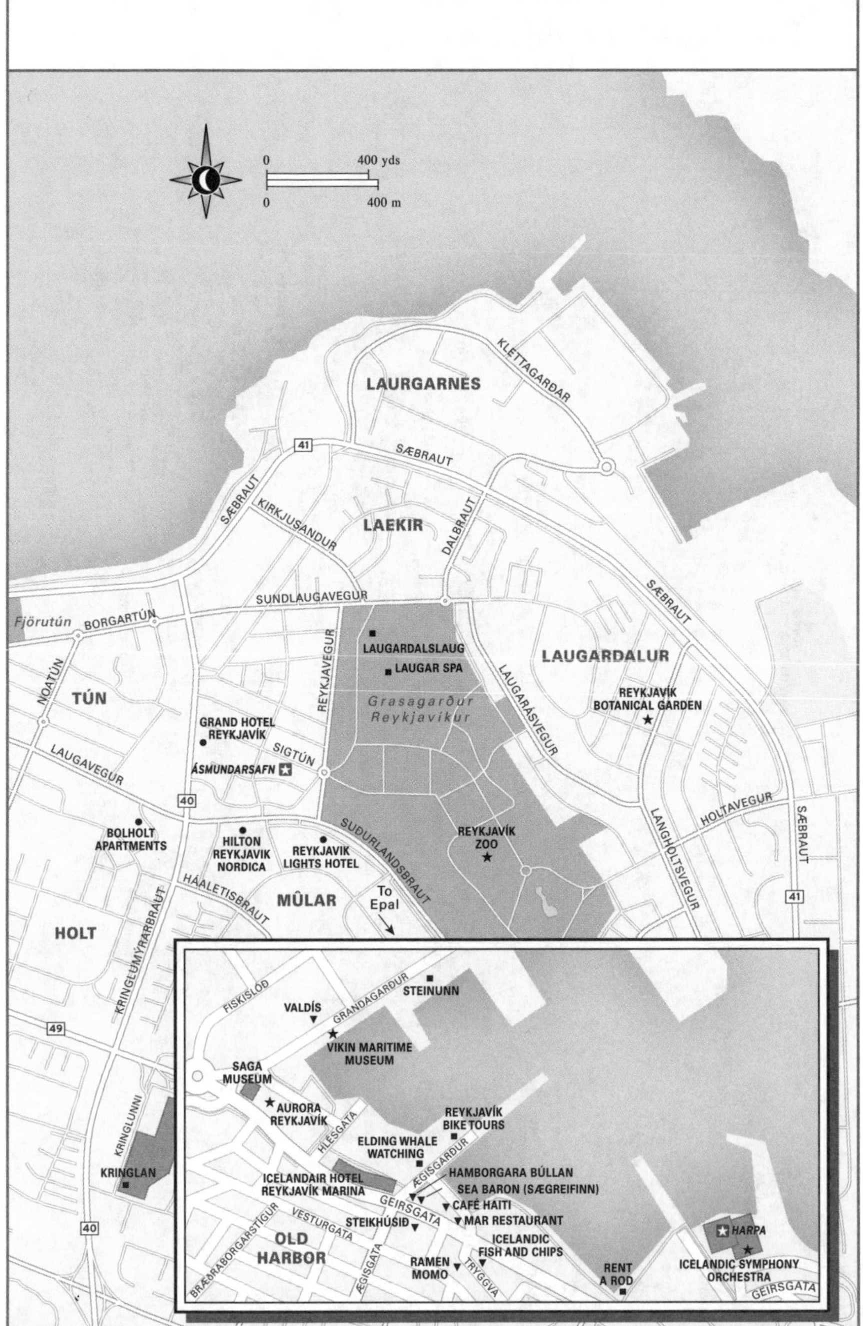
0 400 yds
0 400 m
LAURGARNES
KLETTAGARÐAR
SÆBRAUT
41
LAEKIR
KIRKJUSANDUR
DALBRAUT
SUNDLAUGAVEGUR
Fjörutún
BORGARTÚN
LAUGARDALSLAUG
LAUGAR SPA
Grasagarður Reykjavíkur
LAUGARDALUR
REYKJAVÍK BOTANICAL GARDEN
LAUGARÁSVEGUR
REYKJAVEGUR
NOATÚN
TÚN
GRAND HOTEL REYKJAVÍK
SIGTÚN
LAUGAVEGUR
ÁSMUNDARSAFN
40
HOLTAVEGUR
LANGHOLTSVEGUR
BOLHOLT APARTMENTS
HILTON REYKJAVIK NORDICA
REYKJAVIK LIGHTS HOTEL
SUÐURLANDSBRAUT
REYKJAVÍK ZOO
HÁALETISBRAUT
MÛLAR
To Epal
HOLT
KRINGLUMÝRARBRAUT
49
FISKISLÓÐ
GRANDAGARÐUR
STEINUNN
VALDÍS
VIKIN MARITIME MUSEUM
SAGA MUSEUM
AURORA REYKJAVÍK
HLESGATA
REYKJAVÍK BIKE TOURS
ELDING WHALE WATCHING
ÆGISGARÐUR
KRINGLUNNI
KRINGLAN
ICELANDAIR HOTEL REYKJAVÍK MARINA
HAMBORGARA BÚLLAN
SEA BARON (SÆGREIFINN)
GEIRSGATA
CAFÉ HAITI
MAR RESTAURANT
VESTURGATA
STEIKHÚSIÐ
OLD HARBOR
BRÆÐRABORGARSTÍGUR
ÆGISGATA
ICELANDIC FISH AND CHIPS
RAMEN MOMO
TRYGGVA
RENT A ROD
HARPA
ICELANDIC SYMPHONY ORCHESTRA
GEIRSGATA

Downtown Reykjavík

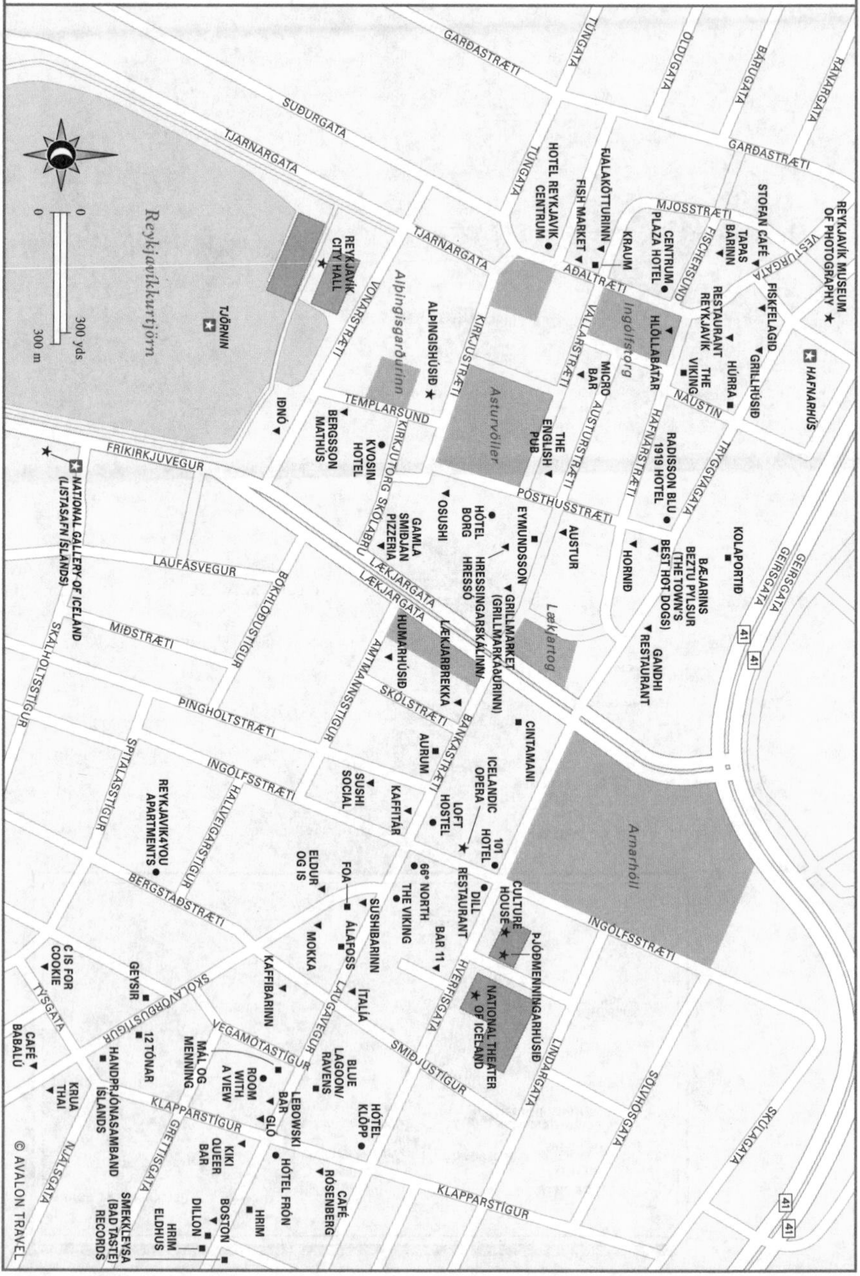

GARÐASTRÆTI
TÚNGATA
ÖLDUGATA
BÁRUGATA
RÁNARGATA
SUÐURGATA
TJARNARGATA
GARÐASTRÆTI
HOTEL REYKJAVIK CENTRUM
FJALAKÖTTURINN
FISH MARKET
KRAUM
CENTRUM PLAZA HOTEL
MJOSSTRÆTI
FISCHERSUND
STOFAN CAFE
TAPAS BARINN
RESTAURANT REYKJAVIK
FISKFELAGID
REYKJAVÍK MUSEUM OF PHOTOGRAPHY
VESTURGATA
HAFNARHÚS
GRILLHÚSID
HÚRRA
THE VIKING
NAUSTIN
HLÖLLABÁTAR
Ingólfstorg
AÐALSTRÆTI
VALLARSTRÆTI
MICRO BAR
AUSTURSTRÆTI
HAFNARSTRÆTI
RADISSON BLU 1919 HOTEL
TRYGGVAGATA
KOLAPORTID
GEIRSGATA
BÆJARINS BEZTU PYLSUR (THE TOWN'S BEST HOT DOGS)
GANDHI RESTAURANT
HORNID
AUSTUR
THE ENGLISH PUB
Austurvöllur
KIRKJUSTRÆTI
ALÞINGISHÚSID
Alþingisgarðurinn
TJARNARGATA
VONARSTRÆTI
REYKJAVÍK CITY HALL
Reykjavíkurtjörn
TJÖRNIN
300 yds
300 m
TEMPLARSUND
IDNÓ
BERGSSON MATHÚS
KVOSIN HOTEL
KIRKJUTORG
PÓSTHUSSTRÆTI
EYMUNDSSON
HÓTEL BORG
HRESSINGARSKÁLINN
HRESSO
GRILLMARKET (GRILLMARKAÐURINN)
OSUSHI
GAMLA SMIÐJAN PIZZERIA
SKÓLABRÚ
FRÍKIRKJUVEGUR
NATIONAL GALLERY OF ICELAND (LISTASAFN ÍSLANDS)
LAUFÁSVEGUR
LÆKJARGATA
Lækjartorg
LÆKJARBREKKA
HUMARHÚSID
AMTMANNSSTÍGUR
BÓKHLÖÐUSTÍGUR
MIÐSTRÆTI
SKÓLSTRÆTI
BANKASTRÆTI
CINTAMANI
AURUM
ICELANDIC OPERA
LOFT HOSTEL
101 HOTEL
Arnarhóll
ÞINGHOLTSSTRÆTI
INGÓLFSSTRÆTI
SUSHI SOCIAL
KAFFITÁR
SKÁLHOLTSSTÍGUR
SPÍTALASTÍGUR
REYKJAVIK4YOU APARTMENTS
HALLVEIGARSTÍGUR
ELDUR OG IS
FOA
66° NORTH
THE VIKING
DILL RESTAURANT
CULTURE HOUSE
ÞJÓÐMENNINGARHÚSID
INGÓLFSSTRÆTI
BERGSTAÐASTRÆTI
SUSHIBARINN
ÁLAFOSS
MOKKA
BAR 11
HVERFISGATA
NATIONAL THEATER OF ICELAND
LINDARGATA
SÓLVHÓLSGATA
SKÚLAGATA
C IS FOR COOKIE
GEYSIR
KAFFIBARINN
ÍTALÍA
LAUGAVEGUR
SKÓLAVÖRÐUSTÍGUR
TÝSGATA
CAFÉ BABALÚ
12 TÓNAR
HANDPRJÓNASAMBAND ÍSLANDS
VEGAMÓTASTÍGUR
MÁL OG MENNING
ROOM WITH A VIEW
BLUE LAGOON
RAVENS
LEBOWSKI BAR
GLÓ
HÓTEL KLÖPP
SMIÐJUSTÍGUR
KRUA THAI
KLAPPARSTÍGUR
GRETTISGATA
KIKI QUEER BAR
HÓTEL FRÓN
CAFÉ RÓSENBERG
BOSTON
HRIM
DILLON
HRIM ELDHUS
SMEKKLEYSA (BAD TASTE) RECORDS
NJÁLSGATA
KLAPPARSTÍGUR
41

(1885-1972), best known for his dark and moody paintings of Iceland's landscapes. Kjarval was a master of capturing the country's raw nature in the winter light. The majority of Kjarval's collection was left to the city of Reykjavík after his death. The other wing of the museum features various Icelandic artists, ranging from well-known modern artists to some of the country's best and brightest art students. The museum is one level with a coffeehouse in the middle of the two wings, and the high ceilings and wall of windows here creates an interesting space. A large field behind the museum sometimes serves as a spot for sculpture exhibitions.

ÁSMUNDARSAFN

Ásmundarsafn (Sigtún, tel. 354/553-2155, www.artmuseum.is) is an impressive sculpture museum exclusively featuring the works of Ásmundur Sveinsson (1893-1982), who worked with materials including wood, copper, and iron. Ásmundur's work is housed in a gorgeous stark-white domed building. An exhibit features what his workshop looked like and contains renderings of projects, as well as his masterpiece, a chair carved out of wood; the level of detail in the craftsmanship of the chair is spectacular. An outdoor sculpture garden features interesting works of human forms among trees, shrubs, and flowers.

Culture House
(Safnahúsið)

Culture House (Hverfisgata 15, tel. 354/545-1400, www.culturehouse.is, 10am-5pm daily, 2,000ISK) is a stately white neoclassical building that opened as a museum in 1909. It is home to significant medieval manuscripts, including unique sagas, narratives, and poems from early settlers. Guided tours of exhibitions on Mondays and Fridays at 3pm last about an hour, or you can tour on your own. Rotating exhibitions throughout the year can include paintings, photography, or literary works. The exhibits do an excellent job of placing the manuscripts, literature, and artwork in context, giving visitors a great overview. Be sure to check the website to see what's on view. Culture House also plays host to conferences, gatherings, and readings throughout the year, including Reykjavík's annual design festival, DesignMarch, in the spring. The cafeteria serves light meals, and the traditional meat soup is delicious.

★ Hallgrímskirkja

Hallgrímskirkja (Hallgrímstorg, tel.

Hallgrímskirkja

354/510-1000, www.hallgrimskirkja.is, 9am-9pm daily May 1-Sept. 30, 9am-5pm daily Oct 1-Apr. 30, free) is one of the most photographed, and most visited, sites in Reykjavík. The "Church of Hallgrímur" is a national monument dedicated to Hallgrímur Pétursson (1614-1674), a poet cherished and celebrated by Icelanders. Hallgrímur is best known for 50 hymns that he wrote, *Hymns of the Passion,* about the passion of Christ. These hymns are familiar to all Icelanders, and are read annually on Icelandic radio before Easter.

The church is a modern structure, made out of concrete, with basalt-style columns at the bottom coming to a point at the top. Standing 73 meters, the Lutheran church was designed by state architect Guðjón Samúelsson. Work started on the building in 1945, and was completed in 1986. Hallgrímskirkja, still an active church that holds services, is a must-see for tourists. The interior is home to a gorgeous organ constructed by Johannes Klais Organworks in Germany, as well as beautiful stained glass windows. Concerts ranging from choirs to organ performances are frequently held; be sure to check the website for upcoming concerts. An annual Christmas concert features traditional songs sung in English.

The highlight of a trip to Hallgrímskirkja for many is a visit to the top of the **tower** (9am-9pm daily May 1-Sept. 30, 9am-5pm daily Oct.1-Apr. 30, 900ISK), which has spectacular views of the city. An elevator takes you up.

Einar Jónsson Museum

The **Einar Jónsson Museum** (Eiríksgata 3, tel. 354/561-3797, www.lej.is, 10am-5pm daily, 1,000ISK, free for children under 18) houses the works of one of Iceland's most celebrated sculptors, Einar Jónsson (1874-1954). Situated across the street from Hallgrímskirkja, the museum features work ranging from Christian-themed sculptures to those depicting Iceland's rich folklore. Einar worked almost entirely with plaster, which was rare for the period. The outdoor sculpture garden is beautiful, whether the sun is shining or if it is under a layer of snow. The garden makes the museum a very special visit. Plan to spend about an hour checking out the art inside, and if the weather is nice, spend additional time outside in the garden.

Icelandic Phallological Museum

(Hið Íslenzka Reðasafn)

The **Icelandic Phallological Museum**

the Saga Museum's restaurant

Reykjavík Walking Tour

Reykjavík is a small, walkable city with a lot to see. While spending at least one day in Reykjavík is recommended, you can see quite a bit in just an hour, which is approximately how long this walk takes without stops. It's ideal to complete this five-kilometer walking tour in the early afternoon, but monitor the weather and decide when it's best for you to go.

- Start your leisurely self-guided walking tour at **Hallgrímskirkja,** where you can explore the interior and head to the top of the tower for a fantastic view over the city.
- Then walk down Skólavörðustígur, the street directly across from the church entrance, to check out some quirky shops and cafés. **Café Babalu** is a nice stop on Skólavörðustígur for a cup of coffee and slice of dynamite carrot cake.
- Continue walking down Skólavörðustígur until you hit **Laugavegur,** the city's main drag and center of life in downtown Reykjavík, and turn left.
- Proceed until you meet Lækjargata street, where you'll turn left and head to **Tjörnin,** a pretty pond where you can watch ducks and swans.
- Walk clockwise around the perimeter on a pondside path, and loop past **Reykjavík City Hall** at the pond's northwest corner.
- Follow Tjarnargata street from here for one block, turning right on Kirkjustræti to see Iceland's Parliament House, **Alþingishúsið,** near Austurvöllur square.
- Then it's time to head toward the harbor; backtrack slightly the way you came, heading west down Kirkjustræti, and turn right onto Aðalstræti, continuing on it as it becomes Vesturgata. Turn right on Mjóstræti and left onto Tryggvagata, crossing the road here and heading east on Geirsgata. In about 400 meters you'll link up with the Sculpture & Shore Walk, a waterfront path that leads to **Harpa** concert hall, a striking architectural gem.
- After some time exploring the building or taking pictures, head 600 meters further southeast along the waterfront walkway to see ***Sólfar,*** a popular sculpture and another excellent photo opportunity.
- Next, cross Sæbraut at the pedestrian crossing east of the sculpture and turn left onto Skúlagata, continuing about 150 meters until you see **Kex Hostel** on the right; stop for a coffee, beer, snack, or chance to chat with locals and other tourists at this hip and wildly popular spot's bar and lounge area.
- Afterward, exit the hostel to the left and head south on Vitastígur for a couple of blocks, turning right back onto Laugavegur to check out more shops like **Smekkleysa (Bad Taste) Records** or **Mál og Menning** bookshop. You're back in the center of town and will soon connect with the portion of Laugavegur covered earlier in the walk.

(Laugavegur 116, tel. 354/561-6663, www.phallus.is, 10am-6pm daily, 1,500ISK) is just as weird as it sounds. Guests can view the penises of 200 animals, including the arctic fox, walrus, seal, and polar bear. After the museum was moved to its current location in Reykjavík (from Húsavík in North Iceland), the curator unveiled his latest acquisition—a human member. The museum has members on display in glass cases, and preserved bones of certain mammals are hanging on the wall. The highlight is also a unique photo op: the huge whale specimen on display. Some people find the museum humorous, while others are a bit freaked out. Looking for unique postcards, T-shirts, and souvenirs? Look no further.

National Museum of Iceland
(Þjóðminjasafn Íslands)

The **National Museum of Iceland** (Suðurgata 41, tel. 354/530-2200, www.nationalmuseum.is, 10am-5pm daily, 2,000ISK) is Reykjavík's main heritage and history museum, housing everything from tools and clothing of the settlement era to models of Viking-era ships. This is the best museum in the city to get insight on the history of the Icelandic nation and its people. The artifacts and exhibitions are well presented with clear information in English. Budget about two hours to take in all the exhibits.

Saga Museum

The **Saga Museum** (Grandagardi 2, tel. 354/511-1517, www.sagamuseum.is, 10am-6pm daily, 2,100ISK) has 17 exhibits covering everything from Iceland's first inhabitants to the nation's conversion to Christianity to the Reformation. Special emphasis is placed on important characters in Iceland's history, such as Ingólfur Arnarson, who is believed to have been Iceland's first settler. There are interactive displays as well as artifacts on view and even a Viking dress-up area that is great for kids; they can play with replicas of traditional clothing and plastic swords. An audio guide in English, German, French, or Swedish is available to accompany your walk around the museum. The in-house restaurant, **Matur og Drykkur,** serves traditional Icelandic food with a modern twist. Budget two hours for this museum.

Nordic House
(Norræna Húsið)

Nordic House (Sturlugata 5, tel. 354/551-7030, www.nordichouse.is, 9am-5pm Sun.-Tue., 9am-9:30pm Wed.-Sat., free) is home to a library, café, and numerous cultural events during the year. Literary and film festivals are held at the building, as well as fashion and music events. Most tourists visit Nordic House for the structure itself. The building, which was opened in 1968, was designed by noted Finnish architect Alvar Aalto, and several of his signature traits are reflected in the design, including the use of tile, white, and wood throughout the building. The one-story building's exterior features a blue ceramic roof.

Reykjavík Museum of Photography
(Ljósmyndasafn Reykjavíkur)

The **Reykjavík Museum of Photography**

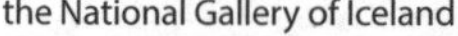
the National Gallery of Iceland

(Tryggvagata 15, tel. 354/563-1790, www.photomuseum.is, 10am-6pm Mon.-Thurs., 11am-6pm Fri., 1pm-5pm Sat.-Sun., 1,000ISK) has an extensive collection of photographs, as well as items and documents related to the practice of photography, from professional and amateur photographers in Iceland. The collection is divided into three categories: landscape, press, and portrait photography. The museum is small, but there are a lot of treasures to be found, including the oldest photo in the museum's collection, a landscape photo dating from 1870. Iceland's most famous landscape photographer, Ragnar Axelsson, regularly has photos on exhibit.

★ National Gallery of Iceland

(Listasafn Íslands)

If you have time for only one art museum, make it the **National Gallery of Iceland** (Fríkirkjuvergur 7, tel. 354/515-9600, www.listasafn.is, 10am-5pm daily, 1,500ISK). The National Gallery has a large and varied collection, and houses the country's main collection of Icelandic art. It places particular emphasis on 19th- and 20th-century Icelandic and international art. Here you will see everything from traditional landscape paintings to art depicting the sagas to works by modern Icelandic artists. Works from international artists on display include some from Pablo Picasso and Richard Serra. The stately white building is a stone's throw from Tjörnin (the Pond), so if the weather is fair, taking a leisurely stroll after visiting the museum is quite nice.

Reykjavík City Hall

(Ráðhús Reykjavíkur)

Reykjavík City Hall (Tjarnagata 11, tel. 354/411-1111, www.visitreykjavik.is) is more than just a building that houses the mayor and other officials. Built in 1992, the large white structure has a wall of windows overlooking the Pond. On the ground floor, visitors will find an information desk with maps and tourist brochures, as well as a cozy café with a great view of the Pond and city. A large hall is often used for art exhibitions and markets, and a huge model of Iceland is a favorite among tourists and worth a visit.

★ Tjörnin

Tjörnin (the Pond) is a small body of water, rich with birdlife, situated next to Reykjavík City Hall. The scenic strip of colorful houses

Reykjavík harbor

surrounding the Pond begs to be photographed. When the weather is nice, a walk around the Pond, which is about 1.5 kilometers around, is delightful. Sculptures and benches dot the perimeter. Birdlife is plentiful, with arctic terns, ducks, gulls, and swans. Feeding the birds is not allowed, so don't be that tourist who empties a bag of stale bread at the edge. In the winter, the water freezes and it becomes a popular spot for ice-skating.

Alþingishúsið

Alþingishúsið, or Parliament House, is the meeting place of the national parliament members of Iceland. Iceland's democracy dates back to the year 930, when parliament members met at Þingvellir; the parliament was moved to Reykjavík in 1844. Situated near Austurvöllur park, the stone building was designed by Danish architect Ferdinand Meldahland and built in 1881. Currently, only the debating chamber and a few small meeting rooms are actually located in the building. Offices of most of Alþingi's members are in other buildings in the area around Austurvöllur, which is actually the address of the building. It's not possible to attend sessions of parliament.

OLD HARBOR

Reykjavík's old harbor has been undergoing a transformation over the past few years, and it's become a dynamic place to visit, with shops, museums, new hotels, and the Ólafur Elíasson-designed Harpa concert hall.

★ Harpa

Harpa (Austurbakki 2, tel. 354/528-5000, www.harpa.is) is a striking glass structure that hosts rock concerts, operas, the Icelandic Symphony, and international conferences. Designed by Icelandic-Danish artist Ólafur Elíasson, the concert hall's exterior features individual glass panels that light up during the darkness of winter, sometimes blinking in a pattern or simply changing colors, and the building's waterside location lends itself to lovely reflections. Since opening its doors in 2011, Harpa has been lauded by design organizations and magazines around the world. Daily 30-minute guided tours of the building are available (1,500ISK, year-round) eight times a day mid-June-August and three times a day from the end of August to mid-June. It's also just a fun place to explore and take pictures of, even if you're not going to attend a concert or conference. **Smurstöðin** (10am-6pm

Harpa

daily), a café on the bottom floor, serves coffee, soft drinks, light meals, and cakes, and **Kolabrautin** (4pm-11pm daily), a formal restaurant on the 4th floor, has stunning views of the harbor.

Höfði House

Höfði House (Borgartún) is one of Reykjavík's most historically significant buildings and worth a photo or two. Built in 1909, the stately white building was initially used as the French consulate, and later served as a sort of guesthouse for famous folks passing through including Winston Churchill, Queen Elizabeth II, and even actress Marlene Dietrich. Perhaps its most famous use was as the backdrop for a 1986 meeting between U.S. president Ronald Reagan and the head of the Soviet Union, Mikhail Gorbachev. Today, Höfði is owned by the city of Reykjavík and is used for official receptions and meetings. Although the house is not open to the public, visitors are welcome to explore the exterior of the building.

★ *Sólfar*

Situated near a coastal path popular with cyclists and runners, ***Sólfar*** (by Sæbraut street) is a huge stainless steel sculpture described as a dreamboat. Before Harpa was built, *Sólfar* was the top spot to take photos near the harbor. It remains a big draw for tourists and is definitely worth a visit. Icelandic sculptor Jón Gunnar Árnason (1931-1989) wanted to convey a sense of undiscovered territory, hope, progress, and freedom, and built the piece as an ode to the sun, hence the name, translated as *Sun Voyager*. The sculpture was unveiled in 1990, just months after the artist's death. The view of Mount Esja, the sea, and passing boats is the perfect backdrop for photos. On clear days, you can see the town of Akranes across the bay.

Aurora Reykjavík

Aurora Reykjavík (Grandagarður 2, tel. 354/780-4500, www.aurorareykjavik.is, 9am-9pm daily, 1,600ISK) gives you a chance to check out northern lights in any season. If you can't make it to Iceland in the wintertime, this is the next best thing. The multimedia exhibition gives a history of the aurora borealis, relates stories of northern lights from around the world, and provides an introduction to northern lights photography. The highlight of the center is a 13-minute film that shows some of the most majestic northern lights displays over the island.

Sólfar, the *Sun Voyager*, by sculptor Jón Gunnar Árnason

Vikin Maritime Museum

Vikin Maritime Museum (Grandargarður 8, tel. 354/517-9400, www.borgarsgusafn.is, 10am-5pm daily, 1,600ISK) is Reykjavík's main museum devoted to the city's fishing history. The exhibitions show the progression from rowboats to modern trawlers and describe the vessels used, trading routes, and the construction of Reykjavík's harbor. There are daily tours of the coastal vessel *Odinn* available at 11am, 1pm, 2pm, and 3pm that last about an hour. The exhibitions cover the city's fishing history from the settlement to the present day. The museum café has great views of the harbor and offers an outdoor eating area when the weather cooperates.

OUTSIDE THE CITY CENTER

Reykjavík Zoo (Fjölskyldu- og Húsdýragarðinum)

The **Reykjavík Zoo** (Laugardalur, tel. 354/575-7800, www.mu.is, 10am-6pm daily June-late Aug., 10am-5pm daily late Aug.-May, 860ISK adults and teenagers, 650ISK children 5-12, free for children 4 and under) is more park than zoo. You won't see monkeys or polar bears, but exhibits house horses, pigs, goats, sheep, and other farm animals. The main attraction is a pair of seals. It's a pleasant place to walk around and bring children, but it isn't much of a tourist destination; if you're not on a long trip with small children, you can skip the zoo and not feel bad about it. Inside is a tiny aquarium that houses mainly fish. In the summer months, you'll see Icelandic families taking a stroll, looking at the animals, and visiting a small play area for children. There isn't an official petting zoo, but it's common to see parents holding their children up to pet horses in a penned area.

Reykjavík Botanical Garden (Grasagardur Reykjavíkur)

The **Reykjavík Botanical Garden** (Laugardalur, tel. 354/411-8650, www.grasagardur.is, 10am-10pm daily May 1-Sept. 30, 10am-3pm daily Oct. 1-Apr. 30, free) is a beautiful spot tucked away in a quiet part of the city. East of downtown Reykjavík, the neighborhood is more residential. During the summer months, the garden is chock-full of bright flowers, hardy plants, peaceful ponds, and thriving birdlife. The café within the garden, Café Flora, is a little-known spot among tourists. You will find locals sipping on coffee drinks and enjoying light meals while taking in the view from grand windows. If you're not visiting in the summer, you can skip the garden.

★ Perlan

Perlan (Öskjuhlíð, tel. 354/562-0200, www.perlanmuseum.is), nicknamed "the Pearl," is the distinctive, dome-shaped structure in Reykjavík's skyline. It offers one of the best views of the city skyline from its outdoor viewing platform (10am-10pm daily, 490ISK)—you can walk the perimeter and get a perfect panorama. The interior underwent a significant renovation in 2017, and the public building now hosts exhibits (2,900ISK), kicked off by an installation on glaciers and ice caves. A planetarium and northern lights exhibition are planned for fall 2018. Perlan also has a café that serves coffee and light meals as well as a souvenir shop.

Sports and Recreation

TOP EXPERIENCE

WHALE-WATCHING

Whale-watching is in some ways the best part of natural Reykjavík, in that you get to see a slice of nature just minutes from shore. **Elding Whale Watching** (Ægisgarður 5, tel. 354/519-5000, www.elding.is), which has 12 boats in Reykjavík, offers tours year-round and boasts a 95 percent chance of seeing whales in the summer, and 80 percent chance in the winter. Guides are enthusiastic, and the business is one of the oldest at the harbor. Tourists relish the sightings of minke and humpback whales, dolphins, porpoises, and various seabirds, including puffins and arctic terns. Make sure you dress warmly, even in the summer, as it can get quite cold on the open waters. Tours are about three hours and cost 10,990ISK for adults and 5,495ISK for children 7-15, free for children 6 and under. **Special Tours** (Ægisgarður 13, tel. 354/560-8800, www.specialtours.is) has a fleet of five boats of different speeds and sizes and also runs year-round tours from Reykjavík harbor, with five daily departures May-August and 1-2 daily departures the remainder of the year. Tours are about three hours and cost 10,990ISK per person. Both companies have environmentally responsible whale-watching policies.

BIKING

Reykjavík is a wonderful city to see by bicycle—that is, when the weather holds up. Over the past few years, there has been an initiative to designate more bike lanes and establish more places to lock up your bicycle along the streets. This isn't Amsterdam, but Reykjavík has come a long way. If you're in town and would like to rent a bike for an independent ride, or join a tour, **Reykjavík Bike Tours** (Ægisgarður 7, tel. 354/694-8956, www.icelandbike.com) will get you going. Its "Classic Reykjavík Bike Tour" (7,500ISK) covers about seven kilometers and takes a good 2.5 hours. Along the tour, you will see the University of Iceland campus, Reykjavík's Catholic cathedral, the parliament house, the old harbor, and more. Bicycle rentals start at 3,500ISK for four hours.

BIRD-WATCHING

For bird-watchers, the "Puffin Express" tour, which leaves from Reykjavík harbor May through mid-August, is operated by **Special Tours** (tel. 354/560-8800, www.specialtours.is). The owners have been running bird-watching tours since 1996, provide binoculars on board, and have a 100 percent sighting success rate. The guides have a soft spot for the funny black and white birds with the brilliant beaks and take great pride in telling you all about them. A one-hour boat tour is 5,700ISK for adults and 2,850ISK for children.

FISHING

If you'd like to try your hand at reeling in one of Iceland's freshest fish during the summer, you can rent equipment at Reykjavík harbor from **Rent a Rod** (tel. 354/869-2840, www.rentarod.is, 10am-6pm Mon.-Fri., 11am-5pm Sat.-Sun. June-Aug.). For 2,990ISK, you can rent a rod with reel and line for two hours, including bait, single-use gloves, and map of the harbor. You can catch trout, salmon, cod, pollock, and haddock. The staff could also arrange for fishing day tours out of the harbor. For sea angling tours, check out **Elding Whale Watching** (Ægisgarður 5, tel. 354/519-5000, www.elding.is), which offers a tour with a "gourmet" twist, where you can cook and eat your catch on board the boat. The tour is available May-August. The tour is about three hours, departs daily from Reykjavík harbor at 11am, and costs 17,800ISK.

SWIMMING

Swimming is a central part of Icelandic culture, and if you don't visit a pool or two during your stay in Iceland, you're missing out. Icelanders treat the pools as places for social gatherings. Visitors will see groups of friends and/or family in the pools and relaxing in hot tubs, chatting, laughing, and catching up. Each pool has its own character and local flavor, and some pools are more child-friendly than others, with slides and bigger areas designated for children. And, for roughly $5, it's a great way to spend a few leisurely hours. The pools listed here are recommended.

Laugardalslaug (Sundlaugavegur 30, tel. 354/411-5100, 7am-10pm Mon.-Fri., 8am-8pm Sat.-Sun., 950ISK) is the biggest pool facility in Reykjavík, and the one that gets the most tourists. The heated 50-meter outdoor pool is a big draw, along with the hot tubs, steam bath, and sauna. It's very crowded in the summer months (June-August) and can be loud because the giant waterslide in the children's pool is a favorite among local kids.

Sundhöllin (Barónstígur, tel. 354/551-4059, 7am-10pm Mon.-Fri., 8am-7pm Sat.-Sun., 950ISK) is the only indoor pool in Reykjavík and popular among locals and tourists alike. The outdoor sundeck overlooking Hallgrímskirkja is a great spot to spend a couple of hours when the sun is shining. Sundhöllin also has a steam room and two hot tubs. Given its proximity to the city center, the pool gets a lot of traffic.

Vesturbæjarlaug (Hofsvallagata 104, tel. 354/566-6879, 7am-10pm Mon.-Fri., 8am-10pm Sat.-Sun., 950ISK) is situated in a quiet neighborhood west of the city center. If you're looking to beat the crowds and experience the pool culture among locals, this is the spot. Facilities include a 25-meter pool, a few hot tubs, and a sauna.

SPAS

If you're after something more luxurious than a local swimming pool, there are a couple of spas in Reykjavík where you can relax and get treatments. Many tourists opt to spend an afternoon at the Blue Lagoon near Grindavík, and several buses depart from the bus station BSÍ (www.bsi.is). But if you want to beat the crowds, a local spa is a great option.

Laugar Spa (Sundlaugavegur 30A, tel. 354/553-0000, www.worldclass.is, 6am-11pm Mon.-Fri., 8am-9:30pm Sat., 8am-7:30pm Sun.) is Reykjavík's largest private spa, offering an extensive menu of treatments including facials, body massage and scrub, tanning treatments, waxing and nail services, and clay wrap treatments. The spa is marketed as an "aquatic heaven," and it's as good as it sounds. The entrance to the spa is reminiscent of a cave, with the soothing sound of water drops falling from a six-meter-wide waterfall. Inside, six sauna rooms are kept at different temperatures, each with its own unique theme. The treatment rooms feature muted hues and calming music. There is an on-site gym, as well as a café serving fresh, healthy meals.

Icelandair Hótel Reykjavík Natura's **Soley Natura Spa** (Nautholsvegur 2, tel. 354/444-4085, www.icelandairhotels.com, 10am-8pm Mon.-Fri., 10am-7pm Sat., noon-5pm Sun.) has an earthy atmosphere with natural hues and lots of wood furnishings. It's Scandinavian to a T. Guests have access to a heated pool, hot tub, and sauna before and after treatments. Massage options include lymphatic massage, hot stone massage, reflexology, and pregnancy massage. Beauty treatments include waxing services, manicures and pedicures, and facials. Access is 3,000ISK for hotel guests, 4,900ISK for non-guests. The spa is only open to guests 16 years of age and older.

Entertainment and Events

TOP EXPERIENCE

NIGHTLIFE

Reykjavík may be small, but its nightlife is epic. Whether you're up for some live music, want to dance, or are interested a classic pub crawl, Reykjavík will not disappoint. The main drag, Laugavegur, is ground zero for the hottest clubs and bars in town. If you are up for dancing, Kiki Queer Bar is your spot. If you fancy a whiskey bar, Dillon is the place. If you want to catch a hot Reykjavík band performing live, Húrra is your best bet. Be prepared for it to be a late night and for your wallet to take a hit. Locals don't venture out until around midnight, and drinks are expensive. Expect to pay upwards of 1,000ISK for a pint of beer and 2,200ISK for a cocktail; for this reason, cocktail bars are scarce, and beer is the favored beverage. But, for such a small city, you can't help but be impressed by the number of hot spots catering to different genres. Your biggest challenge will be narrowing down your options!

Bars

Austur (Austurstræti 7, tel. 354/568-1907, 8pm-1am Wed-Thurs., 8pm-4:30am Fri.-Sat.) was once the hottest club in Reykjavík, but a dress code and competition from other clubs have knocked it down a couple of pegs. It's still a place to mingle with locals and dance the night away to trendy dance music.

Boston (Laugavegur 28B, tel. 354/577-3200, 2pm-1am Sun.-Thurs., 2pm-3am Fri.-Sat.) is best known as a hangout for local artists, writers, hipsters, and hangers-on. The bar has an unassuming exterior, but inside await good drinks and hot music, mainly rock. If there's a concert on the night you go, expect to stand shoulder to shoulder. It's a tight spot and doesn't take too long to draw a big crowd.

Hressingarskálinn (Austurstræti 22, tel. 354/561-2240, www.hresso.is, 9am-1am Sun.-Thurs., 10am-4:30am Fri.-Sat.), simply known as Hresso, is a casual restaurant by day, serving up hamburgers and sandwiches. Free Wi-Fi attracts writers, tourists, and locals, who are known to spend hours sipping endless cups of coffee. By night, Hresso transforms into a dance club, with hot DJs and live bands. Expect trendy dance music.

Lebowski Bar (Laugavegur 20, tel. 354/552-2300, www.lebowski.is, 11:30am-1am Sun.-Thurs., 11:30am-4am Fri.-Sat.) pays not-so-subtle homage to the Coen brothers movie *The Big Lebowski.* Inside there is bowling paraphernalia, posters from the film, and even a rug hanging on the side of the bar. It's a casual eatery during the day, like many of Reykjavík's bars, but at night it transforms into a pretty wild scene, playing the latest dance music. There's a dance floor in the back of the room. The cost of a White Russian, the cocktail famously featured in the film, costs 1,700ISK.

The English Pub (Austurstræti 12b, tel. 354/578-0400, www.enskibarinn.is, noon-1am Mon.-Fri., noon-4:30am Sat.-Sun.) is part English pub, part sports bar. There's a nice selection of Icelandic and foreign beer, and Guinness is on tap. If there's a soccer game being played anywhere in the world, it will likely be shown on one of the many screens in the bar. If there's a Premier League game on, expect a crowd of expats, tourists, and locals.

Kaffibarinn (Bergstaðastræti 1, tel. 354/551-1588, 5pm-1am Sun.-Thurs., 3pm-3am Fri.-Sat.) has been a Reykjavík institution since scenes from the indie film *101 Reykjavík* were filmed here. Damon Albarn, the Blur front man, used to own a stake in the bar. It's a tiny space, with a rich red exterior that gets jam-packed during the weekends, but it's one of those places that it's cool to say you were there. Expect trendy dance music to be blaring as you enter.

Micro Bar (Austurstræti 6, tel.

354/847-9084, 4pm-midnight daily) is a beer lover's paradise. The bar carries about 80 different beers from countries including Belgium, Germany, Denmark, and the United States. The big draws are the wide selection of Icelandic beers on tap and the number of Icelandic craft beers available. Stop by and try a local stout, pale ale, or lager. The atmosphere is relaxed and relatively quiet, with dim lighting and a large wood bar. You'll find locals at the tables enjoying a beer and conversation with friends.

Kiki Queer Bar

Gay and Lesbian

Kiki Queer Bar (Laugavegur 22, tel. 354/571-0194, www.kiki.is, 8pm-1am Thurs., 8pm-4:30am Fri.-Sat.) is Reykjavík's only gay bar and was a welcome addition to the scene. Many locals will tell you this is *the* place to go to dance because it attracts some of the best local and visiting DJs. You can expect music ranging from Lady Gaga to the latest Icelandic pop music.

Live Music

Bar 11 (Hverfisgata 18, tel. 354/690-6021, noon-1am Sun.-Thurs., noon-3am Fri.-Sat.) has earned its reputation as Reykjavík's leading rock bar by featuring a steady stream of up-and-coming rock bands as well as local favorites. The decor is dark, with skulls and black furnishings, but the attitude is light and fun.

Café Rósenberg (Lækjargata 2, tel. 354/551-8008, 11am-1am Sun.-Thurs., 11am-3am Fri.-Sat.) hosts jazz, pop, rock, and folk acts from all around Iceland. You have a good chance to catch local favorites like KK, Ellen, and Svavar Knutur here, as well as international acts. The staffers are warm and friendly music lovers who take pride in booking varied acts and running a laid-back café that serves classic Icelandic comfort food.

Dillon (Laugavegur 30, tel. 354/511-2400, 2pm-1am Sun.-Thurs., 2pm-3am Fri.-Sat.) looks and feels like a dive bar. Rockers, metalheads, and hipsters unite, listening to live bands and sipping from the fine collection of more than 150 whiskeys available. Guests can find Scotch and bourbon as well as small-batch Icelandic whiskeys. When there isn't live music, locals DJs keep the music flowing. The interior is a little rough, with lots of wood and not many places to sit, and the music is always loud.

Húrra (Tryggvagata 22, tel. 354/691-9662, 5pm-1am Sun.-Thurs., 5pm-4:30am Fri.-Sat.) is a colorful spot featuring a steady stream of Iceland's hottest bands taking the stage, playing everything from rock and dance to pop and hip-hop, depending on the night.

Kex Hostel (Skúlagata 28, tel. 354/561-6060, www.kexhostel.is) has become a Reykjavík institution over the past few years. The building, formerly a biscuit factory, is a great space, complete with mid-century furniture, vintage wall maps, and a lot of curiosities. A small stage in the entryway hosts up-and-coming bands while guests drink and hang out at the **bar** (11:30am-11pm daily). A back room serves as a venue for more formal concerts. If you're in your 20s and aren't bothered by hipsters, this is your place. Since this is a hostel, it's open 24 hours, so check listings at www.grapevine.is for concert times.

Loft Hostel (Bankastræti 7, tel. 354/553-8140, www.lofthostel.is) has earned a reputation as a place to see and be seen. The 4th-floor bar/café hosts up-and-coming bands, established live acts, and DJs. An outdoor deck overlooks Bankastræti and is packed with locals and tourists alike when the sun is shining during the day, and filled with mingling concertgoers at night. Since this is a hostel, it's open 24 hours, so check listings at www.grapevine.is for concert and event times.

PERFORMING ARTS

Icelandic Opera

(Íslenska Óperan)

The **Icelandic Opera** (Ingólfsstræti 2A, tel. 354/511-6400, www.opera.is) has been thriving since productions moved in 2011 to the exquisite Harpa concert hall by the harbor. Productions have become more elaborate, and entire runs have been selling out. If you are an opera fan, check the website to see the current and upcoming shows. Past performances include *Carmen, Il Trovatore, La Boheme,* and *The Magic Flute.*

Icelandic Symphony Orchestra

(Sinfóníuhljómsveit Íslands)

The **Icelandic Symphony Orchestra** (Austurbakki 2, tel. 354/545-2500, www.sinfonia.is) consists of 90 full-time members and performs about 60 concerts each season, including subscription concerts in Reykjavík, family concerts, school concerts, and recordings, as well as local and international tours. Based in the Harpa concert hall, the symphony has performed works by Igor Stravinsky, Sergei Rachmaninoff, and Pyotr Tchaikovsky.

National Theater of Iceland

(Þjóðleikhúsið)

The **National Theater of Iceland** (Hverfisgata 19, tel. 354/551-1200, www.leikhusid.is) has been a Reykjavík mainstay since its opening in 1950. The emphasis is on Nordic/Scandinavian plays and musicals, but some foreign works are translated into Icelandic. In 2017, the theater put on productions of *Othello* and *Peter and the Wolf* in the 500-seat main stage. The exterior is a cold, concrete-gray building, but inside is a different story. The interior is modern, the theater is comfortable, and there's a lovely lounge area with plush seats and small tables where you can have a drink and wait for the show to begin.

FESTIVALS AND EVENTS

Spring

The **Reykjavík Fashion Festival** (www.rff.is) showcases fashion lines from established designers as well as up-and-comers every March for four days. Along with runway shows and special exhibitions, the festival welcomes international designers as guest speakers. The focus in recent years has been on Icelandic designers and Icelandic guest speakers.

Coinciding with the Reykjavík Fashion Festival is **DesignMarch (HönnunarMars)** (www.designmarch.is), a broader event that covers everything from product design to graphic design. With pop-up stores around the city and exhibitions held in museums and open-air spaces, the festival attracts people from around the world to check out the latest and greatest in Icelandic design.

You may not expect Reykjavík to be a blues town, but don't tell that to locals. The **Reykjavík Blues Festival (Blúshátið í Reykjavík)** (www.blues.is) is a weeklong event held in early April. It mixes local talent with acclaimed international acts like Michael Burks, Lucky Peterson, Pinetop Perkins, and Magic Slim and the Teardrops.

Gamers rejoice! The **EVE Fanfest** takes over the city every May, celebrating the beloved video game *EVE,* which is the creation of local company CCP. Thousands of gamers, nerds, and curious locals gather, attend roundtable discussions, play live tournaments, and indulge in a pub crawl.

Summer

Delighting locals and tourists since 1970, the **Reykjavík Arts Festival (Listahátíð í Reykjavík)** (www.artfest.is) manages to keep the program fresh, showcasing visual and performance artists from around the globe. The festival spans two weeks over late May and early June and holds events in different cultural venues as well as outdoor exhibitions.

Reykjavík Pride (Hinsegin Dagar) (www.reykjavikpride.com) is a citywide celebration of human rights, diversity, and culture. It garners a huge turnout every year. Each August, the city hosts rainbow-themed events ranging from concerts to guest speakers. It's known as the highest-profile event for Iceland's gay, lesbian, bisexual, and transgender community. Hundreds of volunteers organize the event, and people from around the country congregate to celebrate their fellow citizens.

Since 1990, the **Reykjavík Jazz Festival (Jazzhátíð Reykjavíkur)** (www.reykjavikjazz.is) has been delighting horn section enthusiasts. International artists like Aaron Parks and Chris Speed are invited to put on concerts and jam with locals over five days in mid-August. There are off-venue free events throughout the city, and this is a popular festival among the locals. Headline concerts take place at the concert hall Harpa.

Independent choreographers launched the **Reykjavík Dance Festival** (www.reykjavikdancefestival.com) in 2002, and the annual event is still going strong today. The focus is on bringing contemporary dance closer to the people. The weeklong event held every August showcases local talent as well as international dancers.

Reykjavík Culture Night (Menningarnótt) (www.culturenight.is) has the darling slogan "come on in," which is a reference to the island's old-fashioned customs of hospitality. Culture Night actually starts during the day, with select residents opening up their properties to offer waffles and coffee to their neighbors and visitors. Hundreds of events around the city range from cultural performances to free museum events. The festival culminates with a huge outdoor concert that features some of the biggest names in Icelandic rock and pop music. It's held at the end of August.

Fall

Beginning at the end of September, the **Reykjavík International Film Festival** (www.riff.is) takes place over 11 days, during which films from more than 40 countries are screened. They range from short films to full-length features and documentaries, and the festival is a great venue to discover new talent. Invited special guests have included American director Jim Jarmusch and English director Mike Leigh.

Iceland Airwaves (www.icelandairwaves.is) has been delighting music lovers since 1999. The five-day festival, held in late October/early November, has hosted an impressive list of performers, including Sigur Rós, Björk, and Of Monsters and Men, as well as international artists including Robyn, Kraftwerk, and Flaming Lips. There are also off-venue performances held for free in bars, bookstores, record shops, and coffeehouses—so if you don't score tickets to the festival, you can still check out some amazing music. A detailed off-venue schedule is published along with on-venue appearances.

Winter

Sónar Reykjavík (www.sonarreykjavik.com) is the new kid on the block in Reykjavík music festivals. Launched in 2013, Sónar features rock, pop, punk, electronic, and dance music performances in Harpa concert hall. Artists have included GusGus, Squarepusher, and Hermigervill. The festival takes place in mid-February.

The annual **Reykjavík Food & Fun Festival** (www.foodandfun.is) showcases the culinary exploits of world-renowned chefs collaborating with local Icelandic chefs. There are competitions, exhibitions, and lots of eating. It takes place at the end of February.

Shopping

Reykjavík may not strike you as a shopping destination, but there are quite a few local brands, like clothing labels 66 North and Cintamanti, that are quite popular. If you're up for some shopping, be sure to take a stroll on Laugavegur: The street is chock-full of design shops, jewelers, boutiques, and bookstores.

ART/DESIGN

Aurum (Bankstræti 4, tel. 354/551-2770, www.aurum.is, 10am-6pm daily) is the place to go for unique Icelandic jewelry. Shoppers are treated to an impressive display of rings, necklaces, and earrings made from silver, gold, or lava stones. Aurum's jewelry is distinctively Icelandic, with pieces inspired by the raw nature of the island. An adjoining section is dedicated to modern toys, knitwear, accessories, and home goods.

Epal (Laugavegur 70, tel. 354/551-3555, www.epal.is, 10am-8pm Mon.-Sat, noon-8pm Sun.) is the original design store in Iceland, stocking everything from furniture to light fixtures to bedding and small goods. At Epal, which was founded in 1975, you'll find Icelandic designers as well as international brands, including Fritz Hansen, Georg Jensen, Marimekko, OK Design, and Tin Tin. Other than the downtown Reykjavík store, Epal has three other stores at Skeifan, Keflavík International Airport, and Harpa concert hall.

Foa (Laugavegur 2, tel. 354/571-1433, 10am-6pm Mon.-Sat., 1pm-5pm Sun.) carries indie design brands that can't be found in many other stores. For instance, hand-carved wooden swans by local artist Bjarni Þór are on sale along with small woolen goods for kids and individual letterpress cards. It's a fun store to wander around and pick up something unique.

Hrim Hönnunarhús (Laugavegur 25, tel. 354/553-3003, www.hrim.is, 10am-6pm Mon.-Sat., 1pm-5pm Sun.) is where you go for one-stop shopping for design lovers, whether you're looking for accessories, playful paper goods, or housewares. There is an emphasis on Icelandic design, especially when it comes to jewelry and home goods, but there are also foreign-made items as well. For instance, Hrim has an impressive Lomography camera display for those looking for lo-fi film or a new Diana plastic camera. The staff is friendly and eager to help you find that perfect purchase.

Hrim Eldhus (Laugavegur 32, tel. 354/553-2002, 10am-6pm daily) opened in 2014 after the success of parent shop Hrim, down the block. Eldhus, which means "kitchen" in Iceland, focuses on modern design accessories for the kitchen and dining room. The adorable store stocks goods from local Icelandic designers as well as designers from its Scandinavian and Nordic neighbors. This store is stocked with nothing you really need, but everything you want.

Kraum (Laugavegur 18, tel. 354/779-6161, www.kraum.is, 9am-9pm Mon.-Fri., 10am-9pm Sat- Sun.) has been voted "the best place to stock up on local design" by local newspaper *Reykjavík Grapevine* for straight five years. Kraum stocks everything from the adorable independent children's clothing line As We Grow to handbags made from fish leather. They also carry pillows, jewelry, candleholders, and woolen goods. If you're going to visit one design shop in Reykjavík, it should be Kraum, as it has the largest and most diverse selection of goods.

BOOKSTORES

Reykjavík was named a UNESCO City of Literature in 2012, and the title was well deserved. Locals like to boast that 1 in 10 Icelanders will publish a book in their lifetime and that Iceland has the highest number of Nobel Prize winners for literature per capita. That would be one winner—Halldór

Laxness for *Independent People.* Due to the importance of literature to the city and the exceptionally high literacy rate of its citizens, Reykjavík boasts an unusually large number of bookstores.

Eymundsson (Austurstræti 18, tel. 354/540-2000, www.eymundsson.is, 10am-10pm daily) is the oldest and largest bookstore chain in Reykjavík, dating back to 1872. The main shop on Austurstræti has four levels, with an impressive magazine section, tourist books on Iceland, and a large English-language book section.

Mál og Menning (Laugavegur 18, tel. 354/515-2500, www.malogmenning.is, 9am-10pm daily), which means "Language and Culture," is a favorite among Reykjavík locals. The three-level store sells fun tourist wares on the ground floor next to the magazine section. Upstairs is a collection of art and photography books, along with hundreds of English-language novels and nonfiction reads. The top floor also houses a café, where people sip lattes as they flip through magazines and newspapers.

MUSIC

Icelandic music is more than Björk and Sigur Rós, and a few choice music shops will help you discover local favorites as well as up-and-coming Icelandic artists.

A lot more than a record shop, **12 Tónar** (Skólavörðustígur 15, tel. 354/511-5656, www.12tonar.is, 10am-6pm Mon.-Sat., noon-6pm Sun.) is a place to mingle with other music lovers and sample new Icelandic music with private CD players and headphones, all while sipping on a complimentary cup of coffee. The shop was founded in 1998 and is an integral part of Reykjavík's music culture; the owner also runs an independent music label, and the shop is often used as a music venue during Reykjavík's annual autumn music festival, Iceland Airwaves. This is a landmark, a cultural institution.

If you like vinyl, **Lucky Records** (Rauðarárstígur 10, tel. 354/551-1195, www.luckyrecords.is, 10am-6pm Mon.-Fri., 11am-5pm Sat.-Sun.) is the place for you. The shop has the largest collection of new and used vinyl in the city, with an extensive Icelandic selection as well as foreign rock, pop, hip-hop, jazz, soul, and everything else you could imagine. Bands and DJs frequently play free concerts at the shop, and it's a fun place to spend a couple of hours. There's a turntable and headphones, with which you're welcome to sample used records.

Hrim Eldhus

Smekkleysa (Bad Taste) Records (Laugavegur 28, tel. 354/534-3730, www.smekkleysa.net, 10am-6pm Mon.-Fri., 10am-5pm Sat., noon-5pm Sun.) was born from the legendary Smekkleysa record label that has released albums from the Sugarcubes (Björk's former band), Sigur Rós, and scores of other Icelandic artists. Its record shop, while small, has a great collection of Icelandic music on CD and vinyl, as well as a DVD section, box sets, and classical music on CD.

Reykjavík Record Shop (Klapparstígur 35, tel. 354/561-2299, 11am-6pm Mon.-Fri., 1pm-6pm Sat.) is a small shop specializing in vinyl that has an impressive selection of local music as well as international artists. You can browse new and used records, as well as CDs, books, and T-shirts.

CLOTHING/KNITWEAR

Perhaps Iceland's best-known and oldest brand, **66 North** (Bankastræti 5, tel. 354/535-6600, www.66north.com, 9am-10pm daily) has been keeping Icelanders warm since 1926. You will find hats, rainwear, gloves, fleece, vests, and parkas in colors ranging from basic black (a favorite among Icelanders) to lava orange. Heavy parkas cost an arm and a leg (around $500), but you pay for the Thermolite insulation and design details. If you're not looking to make a fashion investment, you can grab a hat for about $25.

Cintamani (Bankastræti 7, tel. 354/533-3390, www.cintamani.is, 9am-9pm daily) has been dressing Icelanders in colorful, fashionable designs since 1989. Ranging from base layers to outerwear, Cintamani is a bit more playful than 66 North, with more prints and brighter colors. The emphasis is not just on style, but warmth as well with top-notch insulation.

Farmers & Friends (Laugavegur 37, tel. 354/552-1960, www.farmersmarket.is, 10am-10pm Mon.-Fri., 11am-7pm Sat., 11am-5pm Sun) is the flagship store of the wildly popular Farmer's Market clothing label. If you are looking for sweaters other than the traditional garb available at Handprjónasamband Íslands (Handknitting Association of Iceland), Farmer's Market offers everything from cardigans to capes in stylish colors and patterns. The label, which was launched in 2005, is focused on combining classic Nordic design elements with a modern aesthetic.

Geysir (Skólavörðustígur 16, tel. 354/519-6000, www.geysir.com, 10am-7pm Mon.-Sat., 11am-5pm Sun.) features clothes that combine beauty with the utility of Icelandic

coffee at Mál og Menning bookshop

wool. Warm sweaters, cardigans, capes, and blankets are on offer at the flagship Reykjavík shop, not too far from Hallgrímskirkja. The clothes have a traditional look with some modern twists.

Handknitting Association of Iceland (Handprjónasamband Íslands) (Skólavörðustígur 19, tel. 354/552-1890, www.handknit.is, 9am-6pm Mon.-Fri., 9am-4pm Sat., 11am-4pm Sun.) is a collective of Icelanders that knit and sell sweaters, scarves, shawls, hats, mittens, and other woolen goods. If you are looking for an authentic, traditional Icelandic sweater, and are willing to pay top dollar, this is your place. There are a lot of colors and patterns to choose from in an array of sizes.

Kolaportið (Tryggvagata 19, tel. 354/562-5030, www.kolaportid.is, 11am-5pm Sat.-Sun.) is Reykjavík's only flea market, and, boy, do they go all out in this space. You can find everything from secondhand traditional Icelandic sweaters to used CDs and vinyl records to books and even fresh and frozen fish. A very popular place, it's usually packed, regardless of the weather or season.

KronKron (Laugavegur 63b, tel. 354/562-8388, www.kronkron.com, 10am-6pm Mon.-Thurs., 10am-6:30pm Fri., 10am-5pm Sat.) is a hip shop that focuses on up-and-coming designers. Fashions for men and women range from fun and flirty to chic and modern. You can find elegant dresses, fashion-forward sweaters, and unique accessories. The clientele ranges from teens to young professionals, which shows the range of duds available.

GIFTS AND SOUVENIRS

Álafoss (Laugavegur 8, tel. 354/562-6303, www.alafoss.is, 9am-10pm daily) is best known for its huge factory wool store in the Reykjavík suburb of Mosfellsbær, but this small downtown outpost is great for picking up yarn for knitting projects and small wool souvenirs to bring home. You can find socks, hats, magnets, shot glasses, soft toys, candy, and handmade Icelandic soap, among many other goodies.

Blue Lagoon (Laugavegur 15, tel. 354/420-8849, www.bluelagoon.com, 10am-6pm Mon.-Fri., 10am-4pm Sat., 1pm-5pm Sun.) is a tiny shop on the main street that carries all of the Blue Lagoon's skin-care line. If you can't make it to the actual Blue Lagoon near Grindavík, don't fret, because you can take home some of the essence that makes the site so special. The shop is decked out in cool blue hues and lots of lava stones, and the

12 Tónar music shop

shelves are filled with everything from a nourishing algae mask to mineral bath salts.

The Little Christmas Shop (Laugavegur 8, tel. 354/552-2412, 10am-6pm Mon.-Fri., 10am-5pm Sat., 10:30am-2pm Sun.) is a small shop where it's Christmas all year round. A pair of stone Santa shoes outside the store draws you into a world of Christmas tree ornaments, ceramic Yule Lads figurines, soft toys, dishes, and just about everything with a Christmas theme. No matter what the season, it's a joyous shop to visit and will get you buying Christmas ornaments in July.

Polar Bear Gift Store (Laugavegur 38, tel. 354/578-6020, www.isbjorninn.is, 10am-8pm daily) is bound to catch your attention with its huge toy polar bear models outside the store. While polar bears are not indigenous to Iceland, don't let that fact stop you from checking out the cute wares inside. You can pick up T-shirts, hats, magnets, keychains, and other souvenirs.

Ravens (Laugavegur 15, tel. 354/551-1080, www.ravens.is, 10am-7pm Mon.-Sat., 11am-5pm Sun.) is a unique shop that houses all sorts of good stuff that you can't find anywhere else. You can find arctic fur, authentic Inuit art, lambskin rugs, custom-made knives, sculptures, and leather accessories. You won't find mass-produced souvenirs here.

The Viking (Hafnarstræti 3, tel. 354/551-1250, www.theviking.is, 9am-7pm Mon.-Fri., 9am-6pm Sat.-Sun.) is exactly what you would expect from a souvenir shop in Reykjavík. T-shirts, mugs, stuffed puffins and polar bears, wool products, Viking helmets, and just about everything in between can be found here. If you're looking for unique and sophisticated trinkets, this isn't your spot. But, if you're up for fun and affordable items, you will likely find them here.

Vínberið (Laugavegur 43, tel. 354/551-2475, 9am-6pm Mon.-Fri., 10am-6pm Sat., noon-5pm Sun.) is a sweets shop stocked with everything from chocolates to rhubarb toffee. There's a good mix of local and foreign brands, and it would be almost impossible to not find something you like. Gift options include treats wrapped in pretty packaging. In the back there are spices and baking products, and in the summer there is frequently a mini outdoor fruit market just outside the shop. One sweet that is wildly popular among Icelanders is black licorice. You can find a selection of licorice candies with or without a chocolate coating.

Handknitting Association of Iceland

SHOPPING MALLS

Kringlan (Kringlunni 4-12, tel. 354/568-9200, www.kringlan.is, 10am-6:30pm Mon.-Wed., 10am-9pm Thurs., 10am-7pm Fri., 10am-5pm Sat.-Sun.) resembles just about any mall in America. There are clothing stores, a bank, a movie theater, and a food court packed with teenagers and shoppers. If the weather is particularly bad and you want to get some shopping done, it's a good destination. There's a 66 North shop in Kringlan, as well as some other Icelandic brands. Kringlan is a five-minute drive east from downtown Reykjavík, and it can be reached by Strætó bus numbers 1, 2, 3, 4, 6, 13, and 14. One-way bus fare is 350ISK, and it takes about 10 minutes from downtown Reykjavík.

Smáralind (Hagasmári 1, tel. 354/528-8000, www.smaralind.is, 11am-7pm Mon.-Thurs., 11am-9pm Fri., 11am-6pm Sat., 1pm-6pm Sun.) is located in the Reykjavík suburb Kópavogur and is one of the main shopping centers in the region for locals. You will find everything from Adidas sneakers to Levi's, but for double the price than back home. However, it offers a movie theater and an entertainment area with rides for kids if that strikes your fancy.

The Little Christmas Shop

Food

Reykjavík's culinary charm may be surprising to some. While there are traditional Icelandic restaurants serving up fresh fish and tender lamb fillets, there are also fantastic eateries specializing in food you may not expect to see in Iceland. For instance, there's an impressive collection of Asian and Mediterranean restaurants, which have authentic menus that incorporate the great ingredients found in Iceland. If you're in the mood for tapas, there's a place to have an exquisite meal. Craving sushi? You will not be disappointed. As for Icelandic cuisine, there are upmarket restaurants catering to foodies as well as fast-food joints offering quick, affordable bites.

ICELANDIC

Bergsson Mathús (Templarasund 3, tel. 354/571-1822, www.bergsson.is, 7am-10pm daily, 2,400ISK) is known for its fantastic brunch menu and light, flavorful dishes. Try the roast beef on a bed of salad or the spinach lasagna. The eatery is also a popular coffee spot for locals.

Fjalakötturinn (Aðalstræti 16, tel. 354/514-6060, www.fjalakotturinn.is, lunch 11:30am-2pm daily, dinner 6pm-10pm Sun.-Thurs., 6pm-11pm Fri.-Sat., 3,800ISK) is housed inside Hotel Centrum in downtown Reykjavík, but it's not only a popular place for hotel guests to visit. The inventive food, modern decor, intimate tables, and gorgeous pictures of Iceland's landscape make this spot a winner. Fresh fish including salmon, trout, catfish, and lobster is on the menu, as is rack of lamb.

Iðnó (Vonarstræti 3, tel. 354/562-9700, www.idno.is, noon-10pm daily, 3-course menu from 7,900ISK) is a historic building that houses local theater productions as well as a fine restaurant. Situated close to Tjörnin and the city hall, the restaurant is pricey, but the food is memorable. The smoked salmon on blinis with caviar is exquisite, as is the ginger-glazed breast of duck.

★ **Lækjarbrekka** (Bankastræti 2, tel. 354/551-4430, www.laekjarbrekka.is, 11:30am-10pm daily, entrées from 3,800ISK) occupies a historic building that dates back to 1834. Today, Lækjarbrekka is one of the best-known downtown restaurants catering to tourists. Fresh fish dishes are on the menu alongside some of Iceland's most adventurous cuisine. You'll find fermented shark, whale meat, puffin, and Icelandic horse fillets on offer. For tamer choices, the pan-fried fillet of lamb and arctic char are splendid.

Restaurant Reykjavík (Vesturgata 2, tel. 354/552-3030, www.restaurantreykjavik.is, 11:30am-10pm daily, entrées from 4,000ISK) is known for its fantastic fish buffet (6,950ISK), which starts every day at 6pm. This is a favorite among tourists looking to sample traditional Icelandic fish dishes as well as international classics. The restaurant is housed in a huge yellow building with lots of seating, so you're not likely to have to wait for a table. The fish buffet features everything from salmon, cod, lobster, fish balls, trout, and caviar to shrimp and crab specialties. An à la carte menu offers beef, lamb, fish, and vegetarian options.

Icelandic Bar (Íslenski Barinn) (Ingólfsstræti 1, tel. 354/517-6767, www.islenskibarinn.is, 11:30am-1am Sun.-Thurs., 11:30am-3am Fri.-Sat., entrées from 2,600ISK) takes classic Icelandic ingredients like lamb, whale, and puffin and puts a creative spin on the dishes with interesting flavor combinations. For example, the restaurant serves a sweet and savory dish of grilled puffin with blueberries, pickled red onions, *skyr,* and herbs. Guests can also order items like local salmon, traditional lamb meat soup, and the famous Icelandic hot dog. The reindeer burger is highly recommended.

Matur og Drykkur (Grandagarður 2,

tel. 354/571-8877, www.maturogdrykkur.is, 11:30am-10:30pm daily, entrées from 3,200ISK) has an eclectic menu that includes items such as double-smoked lamb with buttermilk and nutmeg, a whole cod's head cooked in chicken stock with dulse (a type of seaweed), and rutabaga soup with red beet caviar and sunflower seeds. The restaurant, which is housed in the Saga Museum, has a casual atmosphere with reminders of the fishing industry—appropriate, because the building used to be a saltfish factory.

★ **Dill Restaurant** (Hverfisgata 12, tel. 354/552-1522, www.dillrestaurant.is, 6pm-10pm Wed.-Sat., entrées from 11,900) is Iceland's first restaurant to receive a Michelin star and has been a hit with tourists and locals for years. The rotating menu features meat, fish, and creative vegetarian options. Decor is minimalist, allowing the food to take center stage. Be sure to book a table far in advance (at least six weeks), as this is the toughest reservation in Iceland. You can book online or by phone; groups of eight or more must email the restaurant (dillrestaurant@dillrestaurant.is).

SEAFOOD

★ **Fish Market** (Aðlstræti 12, tel. 354/578-8877, www.fiskmarkadurinn.is, 5pm-11pm daily, entrées from 5,100ISK) stands out among a number of fantastic seafood restaurants in Reykjavík. What makes Fish Market special is the way the chef combines ingredients. The grilled monkfish comes with crispy bacon, cottage cheese, tomato yuzu pesto, and crunchy enoki mushrooms. It's a vision, as is the salted cod with lime zest with potato puree, dried cranberries, and celery salad.

Fiskfelagid (Fish Company) (Vesturgata 2a, tel. 354/552-5300, www.fiskfelagid.is, 11:30am-10:30pm Mon.-Thurs., 11:30am-11:30pm Fri., 5:30pm-10:30pm Sat.-Sun., entrées from 4,600ISK) has a striking, chic interior with modern wooden tables and chairs, candleholders throughout the space, and personal notes and photos adorning the walls. There are comfortable couches in the lounge, where you're welcome to sip a cocktail while waiting for a table. The food is flawless, ranging from pan-fried prime lamb and oxtail with artichoke puree to blackened monkfish and fried langoustine with lobster spring rolls.

The Lobster House (Amtmannsstígur 1, tel. 354/561-3303, www.thelobsterhouse.is, 11:30am-10pm Mon.-Sat., 5pm-10pm Sun., entrées from 4,400ISK) is the place for—you guessed it—lobster. You can't make a bad choice: grilled lobster tails with garlic butter, lobster soup, slow-cooked monkfish and smoked lobster with potato salad, lobster tempura, and lots of other options. If you're not a fan of lobster, don't fret. There are lamb, pork, and other fish options on the menu.

Icelandic Fish & Chips (Tryggvagata 11, tel. 354/551-1118, www.fishandchips.is, 11:30am-9pm daily, entrées from 1,390ISK) serves up a wonderful range of fresh seafood: cod, plaice, blue ling, haddock, redfish, wolffish, and shellfish. For an authentic Icelandic fish-and-chips meal, go for the cod. The biggest draws, however, are the "skyronnaise dips," in which Iceland's famous soft cheese, *skyr,* is blended with an array of spices, including basil, coriander, ginger, and tarragon. The truffle and tarragon dip is heavenly.

MAR Restaurant (Geirsgata 9, tel. 354/519-5050, www.marrestaurant.com, 11:30am-11pm daily, entrées from 2,900ISK) offers South American-inspired dishes ranging from prosciutto-wrapped monkfish with fennel seeds to lamb fillet with leeks, carrots, and beets. The banana crème brûlée with chocolate sorbet is recommended for dessert. The atmosphere is casual, with wood tables and minimalist design, and the harbor location is great.

★ **Sea Baron (Sægreifinn)** (Geirsgata 8, tel. 354/553-1500, www.saegreifinn.is, 11:30am-10pm daily, entrées from 1,600ISK) has been a Reykjavík institution for years. With its prime location by the harbor, the Sea Baron is known for its perfectly spiced, fresh lobster soup, which comes with a side of bread and butter. Fish kebabs on offer include scallops, monkfish, and cod. Whale meat is also

the Sea Baron restaurant

available if you're so inclined. Inside, visitors will find a hut-like atmosphere with fishing relics, photos, and equipment. A net hangs from the ceiling, and charming knickknacks are displayed.

ASIAN

Bambus (Borgartún 16, tel. 354/517-0123, www.bambusrestaurant.is, 11:30am-11pm Mon.-Fri., 5pm-10pm Sat.-Sun., entrées from 1,750ISK) is a delightful Asian fusion restaurant mixing Thai, Japanese, and Indian influences. Dishes incorporate everything from curry to teriyaki and coconut milk. A salad with chicken, sweet chili, and mango is spectacular. The restaurant is decorated in minimalist, Asian-influenced style.

Gandhi Restaurant (Posthusstræti 17, tel. 354/511-1691, www.gandhi.is, 5:30pm-10pm daily, entrées from 3,000ISK) features the creations of two chefs from southwest India. Combining local Icelandic ingredients with traditional Indian spices, the menu offers authentic dishes like chicken vindaloo and fish masala as well as vegetarian options. The food is fresh and perfectly spiced. The butter chicken is gorgeous, rivaling that of the top Indian restaurants in London.

Krua Thai (Skólavörðustígur 21, tel. 354/551-0833, www.kruathai.is, 11:30am-9:30pm Mon.-Fri., noon-9:30pm Sat., 5pm-9:30pm Sun., 1,500ISK) has all your favorite Thai classics, ranging from chicken pad thai to spring rolls and noodle soups. During weekdays, the restaurant has a three-course lunch special for just 1,400ISK.

Noodle Station (Laugavegur 103, tel. 354/551-3198, 11am-10pm daily, 1,580ISK) is a popular spot for Reykjavík natives, students, and tourists. People flock to the tiny shop for one of the tastiest and cheapest meals you can find in downtown. Noodle soup is available with chicken or beef or as a vegetarian option. The smell of spices wafting down Skólavörðustígur will draw you in.

Osushi (Pósthússtræti 13, tel. 354/561-0562, www.osushi.is, 11:30am-10pm Mon.-Thurs., 11:30am-11pm Fri.-Sat., 3pm-10pm Sun., bites 300-500ISK) is a sushi train with bites snaking their way around. Diners are treated to everything from deep-fried shrimp tempura rolls to tuna sashimi and grilled eel bites. For kids, there are chicken teriyaki kebabs, spring rolls, and even a chocolate mousse for dessert.

Ramen Momo (Tryggvagata 16, tel. 354/571-0646, www.ramenmomo.is, 11am-10pm daily, 1,890ISK) is an adorable hidden restaurant not too far from the harbor. Owned and operated by a Tibetan immigrant, Ramen Momo serves up glorious chicken, beef, or vegetarian ramen soup and dumplings. The nondescript eatery has an authentic feel to it, and your taste buds will thank you.

Sushibarinn (Laugavegur 2, tel. 354/552-4444, www.sushibarinn.is, 11:30am-10pm Mon.-Sat., 5pm-10pm Sun., rolls from 1,990ISK) has not only sushi roll staples like California, volcano, and shrimp tempura rolls, but also some creative combinations, including the Rice Against the Machine roll, which has salmon, cream cheese, red onions, and chili. For those who are inclined, whale sushi is on the menu as well.

Sushi Social (Þingholtsstræti 5, tel. 354/568-6600, www.sushisamba.is, 5pm-11pm Sun.-Thurs., 5pm-midnight Fri.-Sat., rolls from 2,500ISK) combines Japanese and South American elements to create inventive and delicious sushi rolls and entrées. You'll find traditional fresh seafood like tuna, salmon, crab, lobster, and shrimp, along with South American influences like spicy salsa, jalapeño mayo, and chimichurri. Main entrées include baked vanilla-infused cod and grilled beef tenderloin with mushroom sauce, jalapeño, and coriander.

MEDITERRANEAN

Gamla Smiðjan (Lækjargata 8, tel. 354/578-8555, www.gamlasmidjan.is, 11:30am-11pm daily, large pizzas from 1,990ISK) is a wildly popular pizza place among the locals, which is telling. While Reykjavík isn't known for its pizza, this place is pretty darn good. You have a choice of an obscene number of toppings, ranging from classic pepperoni to more exotic options like tuna fish and banana. It has a laid-back atmosphere and decent service.

Hornið (Hafnartsræti 15, tel. 354/551-3340, www.hornid.is, 11am-11:30pm daily, large pizzas from 1,890ISK), with its yellow and blue walls, looks like a bistro from the outside, and the interior reveals a relaxed atmosphere with friendly service and yummy pizzas. Classic pizzas include pepperoni, four cheese, and vegetable, but there are also adventurous creations like the Pizza Pecatore, which has shrimp, mussels, and scallops on top. If you're not up for pizza, entrées include salted cod with risotto and fillet of lamb with vegetables.

Ítalía (Laugavegur 11, tel. 354/552-4630, www.italia.is, 11:30am-11pm daily, pasta dishes from 2,900ISK) is a cute Italian restaurant right on the main street, Laugavegur. The menu offers classics like spaghetti Bolognese, lasagna, and mushroom ravioli as well as options that incorporate local ingredients, like smoked salmon with toasted bread and pan-fried salted cod with onions. Pizza and calzones are also on the menu.

Tapas Barinn (Vesturgata 3b, tel. 354/551-2344, www.tapas.is, 5pm-11:30pm Sun.-Thurs., 5pm-1am Fri.-Sat., 4,990ISK) has many delightful choices, but if you'd like to taste its best Icelandic dishes, go for the "gourmet feast" in which the chef prepares dishes with smoked puffin, Icelandic sea trout, lobster tails, grilled Icelandic lamb, minke whale with cranberry sauce, and pan-fried blue ling with lobster sauce. The seven plates, along with a shot of the famous Icelandic spirit Brennivin and a chocolate *skyr* mousse dessert, will only set you back 7,990ISK. If you would like more traditional tapas, there are lots of options, including salmon and bacon-wrapped scallop bites.

STEAK HOUSES

Argentina (Barónsstígur 11A, tel. 354/551-9555, www.argentina.is, 4pm-midnight Sun.-Thurs., 4pm-1am Fri.-Sat., entrées from 4,550ISK) is warm and inviting the second you step through the door, with leather couches, a roaring fireplace, and the smell of choice cuts of meat wafting through the air. You can choose from rib eye, T-bone, slow-cooked ox flank, beef rump, porterhouse, and peppered beef tenderloin, among other cuts. Chicken, lamb, and seafood round out the menu, and there is an excellent wine list.

Steikhúsið (Tryggvagata 4, tel. 354/561-1111, www.steik.is, 5pm-10pm Sun.-Wed., 5pm-11pm Thurs.-Sat., steaks from 3,990ISK) has made a big impact on Reykjavík's restaurant scene. Guests can choose from beef rib eye, porterhouse, and T-bone cuts or lamb fillets, with tasty sauces including béarnaise, creamy pepper, and blue cheese. There are also fish entrées on offer as well as a dynamite hamburger with brie, pickled vegetables, mango chutney, chipotle, and bacon. For the adventurous, the surf-and-turf features minke whale and horse meat grilled in a coal oven.

★ **Grillmarket (Grillmarkaðurinn)** (Lækjargata 2a, tel. 354/571-7777, www.grillmarkadurinn.is, 11:30am-11pm daily, entrées from 4,800ISK) is an upscale restaurant specializing in all things meat. Expect dishes like grilled rack of lamb, dry-aged rib eye steaks, and beef tenderloin. But the restaurant also offers spectacular fish courses like salmon, cod, and fresh langoustine tails. The decor is modern yet rustic with Scandinavian design and a lot of wood. If you are after a top-notch carnivore's dinner, this is your place.

VEGETARIAN

Gló (Engjateigi 19, tel. 354/553-1111, www.glo.is, 11am-9pm daily, 2,500ISK) has a spectacular menu featuring not just vegetarian and vegan options, but also a killer raw food selection. Expect to see staples like tofu and hummus served in creative ways, and there's also an excellent salad bar. The meat dish option can be great if you're traveling with a carnivore. The decor is modern and chic and the staff friendly.

Kaffi Vinyl (Hverfisgata 76, tel. 354/537-1332, 8am-11pm daily, 1,200ISK) is a vegan café and one of the hippest places to hang out in downtown Reykjavík. Music is always playing, and artists and musicians mingle among tourists and locals. Stop by to enjoy tasty coffee drinks, beers, and light meals.

Garðurinn (Klapparstigur 37, tel. 354/561-2345, 11am-8pm Mon.-Fri., noon-5pm Sat.) is a lovely café inhabiting a quiet corner downtown. It has an eclectic rotating menu of vegetarian meals including items like curry, vegetable chili, and lentil patties, all at affordable prices. You can also expect soups, sandwiches, cakes, teas, and coffee.

FAST FOOD

You have to visit ★ **Bæjarins Beztu Pylsur (The Town's Best Hot Dog)** (Tryggvatagata 1, tel. 354/511-1566, www.bbp.is, 10am-1am Sun.-Thurs., 10am-4:30am Fri.-Sat., 450ISK). Even if you don't eat hot dogs, you should get a look at the tiny shack that has long been delighting tourists, locals, food critics, and even U.S. president Bill Clinton. Located close to the harbor, the hot dog stand serves up lamb meat hot dogs, with fresh buns and an array of toppings. If you're out for a late-night bar crawl and get hungry, the stand is open until 4am on weekends.

Grillhusið (Tryggvagata 20, tel. 354/562-3456, www.grillhusid.is, 11:30am-10pm Sun.-Thurs., 11:30am-11pm Fri.-Sat., 2,500ISK) is part diner, part TGI Friday's, with Americana displayed on the walls and an extensive menu ranging from hamburgers to fish-and-chips to salads and sandwiches. There is an interesting array of burgers on offer, and the lamb and béarnaise burger is a personal favorite.

Hamborgara Búllan (Geirsgata 1, tel. 354/511-888, www.bullan.is, 11:30am-9pm daily, burgers from 990ISK) is a corner burger joint situated in the old harbor district, close to where the whale-watching tours depart. The food is tasty, the service quick, and the decor a little kitschy, making this a great spot to grab a quick bite to eat. A special includes a hamburger, fries, and soda for 1,590ISK, which is pretty cheap for a meal in downtown Reykjavík.

Hlölla Bátar (Ingólfstorg, tel. 354/511-3500, www.hlollabatar.is, 11:30am-10pm daily, sandwiches from 1,590ISK) has hot and cold hero/hoagie sandwiches on offer, including barbecue, curry, ham and cheese, and veggie boats. It's a great place to get something quick and fuel up before you continue exploring the city.

Icelandic Hamburger Factory (Islenska Hamborgarafabrikkan) (Höfðatún 2, tel. 354/575-7575, www.fabrikkan.is, 11am-10pm Sun.-Thurs., 11am-midnight Fri.-Sat., burgers from 2,195ISK) is a wildly popular hamburger joint. It has the look and feel of a casual eatery, but the hamburgers are pretty special. They range from classic hamburgers with lettuce, cheese, and tomatoes to more creative concoctions like the surf-and-turf, which combines a beef patty with tiger prawns, garlic, Japanese seaweed, cheese, lettuce, tomatoes, red onions, and garlic-cheese sauce. Other options include chicken and lamb, as well as a whale meat burger.

Roadhouse (Snorrabraut 56, tel.

354/571-4200, www.roadhouse.is, 11:30am-9:30pm Mon.-Thurs., 11:30am-11pm Fri.-Sat., noon-9:30pm Sun., burgers from 2,395ISK) does its best to depict an American-style hamburger joint. It's kitschy, cute, and familiar, with Americana hanging on the walls, ranging from old license plates to Elvis Presley posters. The food is exceptional "fast food," with choice burgers featuring everything from crumbled blue cheese to jalapeños and fried onions. A favorite among Icelanders is the Texas mac-and-cheese burger, with a patty, macaroni and cheese, bacon, and barbecue sauce piled on top. The pork baby-back ribs are memorable.

CAFÉS

Café Babalu (Skólavörðustígur 22, tel. 354/555-8845, www.babalu.is, 11am-11pm daily, 1,200ISK) is a charming coffeehouse decorated with vintage wood furnishings and kitschy knickknacks. Other than coffee drinks, the two-floor café serves light meals including soup, panini, and crepes. This is a favorite among tourists, and in the summer months, there's an outdoor eating area on the 2nd floor.

Café Haiti (Geirsgata 7, tel. 354/588-8484, www.cafehaiti.is, 6am-9pm Mon.-Thurs., 6am-10pm Fri., 7am-10pm Sat., 7am-8pm Sun., light meals from 1,990ISK) is owned and operated by a delightful Haitian woman who has called Iceland home for years. The atmosphere is warm and inviting, with comfortable couches and chairs among the tables and even a little stage area up front hosting regular concerts. In addition to coffee and tea, light meals of soup and sandwiches are available, as well as sweet treats like cakes and cookies. A house favorite is specially brewed Arabic coffee that takes some time, but it's well worth the wait.

C Is for Cookie (Tysgata 8, tel. 354/578-5914, 7:30am-6pm Mon.-Fri., 10am-5pm Sat., 11am-5pm Sun., 500ISK) is a nondescript café on a quiet side street in the city. For that reason, along with a stellar cup of coffee, it's a favorite among locals. When the weather is good, people congregate in a park adjacent to the coffeehouse and at tables and chairs outside. Freshly baked treats include Icelandic pancakes, brownies, and, of course, cookies.

Kaffitár (Bankastræti 8, tel. 354/511-4540, www.kaffitar.is, 7am-6pm daily, 500ISK) is the closest thing Iceland has to a coffee chain like Starbucks. There are locations in the city center, Keflavík airport, and a smattering of other sites. They also sell coffee beans and ground coffee in supermarkets and takeout

Café Babalu

Mokka

coffee at gas stations. The city-center location is bright, colorful, and usually crowded. The coffee is fresh and the cakes and other sweets are delicious. You can't go wrong at Kaffitár.

Mokka (Skólavörðustígur 3A, tel. 354/552-1174, www.mokka.is, 9am-6:30pm daily, 500ISK) is the oldest coffeehouse in Reykjavík and retains a faithful following. It's busy all day, with tourists as well as artists, writers, and other folks stopping by for a cup of coffee and Mokka's famous waffles with fresh cream and homemade jam. Art and photography exhibitions are frequently held at the coffeehouse, so stop by and have a look at the walls.

Reykjavík Roasters (Karastigur 1, tel. 354/517-5535, www.reykjavikroasters.is, 8am-6pm Mon.-Fri., 9am-5pm Sat.-Sun., 500ISK) is a charming corner coffeehouse situated in a great part of town. Just a stone's throw from Hallgrímskirkja, Reykjavík Roasters is a wonderful spot to sit down for a coffee to break up a busy day of sightseeing. Decorated with vintage couches and chairs and wood tables with delicate tablecloths, the coffeehouse is packed with tourists and locals chilling out, drinking lattes, and taking advantage of the free Wi-Fi. During the summer months, when the weather is cooperating, there's an outside sitting area where guests can enjoy their drinks while soaking in the sun.

Stofan Café (Vesturgata 3, tel. 354/863-8583, 9am-11pm Mon.-Wed., 9am-midnight Fri.-Sun., 9am-10pm Sun., 500ISK), a hot spot near the harbor, has plenty of couches, chairs, and tables to accommodate its legion of fans. The café serves coffee drinks, local beers, and cakes and light meals. It's common to catch locals enjoying their drinks while curling up with a good book on a vintage armchair.

Brauð & Co (Frakkastígur 16, tel. 354/456-7777, 6am-6pm daily) is the hippest bakery in Reykjavík. You can get great pastries, breads, and cookies, as well as a delicious cup of coffee, plus do some fun people-watching in the heart of downtown. Many of the employees and owners are connected to the music industry.

Sandholt (Laugavegur 36, tel. 354/551-3524, www.sandholt.is, 6:30am-9pm daily) is a lovely place to have a coffee and fresh-baked pastry, sandwich, or panini. The bakery also has fine chocolates and other packaged goodies, like jams and cookies, which make good souvenirs.

ICE CREAM

Eldur og Is (Skólavörðustígur 2, tel. 354/571-2480, 8:30am-11pm daily, 1,000ISK) offers soft-serve and Italian-style ice cream with flavors including the basics: vanilla, chocolate, and strawberry, as well as coffee, pistachio, and several others. A crepe bar inside has delicious combinations, including the Nutella and nut special crepe. This place has a central location and a good reputation, so it can be a bit crowded. The sofas and armchairs inside make it very comfortable.

Ísbúðin Valdís (Grandagarður 21, tel. 354/586-8088, www.valdis.is, 11:30am-11pm daily, from 450ISK) draws a crowd during sun-soaked summer days and the dim, windy dog days of winter. It's always busy here and for good reason. The harbor location and its creative and delicious ice cream flavors make this a favorite among locals and tourists. Flavors include coconut, white chocolate, vanilla coffee, Oreo, and local favorites black licorice and rhubarb. During the summer, there are tables and chairs outside the shop, where scores of people enjoy their cones.

Accommodations

Accommodations in Reykjavík fall into three categories: hotels, guesthouses, and self-catering apartments. The city isn't known for luxurious hotels, but there are a few "upmarket" choices; however, they remain "no-frills" when compared to other cities in Europe. By and large, expect to pay a lot during the high season (June-August). While most of the options are downtown, there are a few outside the 101 postal code. However, given how small Reykjavík is, most options are within walking distance or are within a short bus ride to downtown.

HOTELS

Under 25,000ISK

Fosshótel Baron (Baronsstígur 2-4, tel. 354/562-3204, www.fosshotel.is, rooms from 21,000ISK) may not be pretty from the exterior, but it's clean, convenient, and in a good location in downtown Reykjavík. The 120 rooms range from standard singles and doubles to apartment-style accommodations that have kitchenettes and mini refrigerators. The lobby looks a little depressing, but the accommodating staff and the location make up for it. Guests have access to free Wi-Fi, free and plentiful parking, and an adequate included breakfast.

Hilton Reykjavík Nordica (Suðurlandsbraut 2, tel. 354/444-5000, www.hiltonreykjavik.com, rooms from 23,000ISK) is a 252-room four-star hotel situated in the financial district, about a 10-minute walk from downtown Reykjavík. It attracts business travelers as well as families and individuals thanks to its comfortable rooms, top-notch service, luxurious spa, and memorable in-house restaurant, Vox.

★ **Hótel Frón** (Laugavegur 22A, tel. 354/511-4666, www.hotelfron.is, rooms from 20,000ISK) couldn't have picked a better location if it tried. Located on the high street Laugavegur, the hotel has single, double, and apartment-style studios that are clean, bright, and comfortable. The apartments come with small kitchens, and a couple of them feature Jacuzzi bathtubs. It's also conveniently close to the bars on Laugavegur—though this means it can be quite noisy on Friday and Saturday nights.

Hótel Klöpp (Klapparstígur 26, tel. 354/595-8520, www.centerhotels.is, rooms from 18,000ISK) offers fresh rooms on a quiet corner in the city center. Some rooms feature warm, bright hues including red walls, while others are stark white, clean, and cool. All rooms have hardwood floors and small private bathrooms. Guests have access to free Wi-Fi, assistance with booking tours is provided, and the friendly staff even offers a northern lights wake-up service in the winter when the aurora borealis is visible.

Reykjavík Lights Hotel (Suðurlandsbraut 16, tel. 354/513-9000, www.keahotels.is, rooms from 25,000ISK) is a concept design hotel with 105 rooms, including singles, doubles, triples, and group rooms. Just past the reception area is an airy lobby that houses a bar and the common eating area. Rooms are large, featuring Nordic-style decor and luxurious beds. The bathrooms are modern and stark white with showers. Located outside of the city center, it's about a 10-minute walk to downtown.

Radisson Blu Saga Hotel (Hagatorg, tel. 354/525-9900, www.radissonblu.com, rooms from 24,000ISK) has a dynamite location in the city center, close to the Reykjavík Art Museum and the famous Bæjarins Beztu Pylsur hot dog stand. Rooms are larger than average, many with a maritime theme that's charming. Beds are lush, and the 209 rooms are stocked with bath products from Anne Semonin. Amenities include free Wi-Fi, access to the spa and health center, and two in-house restaurants: Grillið for fine dining and Restaurant Skrudur for more casual meals.

Icelandair Hótel Reykjavík Natura (Hlídarfótur, tel. 354/444-4500, www.icelandairhotels.com, rooms from 19,000ISK) pays homage to Reykjavík's rich art culture with murals and sculptures throughout the building. Built in 1964 but renovated in 2012, the hotel has been a favorite among business travelers due to its proximity to the airport and conference facilities. The in-house restaurant Satt offers a delicious breakfast buffet and meals throughout the day. The main attractions, for many, are the indoor swimming pool and Soley Natura Spa, where guests can get massages, manicures, pedicures, and facial treatments. The hotel is a 20-minute walk to downtown Reykjavík, but guests are given free passes for the city bus, which stops just outside the hotel.

Over 25,000ISK

Centrum Plaza Hotel (Aðalstræti 4, tel. 354/595-8500, www.centerhotels.is, rooms from 30,000ISK) is in the heart of Reykjavík. Many of the 180 rooms have spectacular views of the city, but with that comes quite a bit of noise during the weekends. The rooms are cozy and sparsely decorated but clean and bright. The bathrooms are small, with a shower, and each room has a flat-screen TV and free Wi-Fi. The clientele is a mix of business and leisure travelers. A lounge downstairs tends to be sleepy because of the proximity of popular bars downtown.

Award-winning ★ **101 Hotel** (Hverfisgata 10, tel. 354/580-0101, www.101hotel.is, rooms from 59,000ISK) is quite posh for Reykjavík. In 2017, the *Daily Telegraph* named it one of the best luxury hotels in the city. Rooms are cozy and stylish at the same time with a black-and-white color palette, wood floors, and in-room fireplaces. And while the rooms are pricey, the amenities are pretty great. Each room has a large walk-in shower, flat-screen TV with satellite channels, free high-speed Wi-Fi, a CD/DVD player with a Bose iPod sound dock, and bathrobes and slippers. The restaurant offers an eclectic menu with creations ranging from mussels and pommes frites to Icelandic cod with saffron risotto.

Grand Hotel Reykjavík (Sigtún 38, tel. 354/514-8000, www.grand.is, rooms from 27,000ISK) is a huge 311-room high-rise hotel just a few minutes from downtown Reykjavík. This is a favorite among business travelers and conference attendees because the hotel has meeting rooms and conference facilities. The rooms are large, with hardwood floors and comfortable yet uninspiring furnishings. The restaurant is pricey; dishes range from lamb fillets with mushrooms to duck breast with parsnip.

Hlemmur Square (Laugavegur 25, tel. 354/415-1600, www.hlemmursquare.com, rooms from 28,000ISK) bills itself as an upmarket hostel. As the name suggests, the hotel is right next to Hlemmur bus station, which is downtown's most extensive station and provides bus transfers to just about every part of the city. Other than being in a killer location, Hlemmur Square has a popular lounge that attracts both hotel guests and locals. This is a great spot for twentysomethings to meet fellow travelers and socialize.

★ **Hótel Borg** (Posthússtræti 9-11, tel. 354/551-1440, www.hotelborg.is, rooms from 30,000ISK) is a popular choice for celebrities and politicians passing through Reykjavík. Why? Built in 1930, the 56-room four-star downtown hotel is at once elegant, modern, and steeped in old-time charm. Hotel Borg's rooms have custom-made furniture, flat-screen satellite TVs, and very comfortable beds. The in-house restaurant, Silfur, is a favorite, and a café/bar serves light meals.

Hotel Holt (Bergstaðastæti 37, tel. 354/552-5700, www.holt.is, rooms from

40,000ISK) offers spacious, tastefully decorated rooms, some with a balcony. Holt is one of the few hotels in downtown Reykjavík that offers room service, and its service and amenities are comparable to upscale hotels in large European cities. Guests also have free access to Iceland's largest health club (World Class Fitness), free parking, free Wi-Fi, and a staff eager to assist with tour bookings and recommendations for sights and restaurants.

★ **Icelandair Hótel Reykjavík Marina** (Myrargata 2, tel. 354/560-8000, www.icelandairhotels.com, rooms from 26,000ISK) is in a great location by the harbor district, close to the whale-watching tours, restaurants, and museums. One of the most design conscious of the Icelandair Hótels chain, Reykjavík Marina displays art throughout the lobby, restaurant, and rooms, featuring everything from murals by local Icelandic artists to impressive wood sculptures. Rooms are minimalist and modern, the staff is warm, and the hotel is home to one of the hippest hotel bars in the city, Slipp Bar.

Kvosin Hotel (Kirkutorg 4, tel. 354/571-4460, www.kvosinhotel.is, rooms from 30,000ISK) is a gorgeous modern boutique hotel situated close to the Pond and parliament in downtown Reykjavík. Rooms come in four adorably described sizes: normal, bigger, biggest, and larger than life. All rooms feature mini refrigerators, a Nespresso machine, Samsung Smart TV, and skin-care amenities from Aveda. The rooms are sleek and Scandinavian cool with accents from local Icelandic designers. A delicious breakfast is included and served downstairs at the Bergsson restaurant.

Radisson Blu 1919 Hotel (Posthússtræti 2, tel. 354/599-1000, www.radissonblu.com, rooms from 27,000ISK) is an 88-room hotel that occupies a central location in the capital. Built in 1919, the hotel has undergone a couple of renovations, but it has maintained a lot of its charm. The rooms are large, with hardwood floors, sizable bathrooms, comfortable beds, and free high-speed Wi-Fi. Guests who reserve a suite are treated to a king-size bed, Jacuzzi bathtub, and bathrobe with slippers. Guests also have access to a fitness center with some basic machines. The in-house restaurant is dynamite, with a menu ranging from fresh fish caught off of Iceland's shores to lamb fillets and duck breast entrées.

GUESTHOUSES

Under 25,000ISK

Reykjavik Hostel Village (Flókagata 1, tel.

Hótel Borg

354/552-1155, www.hostelvillage.is, rooms from 15,000ISK) offers rooms in five different residential houses. Rooms include dorm accommodations, singles, doubles, triples, and apartment-style studios. The decor is simple, with neutral colors and wood furnishings. It's a five-minute walk to Laugavegur, the main drag, and the prices are reasonable, making this a great option for budget travelers.

★ **Loft Hostel** (Bankastræti 7, tel. 354/553-8140, www.lofthostel.is, private rooms from 23,000ISK) has a reputation as a place to see and be seen. Rooms range from dorm accommodation to privates, but the big draw is the 4th-floor bar/café that hosts up-and-coming bands, established live acts, and DJs. An outdoor deck overlooks Bankastræti in downtown Reykjavík, and it's packed with locals and tourists alike when the sun is shining.

Sunna Guesthouse (Thórsgata 26, tel. 354/511-5570, www.sunna.is, rooms from 19,000ISK) offers several types of accommodations: one- and two-bedroom apartments, studios, rooms with private bathrooms, and rooms with shared bathroom facilities. All rooms are decorated in a light, minimalist style with muted colors and wood furniture. The location is key, as it's right across the street from Hallgrímskirkja in downtown Reykjavík. Guests have access to a shared kitchen to prepare meals, and a breakfast buffet is included in the price. The breakfast accommodates vegetarians as well as those with gluten allergies.

★ **Kex Hostel** (Skúlagata 28, tel. 354/561-6060, www.kexhostel.is, private rooms from 22,000ISK) is a lot more than a hostel; it's where music lovers, hipsters, and the beautiful people of downtown Reykjavík congregate, meeting for drinks and live music. The hostel offers options ranging from dorm accommodations to private rooms, all with shared bathroom facilities. That said, most people don't stay for the style or comfort of the rooms, but for the Kex experience. The front lounge houses vintage wall maps, mid-century furniture, and a small stage for live bands to plug in and play. The back room is a converted gym that hosts concerts, fashion and vinyl markets, and even food festivals.

APARTMENTS

Under 25,000ISK

Bolholt Apartments (Bolholt 6, tel. 354/517-4050, www.stay.is, rooms from 18,000ISK) offers comfortable, simple rooms just a 10-minute walk from downtown Reykjavík, which makes this well-managed apartment complex very popular. Guests have private bathrooms, small kitchenettes, and access to free Wi-Fi and free parking. A common lounge has a pool table and a couple of sofas great for unwinding and meeting fellow travelers. Bolholt is an excellent option for independent, budget-conscious travelers.

Einholt Apartments (Einholt 2, tel. 354/517-4050, www.stay.is, rooms from 18,000ISK) has stylish, minimalist apartments with private bathrooms and kitchenettes. Its clientele ranges from more mature travelers to twentysomething backpackers. Einholt is a great downtown spot for the independent traveler to spend a couple of nights or a longer stay to get to know Reykjavík.

The **Reykjavík4You Apartments** (Laugavegur 85, www.reykjavik4you.com, rooms from 25,000ISK) offer great spaces in a central location. Studios and one- and two-bedroom apartments are available, and all are stocked with well-equipped kitchens, spacious bathrooms, and bright decor. Apartments are clean and comfortable, with lots of light in the summer months.

Room with a View (Laugavegur 18, tel. 354/552-7262, www.roomwithaview.is, rooms from 20,000ISK) is right next to the popular bookstore Mál og Menning and near all the great bars downtown. Rooms range from small singles to three-bedroom apartments for groups. Rooms are clean and modern, some with private bathroom facilities. Guests have access to two hot tubs as well as a common kitchen area. Be advised that because of the proximity of bars and restaurants, it can be quite noisy on Friday and Saturday nights. If you're looking for a quiet room on a sleepy street, this isn't it.

Information and Services

VISITORS CENTERS

Reykjavík Official Tourist Information Centre (Tjarnargata 11, tel. 354/411-6040, 8am-8pm daily) is downtown inside Reykjavík City Hall. The office has brochures, a friendly and knowledgeable staff, and maps. You can book excursions from here as well.

MEDIA

The ***Reykjavík Grapevine*** is Iceland's only English-language newspaper, and it's geared toward tourists, hipsters, and music-loving locals. There are listings for bands and DJ club dates, information about what's on at museums and art galleries, and articles ranging from humorous to informative to sarcastic on what's going on in Reykjavík. To get the pulse of the city, pick up a copy in bookstores, museums, and shops, or check it out online at www.grapevine.is. In summertime, the newspaper comes out every other week, and in the winter it's monthly.

EMERGENCY SERVICES

The telephone number for emergencies is 112. If you are having a medical emergency, are stranded by car trouble, or are experiencing a safety issue or any other pressing, dire emergency, dial this number.

MEDICAL SERVICES

Landspitali (Norðurmýri, tel. 354/543-1000, www.landspitali.is) is the national hospital of Iceland. It houses day-patient units, an emergency room, and clinical services. If you are experiencing a medical emergency, dial 112 for an ambulance.

For a pharmacy, visit **Lyf og Heilsa** (Haaleitisbraut 68, tel. 354/581-2101, 8am-midnight Mon.-Fri., 10am-midnight Sat.-Sun.). Keep in mind that over-the-counter medication and aspirin are only available at a pharmacy, not in supermarkets or convenience stores like in other countries.

Transportation

GETTING THERE

Air

Iceland isn't as difficult to reach as you may think. Smack-dab in the mid-Atlantic, Reykjavík is just a short flight for many North Americans and Europeans, about five hours from New York City and three hours from London. The majority of international travel is handled through **Keflavík International Airport** (KEF), which is about 50 minutes west of Reykjavík.

Reykjavík City Airport (Þorragata 10, tel. 354/569-4100, www.isavia.is) is the city's domestic airport, with regional connections to towns throughout the country, including Akureyri and the Westfjords. The only international flights are to the Faroe Islands and Greenland.

Several airlines have offices in Reykjavík: **Air Iceland Connect** (Reykjavíkurflugvöllur, tel. 354/570-3000, www.airicelandconnect.com), **Eagle Air** (Reykjavíkurflugvöllur, tel. 354/562-4200, www.eagleair.is), **Icelandair** (Reykjavíkurflugvöllur, tel. 354/505-0100, www.icelandair.is), and **Wow Air** (Katrinartun 12, tel. 354/590-3000, www.wowair.is).

GETTING TO AND FROM THE AIRPORT

The **Fly Bus** (tel. 354/580-5400, www.flybus.is) runs regularly from **Keflavík International Airport** to **BSÍ** (Vatnsmýrarvegur 10, tel. 354/562-1011, www.bsi.is), Reykjavík's main bus station, where you can get a shuttle to the downtown hotels.

It takes about 50 minutes to get from Keflavík to BSÍ bus station, and buses depart about 40 minutes after flights land. One-way tickets cost 2,500ISK. (BSÍ is also the main departure site for day-tour bus trips with various companies, including Reykjavík Excursions.) **Taxis** are also available at Keflavík; the fare from the airport to Reykjavík is upward of 15,000ISK.

Strætó (www.straeto) bus numbers 15 and 19 stop at the **Reykjavík City Airport** near the Air Iceland and Eagle Air terminals, respectively. Taxis are also available on-site.

GETTING AROUND

Bus

Reykjavík's bus system is convenient, reliable, and an affordable way to get around the city. The bus system, called **Strætó** (www.straeto.is), which means "street" in Icelandic, runs about 30 bus lines within the city center as well as to outlying areas like Kópavogur and Hafnarfjörður. The bright yellow buses cost 350ISK per ride within the city limits, and you can ask for a free bus transfer if you need to switch buses to get to your destination. You must pay with exact change; bus drivers don't make change. Buses run daily 7am-11pm. Be sure to check the website at www.straeto.is for information on holiday schedules and delays due to weather.

If you plan to use the bus a fair amount, you can buy nine tickets for 3,000ISK at **Hlemmur bus station** (Laugavegur, tel. 354/540-2701). Hlemmur is Strætó's central downtown station, where you can catch or connect to any bus you're looking for. Think of it as Reykjavík's equivalent of New York's Times Square subway station. Another great option is the **Reykjavík Welcome Card,** which grants you free access to the city's swimming pools, almost all the city's museums, and unlimited city bus rides. You can purchase a card for one or three days for 900ISK and 2,200ISK, respectively. If you will be spending a lot of time in Reykjavík, this is a great option to save a lot of money. Cards can be purchased at tourist offices and bus stations.

Strætó's blue long-distance buses depart from **Mjodd station** (tel. 354/557-7854), eight kilometers southeast of the city center, traveling to several regions around the country.

Taxi

The two things you need to know about taxis in Reykjavík is that they are expensive, and you have to call ahead for one (for instance, a ride from the BSI bus station to Harpa takes about eight minutes and costs roughly 2,000ISK). **Hreyfill** (tel. 354/588-5522, www.hreyfill.is) and **BSR** (tel. 354/561-0000, www.taxireykjavik.is) are two popular taxi companies in the city. Taxis arrive 5-10 minutes after you call, and the price on the meter is inclusive—you don't tip in Iceland. Cab prices rival those in New York City: It's rare to spend less than 2,000ISK on a taxi ride, even for short distances. There are a couple of cab stations downtown where you don't have to call ahead—just outside Hlemmur bus station and near Lækjartorg, a square in downtown Reykjavík where Lækjargata, Bankastræti, and Austurstræti streets meet. The taxi stands are hard to miss, as the cabs can be lined up 10 deep.

Car

There is no shortage of companies in Iceland eager to rent you a car, and many of them make it quite easy, with offices at Keflavík International Airport, BSÍ bus station, and around the city. They include the following: **Avis** (Knarrarvogur 2, tel. 354/591-4000, www.avis.is), **Budget** (Vatsmýrarvegur 10, tel. 354/562-6060, www.budget.is), **Europcar** (Hjallahrauni 9, tel. 354/565-3800, www.europcar.is), and **Hertz** (Reykjavík City Airport, tel. 354/505-0600, www.hertz.is).

Be advised that parking isn't easy in Reykjavík. Most locals have cars, and street parking can take some time. However, there are several parking garages and lots available around the city, and parking at a garage will cost less than 100ISK per hour.

Bicycle

Reykjavík has made great strides in becoming more bicycle friendly over the past few years. There are new bicycle lanes throughout the city as well as new bike racks to lock up your ride outside shops. Be aware that bike theft is rampant, so be proactive and lock up your bicycle; if you leave it unattended and unlocked, it'll disappear. Other than bike theft, the only concern for cyclists is weather, which changes often. You can start your ride during calm and sunny skies, but within minutes that could change to rain and wind.

In Reykjavík, Wow Air sponsors a **city bike program** (www.wowcitybike.com). Visitors can rent the purple bicycles from several kiosks around the city, including near Laugardalslaug. The station map can be accessed on the website. Rates start at 350ISK for 30 minutes; an additional 30 minutes costs 500ISK.

Walking

Reykjavík is an inherently walkable city—depending on the weather, of course. Because of its small size, it's a perfect place to roam, to pop into quaint shops, visit museums, and photograph its many statues. You can start at the harbor and make your way to Tjörnin, up to Hallgrímskirkja, and beyond.

A walking tour by **I Heart Reykjavík** (Mjóahlíð 14, tel. 354/854-4476, www.iheartreykjavik.net) is designed to tell you about the history of Reykjavík and some of the quirky characters who inhabit the city. The three-hour tour is 6,000ISK, and you can book at www.tours.iheartreykjavik.net. Tours are offered daily.

Greater Reykjavík

MOSFELLSBÆR

Just 15 minutes from downtown Reykjavík, Mosfellsbær is a quaint, placid town with a picturesque bay, beautiful mountains, and clean streams and rivers. About 10,000 people live in Mosfellsbær, and despite its proximity to downtown it feels remote enough to make it seem like you're in the countryside.

Sights

ÁLAFOSS WOOL FACTORY SHOP

The **Álafoss Wool Factory Shop** (Álafossvegur 23, tel. 354/566-6303, www.alafoss.is, 8am-8pm daily) is home to the Álafoss wool brand, which was established in 1896 and was for decades the leading manufacturer and exporter of Icelandic wool products. The shop is located in the old factory house by the Álafoss waterfall, which was used to drive the mills. The shop sells wool skeins, scarves, hats, sweaters, and blankets, along with some other small goods. You can also purchase a sheep skin as well as other Icelandic design products. The prices are comparable to those in downtown Reykjavík, but the selection is better and bigger. The site also includes an exhibition of old knitting machinery and photographs from the mill's early days.

GLJÚFRASTEINN

Gljúfrasteinn (Pósthólf 250, tel. 354/568-8066, www.gljufrasteinn.is, 9am-5pm daily June 1-Aug. 31, 10am-4pm Tues.-Sun. Sept. 1-May 31, 900ISK) was the home of Icelandic novelist and national treasure Halldór Laxness. Halldór, who was awarded the Nobel Prize for Literature in 1955 for his novel *Independent People,* lived at this home from 1945 until his death in 1998. It has been preserved as a museum, giving visitors a glimpse into his life, including the library and study where he wrote several of his works. The white two-story concrete building is well preserved, but it feels lived in with lots of personal artifacts decorating the home, including books, clothing, and furniture. There is a short multimedia presentation about Halldór's life and work, available in English, Icelandic,

Greater Reykjavík

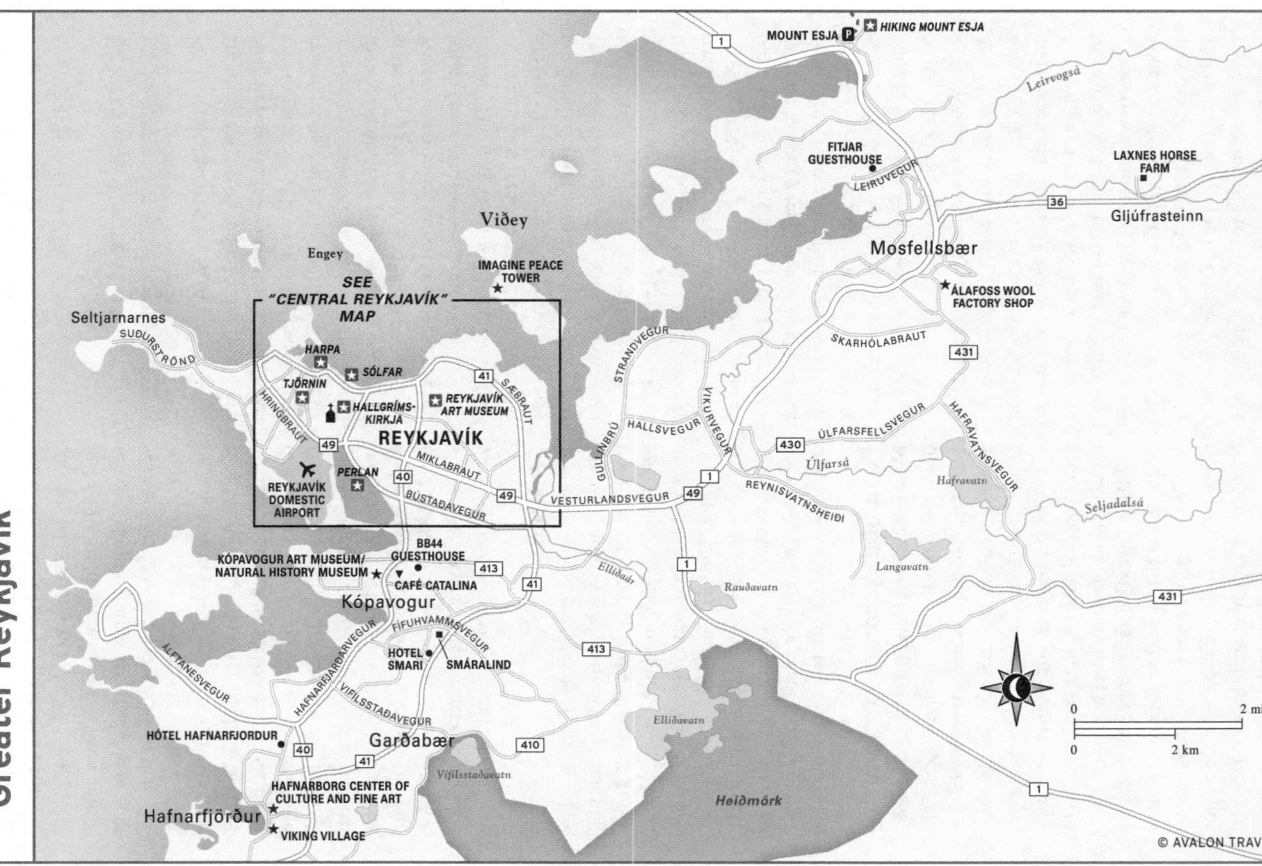

and Swedish. Guided tours of the house and grounds take about an hour. You can purchase many of his books at the museum, translated into English and German.

Sports and Recreation

TOP EXPERIENCE

★ HIKING MOUNT ESJA

Standing 914 meters high, Mount Esja looms over Reykjavík. It's a favorite among locals and the subject of thousands of picturesque photographs snapped by tourists. Hiking Esja is a popular pastime and a few paths ascend the mountain. The most popular path begins at the car park, which is at about 780 meters. From there, you can cross the Mógilsa stream, which leads to a steeper stretch named "steinnin." The hike is eight kilometers round-trip and considered easy, but be aware that the last stretch to the top is pretty steep; there are handrails to lessen the challenge. When you reach the top of this path, you can sign a guestbook. It's fun to read through all the names and see where people have traveled from to climb the mountain. At a leisurely pace, the hike takes about two hours total.

Please take precautions before you head out. Make sure you check the weather forecast and let your guesthouse or hotel know of your plans. Remember that the weather can be fickle. It may be beautiful out with sunny skies, but it could turn very windy and rainy quickly. Bring water, proper footwear, and waterproof clothing with you.

Getting to Esja is pretty easy, even if you don't have access to a car. It's just 20 minutes (10.7 kilometers) north of Mosfellsbær and is accessible from Route 1. Drive through Mosfellsbær and you'll see signs pointing to the car park. You can also take the **Strætó** 57 bus (www.straeto.is) from the bus station Mjodd in Reykjavík. The bus fare is 880ISK and the bus departs 12 times a day. It's a 30-minute ride. Let the bus driver know that you are heading to the base of Esja (the bus stop is Esjumelar) and you will get dropped off at the car park.

HORSE RIDING

If you're staying in Reykjavík and want to do some horseback riding, **Laxnes Farm** (off Rte. 36, tel. 354/566-6179, www.laxnes.is) is just a 15-minute drive northeast from downtown. Icelandic horses are available to ride year-round for different tour lengths. The staff is warm and friendly and shows a great deal of love and respect for the horses they care for. A popular tour is called the "Laxnes Special"; you will be picked up at your hotel or guesthouse in Reykjavík and taken to the farm, where you will meet your guide and horse. You are given all the gear you need, including helmets, rain clothes, and boots, and are taken on a glorious two-hour tour (11,900ISK) that has spectacular landscape views. The Laxnes Farm is close to Halldór Laxness's home, but they are not related.

SWIMMING

If you're planning to stay in town for a few hours or more, check out the local swimming pool, called **Varmárlaug** (Þverholt 2, tel. 354/566-6754, 6:30am-8pm Mon.-Fri., 9am-6pm Sat.-Sun. in summer, 4pm-9pm Mon.-Fri. in winter, 750ISK). The pool isn't as impressive as some of the pools in the Reykjavík city center, but the water is warm and the facilities are clean. You're likely to see locals taking a dip, but not many tourists.

Food and Accommodations

Mosfellsbakarí (Háholti 13-15, tel. 354/566-6145, www.mosbak.is, 7am-6pm Mon.-Fri., 8am-4pm Sat.-Sun., pastries from 600ISK) is a decadent bakery known for its chocolate creations. Located in the center of town, it does a roaring business. In addition to its indulgent cakes and pastries, the bakery offers light meals, including sandwiches and soup.

Fitjar Guesthouse (Fitjar, tel. 354/691-5005, www.fitjarguesthouse.com, rooms from 16,000ISK) is a six-room guesthouse on a quiet street in Mosfellsbær. Three rooms have private bathroom facilities with a shower, and three rooms share bathroom accommodations. Rooms are clean and comfortable, but the decor is nothing to write home about. This is a great spot to spend a night before you continue on your journey. Guests have access to free Wi-Fi, a television, a common room, fully equipped kitchen, and laundry facilities.

Information and Services

Mosfellsbær's **tourist information office** is based inside the **Mosfellsbær public library** (Þverholti 2, tel. 354/566-6822, www.mosfellsbaer.is, 9am-5pm daily), which is housed in a shopping area. It's a great place to gather some tourist brochures and maps as well as buy some food at the grocery store inside the shopping center.

Transportation

Mosfellsbær is just a 15-minute drive from downtown Reykjavík. It's 14 kilometers northeast of Reykjavík via Route 49.

By bus, take the 15 bus to the Haholt stop, which is in the center of town. Check www.straeto.is for more bus information. Depending on the time of day, buses run every 30 minutes to every hour, and it takes 30 minutes from downtown Reykjavík to Mosfellsbær. A single ride on the bus is 440ISK.

KÓPAVOGUR

Kópavogur is a quiet suburb home to families, young professionals, and immigrants, and it attracts people traveling on business or shoppers headed to the Smáralind mall or the island's only IKEA and Costco. There are a couple of museums worth checking out for local art and history.

Sights

KÓPAVOGUR ART MUSEUM (Gerðarsafn)

The **Kópavogur Art Museum** (Hamraborg 4, tel. 354/570-0440, www.gerdarsafn.is, 11am-5pm Tues.-Sun., 500ISK) is named Gerðarsafn in Icelandic, after sculptor Gerður Helgadóttir, who passed away in 1975. In 1977, her heirs donated roughly 1,400 of her works to the municipality of Kópavogur on the condition that a museum bearing her name would be opened. The museum opened in 1994. Gerður's black-iron works in the 1950s made her a pioneer of three-dimensional abstract art in Iceland. Around 1970 Gerður returned to working with plaster, terra cotta, and concrete, using simple circles with movement in many variations. Other works on display range from contemporary to landscape art. It's a pretty museum with varied works of art, and it's worth a visit if you're in the neighborhood.

NATURAL HISTORY MUSEUM (Náttúrúfræðistofa)

The **Natural History Museum** (Hamraborg 6A, tel. 354/570-0430, www.natkop.is, 9am-6pm Mon.-Thurs., 11am-5pm Fri.-Sat., free) is a great place to bring kids to learn about the animals and geology of Iceland. The exhibits fall into two categories: zoological and geological. The geology section, where you learn about the major rock types and minerals of Iceland, is of more interest to adults. The zoological part focuses on the mammals, fish, birds, and invertebrates of the country. It's educational and entertaining, and kids love the exhibitions on seals, foxes, and cute birds like puffins.

Sports and Recreation

SWIMMING

The **Kópavogur Swimming Pool** (Borgarholtsbruat 17, tel. 354/540-0470, 6:30am-10pm Mon.-Fri., 8am-7pm Sat.-Sun., 500ISK) is frequented by locals and their children and has a very family-friendly atmosphere. Amenities include a 50-meter outdoor pool, two smaller indoor pools, three waterslides, seven hot pots, and a steam bath. You aren't likely to see crowds or tourists, so if you're looking to just swim, this is a good spot.

Food and Accommodations

Smáralind (Hagasmara 1, tel. 354/528-8000, www.smaralind.is, 11am-7pm Mon., Wed., and Fri., 11am-9pm Thurs., 11am-6pm Sat., 1pm-6pm Sun.) is Iceland's largest shopping mall, and in addition to a food court, there are casual eateries TGI Friday's and Café Adesso, coffee shop Kaffitár, and Serrano, which serves Mexican-style food.

Hótel Smári (Hlíðarsmára, tel. 354/558-1900, www.hotelsmari.is, rooms from 23,000ISK) is a 48-room block hotel situated right next to the huge mall Smáralind. The rooms need an update, as they have a 1980s style with carpeting, orange hues, and shiny lamps. But the rooms are clean and spacious, and comfortable for a short stay.

BB44 Guesthouse (Borgarholtsbraut 44/Nýbýlavegur 16, tel. 354/554 4228, www.bb44.is, doubles 20,800ISK) offers eight guest rooms in two locations. The single, double, and family rooms have free Wi-Fi, shared kitchen facilities, and free parking. Rooms are very basic, with standard beds, desks, and simple chairs. The location is prime, just a 10-minute walk from downtown Kópavogur, where there are museums, restaurants, and the town's swimming pool. Guests have access to a hot tub at the guesthouse.

Information and Services

The town's **service and administration center** (Fannborg 2, tel. 354/570-1500) is open 8am-4pm Monday-Thursday and 8am-3pm Friday.

Transportation

Kópavogur is just a 10-minute ride (5 kilometers) south from downtown Reykjavík by car. You take Route 40 to Route 49.

City buses go to Kópavogur, including buses 1, 2, and 28. Buses leave every 30 minutes or so, the fare is 440ISK one-way, and it takes about 20 minutes by bus. Check www.straeto.is for more bus information.

HAFNARFJÖRÐUR

Hafnarfjörður is a picturesque fishing town that about 30,000 people call home. Attractions include a scenic harbor, pretty parks, and the famous Viking Village, a restaurant and hotel that plays host to numerous Viking-related events.

Sights

HAFNARFJÖRÐUR MUSEUM

Hafnarfjörður Museum (Vesturgata 8, www.hafnarfjordur.is, 11am-5pm daily June 1-Aug. 31, 11am-5pm Sat.-Sun. rest of year, free) houses a collection of cultural artifacts and photographs that are significant to the town. The museum consists of six houses and nine exhibitions that showcase life in the town's early days. The six houses date from 1803 to 1906 and include the oldest house in the town, Sivertsen's House.

HAFNARBORG CENTER OF CULTURE AND FINE ART

Hafnarborg Center of Culture and Fine Art (Strandgata 34, tel. 354/555-0800, www.hafnarborg.is, noon-5pm Wed.-Mon., free) consists of two galleries with rotating exhibitions ranging from contemporary art by modern Icelandic artists to works by some of the island's most celebrated artists of years past.

VIKING VILLAGE (Fjörukráin)

Viking Village (Strandgata 55, tel. 354/565-1213, www.vikingvillage.is) is great fun for kids and adults alike. The closest thing Iceland has to a theme park, the Viking Village celebrates the island's history—with a sense of humor. It's kitschy, with lots of Viking horns, reproduced wood huts, and wooden furnishings. Guests can stay at the hotel, visit the gift shop, stay for a meal at the restaurant, or just check out the decor.

The Viking Village takes center stage every mid-June when the space hosts the **Viking Festival,** which takes place over five days. There are performances of jousts with participants in Viking costumes, food stands, metalwork demonstrations, and woolen goods and jewelry for sale.

Sports and Recreation

HORSE RIDING

This town is a lovely place to ride a horse. With its rolling landscape and picturesque views, it doesn't get much better than this in the greater Reykjavík area. **Íshestar** (Sörlaskeið 26, tel. 354/555-7000, www.ishestar.is) is a local company that offers an array of tours year-round. It provides transportation to the riding center from your accommodation and all gear needed to ride. A half-day tour goes for about 19,500ISK. **Extreme Iceland** (Skutuvogur 13a, tel. 354/588-1300, www.extremeiceland.is, 19,500ISK) also offers a day tour from Hafnarfjörður, with 4-5 hours of riding along the Reykjanes Peninsula.

SWIMMING

Take a dip with the locals at the **Suðurbæjarlaug** pool (Hringbruat 77, tel. 354/565-3080, 6:30am-9:30pm Mon.-Fri., 8am-5:30pm Sat.-Sun., 600ISK), which has an outdoor pool with a waterslide, a steam bath, and a few hot tubs.

Food

Viking Restaurant (Fjörugarðurinn) (Strandagata 55, tel. 354/565-1213, www.fjorukrain.is, 2,400ISK) at the Viking Village is a restaurant that serves traditional Icelandic fare like lamb and fish dishes in a fun, Viking-themed atmosphere. There are lots of wood furnishings and medieval accents displayed throughout the space. You can book a Viking performance in advance for groups of any size for a fee, which includes the guests being "kidnapped" from their bus, brought into a "cave" in the restaurant, served mead, escorted to dinner, and entertained with singing and music. The restaurant is open for dinner 6pm-10pm daily.

Osushi (Reykjarvíkurvegi 60, tel. 354/561-0562, www.osushi.is, 11:30am-9:30pm Mon.-Thurs., 11:30am-10pm Fri.-Sat., 3pm-9:30pm Sun., bites from 400ISK) is the Hafnarfjörður outpost of the popular downtown Reykjavík sushi train. Individual bites on offer range from fresh salmon farmed from Iceland's shores to eel and shrimp-based pieces.

Súfistinn (Strandgata 9, tel. 354/565-3740, 8am-11:30pm Mon.-Thurs., 8am-midnight Fri., 10am-midnight Sat., 1pm-midnight Sun., 800ISK) is a cozy café that sells stellar coffee drinks, fresh pastries, and light meals. Situated by the central downtown shopping area and performance hall, it's a perfect place to grab a blueberry muffin and latte or a soup or sandwich.

Accommodations

Hótel Hafnarfjörður (Reykjavíkurvegur 72, tel. 354/540-9700, www.hhotel.is, rooms from 26,000ISK) is a 70-room hotel with

Hafnarfjörður

comfortable rooms ranging from single rooms to family suites. The hotel has a business traveler/corporate feel to it, but you can't beat the amenities and location. Rooms feature neutral hues, simple furnishings, and private bathrooms. Some rooms have a kitchenette for self-catering needs. Continental breakfast, Wi-Fi, parking, and access to a nearby fitness center are included in the price.

Hótel Viking (Strandgata 55, tel. 354/565-1213, www.vikingvillage.is, rooms from 16,000ISK) at the Viking Village has 42 hotel rooms and 14 "Viking cottages" next to the hotel. All rooms and cottages include private bathrooms, comfortable beds, televisions, and stylish Viking accessories. The hotel features artworks from Iceland, Greenland, and the Faroe Islands. Guests have access to free Wi-Fi, free parking, and an on-site hot tub. Breakfast is included in the price.

Information and Services

The tourist information center is situated in **Hafnarfjörður Town Hall** (Strandgata 6, tel. 354/585-5555, www.hafnarfjordur.is, 8am-5pm Mon.-Fri. year-round, 10am-3pm Sat.-Sun. June-Aug.). You can arrange for transportation, buy tickets to local tours, and peruse brochures about the town's sights.

Transportation

Hafnarfjörður is just a 15-minute drive (11 kilometers) south from downtown Reykjavík. Take Route 40 to get there.

City bus 1 stops in town. Check www.straeto.is for bus schedules and information.

VIÐEY ISLAND

Viðey is a little gem of an island accessible by ferry. Historically, the island was inhabited by an Augustine monastery from 1225 to 1539 and was a pilgrimage destination in the Middle Ages. The island is home to one of the oldest buildings in Iceland—**Viðeyjarstofa** (Höfuðborgarsvæði), which dates back to 1755 and served as a home to many of Iceland's most powerful men over generations. The building, made from white stone with a black roof, is open to the public. The island, which is just 1.6 square kilometers in size, hosts unspoiled nature with vast stretches of grassy plains and rich birdlife, as well as the Imagine Peace Tower, an installation created by Yoko Ono.

Imagine Peace Tower

The **Imagine Peace Tower** (www.imaginepeacetower.com) is an outdoor installation created by artist Yoko Ono in memory of her

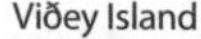
Viðey Island

late husband, John Lennon. Ono chose Iceland because it's one of the most peaceful countries in the world. The base of the tower is 10 meters wide, and the words "imagine peace" are inscribed on the structure in 24 languages. A vertical beam of light shines from the structure 4,000 meters into the sky and is visible from miles away. It was unveiled on October 9, 2007, Lennon's 67th birthday. It's lit every year October 9-December 8, the latter of which is the anniversary of Lennon's death.

Transportation

In the summer, **Elding** (tel. 354/533-5055, www.videy.com) operates a ferry with eight daily departures mid-May through September from Skarfabakki pier, Harpa, and Ægisgarður pier. Ferries run in the afternoon. During the rest of the year the ferry runs three departures on Saturdays and Sundays from Skarfabakki to Viðey. The ferry ride costs 1,500ISK for adults or 750ISK for children 7-17, and takes about 10 minutes.

Reykjanes Peninsula and the South

South Iceland is the country's busiest tourist destination, but it still feels untouched and exotic in many places—a hiker's paradise.

Glaciers, mountains, and two active volcanoes (Katla and Hekla) beckon. A wide and diverse region, the south is home to well-known sights like Þingvellir National Park and the Geysir hot springs, both on the popular Golden Circle tour, and lesser-known gems like the Laugavegurinn hiking trail, an area with colorful mountains, waterfalls, and lava-shaped landscapes.

The terrain is rugged, even desert-like in some areas, while heather, moss, and lichen cover lava stones for miles. Hiking trails are well developed and the land mostly level, making for a relatively easy hiking locale. Trails are situated in picturesque areas with plenty of bird-watching opportunities in the summer, and the lack of trees means visitors have an uninterrupted view of the landscape.

Steeped in history, Þingvellir National Park is commonly referred to as the site of the world's first democracy. It's said that a group of settlers met as a democratic legislature here close to a millennium ago. Geology buffs will be thrilled to visit the Mid-Atlantic Ridge, a fault line that lies in Þingvellir. Visitors can literally plant one foot on Europe's side and the other in North America. Outside of Reykjavík, Þingvellir is the most visited site in Iceland.

Home to Iceland's only international airport, the Reykjanes Peninsula is one part of the country that visitors are sure to see. Reykjanes is also home to the famous heated waters of the Blue Lagoon, where you can soak away your jet lag.

PLANNING YOUR TIME

The dynamic Reykjanes Peninsula and southern coast region is defined by its vast lava fields, numerous hot springs, geothermal energy, and rugged terrain. Most tourists plan to visit at least two sites other than Keflavík airport—the Mid-Atlantic Ridge at Þingvellir National Park and the glorious Blue Lagoon, where you can soak in geothermally heated water.

If you are planning to spend one night in

Previous: Mount Hekla; Gullfoss. **Above:** church in Vík.

Look for ★ to find recommended sights, activities, dining, and lodging.

Highlights

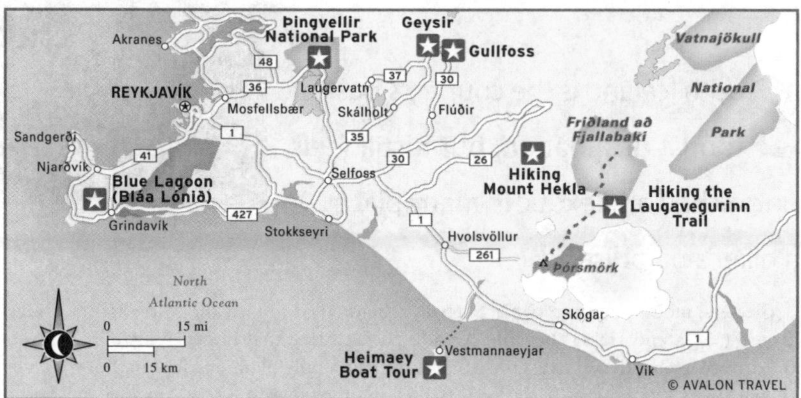

★ **Blue Lagoon (Bláa Lónið):** This gorgeous, geothermally heated spring heals the skin and soothes the body (page 86).

★ **Þingvellir National Park:** Appealing to both geology buffs and history enthusiasts, this park is home to the rift valley that marks the crest of the Mid-Atlantic Ridge as well as the site where Iceland's first parliament gathered (page 90).

★ **Geysir:** Make the trip to see the Strokkur geyser shoot steam and boiling water up to 30 meters, a natural phenomenon that occurs every 10 minutes or so (page 94).

★ **Gullfoss:** If you have time to see only one waterfall in Iceland, this should be it (page 96).

★ **Hiking Mount Hekla:** One of Iceland's most active volcanoes offers stunning views. On a clear day, you can see as far as the Vatnajökull glacier (page 104).

★ **Hiking the Laugavegurinn Trail:** See vast glaciers, bubbling hot springs, and towering mountains on this 55-kilometer, four-day hike, one of the most popular trails on the island (page 106).

★ **Heimaey Boat Tour:** Take a tour from the harbor of lovely Heimaey, the only inhabited island in the Westman Islands, to see rocky lava coastline, bird cliffs, and ocean caves (page 115).

Reykjanes Peninsula and the South

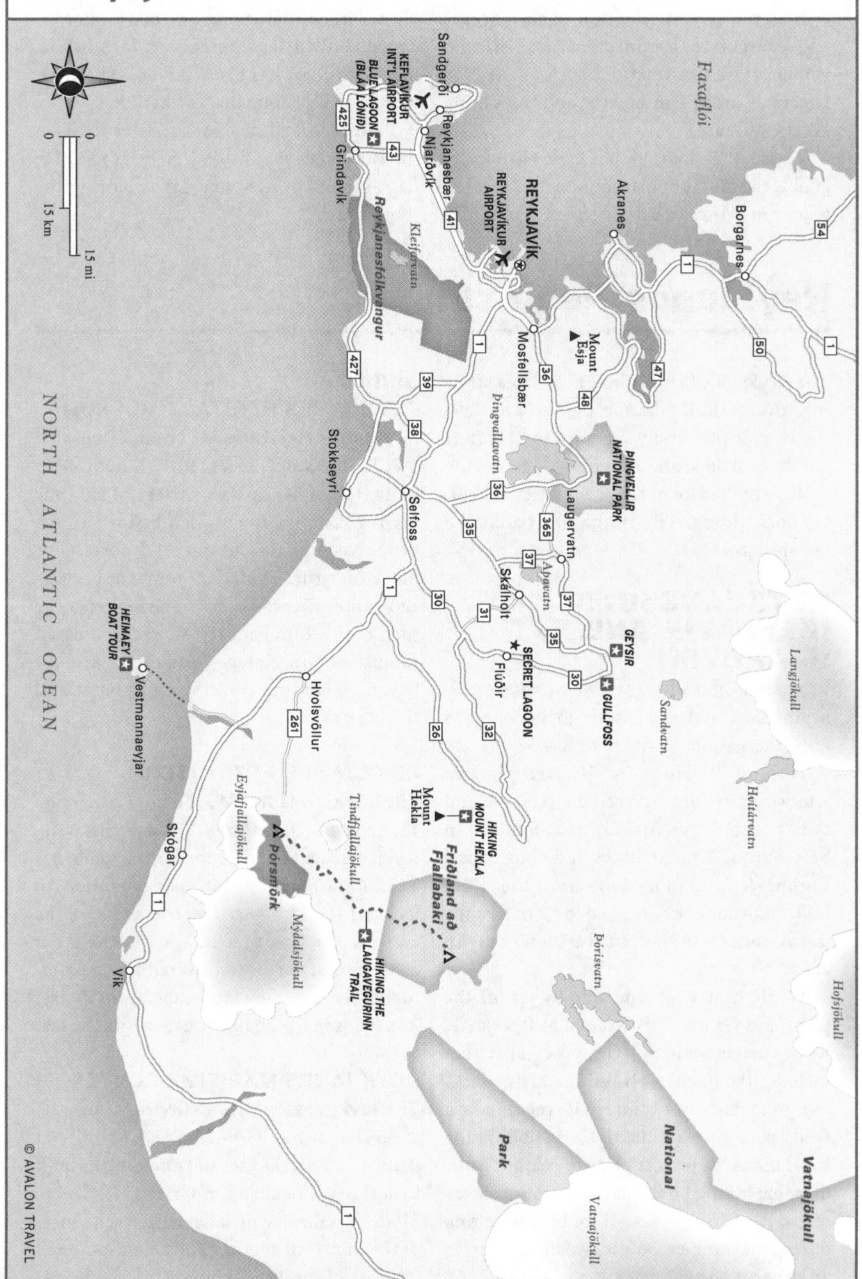
Faxaflói
Borgarnes
Akranes
REYKJAVÍK
REYKJAVÍKUR AIRPORT
Sandgerði
KEFLAVÍKUR INT'L AIRPORT
BLUE LAGOON (BLÁA LÓNIÐ)
Reykjanesbær
Njarðvík
Grindavík
Kleifarvatn
Reykjanesfólkvangur
Mosfellsbær
Mount Esja
Þingvallavatn
ÞINGVELLIR NATIONAL PARK
Laugervatn
Apavatn
Skálholt
GEYSIR
GULLFOSS
SECRET LAGOON
Flúðir
Sandavatn
Langjökull
Hvítárvatn
Hofsjökull
Stokkseyri
Selfoss
Hvolsvöllur
HEIMAEY BOAT TOUR
Vestmannaeyjar
Eyjafjallajökull
Tindfjallajökull
Mount Hekla
HIKING MOUNT HEKLA
Friðland að Fjallabaki
Þórsmörk
HIKING THE LAUGAVEGURINN TRAIL
Mýdalsjökull
Þórisvatn
Skógar
Vík
Vatnajökull National Park
Vatnajökull
NORTH ATLANTIC OCEAN
0 15 mi
0 15 km
1
54
50
47
36
48
41
43
425
427
39
38
365
37
35
30
31
32
26
261

the region, base yourself in Keflavík, where there are several guesthouses and hotels, as well as the largest selection of restaurants and shops on the peninsula. From Keflavík, you are close to attractions such as the Blue Lagoon, Garður lighthouses, and the Viking World museum.

The south is home to the Golden Circle, arguably the most popular tour on the island. It takes you to three must-see sites: the towering Gullfoss waterfall, Þingvellir National Park, and Geysir. The Golden Circle can be accomplished in one day, either by a bus tour or independently using a rental car. Meanwhile, the south coast has black-sand beaches, waterfalls, and quaint villages like Vik.

Plan to spend at least an afternoon on the Reykjanes Peninsula (likely, at the Blue Lagoon) and at least one day exploring the south coast.

Reykjanes Peninsula

The Reykjanes Peninsula is home to a striking, dramatic landscape comprising lava fields, volcanic craters, geothermal waters and hot springs, and lava caves. The region is also a hotbed for outdoor activities, including horse riding, ATV riding, and bathing in hot springs.

REYKJANESBÆR (KEFLAVÍK AND NJARÐVÍK)

Reykjanesbær is where every tourist's journey begins in Iceland, as it is home to the country's only international airport, Keflavík.

During World War II, British and American troops arrived in Iceland and built the country's first air base. Situated in between the United States and continental Europe, Iceland's location served the Allies well. Some may be surprised to learn that the last American troops left the island only in 2006.

While it may be tempting to get off the plane and get on a bus straight to Reykjavík, Reykjanesbær, which is a municipality that includes the towns **Keflavík** and **Njarðvík,** is a great place to explore. The region's lava fields, majestic sea cliffs, and accessible hiking trails make it a perfect place to roam. Throw on some hiking boots and have your camera ready. It's also a great spot for bird-watching during the summer months, when you can see arctic terns and gannets.

Sights

REYKJANES HERITAGE MUSEUM

Reykjanes Heritage Museum (Duusgata 2-8, Keflavík, tel. 354/421-6700, noon-5pm daily, 1,500ISK) hosts a variety of exhibits highlighting the town's rich history as one of Iceland's main commercial ports. The museum's turf-roofed stone farm cottage shows how life was lived in the region at the turn of the 20th century. Its reconstructed rooms contain vintage furnishings and artifacts, including cooking equipment and fishing gear.

REYKJANES ART MUSEUM

The **Reykjanes Art Museum** (Tjarnargata 12, Keflavík, tel. 354/421-6700, www.listasafn.reykjanesbaer.is, noon-5pm daily, 1,500ISK) is a charming museum that hosts exhibitions of local artists. The museum gives a taste of the region's eclectic art scene. You can check out contemporary art as well as traditional paintings of the sweeping landscape, from its vast lava fields to the quaint houses along the sea.

REYKJANES MARITIME CENTER

The **Reykjanes Maritime Center** (Duusgata 2, Keflavík, tel. 354/421-6700, noon-5pm daily, 1,500ISK) houses 100 model boats built by a retired local sailor, Grímur Karlsson. Models on display include masted schooners of the mid-19th century and steam-powered trawlers of the 20th century. Information is

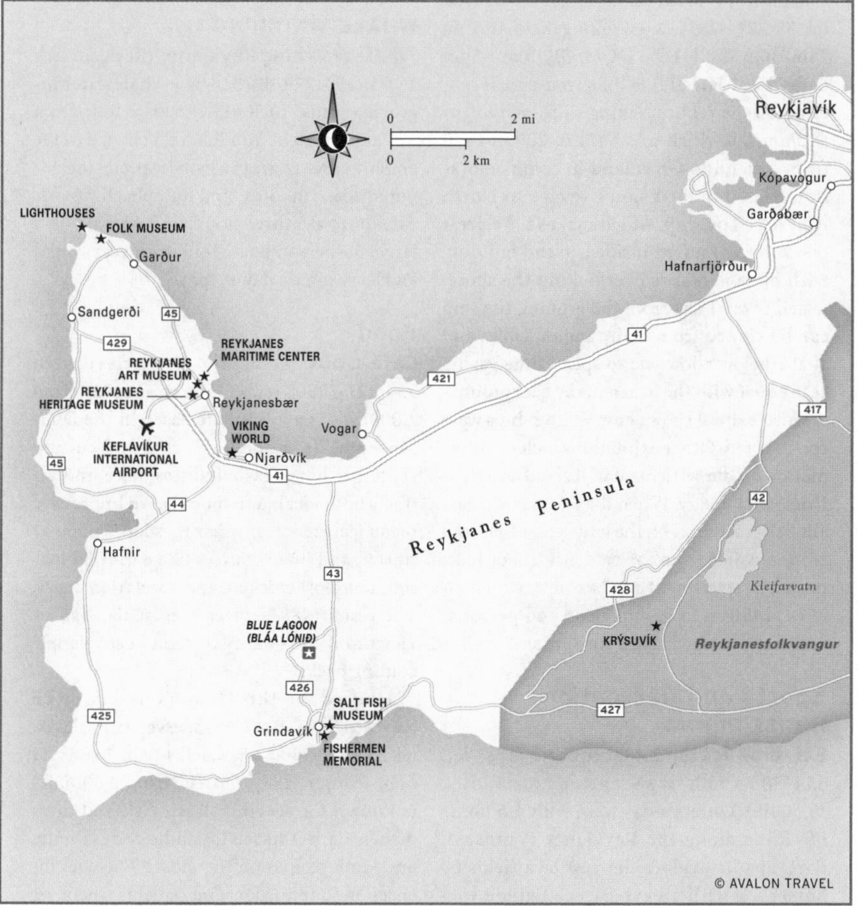

available on the types of boats and when they were used.

ICELANDIC MUSEUM OF ROCK 'N' ROLL

Icelandic Museum of Rock 'n' Roll (Hjallavegur 2, Keflavík, tel. 354/420-1030, www.rokksafn.is, 11am-6pm daily, 1,500ISK) is a perfect stop for those who love the music of Björk, Sigur Rós, Kaleo, and Of Monsters and Men, and are interested in learning about other rock and pop acts from Iceland. Visitors can listen to the music of local artists, see instruments, and check out costumes that have been worn by well-known local musicians, including one of Iceland's biggest pop stars, Páll Óskar. Guests can also learn about the histories of some of the island's most popular bands and singers. Interactive displays include a sound lab where you can have a karaoke-style sing-along or play drums, guitar, or bass. A café and music shop are also on-site.

VIKING WORLD (Vikingaheimar)

The **Viking World** (Vikingabraut 1, Njarðvík, tel. 354/894-2874, www.vikingaheimar.com, 7am-6pm daily Feb. 1-Oct. 31, 10am-5pm daily Nov. 1-Jan. 31, 1,500ISK) museum is centered on the replica Viking ship *Íslendingur (Icelander)*, which was built in 2000 to sail from Iceland to Greenland in commemoration of Leifur Eiríksson's voyage to North America. The ship, which makes for a great photo op, is housed inside a grand building with huge windows overlooking the shore. Lifted several feet from the ground, the ship can be viewed from many angles; tables and chairs below allow you to spend time gazing at the boat with the ocean in the background. A video exhibit shows how Viking ships were constructed. Other exhibitions include information on the settlement of Iceland as well as Norse mythology. When the weather is pleasant, it's great to sit on the large grass field and enjoy a coffee from the café inside. For kids, there's a "settlement zoo" exhibit, which allows children to get up close and personal with baby lambs, calves, and birds.

Sports and Recreation

HORSE RIDING

Extreme Iceland (Skutuvogur 13a, tel. 354/588-1300, www.extremeiceland.is, 19,500ISK) offers a day tour, with 4-5 hours of riding along the Reykjanes Peninsula. Participants explore the vast lava fields by horseback with an experienced guide who takes you along rivers, mountains, even a volcano ridge. The tour is offered year-round and departs from Hafnarfjörður. The tour cost includes all necessary riding equipment.

SWIMMING

The **Vatnaveröld Swimming Pool** (Sunnubraut 31, Keflavík, tel. 354/421-1500, 7am-8pm Mon.-Fri., 8am-6pm Sat.-Sun., 600ISK) in Keflavík is complete with hot tubs, heated pools, and a great swimming area for children. It's a wildly popular spot for locals and gives you a peek into an integral part of Icelandic society.

WHALE-WATCHING

Whale Watching Reykjanes (Reykjanesveg 2, tel. 354/779-8272, www.whalewatchingreykjanes.is, 10,900ISK) runs a tour from Keflavík Harbor. You'll have a chance to see dolphins and an array of whale species including minke, fin, orca, and humpback whales. The tours are three hours and operate on a large, 90-person boat. Tours run year-round and leave once a day at 1pm.

Food

Café Duus (Duusgata 10, Keflavík, tel. 354/421-7080, www.duus.is, entrées from 2,000ISK) is a lovely café based in the Duus Museum, Reykjanesbær's arts and culture center. It has a casual atmosphere and attracts both locals and tourists. An impressive menu features creamy lobster soup, a popular starter, and main courses like pan-fried lobster, tandoori chicken, and vegetarian curry. The restaurant features spectacular harbor views and the quality of food keeps people coming back.

Housed in the Hótel Keflavík, **KEF Restaurant & Bar** (Vatnsnesvegur, Keflavík, tel. 354/420-7000, www.kef.is, 5am-10am and 6pm-9:30pm daily, entrées from 3,500ISK) is known for serving classic fish and meat dishes. Expect to see Icelandic cod, salmon, and lamb recipes on the menu. The chef focuses on sourcing local ingredients whenever possible. It opens for breakfast at 5am for early birds. During the winter, if the northern lights decide to make an appearance, the restaurant's glass façade allows expansive views of the lights dancing and flickering in the deep black sky.

Situated in the heart of the town, **Langbest** (Keilisbraut 771, Keflavík, tel. 354/421-4777, www.langbest.is, 11:30am-9:30pm daily, entrées from 1,600ISK) serves up pizza, sandwiches, and fish-and-chips. It's a great place to stop for something quick and affordable.

Accommodations

At **Hótel Berg** (Bakkavegur 17, Keflavík, tel. 354/422-7922, www.hotelberg.is, rooms from 30,000ISK), modernized rooms are comfortable and have flat-screen televisions and free Wi-Fi. If you get one of the two loft suites during the winter months, you might catch a glimpse of the northern lights from the skylight.

Rooms at **Hótel Keflavík** (Vatnsvegur 12, Keflavík, tel. 354/420-7000, www.kef.is, rooms from 34,000ISK) are a bit small, but each room has a private bathroom, comfortable bed, and sweeping views of the lava fields. Staff is warm and helpful, and an in-house restaurant serves traditional Icelandic fare as well as some international favorites.

Keflavík's centrally located **Hótel Keilir** (Hafnargata 37, Keflavík, tel. 354/420-9800, www.eng.hotelkelir.is, rooms from 24,000ISK), boasts modern, minimalist decor, average-sized rooms, and small bathrooms. A family suite is available that can comfortably sleep five people. This hotel is a good budget option and just a five-minute drive from the airport.

Start Hostel (Lindarbraut 637, tel. 354/420-6050, www.starthostel.is, rooms from 16,000ISK) offers a mix of doubles, quadruples, family rooms, and dorm beds. The rooms are clean but bare bones, with just beds and a small table. Some rooms have private bathrooms, others share facilities, and there is a common room with a kitchen, luggage storage, free parking, and free Wi-Fi. Guests have access to laundry machines and Keflavík International Airport is just an eight-minute drive away.

Information and Services

Reykjanesbær's **tourist office** (Hafnargata 36, tel. 354/421-5660, www.visitreykjanes.is, 1pm-6pm daily) offers a booking service for tours and has brochures on activities, restaurants, and sights in the region.

Transportation

Reykjanesbær is 49 kilometers southwest from Reykjavík. By car, take Route 41, which is paved, to reach the region. It's about a 50-minute drive.

The **Fly Bus** (tel. 354/580-5400, www.flybus.is) runs regularly from **Keflavík International Airport** to the BSÍ bus station in Reykjavík, from where you can get a shuttle to your downtown hotel. It takes about 50 minutes to get from Keflavík to BSÍ bus station, and buses depart about 40 minutes after flights land. One-way tickets cost 2,500ISK.

If you are staying in Reykjanesbær, be sure to contact your hotel or guesthouse to see if there is a shuttle to pick you up at the airport. If not, taxis are available at the airport.

There are tours for sights in Reykjanesbær, but if you want the freedom to roam, renting a car is essential.

GARÐUR

Garður is a placid seaside town on the northwest tip of Reykjanes and a great place to spend a couple of hours. Garður is best known for a pair of lighthouses. On sunny summer days, locals and tourists picnic by the lighthouses, basking in the sun and enjoying the serenity and scenery. The lighthouses are a great spot to catch a glimpse of the northern lights in the winter, as the location is away from the bright lights of downtown.

Sights

LIGHTHOUSES

The highlight of Garður is the two lighthouses, each with unique charm. The older, more traditional red-striped lighthouse was built in 1847, and the newer square-designed one was built in 1944 in a more modern Nordic style. This is a popular destination for photos. Fishing boats can often be seen from shore, and there is rich birdlife in the region, ranging from hordes of gulls circling in the summer months to ravens dominating the skies in the winter. It's also common to see arctic terns and gannets in the summer. In the winter, the lighthouses appear against a backdrop of mist and mystery, and if you're lucky, you will see northern lights dancing in the night sky.

FOLK MUSEUM
(Byggðasafn Garðskaga)

The **Folk Museum** (Skagabraut 100, tel. 354/422-7220, www.svgardur.is, 1pm-5pm daily Apr. 1-Oct. 31, open by appointment the rest of the year, free) sits amid a rugged landscape with thriving birdlife. The quaint museum houses items that were essential for the livelihood of residents on both land and sea, including tools, fishing items, and maps. It offers a window into what life was like in past generations, reminding visitors that life in Iceland was not easy for early settlers. The museum also has an extensive collection of 60 functional engines provided by local resident Guðni Ingimundarson.

Food and Accommodations

The Old Lighthouse Café (Garðskagi, tel. 354/422-7220, 11:30am-8:30pm daily May-Oct., entrées from 1,800ISK), housed in an actual lighthouse, offers cakes, coffee, soft drinks, and light meals. It's a good place to grab a quick bite, and you can also go to the top of the lighthouse for a great view of the Reykjanes Peninsula, the lava fields, and if you're lucky, maybe a whale in the distance.

Guesthouse Garður (Skagabraut 46, tel. 354/660-7894, www.guesthousegardur.is, apartments from 26,000ISK) is a charming guesthouse with seven apartments ranging from studios to two-bedrooms available year-round. Located close to the harbor, the apartments have private kitchens, bathrooms with showers, free Wi-Fi, and satellite TV. The friendly staff can help arrange local tours, including golfing, bird-watching, and fishing. The cozy guesthouse is just a 10-minute drive to Keflavík airport.

CAMPING

The **Garðskagi campground** (Skagabraut, tel. 354/422-7220, 1,200ISK) is close to the two lighthouses in a quiet stretch of town. Campers have access to running water and toilets year-round.

Transportation

Garður is 55 kilometers west of Reykjavík. By car, take Route 41 to Route 45.

ELDEY ISLAND

Situated about 15 kilometers southwest from the southernmost tip of the Reykjanes Peninsula, Eldey Island is made up of sheer cliffs that jut out of the ocean and reach 77 meters high. Birdlife thrives on the island; Eldey has one of the biggest gannet bird colonies in the world. In recent years, an estimated 70,000 gannets have bred on the island from June to August. The best view of the island is from the Reykjanes Lighthouse; the GPS coordinates are N 63.8151, W 22.7033.

GRINDAVÍK

Grindavík is a placid fishing town steeped in fish trade history. Many of the same families have been trolling these waters for generations, and visitors can see fishers hauling their daily bounty of cod out of the harbor by day and dine on the local catch at night. The Grindavík area's greatest claim to fame, however, is the giant man-made geothermal expanse of the Blue Lagoon.

Sights

TOP EXPERIENCE

★ BLUE LAGOON
(Bláa Lónið)

Built on an 800-year old lava field, the **Blue Lagoon** (Svartsengi, tel. 354/420-8800, www.bluelagoon.com, 8am-10pm daily Jan.1-May 25 and Aug. 21-Oct. 1, 7am-11pm daily May 26-June 29, 7am-midnight daily June 30-Aug. 20, 8am-8pm daily Oct. 2-Dec. 31) covers an area of 8,700 square meters and draws visitors from around the world to soak in its gloriously milky-blue waters amid a dreamlike atmosphere. The heated water, which ranges 37-39°C (98-102°F), is heavenly any time of year. Enjoying the steamy air while soaking during the summer is lovely, especially on sunny days. And in the winter, a visit here is eerie and wonderful; watching as snow falls from the jet-black December sky or as northern lights dance across it while lounging in the hot water is sublime.

The water isn't deep, less than five feet, and the bottom is covered with white silica mud, the result of a natural process of recondensation. It's common to see visitors cover their faces with the mud—it's great for your skin, and all guests receive a free silica mud mask with standard admission. The gift shop sells Blue Lagoon skin products that have ingredients ranging from silica mud to algae found in other parts of Iceland. At the Lagoon Bar, a swim-up bar in the main section of the lagoon, you can purchase drinks to be enjoyed while lounging in the waters. There are also two steam baths on the property, as well as a dry sauna and massage area, and spa treatments are available.

The standard entrance fee is 6,100ISK for those over 14 years of age, 3,400ISK for disabled visitors, and free for children 2-13. Children under the age of 2 are not allowed at the lagoon. You can also upgrade your ticket to include add-ons like an algae mask, your first drink of choice, and a towel to use, but towels, swimsuits, robes, and slippers can also be rented à la carte. Because of the increase in tourism over the past few years, the Blue Lagoon now requires you to book a time slot ahead of your arrival, which you can do on its website. Reserve your time at least several weeks before your trip. Thousands of people visit the site every day, and it can get quite crowded during summer months. For the best chance of avoiding crowds, try to book early in the morning or late in the evening.

Many tours feature a visit to the Blue Lagoon, but if you're traveling independently, it makes sense to visit right after you fly in or before you head home, as it's very close to Keflavík airport. A rejuvenating soak is a great way to kick off your trip or end it on a relaxing note.

Driving from Reykjavík, the Blue Lagoon is about 48 kilometers, roughly 45 minutes, away on paved roads; head southwest on Route 41 and turn left onto Route 43. From Keflavík International Airport, the Blue Lagoon is about 23 kilometers away; take Route 41 and turn right onto Route 43, and you'll arrive in approximately 20 minutes. If you're making your way to or from the airport, note that the Blue Lagoon offers luggage storage. Bus transfers via **Reykjavík Excursions** (tel.

the Blue Lagoon

354/580-5400, www.re.is) can be booked in conjunction with Blue Lagoon entrance tickets; the buses run between both Reykjavík and the Blue Lagoon and Keflavík International Airport and the Blue Lagoon. Buses are available from Reykjavík to the Blue Lagoon, every hour 7am-7pm year-round, with additional services seasonally. From KEF to the Blue Lagoon, there are seven daily departures year-round and added service during the high season.

SALTFISH MUSEUM (Saltfisksetur)

The **Saltfish Museum** (Hafnargata 12A, tel. 354/420-1190, 9am-6pm daily, entrance 1,200ISK) tells the story of Iceland's fish trade from 1770 to 1965, the period when saltfish was Iceland's top export. Photos, fishing equipment, and even a full-size fishing boat from the early 20th century are on display, explaining the economic and cultural importance of saltfish to Iceland. If you're curious about the region, would like to learn more about processing saltfish in the olden days, or would like to get a look at an old-school fishing boat, be sure to stop by.

FISHERMEN MEMORIAL

A sad part of Iceland's fishing history is the stories of men who went out to sea to never return. There's a moving memorial in downtown Grindavík, in the main garden near the Saltfish Museum, showing a mother with her son and daughter waiting for their fisherman husband/father to return home from sea. It's a reminder that the fish used for consumption and trade has come at a high price for many families over the years. The memorial was created by sculptor Ragnar Kjartansson.

Sports and Recreation

ATV RIDING

For those looking for a little adventure, **4x4 Adventures Iceland** (Tangasund 1, Grindavík, tel. 354/857-3001, www.4x4adventuresiceland.is, 13,900ISK) offers a number of ATV/quad bike tours that let you get off the beaten track. Its one-hour Panorama tour takes travelers around the Reykjanes Peninsula and near rocky lava formations, mountains, and even to a view over the Blue Lagoon. No experience is necessary for this year-round tour.

SWIMMING

The **Grindavík Swimming Pool** (Austurvegi 1, tel. 354/426-7555, www.grindavik.is, 7am-8pm Mon.-Fri., 10am-5pm Sat.-Sun. June-Aug., 500ISK) is one of the best pools in South Iceland with its 25-meter pool, hot tubs, tanning beds, waterslide, children's pool, and fitness center.

GOLF

Just four kilometers southwest from the Blue Lagoon, **Húsatóftir Golf Course** (Húsatóftum, tel. 354/426-8720, paller@grindavik.is, greens fees Mon.-Fri. 3,000ISK, Sat.-Sun. 3,500ISK) is an 18-hole facility where visitors can golf late May-early September, depending on the weather. The scenic course offers picturesque views. It can be busy with locals during the high season of June-July, so be sure to call ahead for a tee time.

Food

Hja Hollu (Víkurbraut 62, tel. 354/896-5316, www.hjahollu.is, 8am-5pm Mon.-Fri., 11am-5pm Sat., entrées from 1,890ISK) is modern and casual with a friendly atmosphere and menu chock-full of healthy options like salads and vegan dishes. Guests can also choose from soups, sandwiches, pizzas, and wraps.

The ★ **Lava Blue Lagoon Restaurant** (Svartsengi, tel. 354/420-8800, www.bluelagoon.com, 11:30am-9pm daily, entrées from 5,900ISK) is very much a spa restaurant: ingredients are local, and the recipes are healthy. You will find fresh vegetables and fish as well as lean meats. The menu accommodates a host of dietary requirements. The atmosphere is minimalist chic with cool hues and modern accents. Casual clothing is allowed.

★ **Salthúsið** (Stamphólsvegur 9, tel. 354/426-9700, www.salthusid.is, noon-10pm daily mid-May-mid-Sept., noon-9pm mid-Sept.-mid-May, entrées from 3,300ISK), or "the Salt House," is a favorite among local fishers, residents, and tourists. A lot of saltfish is on the quiet eatery's menu, but guests can also choose from lamb and chicken dishes, as well as burgers, sandwiches, and fish-and-chips. The garlic-roasted lobster with salad and garlic bread is delicious. If you have room, be sure to check out the decadent dessert menu, which includes items such as deep-fried bananas with vanilla ice cream and caramel sauce, and French chocolate cake with fresh cream.

Max's Restaurant (Grindavíkurvegi 1, tel. 354/426-8650, www.nli.is, entrées from 3,200ISK) is the in-house restaurant at the Northern Light Inn. The atmosphere is very much that of a hotel restaurant, with good service and not many surprises, but it charms with huge windows overlooking mountains and lava fields. The menu consists of classic Icelandic food like lamb fillet and fresh fish dishes.

Accommodations

The ★ **Blue Lagoon Silica Hotel** (Svartsengi, tel. 354/420-8806, www.bluelagoon.com/Clinic, doubles from 46,000ISK) is a luxurious hotel connected to the Blue Lagoon. It has 35 bright and airy double rooms, each with private bathrooms and a terrace overlooking the surrounding lava fields. Silica offers luxury beds, modern decor, and beautiful views of the lagoon. Guests have access to a private lagoon open daily 9am-10pm.

Geo Hotel Grindavík (Víkurbraut 58, tel. 354/421-4000, www.geohotel.is, rooms from 22,000ISK) has double and family rooms, all with private bathroom facilities. The hotel's design includes a spacious social area for guests to relax in cozy surroundings. Room walls are painted in muted colors, and there are wood floors and minimalist furniture. Shops and conveniences are nearby in the town center.

Open year-round, **Guesthouse Borg** (Boragarhraun 2, tel. 354/895-8686, www.guesthouseborg.com, rooms from 15,000ISK) is a basic, no-frills guesthouse in the center of Grindavík and the best budget-friendly option in the area. The seven-room guesthouse has shared kitchen facilities, bathrooms, and washing machines, and is a five-minute drive from the Blue Lagoon. It's a clean and comfortable place to stay, but nothing to write home about.

The 32-room guesthouse **Northern Light Inn** (Grindavíkurvegi 1, tel. 354/426-8650, www.nli.is, doubles from 36,000ISK) offers cozy, bright, rooms with free Wi-Fi, satellite TV, and sweeping views. An in-house restaurant serves classic Icelandic fare with plenty of fish and lamb dishes, as well as a couple of vegetarian options. Its proximity to the Blue Lagoon is a big draw for tourists: It's just a 0.7-kilometer walk from the lagoon.

CAMPING

You can camp from mid-May to mid-September at the popular **Grindavík's Campsite** (Austurvegur 26, tel. 354/660-7323, 1,390ISK) by the harbor. It accommodates tents, RVs, and campers, with access to hookups (electricity costs an extra 1,000ISK per night) and a dump station. There's a paved entrance and a large parking area, and the grassy field has beautiful mountain views. The campsite offers laundry facilities, a common eating area, and a playground with swings and a spider net.

Information and Services

The tourist information center is located in the **Saltfish Museum** (Hafnargata 12A, tel. 354/420-1190, 10am-5pm daily). The gas station N1 and grocery chain Netto are situated downtown on Víkurbraut.

Transportation

By car, Grindavík is 50 kilometers from Reykjavík. Drivers should take Route 41 west to Route 43 south, both paved roads. It's about a 50-minute drive.

There are three daily departures from BSÍ bus station (www.bsi.is) in Reykjavík to Grindavík, offered year-round through

Reykjavík Excursions (tel. 354/580-5400, www.re.is, 4,500ISK). There are return buses to Reykjavík as well. The buses go to both the Blue Lagoon and the center of Grindavík (about 1.25 hours).

KRÝSUVÍK

The Krýsuvík geothermal area, which is 35 kilometers south of Reykjavík, is popular among geology buffs and hikers. Gurgling mud pools bubble from the yellow, red, and orange clay-like earth, intertwined with dancing steam and hot springs. The many hiking paths allow you to feel lost in the outer space-like atmosphere. The region gives you a great sense of Iceland's raw, natural geothermal energy, which powers much of the island. Take some time to roam, but be sure to stay within the designated roped-off areas to avoid getting burned by spray and steam. To get to the region, take Route 42 south from Reykjavík. It's about a 40-minute drive on the paved road.

The Golden Circle

TOP EXPERIENCE

If you ask an Icelander which tour you should take if you want a taste of Iceland outside of Reykjavík, he or she will most likely recommend the Golden Circle. Encompassing the three most visited sights in South Iceland, the Golden Circle gives you a slice of Icelandic history at Þingvellir, a view of Iceland's bubbling geothermal activity at Geysir, and a peek at a roaring, powerful waterfall at Gullfoss. The sights are classically Icelandic, and are postcard perfect in summer or winter.

Because of the popularity of the sights, it's pretty easy to get there. You can prebook a tour through many tourism companies, or simply go to Reykjavík's main bus terminal, **BSÍ** (Vatnsmýrarvegur 10, Reykjavík, tel. 354/562-1011, www.bsi.is), and buy a same-day ticket through **Reykjavík Excursions** (tel. 354/580-5400, www.re.is) for 10,900ISK for an eight-hour tour. If you have a rental car and want to view the sights independently, take Route 1 to Route 36 for Þingvellir. Continue on Route 36 then Routes 365, 37, and 35 to Geysir. From Geysir continue on Route 35 to Gullfoss, before looping back toward Reykjavík heading southwest on Routes 35 and 1. In total, the Golden Circle is an approximately 300-kilometer paved circular route, leaving from and returning to Reykjavík.

★ ÞINGVELLIR NATIONAL PARK

The birth of Iceland as a nation happened at Þingvellir. Literally translated to "Parliament Plains," Þingvellir was the site of Iceland's first general assembly, which was said to have been established in the year 930, and was the meeting place of the Icelandic parliament until 1798. Many significant sights are at Þingvellir, including Almannagjá and Law Rock (Lögberg). Þingvellir was established as a national park in 1930.

Visitors also come to the area for its geological significance, as it is the site of a rift valley that marks the crest of the **Mid-Atlantic Ridge.** It's also home to Þingvallavatn, the largest natural lake on the island, which has a surface area of 84 square kilometers. Visiting the park itself is free, but there's a parking fee (500ISK).

Sights

ÞINGVELLIR INTERPRETIVE CENTER

The **Þingvellir Interpretive Center** (tel. 354/482-2660, www.thingvellir.is, 9am-8pm daily June-Aug., 9am-5pm Sept.-Apr., free) gives a great overview of the national park, its history, and its geological significance. Stop in to see the interactive display and then pick up hiking maps at the information center next door.

The Golden Circle

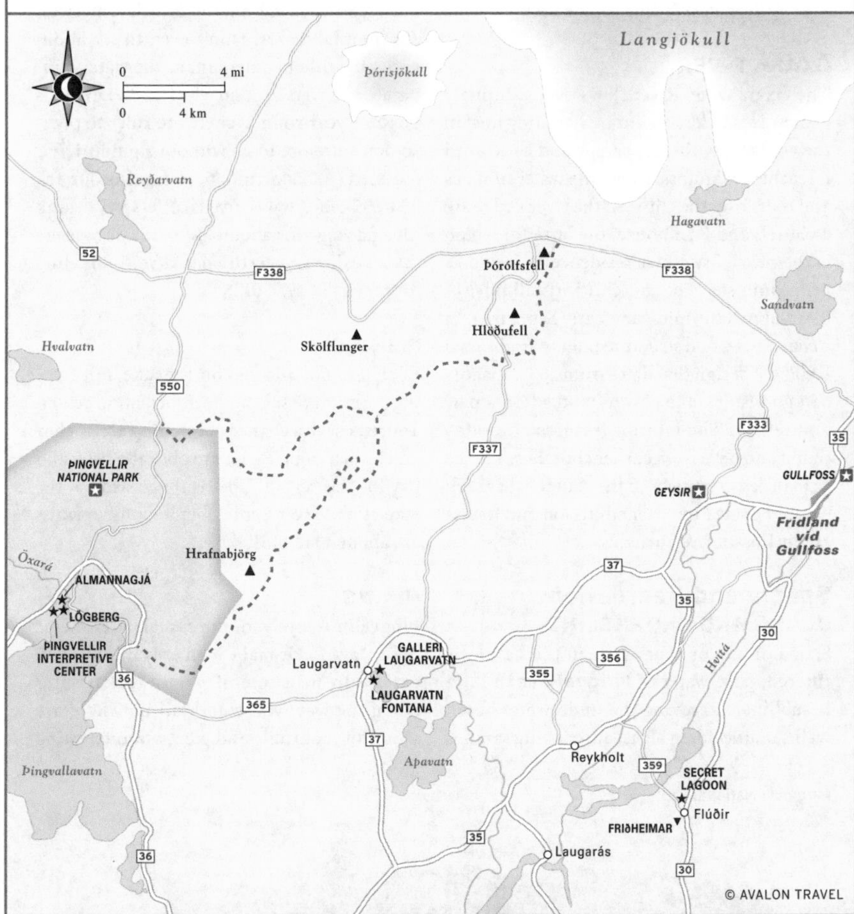

ALMANNAGJÁ

The park's stony, moss-covered landscape is home to Almannagjá (All Man's Gorge), which is the tallest cliff face in the national park and the original backdrop to the Alþing. This rock structure is considered the edge of the North American plate, which visitors can view up close. It's an impressive sight, so be sure you have your camera ready.

LÖGBERG

Lögberg (Law Rock) is where Icelandic democracy began. Iceland's Commonwealth period ran from 930 till 1262, and during that time, the Law Rock was the center of the Alþing (parliament). Members of the Alþing gave speeches and held events at the rock, including confirming of the year's calendar and issuing legal rulings. A man known as the "law speaker," who was responsible for understanding all laws and required to memorize them, read the procedural laws aloud every summer, standing on the rock.

ÖXARÁ RIVER

The Öxará (Axe) River flows over seemingly endless lava fields, emitting a haunting mist in the winter months. It's serene and eerie until it reaches Öxaráfoss, where the water tumbles and roars over the cliffs. At the river's edge are a church and farmhouse, the latter of which is the official summer residence of Iceland's prime minister. The church, **Þingvallakirkja** (9am-5pm daily mid-May-early Sept., free), is a charming wood structure built in traditional Icelandic design that dates from 1859. Visitors can go inside, take photos, and sit on a pew and reflect. The interior features a wooden pulpit and bells from earlier churches. There's a small cemetery behind the church where celebrated poets Einar Benediktsson and Jonasa Hallgrimsson are buried.

Sports and Recreation

DIVING AND SNORKELING

Scuba diving or snorkeling in the naturally filtered, pure water of **Þingvallavatn lake** is sublime. Surveying the underwater basalt walls, multicolored algae, and sloping sands is magical and unique—you're able to snorkel or scuba in the Silfa fissure, the enormous crack between the Eurasian and North American continental plates. Don't even think about going in without a drysuit, as the water temperature hovers around 3°C (37°F). Diving is possible year-round. There are rules to obey, so don't attempt to go without a guide. **Dive Iceland** (Ásbúðartröð 17, Hafnarfjörður, tel. 354/699-3000, www.dive.is) offers a two-tank dive package for about 44,990ISK. Travelers must be dry-suit certified to dive. Snorkeling tours start at 19,990ISK.

FISHING

Boats are not allowed on the lake, but fishing permits are sold at the information center. Tourists have a chance of catching arctic char and brown trout. Be sure to obey the rules and pay for the permit. The fishing season at the lake runs May 1-September 15, and permits are about 40,000ISK.

HIKING

Þingvellir is lovely for the casual hiker. Acres of flat lava fields make it an easy hiking spot, but be sure to be careful of open rock fissures along the way; you could fall in. There are scores of foot trails and plenty of interesting

Þingvellir National Park

rock formations and rugged terrain to see. You can get information about trails and the surrounding area at the visitors center. If you're looking to scale some small mountains, check out **Mount Syðstasúla** (1,085 meters), which is in the northern region of the park and is the park's easiest peak to climb. The view from the top is spectacular. The moderate hike is 13 kilometers round-trip and takes about seven hours.

HORSE RIDING

Þingvellir is a popular spot for riding horses, with several trails that offer the chance to check out some of the more beautiful and geologically significant areas of the park. Seeing the region by horseback is a beautiful way to survey the land. **Reykjavík Excursions** (tel. 354/580-5400, www.re.is) offers a year-round horse-riding day tour in Þingvellir for 23,300ISK.

Food and Accommodations

There are no hotels within Þingvellir National Park. However, there are accommodations in nearby Laugarvatn and Selfoss. If you would like to stay within the park limits, your only option is **camping** at one of Þingvellir's five campgrounds, spread across two areas of the park: the Leirar section, which is a five-minute walk from the Þingvellir information center, and the Vatnskot section, which is by Lake Þingvallavatn. The Leirar campground is divided into four campsites: Fagrabrekka, Syðri-Leirar, Hvannabrekka, and Nyrðri-Leirar. The Vatnskot campground is situated at an abandoned farm by the lake. All campsites have access to toilets, electricity, and cooking facilities. The difference in the two sections is not about amenities, but whether you want to camp close to the lake or stay closer to the information center. Both sections have great landscape views and spacious fields. The campgrounds are open June 1-September 30, and cost 1,300ISK per person.

Information and Services

The **tourist information center** (tel. 354/482-2660, www.thingvellir.is, 9am-8pm daily June 1-Aug. 31, 9am-6pm daily Sept. 1-May 31) is close to the car park. Be advised that there is a service fee of 200ISK to use the bathroom.

Transportation

Þingvellir is 46 kilometers northeast of Reykjavík. By car, take Route 1 to Route 36, which will take you to the northern part of the park.

While there is no public transportation available to get to the park, a number of tours include a stop at Þingvellir. Check out **Reykjavík Excursions** (tel. 354/580-5400, www.re.is) for daily departures.

LAUGARVATN

Laugarvatn, or "Bathing Waters," is a lake situated between Þingvellir and the geothermal hot spot of Geysir. Historically, members of Iceland's parliament (Alþing) visited the springs due to their proximity to where parliament met at Þingvellir for hundreds of years. The lake's water temperature hovers around 104°F, making it a unique and warm swimming experience.

Sights

GALLERI LAUGARVATN

When not enjoying the soothing hot springs or the vistas, steal away for a few minutes at **Galleri Laugarvatn** (Haholt 1, tel. 354/486-1016, www.gallerilaugarvatn.is, 1pm-5pm daily), a charming little gallery that features local handicrafts, ranging from glass tea light holders to unique paper crafts.

LAUGARVATN FONTANA

The **Laugarvatn Fontana** (Hverabraut 1, tel. 354/486-1400, www.fontana.is, 10am-11pm daily June 9-Aug. 20, 11am-10pm daily Aug. 21-June 8, 4,200ISK adults, 2,200ISK children 13-16, free for children 12 and under) is worth a stop before or after you visit Geysir. The facility's sauna captures the steam just as it escapes from the earth. You can bask in the natural sauna and hot springs, enjoying the geothermal energy up close and personal. Towels, bathing suits, and bathrobes can be rented at the spa.

For an experience unique to the region, each day at 2:30pm there is a walk from the reception area to the on-site geothermal bakery. Visitors can watch as the staff digs out rye bread that's been buried in the ground, left to bake naturally in the geothermally heated earth. You can try the bread, served hot from the ground with some butter—it's delicious!

Sports and Recreation

SWIMMING

Situated downtown, the **Laugarvatn Swimming Pool** (Hverabraut 2, tel. 354/486-1251, 10am-10pm Mon.-Fri., 10am-6pm Sat.-Sun. June-mid-Aug., 5pm-8pm Mon., Wed., and Fri., 1pm-5pm Sat. mid-Aug.-May, 600ISK) is popular among locals, and it's a nice break from the summer tourist rush at the Fontana spa nearby. Head here if you would like a quiet spot to take a dip.

Food

At **Restaurant Linden** (Lindarbraut 2, tel. 354/486-1262, www.laugarvatn.is, noon-10pm daily, entrées from 3,600ISK), owner and head chef Baldur Öxdal Halldórsson has created an upscale, fine-dining experience in a town with fewer than 300 residents. Guests have a lot of choices, from Icelandic mainstays to more exotic fare, with dishes ranging from reindeer meat burgers and pan-fried arctic char to tender lamb fillets and smoked cod. The classic decor and friendly staff make this little restaurant a treasure.

Accommodations

Location is key for **Hótel Edda ML Laugarvatn** (Skólatún, tel. 354/444-4810, www.hoteledda.is, mid-June-mid-Aug., rooms from 11,500ISK), as this 101-room hotel is a popular stop for those touring the Golden Circle. Rooms are basic and no-frills, with double beds, IKEA-style furniture, and crisp white bedding. Thirty-two rooms have private bathrooms, while the rest share facilities, and there is free Wi-Fi in common areas. Guests get a 10 percent discount for the geothermal steam baths at the nearby Fontana spa.

Efstidalur II (Bláskógabyggð, tel. 354/486-1186, www.efstidalur.is, rooms from 25,000ISK) is a charming farmhouse bed-and-breakfast with an in-house restaurant, friendly staff, and horse rentals. Situated close to the Fontana spa, the B&B is also in the proximity of the Golden Circle.

Golden Circle Apartments (Laugarbraut, tel. 354/487-1212, www.goldencircleapartments.is, apartments from 19,000ISK) offers 25 apartments that are modern and perfect for families, with fully equipped kitchens, private bathrooms, a TV, free Wi-Fi, and free parking. Apartments are spacious, have new appliances, and are close to town attractions.

One of the busiest hostels in South Iceland, **Laugarvatn Youth Hostel** (Dalsel, tel. 354/486-1215, www.laugarvatnhostel.is, open all year, double rooms from 10,900ISK) can accommodate 140 people in single, double, and family rooms. Ten rooms have private bathroom facilities, while the rest share. Kitchen and laundry facilities are available, and the staff is very warm and helpful. There's also a big hot tub on the property.

Transportation

Laugarvatn is just 77 kilometers northeast from Reykjavík and is easily accessible by car and bus. If driving from Þingvellir, take Routes 36 and 365 to Route 37.

The **Strætó** bus company (tel. 354/540-2700, www.straeto.is) has one daily departure to Laugarvatn year-round, leaving from the Mjodd bus terminal (tel. 354/587-0230) in Reykjavík. The trip is about 2.5 hours, and it costs 2,520ISK.

★ GEYSIR

Iceland's geysers are the most obvious demonstration of the island's natural geothermal energy, and historically, Geysir is the country's most famous example of the phenomenon—it's actually the source of the word "geyser."

Geologists theorized that in the 13th century earthquakes stirred the underground workings of the natural hot springs here, causing them to gush, releasing pressure, steam, and water up to 20 meters into the air.

Visitors to the site today aren't going to see the dormant Geysir erupt—it hasn't blown since 2005. But don't fret, because Geysir's nearby cousin, **Strokkur** (Churn), erupts every seven minutes or so. Crowds gather to watch the frequent eruptions, and the churning, gurgling pool of hot water turning out a rush of pressure from the clay-like earth is an impressive sight; be sure to have your camera ready. Please be careful and stay behind the ropes or you may get hit with hot spray.

After walking around the geothermal area, stop at the **visitors center** (9am-10pm daily). It has a short multimedia exhibition about the geology of the region, a small café serving refreshments, and a souvenir shop.

Food and Accommodations

You can't stay any closer to the geysers than at the **Hótel Geysir** (Geysir, tel. 354/480-6800, www.geysircenter.is, rooms from 23,000ISK). The property features posh suites that have huge Jacuzzi tubs and luxurious beds in a location just two minutes from the geysers. Guests can also stay in chalets on the property that are essentially double rooms. The decor is a bit rustic, but the rooms are comfortable. Visitors have access to an outdoor swimming pool and hot tub. The in-house **restaurant** (8am-10pm daily) serves up delicious dishes ranging from fresh Icelandic cod to lamb and beef entrées. A lunch buffet is popular among tourists. A three-course dinner menu will run you about 8,000ISK.

CAMPING

About 100 meters from the Geysir area is a **campground** (tel. 354/480-6800, 1,700ISK) that has hot showers, pool access, and a common barbecue area. Hótel Geysir operates the campsite, and you pay at the Geysir Shops just across from the campground. For an additional 1,000ISK you can have access to electricity, and the use of the swimming pool and hot tub at Hótel Geysir will run you an additional 500ISK.

Transportation

Geysir is about a 1.5-hour drive east from Reykjavík. You start out on Route 1 and then take Route 35, which takes you directly to the site.

the Strokkur geyser erupting

If following the Golden Circle route, continue from Laugarvatn on Route 37 to Route 35 for Geysir.

★ GULLFOSS

The thundering, roaring waterfall of Gullfoss epitomizes the raw beauty of Iceland. Gullfoss (Golden Falls) tumbles into the Hvíta (White) River, which is a perfect name given the turbulent white water. There are three levels of water at the falls, ranging from 11 to 21 meters, meeting at a 70-meter gorge. If you get too close, expect to get soaked.

Because of Iceland's changing weather, you have a good chance to see a rainbow over the falls, making for a perfect snapshot of your visit. Plan to walk around the site, enjoying not only the wonder of the falls, but also the beautiful surrounding landscape. In the summer, there are miles of lush green grass and frequent rainbows on sunny/rainy days. Be careful; it could be slippery.

No matter what time of year, there are scores of tour buses and independent drivers visiting the falls, and that's for a very good reason: It's gorgeous.

There is an ongoing fight between landowners and the Icelandic government over whether to charge visitors a fee to visit the falls. As of summer 2017, it was undecided and still in the courts.

An on-site café includes a souvenir shop and offers some brochures about the surrounding area.

Food and Accommodations

A short walk from the falls and parking area, **Gullfoss Café (Gullfosskaffi)** (tel. 354/486-6500, www.gullfoss.is, 9am-9:30pm daily, entrées from 1,800ISK) is the place to go when you're in the area. The Icelandic lamb meat soup on the menu is a winner, and a favorite among visitors, but sandwiches, cakes, and coffee are also available.

Hótel Gullfoss (Brattholt, tel. 354/486-8979, www.hotelgullfoss.is, rooms from 27,000ISK) is situated perfectly, just three kilometers from the falls in a remote area. The resort-like atmosphere is comfortable and a great place to spend the night while touring the Golden Circle. Every room has a private bathroom and is classically furnished with comfortable beds. An in-house restaurant and hot tub out back make for a comfortable stay.

On Route 35 between Gullfoss and Selfoss, you might stop for lunch at ★ **Friðheimar** (Bláskógabyggð, tel. 354/486-8894, www.fridheimar.is, noon-4pm daily), located in

Gullfoss

The Secret Lagoon

The **Secret Lagoon (Gamla Laugin)** (Hvammsvegur, tel. 354/555-3351, www.secretlagoon.is, 10am-10pm May 1-Sept. 30, 11am-8pm Oct. 1-Apr. 30, 2,800ISK adults, free for children 14 and under) has become a popular alternative (and cheaper at that) to the Blue Lagoon. It's located in Fluðir, a blip of a village with not much going on, but the Secret Lagoon brings tourists by the thousands while still offering a slightly more intimate, less touristy experience than the Blue Lagoon. The surroundings here are beautiful, with farmland and a geothermal area lush with moss covering lava stones and natural springs bubbling and steaming, just past the water's edge. You can rent towels and swimsuits here, and there is a café with drinks and snacks for sale.

If following the conventional Golden Circle route from Gulfoss down Route 35 back to Route 1, you'll bypass the Secret Lagoon. But if you make a slightly larger circle, jumping off Route 35 and taking Route 30 south instead, you'll pass right by Fluðir; it's about 38 kilometers south of Gulfoss, a 30-minute drive, and afterward you can connect from Route 30 back to Route 1 and Reykjavík.

Reykholt about a half hour and 30 kilometers south of Gullfoss. The farm is home to tomato greenhouses and a restaurant, as well as a horse-breeding operation. It's an ideal place to have lunch: Tomatoes don't get any fresher in Iceland, and the menu takes advantage of this with items like tomato soup and creative Bloody Marys. Call ahead for lunch reservations. Groups of 10 or more can take a tour of the greenhouse with the owner or a staff member. Tours are offered year-round; email fridheimar@fridheimar.is for more information.

Transportation

By car, Gullfoss is 115 kilometers northeast from Reykjavík. The drive takes about 1.5 hours on Routes 1 and 35.

Gullfoss is about 10 kilometers from Geysir on Route 35.

The South Coast

If you're after hot springs and quirky museums, and you have some time to spend before you head to the Golden Circle, look no farther than the southern coast. Small towns like Hveragerði, Selfoss, and Vík have unique charm. Hveragerði is famed as the hot springs capital of Iceland. Selfoss is frequently used as a home base when exploring the Golden Circle, but it also has a couple of museums to check out. Vík boasts black-sand beaches. Outdoor activities like hiking, bird-watching, and jeep tours are popular in this region.

HVERAGERÐI

Some Icelanders affectionately call Hveragerði the "Capital of Hot Springs." It's just 30 minutes outside of Reykjavík, so tourists have no reason not to stop by the region, especially as the town is on the way to the Golden Circle of Gullfoss, Geysir, and Þingvellir. Given its proximity to Reykjavík and its healing hot springs, the town is an all-year destination. After a visit to the springs, think about taking a peek at some of the local greenhouses populating the geothermal area. Tomatoes, cucumbers, and bell peppers are popular greenhouse-grown veggies in the region.

Sights

HVERAGARÐURINN GEOTHERMAL PARK

People flock to Hveragerði for one reason—hot springs. Whether they're under blue skies and sunshine or beset by rain, wind, and snow, the hot springs beckon visitors from around the world. The central geothermal area is in the center of town (Hveramörk 13, 9am-5pm Mon.-Fri., 9am-1pm Sat.-Sun., free). The natural phenomenon is hypnotizing to watch, as water bubbles to the surface. It's a constant reminder that Iceland sits on a hotbed of natural geothermal energy. Follow the path between geysers and hot pools, and at the end of the walk, you can soak your feet in one of the hot springs.

LÁ ART MUSEUM
(Listasafn Árnesinga)

The **LÁ Art Museum** (Austurmork 21, tel. 354/483-1727, www.listasafnarnesinga.is, noon-6pm Thurs.-Sun., free) offers several different exhibitions throughout the year, ranging from modern to traditional art from Icelandic artists local to the region. The museum also has a children's section, focusing on art for young visitors. It's a cute place to visit, especially if you are traveling with kids.

HVERAGERÐI BOTANICAL GARDEN

Hveragerði Botanical Garden (Breiðamörk, tel. 354/483-4000, free), located in the center of town, is a favorite spot for locals and tourists to stroll and enjoy nature. Guests can find a lot of trees (a rarity in Iceland) and walk along the mighty river Varmá. When the weather is good, it's common to see locals chatting and walking the trails, and tourists taking photos of the surroundings. It's also a great spot for birdwatching in the summer.

HVERAGERÐI STONE AND GEOLOGY EXHIBITION

Hveragerði Stone and Geology Exhibition (Breiðamörk 1b, tel. 354/847-3460, www.ljosbra.is, 9am-5pm Mon.-Fri., 10am-5pm Sat.-Sun., 700ISK) is a privately owned stone collection that is not to be missed by geology enthusiasts. Guests can see minerals, lava stones, crystals, and more. The owners are happy to chat about the collection, which goes back generations.

Sports and Recreation
HIKING AND BIKING

Several trails between Hveragerði and Þingvallavatn lead up to Mount Hengill, which is 68 kilometers north of Hveragerði. The 803-meter mountain gives hikers a view of the vast volcanic landscape. Bring your camera and a good pair of boots. There are several active hot spots along the way, so be

the South Coast

The South Coast

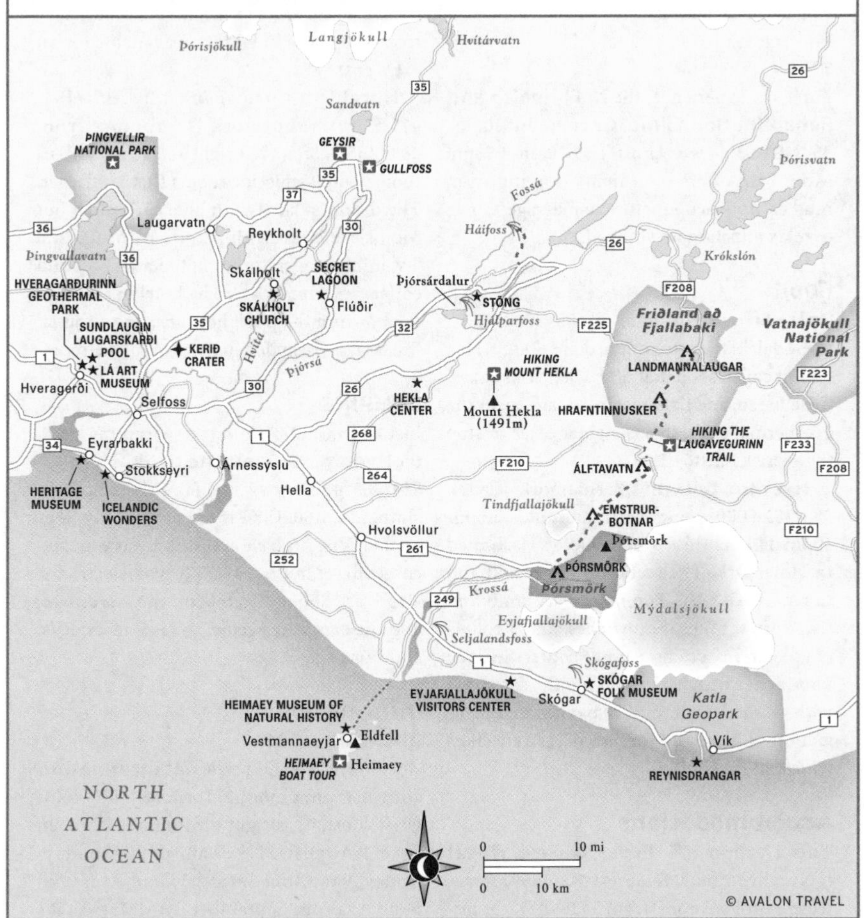

sure to stick to the trail. You can begin the hike at a parking area near a small spring close to the golf course. From here, the hike is about five kilometers round-trip and takes about three hours.

If you are interested in bicycling, Hveragerði-based **Iceland Activities** (tel. 354/777-6263, www.icelandactivities.is) rents bikes in the region and organizes daily bike tours. Day tours last 4-5 hours and cost 17,900ISK per person. Tours and rentals are available year-round.

SWIMMING

If hot springs aren't your bag, there's a lovely swimming pool downtown. The heated pool **Laugaskarð** (Reykjamörk, tel. 354/483-4113, 600ISK) is open 7am-8:30pm daily in summer, 10am-5:30pm daily in winter.

GOLF

The **Hveragerði Golf Course** (Gufudalur, tel. 354/483-5090, greens fees 4,500ISK) is a nine-hole course in a picturesque part of town, set against a backdrop of hot springs. It rents clubs and golf carts, and runs a café with light meals. The course is open May-August; call ahead for a tee time.

SPAS

For a spa experience, the **NLFÍ Health and Rehabilitation Clinic** (Grænumörk 10, tel. 354/483-0300, www.hnlfi.is, 7:30am-4:30pm Mon.-Fri.) offers treatments ranging from mud baths to acupuncture to massage. Come to relax and pamper yourself.

Food

Dalakaffi (Jokutunga, tel. 354/862-8522, www.dalakaffi.is, 1pm-6pm daily, 600ISK) is a quaint coffee shop that offers delicious cakes, fresh bread, and light meals. Located near the geothermal park, this is a great place to stop for a quick bite to eat.

Hver Restaurant (Breiðamörk 1C, tel. 354/483-7000, www.hverrestaurant.is, noon-10pm daily, entrées from 3,900ISK) is located in Hotel Örk. The restaurant is casual and the staff friendly. The menu has lamb and fish dishes, soups, sandwiches, and a couple of vegetarian options. Sample courses include Arctic char with barley and lightly salted cod with mashed potatoes. The bar has a good selection of local and foreign beers as well as wine and cocktails.

Accommodations

The 17-room ★ **Frost & Fire Hotel** (Hverahvammur, tel. 354/483-4959, www.frostogfuni.is, rooms from 24,000ISK) is nestled in the heart of Hveragerði. Each room in the boutique hotel is adorned with works from local Icelandic artists and has private shower facilities and comfortable beds. Guests have access to a spa next to the river that offers treatments, hot tubs, and a swimming pool. The included breakfast is delicious.

Frumskógar (Frumskógar 3, tel. 354/896-2780, www.frumskogar.is, double rooms from 18,000ISK) is a small guesthouse with six apartments (perfect for families), five double rooms, and one single room. Rooms are clean and comfortable, but no-frills. Its location, close to the Ring Road, is excellent. The friendly staff is happy to recommend activities, tours, and attractions. All rooms have free Wi-Fi, and breakfast is available for an extra cost.

Hotel Ork (Breiðamörk 1, tel. 354/483-4775, www.hotelork.is, rooms from 28,000ISK) offers 76 bright and airy standard rooms and 9 superior rooms that are larger. The decor is dated with blue carpeting, but rooms are clean with private bathrooms, a TV, mini refrigerator, complimentary tea and coffee, and free Wi-Fi. The hotel has an outdoor swimming pool, hot tubs, and a sauna. Breakfast is included in the price of the room.

CAMPING

Just two minutes from the swimming pool, the **Hveragerði Campsite** (Reykjamork, tel. 354/483-4605, www.reykjamork-camping@simnet.is, 1,500ISK) is open mid-May-September. Visitors have access to a washing machine, dryer, toilets, and 220-volt electricity. There are about 80 spots on the large field, and the campsite accommodates tents, RVs, and campers.

Information and Services

The South Iceland **regional information center** (Sunnumörk 2-4, tel. 354/483-4601, www.south.is) is right off Route 1. It's open June 1-August 31 8:30am-6pm Monday-Friday, 9am-4pm Saturday, and 9am-2pm Sunday. From September 1 to May 31 it's open 8:30am-5pm Monday-Friday and 9am-1pm Saturday.

Transportation

Hveragerði is 40 kilometers southeast of Reykjavík. The drive takes about 35 minutes on Route 1.

The **Strætó** 51 bus (tel. 354/540-2700, www.straeto.is) from Mjodd bus station in Reykjavík makes about 10 daily stops to Hveragerði year-round, stopping at the Shell gas station downtown. The bus ride is about 55 minutes and costs 1,320ISK.

SELFOSS

Located close to Gullfoss, Geysir, and Þingvellir, Selfoss is a service hub for South Iceland. Many visitors make a stop here to fill up their gas tanks, get a bite to eat, or rest their heads in one of the town's nice hotels or guesthouses. While the town's proximity to the Ring Road and sights in the countryside is a plus, Selfoss has a few attractions of its own that are worth checking out. History buffs will want to drop by the Heritage Museum, which features exhibitions of life in the town and the surrounding sights.

Sights

HERITAGE MUSEUM (Byggðasafn Árnesinga)

The **Heritage Museum** (Eyrargötu 50, tel. 354/483-1504, www.husid.com, 11am-6pm daily May-Sept., 1,000ISK) is housed in one of Iceland's oldest buildings. Built in 1765, it was home to a local Danish merchant and his large family and business. Merchant families lived in the house for nearly two centuries. Today, the museum gives a peek into what life was like in Iceland in the 1870s, with the decor, furniture, tools, and housewares of years past.

BOBBY FISCHER CENTER

The **Bobby Fischer Center** (Austurvegur 21, tel. 354/894-1275, www.fischersetur.is, 1pm-4pm daily May 15-Sept. 15, or by appointment, 1,000ISK) is located is a small white house in the heart of Selfoss. This may sound like an odd museum to find in Iceland, but Bobby Fischer lived in the town for a couple of years after he applied for asylum to the country (after breaking international sanctions to play a chess match in Yugoslavia), which was granted. The museum serves as the home of the local chess club and you'll find Bobby Fischer memorabilia, mostly from his time in Iceland, on display. Bobby lived in Iceland from 2005 until his death in 2008.

KERIÐ CRATER

The **Kerið crater**, which is just 15 kilometers north of Selfoss, is a cool place to stop and take a photo due to the sheer size of the crater lake. The collapsed scoria cone is 70 meters deep and is used for farming fish. There's a nice path along the rim that allows good views, but use caution and stay on the path.

SKÁLHOLT CHURCH

The site of the **Skálholt church** (tel. 354/486-8870, www.skalholt.is) has great significance in Iceland's history, and is a sacred site for many Icelanders. Gissur the White, a wealthy political figure, played an important role in the Christianization of Iceland and the growth of the early church. He built the first church in Iceland at Skálholt around the year 1000. His son, Ísleifur (1006-1080), chose Skálholt as the site of the first Episcopal see in Iceland, and the first bishopric was founded here in 1056 for southern Iceland.

In the 12th century, bishop Klængur Þorsteinsson built a great cathedral at Skálholt, and it served as a cultural center up to the Reformation in 1550. The last Catholic bishop of Iceland, Jón Arason, was executed at Skálholt in 1550, along with his two sons, because he opposed the Reformation forced upon Iceland by King Christian III of Denmark. A memorial stands at the site of the execution. Today, Skálholt is visited for the cathedral, the tomb of bishops, the museum, and the collection of ancient books on view in the tower. The church on the site today dates from 1963 and is a large, stark-white building with a dark top. The design is sharp, clean, and classically Nordic. In the summer months, there are cultural events and concerts open to the public.

The church is open to the public 9am-6pm daily; admission is free. There's a church service every Sunday at either 11am or 2pm.

Skálholt is 39 kilometers northeast of Selfoss. The drive takes about 40 minutes on the paved Route 35.

Sports and Recreation

HORSE RIDING

Sólhestar (Borgargerdi, tel. 354/892-3066, www.solhestar.is) offers year-round horse tours ranging from one-hour rides for 9,000ISK to customized all-day tours for 24,000ISK. Tours feature trails along scenic hot springs, volcanoes, remote beaches, and gorgeous waterfalls.

SWIMMING

The **Sundhöll Selfoss** (Bankavegur, tel. 354/480-1960, sundh@arborg.is, 6:30am-9:30pm Mon.-Fri., 9am-7pm Sat.-Sun., 950ISK) is a pool open year-round; towel and swimsuit rentals are available.

GOLF

The **Kidjaberg Golf Course** (Kidjaberg, tel. 354/486-4495, 8am-10pm daily in summer, greens fees Mon.-Fri. 6,000ISK, Sat.-Sun. 7000ISK) in Selfoss is an 18-hole facility near the Hvitá River with glorious views. A clubhouse and restaurant are on-site. Be sure to call ahead for a tee time, as this is a popular course among locals.

Food

Hafið Bláa (Thorlákshöfn, tel. 354/483-1000, www.hafidblaa.is, 12:30pm-9pm daily, entrées from 2,700ISK), which translates to "the Blue Sea," is a seaside café where you can grab a quick coffee and cake or sit and enjoy a light meal and the beautiful view. The cream of mushroom soup is memorable. Lobster soup, arctic char, and salted cod are also on the menu.

Menam (Eyrarvegur 8, tel. 354/482-4099, www.menam.is, 11:30am-2pm and 5pm-10pm daily, entrées from 2,590ISK) is a nice little Thai restaurant that serves classic chicken, lamb, beef, and seafood dishes. The chicken pad thai is delicious. There's also an international menu with burgers, fish-and-chips, and a soup of the day.

Riverside Restaurant (Eyrarvegur 2, tel. 354/480-2500, www.hotelselfoss.is, 7am-10pm daily, entrées from 3,600ISK) is Hótel Selfoss's in-house restaurant. Guests are treated to fresh, local ingredients and eclectic recipes in an elegant atmosphere. The sesame fried salmon and bacon-covered monkfish are recommended. Vegetarian dishes are available.

Accommodations

★ **Hótel Selfoss** (Eyrarvegur 2, tel. 354/480-2500, www.selfosshotel.is, rooms from 25,000ISK) has the sort of stylish interior you'd expect in Reykjavík, so it comes as a delightful surprise in the countryside. The 99-room hotel has large rooms, including spacious bathrooms, and chic decor. Ten rooms

Skálholt church

are specifically designed for people with disabilities, and it is one of the most wheelchair-friendly hotels on the island. Business travelers are attracted to the hotel for its conference center, while those looking for luxury are thrilled about the in-house spa, which offers a number of treatments. The staff aims to please and is happy to chat and give recommendations about local sights.

Fosstún (Eyrarvegur 26, tel. 354/480-1200, www.fosstun.is, June-mid-Aug., hotel rooms from 21,500ISK) is a no-frills lodging facility that features 12 hotel rooms with private bathrooms and mountain views; 4 rooms in a guesthouse with shared bathrooms, a kitchen, and a common area; and 8 camping pods with access to a kitchen, bathrooms, and hot tubs. A washing machine is available for use, and parking is free. A breakfast buffet is included in the price of accommodation.

Selfoss Hostel (Austurvegur 28, tel. 354/660-6999, www.selfosshostel.is, rooms from 13,000ISK) is one of the nicer hostels on the island. The 60-bed facility has spacious rooms, a common kitchen, small gym, and helpful staff. The hostel has a friendly atmosphere. Guests often meet up with fellow travelers and plan excursions together. Washing machines are available for use, and sheets are provided. A hot tub out back is a nice touch.

Information and Services

The **tourist information center** (Austurvegur 4, tel. 354/482-4241, www.arborg.is, 8:30am-6pm daily June 1-Aug. 31, 9:15am-5pm Mon.-Fri. Sept. 1-May 31) is a great place to pick up pamphlets, arrange tours, and ask questions of the staff.

Transportation

Selfoss is 57 kilometers southeast from Reykjavík. By car, Selfoss is off of the familiar Route 1. The drive takes about 45 minutes.

If you're traveling by bus, the **Strætó** 51 bus (tel. 354/540-2700, www.straeto.is) leaves from bus station Mjodd in Reykjavík several times a day. The ride takes about one hour and costs 1,760ISK. Buses stop and pick up near the main circle (Austurvegur) downtown.

STOKKSEYRI

This small town was home to a thriving fishing industry, but today it's more of a tourist town with a couple of kitschy museums.

Sights

THE GHOST CENTRE

The small **Ghost Centre** (Hafnargata 9, tel. 354/483-1202, www.icelandicwonders.is, 1pm-6pm daily, 1,500ISK) is a fun museum dedicated to Iceland's most famous ghosts and their stories. During the tour, which takes about 40 minutes, you hear 24 ghost stories through a device and headphones that can be listened to in English, French, German, Russian, Japanese, or Icelandic. While you listen to the ghost stories, you look at displays about the various spirits. The phantoms include mountainside ghosts, ancient ghosts, ghosts in animal disguises, infant ghosts, and sea ghosts. The Ghost Bar is at the end of the tour, where you can order a drink and absorb everything you just took in. It's all in good fun, but it's not recommended for children under the age of 12.

ICELANDIC WONDERS

Icelandic Wonders (Hafnargata 9, tel. 354/483-1202, www.icelandicwonders.is, 1pm-6pm daily, 1,500ISK) is next door to the Ghost Centre. Instead of ghosts, this exhibition focuses on Iceland's rich folklore, including elves, trolls, the Yule Lads (Iceland's version of Santa Claus), and northern lights. There's something for everyone at this charming museum, and it is much more child friendly than the Ghost Centre.

Transportation

Stokkseyri is 65 kilometers southeast of Reykjavík and accessible by Route 1. The drive takes about 55 minutes.

MOUNT HEKLA

Hekla's claim to fame is being the most active volcano in the country today. And that's no easy feat, as there are 35 volcanoes currently active in Iceland. Hekla (Hood) should not be confused with nearby Eyjafjallajökull, which wreaked havoc on transatlantic air travel in 2010. Climbing 1,491 meters, Hekla has erupted 5 times in the last hundred years and more than 20 times since Iceland was settled in the 10th century. Its last eruption was in 2000, and local scientists expect it to erupt in the near future, as there were thousands of tremors in 2017. What makes Hekla somewhat unique is that it's a cone volcano, which is less common in Iceland than fissure volcanoes.

Sights and Recreation

★ HIKING MOUNT HEKLA

Scaling Hekla is not as daunting as it looks. In 3.5 hours or so, you can reach the summit via a moderately challenging seven-kilometer trail. Along the way, you cross rough lava fields and see ice and snow as the peak gets nearer. At the top, the view is jaw-dropping. On clear days, you can see the Fjallabak mountains up to Vatnajökull glacier, Europe's largest glacier.

Now for some crucial safety tips. The ideal time to make the climb is August-September, when it's not likely that you'll encounter a lot of snow at the top. Always make sure to check weather conditions before you head out and let someone (such as the concierge of your hotel) know of your travel plans. Also check in with the **tourist information center** in Hella (Thrudvangur 6, tel. 354/487-4800). Make sure you have an adequate amount of drinking water, appropriate clothing, and a charged mobile phone. Mount Hekla is an active volcano, so check with locals and consult with www.safetravel.is before heading out on a hike.

HEKLA CENTER

The **Hekla Center** (Leirubakki, tel. 354/487-8700, www.leirubakki.is, 10am-9pm daily May-Sept., 900ISK) gives visitors a comprehensive look at one of the island's most active volcanoes. The exhibition emphasizes the influence of the volcano on the inhabited areas close to it, including Landsveit, Holt, and Rangárvellir. The center has special educational materials for children as well as tourist information in English. An on-site café offers

hiking Mount Hekla

light meals and coffee. It's an essential place to stop and read up on the region.

Transportation

By car from Reykjavík, head southeast on Route 1 and take unpaved Route 26 toward the town of Hella. The journey from Reykjavík is 93 kilometers, which takes about 1.5 hours.

For those interested in going by bus during the summer months, **Reykjavík Excursions** (tel. 354/580-5400, www.re.is) runs a daily bus that goes to Landmannalaugar, which passes Hekla. The tour takes 12 hours and costs 15,700ISK.

ÞJÓRSÁRDALUR

Þjórsárdalur is a flat valley, but it's quite lush due to its proximity to the Þjórsá River. The region has a lot of pumice because of the numerous eruptions of Mount Hekla over the years.

Sights

HÁIFOSS

Háifoss, a beautiful waterfall near Mount Hekla, drops from a height of 122 meters, making it the second-highest waterfall on the island. Set against the backdrop of the Þjórsá River, Háifoss is a wonderful place to stop and take a picture. It is possible to hike to the waterfall (a moderate, six-hour, 18-kilometer hike round-trip), but there is a parking lot above the cascade, which makes it a car-friendly stop along the way to your next destination. If you are planning to hike it, make sure you have proper footwear and adequate drinking water. A well-maintained trail starts from the car park. From Selfoss, take Route 1 for 14 kilometers to Route 30 for 18 kilometers to Route 32 for about 43 kilometers. Both routes are paved.

HJÁLPARFOSS

Hjálparfoss is another gorgeous waterfall near Mount Hekla. It is about 30 kilometers east of the village Flúðir and can be reached by a gravel road off Route 32 that winds through the Vikrar lava fields.

STÖNG

Stöng, a settlement-era farm, was completely buried by Hekla's eruption in the year 1104. A reconstructed 11th-century longhouse called Þjóðveldisbær was erected in this protected valley (tel. 354/488-7713, www.thjodveldisbaer.is, 10am-6pm daily early June-Aug., remainder of the year open by appointment, 750ISK). For those looking to see a traditional "turf house" with grass on the roof, this is the place to go. The farm, as legend tells it, was the residence of Gaukur á Stöng from *Njál's Saga*. History buffs will want to make a stop, and are welcome to go inside and take a look.

Sports and Recreation

SWIMMING

After erecting the local dam, the Búrfell hydroelectric station used its extra cement to build the open-air **Þjórsárdalur Swimming Pool** (tel. 354/488-7002, 10am-9pm daily June-Aug., 600ISK).

Transportation

Þjórsárdalur is 118 kilometers east of Reykjavík. It's accessible by unpaved Route 32; a four-wheel-drive jeep is needed to get around some choppy parts by the river. It is not recommended to venture out in a compact car, as the likelihood of getting stranded is high. The drive takes about 1.5 hours. Be sure to check weather forecasts before heading out on your journey.

ÞÓRSMÖRK AND LANDMANNALAUGAR

The Þórsmörk (Thor's Woods) region offers a spectacular view of the landscape, ranging from towering mountains to scores of glacial streams and miles of black sand. Be advised that making it to the region is no easy feat. Do not venture out in a compact car. Because of the Krossá River, it is a wet and turbulent ride that requires a jeep. Meanwhile, Landmannalaugar is a major hub for hikers, and for very good reason. There are several well-maintained trails throughout the region that range from day hikes to multiday treks. The landscape is one of wonder with vast valleys, colorful rhyolite mountains, hot springs, and riverbanks.

★ Hiking the Laugavegurinn Trail

The wildly popular hiking route from the Landmannalaugar region to the Þórsmörk area is a 55-kilometer, four-day hike that attracts backpackers and hikers from around the world. If you're coming to Iceland to hike just one trail, this is the one. Its popularity stems from the variety of landscape along the way: bubbling hot springs, vast glaciers, beautiful mountains, stunning waterfalls, and roaring rivers.

At night, hikers can rest their heads in mountain huts, which span the duration of the trail. The huts mark the starting and ending points of each leg of the trail.

To reserve huts, visit the **Volcano Huts** website at www.volcanohuts.com. Huts can sleep 2-16 people, and beds start at 8,200ISK. Huts have running water, cooking facilities, a sauna, pool, and showers. There are campsites that adjoin the mountain huts that are also operated by Volcano Huts. The facilities include a cooking area, toilets, and running water. It's always a good idea to call ahead for camping, and it's required to call ahead for spots in the mountain huts.

For more information about the Laugavegurinn Trail, contact the **Iceland Touring Association (Ferðafélag Íslands)** (www.fi.is).

DAY 1: LANDMANNALAUGAR TO HRAFNTINNUSKER

The Landmannalaugar-Hrafntinnusker leg of the hike spans 12 kilometers, and its estimated walking time is 4-5 hours. It's considered moderately challenging. The trail goes through a rugged lava field, which makes this leg a bit more difficult, to the slopes of the volcano Brennisteinsalda. The landscape offers every color of the rainbow, from deep green moss to the bluest skies to yellow and red earth. After about four hours, you will reach a hot spring, Stórihver, which surges with activity, steam bubbling to the surface. The remainder of the day 1 trail to the Hrafntinnusker hut at Höskuldsskáli might be challenging depending on weather conditions, so be sure to monitor the forecast for snow and wind.

Landmannalaugar

DAY 2: HRAFNTINNUSKER TO ÁLFTAVATN

The Hrafntinnusker-Álftavatn part of the trail is 12 moderately challenging kilometers, with an estimated walking time of about five hours. You start out going through a valley with some small gorges and dips in the land, but be careful where you step, because they may be filled with snow or ice. If the weather is good, a climb up Mount Háskerðingur (1,032 meters) will treat you to a spectacular view of the landscape and the road ahead. The trail continues through a region rich with mountains and glaciers. As you get closer to the Grashagakvísl River, the colors become more vibrant, with bright green moss and lichen alive along the riverbanks. It's a beautiful place to stop, take some pictures, and soak up the scenery.

DAY 3: ÁLFTAVATN TO EMSTRUR

The third day from Álftavatn to Emstrur is a little longer at 15 kilometers and an estimated walking time of seven hours. The moderately challenging trail starts out over the ridge Brattháls, passes into the Hvanngil gorge, and crosses the Bratthálskvísl River by bridge. The landscape is vast and serene. As you continue on to the Kaldaklofskvísl River, there is a bridge for hikers. Past the bridge, you have two options as the trail splits. One branch leads east to Mælifellssandur, and the other path leads south to Emstrur. Most people opt for the southern trail to Emstrur because it's a bit more scenic with mountain views and an interesting rocky landscape. Less than one kilometer from Kaldaklofskvísl from the southern trail, there's another river, Nyrðri Emstruá, where there is a bridge to cross.

DAY 4: EMSTRUR TO ÞÓRSMÖRK

The last leg of the hike, from Emstrur to Þórsmörk, is 15 kilometers, with an estimated walking time of seven hours. Hikers start out by navigating the canyon of Syðri-Emstruá. It's important to note that there is a steep path down to the bridge, so stay aware and be careful where you step while descending. Next, hikers come across the Almenningar region and will have to ford the Þröngá River. After wading through the river, it's a 30-minute walk to the Langidalur huts in Þórsmörk.

TIPS

It can be quite cold and snowy, so it's important to closely monitor the weather and hike in good conditions. Even if there isn't snow, the wind can be unforgiving. Be sure to

Þórsmörk

dress warmly and have good boots. The ideal months for this hike are June and July.

Transportation

Landmannalaugar is 193 kilometers southeast of Reykjavík. Take Route 1 to Route 26 to F225; the latter two roads are unpaved. It's about a 3.5-hour drive.

If starting the hike at Þórsmörk, it's important to note that it is not easy to reach when compared to other destinations in the south. However, it's worth the effort if you're looking for untouched and unspoiled land. There are significantly fewer visitors to Þórsmörk. You will need a jeep to navigate these roads; do not attempt the trip in a compact car.

Þórsmörk is 157 kilometers southeast from Reykjavík. It's reachable by jeep via Route 1 and Route 249. The drive takes about 3.5 hours.

By bus, **Trex** (tel. 354/587-6000, www.trex.is) has daily departures in the summer from Reykjavík to Þórsmörk and to Landmannalaugar for 14,100ISK per person, and it's about a four-hour ride. **Reykjavík Excursions** (www.re.is) offers bus service daily in the summer from Reykjavík to and from Landmannalaugar and to and from Þórsmörk for 15,700ISK.

SELJALANDSFOSS

The mighty Seljalandsfoss is a highlight for many visitors to the south coast. Tourists delight in the spray from the 40-meter falls, and rainbows are frequently seen here due to the changing weather and frequent rain showers. During the summer, the area around the falls is lush with bright green grass, a heavenly sight on bright days. What makes this waterfall unique in a land of spectacular waterfalls is that there's a path that lets you walk behind it. Those who do so are treated to a memorable view, but be prepared to get wet and be sure to wear appropriate footwear. Use caution during the winter, as it can be especially slippery. Seljalandsfoss is about 120 kilometers southeast of Reykjavík, about a 1.75-hour drive, and is right off Route 1.

EYJAFJALLAJÖKULL

Eyjafjallajökull became Iceland's most famous volcano after its eruption in 2010 halted air travel across Europe, stranding tens of thousands of people. For locals, it was a treat to hear foreign newscasters struggle to pronounce the name of the volcano on the nightly news. Clips were regularly shown on Icelandic TV. (For the record, it's pronounced EYE-ya-fyat-lah-YOH-kuht.)

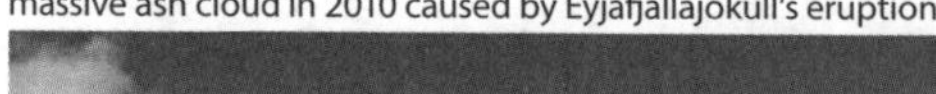

massive ash cloud in 2010 caused by Eyjafjallajökull's eruption

Before Eyjafjallajökull made worldwide headlines, the volcano had been a popular destination to explore, and it remains so today, with a rugged and icy landscape. Eyjafjallajökull is completely covered by an ice cap; magma hitting the ice created the tremendous ash cloud during the eruption. The ice cap covers an area of about 100 square kilometers, which feeds several outlet glaciers. When people joke that "Iceland is green, and Greenland is icy," those who visit the Eyjafjallajökull region will think again. There is a lot of ice in Iceland. The ice cap is the fourth-largest glacier in Iceland.

Eyjafjallajökull is a stratovolcano that ascends to 1,651 meters at its highest point. The volcano is fed by a magma chamber under the mountain, and it is part of a chain of volcanoes stretching across Iceland. Its nearest active neighbors are Katla to the north and Heimaey and Eldfell to the south. The volcano is thought to be related to Katla, in that eruptions of Eyjafjallajökull have generally been followed by eruptions of Katla. However, Katla did not erupt following Eyjafjallajökull's 2010 eruption. Scientists closely monitor the volcanoes' activity, measuring the size and frequency of the tremors.

Eyjafjallajökull (Iceland Erupts) Visitors Center

The **visitors center** (Rte. 1, tel. 354/487-5757, www.icelanderupts.is, 10am-4pm Mon.-Fri. May, 9am-6pm Mon.-Fri. June-Aug., 10am-4pm Mon.-Fri. Sept., 11am-4pm Mon.-Fri. Oct.-Apr., 850ISK) opened on April 14, 2011, exactly one year after the start of the Eyjafjallajökull eruption. Situated at the foot of the volcano, the visitors center features color posters of the eruption, and a short film shows the power of nature and how the region rose from the ashes. The movie hall seats 60 people, and the film is available in multiple languages, including English, German, French, Spanish, and Italian. The center is closed on weekends, Christmas, New Year's, and Easter.

Transportation

Eyjafjallajökull is on the Ring Road, Route 1, and is 140 kilometers east of Reykjavík. Buses do not stop near the volcano, so if you want to get up close and personal, you need access to a car.

SKÓGAR

Skógar is a tiny village of fewer than 40 people. The town suffered a major setback in the

Skógafoss

aftermath of the Eyjafjallajökull eruption, as it was covered in ash and life ground to a halt. The town has since recovered, and tourism to the region is back in full swing. The Skógafoss cascade is the main draw, but there is also a folk museum worth checking out.

Sights

SKÓGAFOSS

Skógafoss is an epic waterfall, one of the biggest in the country. It looms 25 meters high and has a drop-off of 60 meters. According to Viking lore, a local settler buried a treasure chest in a cave behind the waterfall. It was said that locals discovered the chest years later, but it quickly disappeared before they could grasp it. Because of the amount of spray the waterfall produces, as well as the changing weather from sun to rain, it's common to see rainbows over the falls; be sure to have your camera ready. The waterfall is in town, near the southern Ring Road.

SKÓGAR FOLK MUSEUM (Skógasafn)

Skógar Folk Museum (Austur-Eyjafjöllum, tel. 354/487-8845, www.skogasafn.is, 9am-6pm daily June 1-Aug. 31, 10am-5pm daily Sept. 1-May 31, 2,000ISK) is a charming initiative that started in 1949 at the behest of resident Þórður Tómasson, who curated the museum from its inception until his retirement in 2013, at the age of 92. The museum, which houses relics of the past, including tools, fishing equipment, and a fishing boat, does a great job of showing what life has been like in Skógar over the last several decades. A little coffee shop serves a great cup of coffee and delicious pastries.

TOP EXPERIENCE

Hiking the Fimmvörðuháls Trail

The trek through the Fimmvörðuháls pass from Skógar to Þórsmörk is one of the most popular hiking routes in the country. The trail takes hikers up from Skógar, along the Skógá River and its wondrous waterfalls, and up between the two enormous glaciers Eyjafjallajökull and Mýrdalsjökull. There, hikers can see recently formed lava and craters. Heading down from the craters to the stunning Þórsmörk glacier valley, there are some amazing views over the highlands and the surrounding glaciers. The trek is only safely accessible from around mid-June to early September.

This is a demanding hike, with an elevation gain of over 1,000 meters and a total distance of about 25 kilometers. It takes about 8-10 hours. Most tourists hike it one day, but it can be done over two days as well. It's recommended that you start the hike at Skógar and end at Þórsmörk; starting at Skógar is more popular than starting in Þórsmörk because it's easier to get to. There are no facilities along the route, so be sure to have enough food and water, as well as proper gear. Good hiking boots and waterproof clothing are required, and having layers is strongly recommended. You can encounter all types of weather, so be prepared. Guided hikes from mid-June to the end of August are available through **Icelandic Mountain Guides** (tel. 354/587-9999, www.mountainguides.is) for 41,900ISK (includes all gear).

Experienced independent hikers may opt to take a bus run by **Reykjavík Excursions** (tel. 354/580-5400, www.re.is) to Skógar, which leaves twice daily from Reykjavík June 1-August 31. The one-way fare is 6,000ISK. Upon completing the hike, travelers can take a Reykjavík Excursion bus back to Reykjavík from the Básar campsite, in the vicinity of Þórsmörk, for 8,400ISK.

DAY 1: SKÓGAR TO FIMMVÖRÐUSKÁLI HUT

The trek starts at the epic waterfall Skógarfoss, where you'll want to spend some time exploring the area and admiring the thundering falls. The trail officially begins after climbing the makeshift stairs along the waterfall. You'll see a river ahead and a path, and you'll encounter myriad colors in the landscape, from lush greens in the first 7-8 kilometers to the muted grays and browns of the rugged, rocky terrain. Eyjafjallajökull and Mýrdalsjökull glaciers loom ahead as you make your way past gravelly ruts and fields of snow. Keep in mind that even in the summer, you will see snow. The Fimmvörðuskáli Hut, which is signposted and about 30-40 minutes west of the trail, is the halfway mark. The hut (tel. 354/562-1000, www.utivist.is, 6,500ISK) is open mid-June to August 31 and can accommodate 20 people. It has bathrooms, a gas stove, and kitchen accessories. The GPS coordinates are N 63.37.320, W 19.27.093.

DAY 2: FIMMVÖRÐUSKÁLI HUT TO ÞÓRSMÖRK

After a hopefully restful evening and soon after getting back on the trail, you'll make your way between the two glaciers—for many this is a highlight. Observe the smooth curves and jagged edges of the glaciers before getting ready to encounter snow as the elevation rises. The highest point is between the two mountains, Magni and Móði. Pressing ahead, you will encounter the site of the 2010 Eyjafjallajökull eruption and new lava fields created in its aftermath. The path continues through rocky plateaus before descending into valleys as you enter Þórsmörk.

Food and Accommodations

Just a five-minute walk from Skógafoss waterfall, at the foot of Eyjafjallajökull, ★ **Hotel Skogar** (Skogum, tel. 354/487-4880, www.hotelskogar.is, rooms from 24,900ISK) offers 12 rooms in a minimalist Nordic design. Rooms are bright and airy, with wood furniture and shockingly white bedding. It's clean, comfortable, and has a beautiful in-house restaurant in a killer location with stunning views. Breakfast is included, and guests have access to a sauna and outdoor hot tub. The **Hotel Skogar Restaurant** (entrées from 3,100ISK) offers a delicious selection of choice local meats and fish and other fresh ingredients. The restaurant is open for breakfast 8am-10am daily year-round, lunch noon-3pm daily June-August, and dinner 6pm-10pm daily year-round.

Transportation

The tiny village of Skógar is 154 kilometers southeast of Reykjavík and is accessible by Route 1.

Some bus tours include Skógar in their itinerary. **Bus Travel Iceland** (tel. 354/511-2600, www.bustravel.is) offers a "Southern Iceland" nine-hour tour that includes Skógafoss and the town of Vík (12,990ISK).

VÍK

Vík, home to fewer than 400 people, has that small-town feel. The main tourist draws are the Katla Geopark—the region surrounding the mighty Katla volcano—and the area's hauntingly beautiful black-sand beaches.

Sights

REYNISDRANGAR

Reynisdrangar is a cluster of striking basalt sea stacks that jut out from a sandy beach. The stacks sit under the mountain Reynisfjall just outside Vík. It's popular to climb on the stacks and take photos, then roam the black-sand beach picking up stones and admiring the rock formations. Reynisdrangar is about 10 kilometers south of Vík and can be reached by Route 1 and Road 215, both paved roads.

REYNISFJARA

Reynisfjara, from which Reynisdrangar is visible, is probably the most famous black-sand beach in Iceland. The juxtaposition of the white waves crashing on the stark black sand and pebbles is beautiful, with towering basalt columns along the shore next to a small cave. As a popular sight in the south, there tends to be a lot of foot traffic in the area. Pay close attention to the warning signs in the parking lot, as there are sneaker waves that can drag you out to sea; there have been fatal accidents here in recent years. Reynisfjara is about 10 kilometers south of Vík and can be reached by Route 1 and Road 215, both paved roads.

DYRHÓLAEY

Dyrhólaey is a unique rock formation near Reynisfjara. The rock arch rises from the sea, peaking at 120 meters, and offers views of the Reynisfjara black-sand beach, basalt columns, the ocean, and during the summer, seabirds, including puffins. You can drive to Dyrhólaey from Reynisfjara, which is about 20 kilometers west, taking paved Road 215 to paved Route 1 to unpaved Road 218. Visitors can walk to the arch from the small carpark.

KATLA GEOPARK

Vík is the gateway to the Katla Geopark. Iceland's first geopark was designated in 2011 to protect the natural environment, promote local sustainable development, introduce local culture, and emphasize nature tourism. The name comes from one of the island's volcanoes, Katla, which is situated under the glacier Mýrdalsjökull. The geopark is 9,542 square kilometers, which is 9.3 percent of the total area of Iceland. Within the geopark are glaciers, volcanoes, mountains, rivers, waterfalls, and miles of lava fields. Visitors can enjoy hiking, caving, angling, horse riding, glacier walking, and ice climbing. The geopark is open year-round.

One of the best tours offered in the region is a three-hour jeep tour from **Katla Track** (tel. 354/849-4404, www.katlatrack.is), which takes you takes you to see black-sand beaches, the Katla glacier, and Reynisdrangar. The tour is available year-round and costs 29,900ISK per person for a local guide and the jeep. Be sure to dress in warm clothing, rain gear, and good shoes.

Food

★ **Halldorskaffi** (Víkurbraut 28, tel. 354/487-1202, www.halldorskaffi.is, 11am-10pm daily year-round, entrées from 2,400ISK) has it all for a tiny café. There are soups, sandwiches, pizza, hamburgers, and more upscale fish and lamb dishes. A children's menu offers chicken nuggets and hamburgers. The food is eclectic for a local café, and the owner is a big fan of garlic. The lamb sandwich with fresh, marinated meat in pepper sauce with a salad and french fries hits the spot.

Strondin (Austurvegi 18, tel. 354/487-1230, www.strondin.is, entrées from 2,690ISK) is a cozy eatery in the heart of Vík and a great place to stop for home-cooked comfort food. The small restaurant features wood furnishings and decor that conjures the atmosphere of a lodge, with a warm, friendly

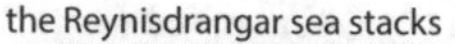

the Reynisdrangar sea stacks

staff and a diverse menu. Guests can choose from pizzas, salads, and main courses like Icelandic cod stew, pan-fried Arctic char, and grilled lamb fillet.

Suður-Vík Restaurant and Café (Suðurvikurvegur 1, tel. 354/487-1515, noon-10pm daily, entrées from 3,000ISK) brings some much-needed food diversity to Vík. The menu is eclectic and includes some tasty Thai dishes that are perfectly spiced. The restaurant is situated in an old house on the top of a hill with amazing views of the landscape, including the sea and mountains.

Accommodations

Hótel Edda Vík (Klettsvegi 1-5, tel. 354/444-4840, www.hoteledda.is, May-Sept., rooms from 24,500ISK) is a 41-room hotel featuring standard rooms that aren't much to look at but are clean and adequate. The hotel could use a renovation, and Wi-Fi and breakfast cost extra, but the location is great, and it is a decent place to lay your head.

Guesthouse Hátún 8 (Hátún 8, tel. 354/487-1211, www.guesthousevik.is, rooms from 22,000ISK) is operated by a local couple who offer two cozy bedrooms with comfortable beds. There's a shared bathroom, and guests have access to free Wi-Fi, a common kitchen, and a dining room. Tourists sometimes opt to eat with fellow travelers and the hosts (meals are available for purchase). The guesthouse is nothing fancy, but the warm owners and great location just off the Ring Road make this place a winner.

Icelandair Hotel Vik (Klettsvegi 1-5, tel. 354/487-1480, www.icelandairhotels.com, rooms from 30,000ISK) is a 78-room hotel close to the major attractions in Vík. It's spacious and has contemporary decor with light colors and lots of windows. Economy, deluxe, and family rooms are available. The hotel also has a cozy bar, and a breakfast buffet is included in the rate.

Transportation

By car, Vík is 185 kilometers southeast of Reykjavík by Route 1. It's about a 2.5-hour ride.

The **Strætó** 51 bus (tel. 354/540-2700, www.straeto.is) departs daily from the Mjodd bus terminal in Reykjavík to Vík. It's about a three-hour ride and costs 6,160ISK.

KIRKJUBÆ-JARKLAUSTUR

Kirkjubæjarklaustur is a small village located between Vík and Höfn. The village, referred to as Klaustur by locals, is home to fewer than 150 people. Many tourists who struggle to find accommodations in Vík choose to stay here.

Sports and Recreation

MOUNTAIN BIKING

Kind Adventure (tel. 354/847-1604, www.kindadventure.is) is a local tour operator that specializes in year-round guided biking tours in the south of Iceland. Its Fatbike Surprise tour (16,000ISK) last 2-3 hours and traverses 10-20 kilometers around Kirkjubæjarklaustur. Guests bike on paved roads, gravel roads, and muddy tracks, depending on the weather and conditions. Scenic lava fields and mountains looming in the distance provide a beautiful backdrop.

SWIMMING

Kirkjubæjarklaustur Swimming Pool (Kirkjubær, tel. 354/487-4656, 10am-8pm daily, 600ISK) is a popular outdoor swimming pool with two hot tubs in the center of town.

Food and Accommodations

Fosshotel Núpar (Núpar, tel. 354/517-3060, www.fosshotel.is, rooms from 31,000ISK) has 30 standard rooms and 30 that boast a view of the glacier Vatnajökull. Rooms are clean, with private bathrooms, a simple desk, and a bedside table. There's an in-house **restaurant and bar** (11am-9pm daily, entrées from 3,000ISK), and breakfast is included in the price of the room.

Icelandair Hotel Klaustur (Klausturvegur 6, tel. 354/487-4900, www.icelandairhotels.com, rooms from

35,000ISK) is a 57-room hotel just off the Ring Road, making this a convenient place to stay when exploring the south coast. It offers twin and queen rooms as well as king junior suites. The rooms feel a little dated with green carpeting and bright bed linens, but it's an adequate three-star hotel. The in-house **restaurant** offers a breakfast buffet every morning (7am-10am daily), as well as lunch (noon-2pm daily) and dinner (6pm-9pm daily). Main courses start at 2,650ISK and include grilled Arctic char, lamb fillet, and pasta dishes.

Magma Hotel (Tunga, tel. 354/420-0800, www.magmahotel.is, rooms from 18,000ISK) is a stylish addition to the area. The 14 self-contained cottage-style rooms are modern, chic, and heavy on Nordic design. Each room is tastefully decorated in muted colors with quality linens, wood furniture, and hardwood floors. Each room has huge windows as well as a patio. Rooms range from doubles to family rooms and have a flat-screen TV with access to Netflix, Marshall speakers, free Wi-Fi, and a private bathroom.

Transportation

By car, Kirkjubæjarklaustur is about 250 kilometers southeast of Reykjavík on Route 1, an approximately three-hour drive.

Heimaey

The Westman Islands (Vestmannaeyjar) are chock-full of rocky ridges and bird-watching opportunities. Heimaey, the only inhabited island, is where all of the sights, restaurants, and museums are located. With fewer than 5,000 residents, it's an isolated community, surrounded by beauty. The other islands remain uninhabited but can be seen from the sea during a boat tour. In the summer months, Heimaey is a popular spot for puffin-watching.

SIGHTS

Eldfell

Eldfell, which means "fire mountain" in Icelandic, is a volcanic cone that reaches 200 meters high. It was formed after the 1973 volcanic eruption on Heimaey, which came without warning and displaced more than 3,000 Icelanders. Ash from the eruption fell for weeks, destroying homes, livestock, and personal possessions. Most of Heimaey's residents left by boat, and thankfully there were no deaths.

Tourists can take a 30-minute ferry ride from Landeyjaharbor in the southern town of Hvolsvöllur to Heimaey to get a close look at Eldfell. **Eimskip** (tel. 354/481-2800, www.eimskip.is) operates the ferry that departs six times a day May-September (3,600ISK round-trip with a car).

Eldheimar

Eldheimar (Gerðisbraut 10, tel. 354/488-2700, www.eldheimar.is, 11am-6pm daily May 6-Oct. 14, 1pm-5pm only Wed.-Sun. Oct. 15-May 5, 2,300ISK) is a fascinating interactive museum about Heimaey's 1973 volcanic eruption. It includes photos, surviving structures, and an overview of the volcanic geology of the region. Videos illustrate the force of the volcanic eruption and destruction left in its wake, and maps light up on the walls, pointing out volcanoes around the island.

Sæheimar

Heimaey's Natural History Museum & Aquarium, **Sæheimar** (Heidarvegur 12, tel. 354/481-1997, www.saeheimar.is, 10am-5pm daily May 1-Sept. 30, 1pm-4pm Sat. Oct. 1-Apr. 30, 1,200ISK adults, 500ISK children 10-17, free for children under 9) is in the center of town and a great spot to take kids. It's filled with tanks of live Icelandic fish, along with stuffed birds such as puffins (always a kids' favorite) and arctic terns.

SPORTS AND RECREATION

★ Boat Tour

Viking Tours (tel. 354/488-4884, www.vikingtours.is) offers a lovely boat tour departing from Heimaey harbor daily at 11am and 4pm (May 15-Sept. 15, 7,400ISK adults, 6,400ISK children 9-14 and seniors, free for children under 9). On the 1.5-hour tour, you'll see the rugged lava coastline, bird cliffs, and ocean caves. Near its conclusion, you'll enter a cave along the harbor, where you'll listen to instrumental music that takes advantage of the cave's acoustics. It's a wonderful way to spend a couple of hours.

Bird-Watching

The island's puffin population is the main attraction for tens of thousands of visitors. Puffins are cute, charismatic, and classically Icelandic. Their bright orange feet, round bodies, and striped bills are irresistible to children and adults alike. Take a walk along the sea cliffs and spend some time with the adorable birds. Prime puffin-watching season is June-August.

Hiking

Heimaey has a little bit of everything. Because of its small size, it's impossible to get lost, but there are moments when you will feel completely isolated, and serene, on your hike. Many choose to roam the base of the Eldfell volcano, watch the personality-packed puffins in the summer, and stroll downtown. You won't find a plethora of arduous treks, but the island is an opportunity for casual strolls and prime picture-taking. There are about 12 kilometers of trails along the coast.

Swimming

The **Heimaey Swimming Pool** (6:15am-9pm Mon.-Fri., 9am-6pm Sat.-Sun. June-Aug., 6:15am-9pm Mon.-Fri. rest of year, 600ISK) has a large indoor swimming pool, three hot tubs, a sauna, and a gym. There's a slide for children and the pool is family friendly. It's open all year.

FOOD

★ **Slippurinn** (Strandvegur, tel. 354/481-1515, www.slippurinn.com, noon-2:30pm and 5pm-10pm daily mid-May-Aug. 27, entrées from 2,790ISK) has received rave reviews since opening in 2015. If you want fine dining

Heimaey, one of the Westman Islands

on the island, this is your place. Only open during the summer months, the restaurant is a mix of modern and rustic, housed in an old machine warehouse near a shipyard. Local ingredients are featured in its scratch-made dishes. Guests will find divine seafood entrées like lobster soup, lemon sole, and a pan-fried fish of the day. Meat eaters can choose from lamb, beef, chicken, and even minke whale. Vegetarian options are limited.

Café María (Skólavegur 1, tel. 354/481-3160, 11:30am-11:30pm Sun.-Thurs., 11am-1am Fri.-Sat., entrées from 2,000ISK) is one of the most frequented restaurants on the island. Diners have a lot to choose from, ranging from local cod and salmon to halibut and monkfish. For those who don't eat fish, there is puffin, lamb, and salad on the menu. It's crowded in the summer months with both tourists and locals.

ACCOMMODATIONS

★ **Hotel Vestmannaeyjar** (Vestmannabraut 28, tel. 354/481-2900, hotel@eyjar.is, rooms from 17,000ISK) offers clean, small rooms with a shared kitchen and bathroom facilities. The hotel has a hot tub out back, arranges bicycle rentals, and has a tour desk that can book excursions. The property underwent a renovation in 2015, and 24 of the 57 rooms are in a new wing, with those rooms offering much more space. There is also a spa on the lower floor that has hot tubs and a sauna, with massages and other treatments on offer. Breakfast is included in the price of the room.

Árný Guesthouse (Illugagata 7, tel. 354/481-2082, www.arny.is, rooms from 15,000ISK) is a small guesthouse that favors wood decor and neutral tones. The beds and furniture are comfortable and homey, and guests have access to a shared kitchen and laundry facilities; bathrooms are also shared. A swimming pool is next to the guesthouse.

INFORMATION AND SERVICES

The **tourist information center** (Strandvegur, tel. 354/488-2555, www.vestmannaeyjar.is, 9am-6pm Mon.-Fri., 10am-5pm Sat.-Sun. June-Aug.) is open during the summer months and is ground zero for pamphlets and booking tours.

TRANSPORTATION

Heimaey Airport (tel. 354/481-3300), which is roughly three kilometers from downtown Heimaey, hosts **Eagle Air** (tel. 354/562-4200, www.eagleair.is) with daily flights to and from Reykjavík. Flights are about 25 minutes and cost 15,000ISK each way.

By ferry, visitors can get to the island through the company **Eimskip** (tel. 354/481-2800, www.eimskip.is, 1,380ISK), which has frequent year-round service, daily May-September. Travelers can bring their cars on the ferry for an extra fee. The ferry departs from Landeyjahöfn in South Iceland, and the ferry ride is about 35 minutes. Landeyjahöfn is 137 kilometers southeast of Reykjavík, accessible by Route 1.

Snæfellsnes Peninsula and the Westfjords

Look for ★ to find recommended sights, activities, dining, and lodging.

Highlights

★ **Settlement Center (Landnámssetur):** This museum in Borgarnes offers a crash-course in the sagas and earliest days of Icelanders (page 124).

★ **Hiking in Húsafell:** Húsafell is a gem of a town in the west, with well-maintained hiking trails offering spectacular views of mountains and glaciers (page 129).

★ **Snæfellsjökull National Park:** Explore the giant glacier that was the setting for Jules Verne's *Journey to the Center of the Earth,* as well as lava-formed landscapes (page 130).

★ **Bird-Watching at the Látrabjarg Cliffs:** Visit one of the best spots on the island to see puffins (page 148).

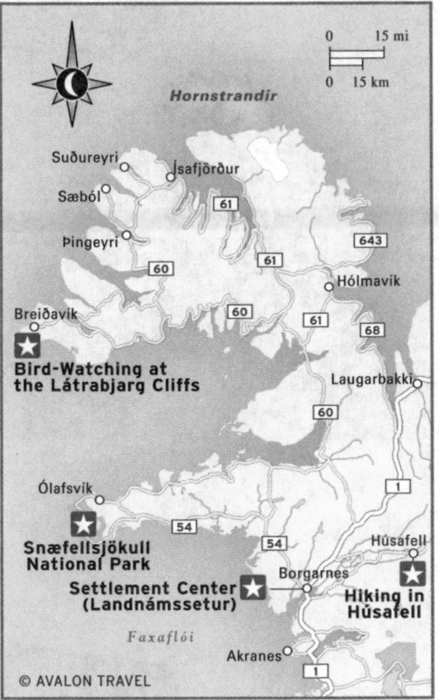

A trip to West Iceland is ideal if you have limited time but want to see some of the countryside. Black-sand beaches, hot springs, quiet fishing towns, and a glacier accessible by foot await you, just 40 minutes from Reykjavík.

Perhaps the most beautiful park in Iceland, Snæfellsjökull National Park is the ultimate tourist treat. The glacier's ice-capped glory invites visitors to put on a pair of crampons and see it for themselves.

On the Snæfellsnes Peninsula, you can see the small fishing towns that serve as the backbone of the country, sustaining the island over the centuries. Without fish, there wouldn't be an Icelandic economy to speak of.

If you are in Iceland for an extended period of time, don't miss the Westfjords, where you'll find steep cliffs with millions of nesting birds, well-maintained hiking paths, quirky museums, and some of the most striking beauty on the island.

PLANNING YOUR TIME

Tourism in the west is still growing, especially in the Westfjords. Independent travelers who rent a car for a day out of Reykjavík frequently make their way to Akranes, Borgarnes, and the Snæfellsnes Peninsula, which gives casual day-trippers a great taste of what the west has to offer, including mountains and charming fishing villages. A trip farther northwest will treat you to pure beauty, along with everything from whale-watching excursions to quirky museums to mountain climbing.

A day is enough for a taste of the west coast. To get a true sense of the western coast and the Westfjords, plan for at least 5-6 days, with one day in Akranes/Borgarnes, two days in the Snæfellsnes Peninsula, and 2-3 days in the Westfjords. While buses stop at several towns, you need a car to see some choice spots in the Westfjords—Hólmavík and Hornstrandir in particular.

Previous: puffins in the Westfjords; West Iceland landscape. **Above:** little free library in the Westfjords.

Snæfellsnes Peninsula and the Westfjords

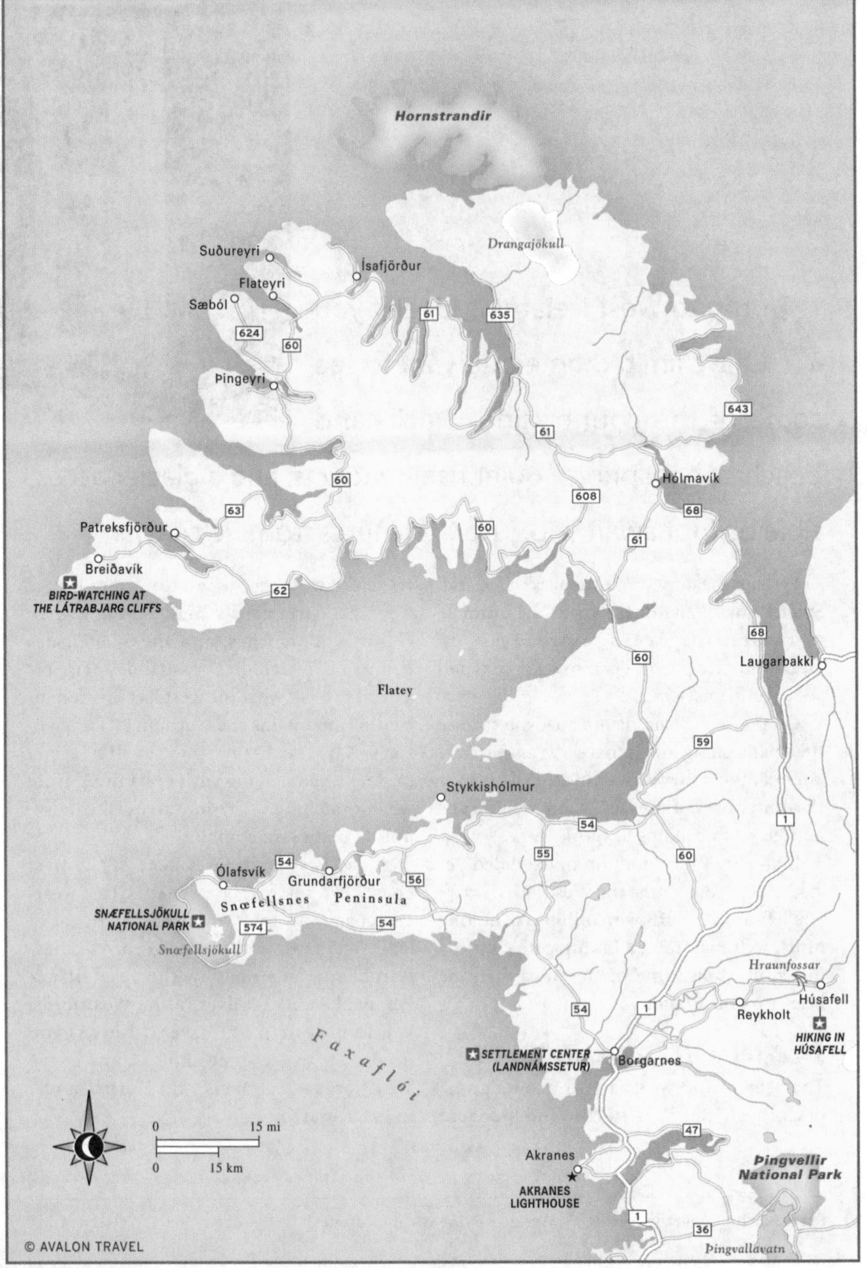
Hornstrandir
Drangajökull
Suðureyri
Ísafjörður
Flateyri
Sæból
624
60
61
635
Þingeyri
643
61
Hólmavík
608
60
68
63
Patreksfjörður
60
61
Breiðavík
BIRD-WATCHING AT THE LÁTRABJARG CLIFFS
62
68
60
Laugarbakki
Flatey
59
Stykkishólmur
54
1
55
60
54
Ólafsvík
Grundarfjörður
56
Snæfellsnes Peninsula
SNÆFELLSJÖKULL NATIONAL PARK
574
54
Snæfellsjökull
Hraunfossar
Húsafell
Reykholt
54
1
HIKING IN HÚSAFELL
Faxaflói
SETTLEMENT CENTER (LANDNÁMSSETUR)
Borgarnes
0
15 mi
0
15 km
47
Akranes
Þingvellir National Park
AKRANES LIGHTHOUSE
1
36
Þingvallavatn

Akranes and Inland

Charming little towns await travelers who pass through the Hvalfjarðargöng (Hvalfjörður Tunnel) from Reykjavík. Before heading to the Snæfellsnes Peninsula, spend some time exploring the region's small fishing villages.

AKRANES

Just a 40-minute drive from Reykjavík, Akranes is a popular detour for those looking to explore the west coast. Start at Akranes, then continue on to Borgarnes, Snæfellsnes, and the Westfjords.

A town of 7,000 people, Akranes is a classic west coast fishing village that also has deep industrial roots. It was once home to the country's only cement factory, and an aluminum smelter lies just outside the town. The town is peaceful, friendly, and home to a lighthouse open to the public; it offers spectacular views of Snæfellsnes on clear days.

Sights

AKRANES LIGHTHOUSE (Akranesviti)

The **Akranes Lighthouse** (Breið 2, 11am-6pm daily, 300ISK) is a delightful place to visit any time of year. Away from bright lights, tourists and townfolk flock to the site in winter to catch a glimpse of the northern lights dancing in the sky. In the summer, locals picnic outside the lighthouse, and when it is open, guests are invited in and can climb to the top. On clear days you can see the Snæfellsnes Peninsula and a spectacular view of Mount Akrafjall. Built in 1947, the lighthouse has been used in recent years to host concerts and art exhibitions. In 2013, the Icelandic band Amiina filmed a video here for a single off of their album *The Lighthouse Project.*

AKRANES MUSEUM CENTRE (Safnasvæðið á Akranesi)

The **Akranes Museum Centre** (Garðarholt 3, tel. 354/431-5566, www.museum.is, 10am-5pm daily June-Aug., 1pm-5pm daily Sept.-May, 800ISK adults, 500ISK seniors, free for 18 and under) comprises two museums: the **Icelandic Sports Museum,** dedicated to the town's rich sports history (primarily soccer) and the **Akranes Folk Museum,** which explores what Akranes was like in the days of settlement in the 10th century.

Outdoors, there are a few houses and boats that are key to the history of the town. One of them, the red house **Neðri-Sýrupartur** was built in 1875, and it's considered the oldest wooden house in the town. Visitors can go inside the houses and explore. The grounds also hold a collection of fishing boats, and a wood building hosts the annual Nordic blacksmithing competition.

A café inside the main museum building serves coffee, soft drinks, and cakes.

Sports and Recreation

TOP EXPERIENCE

HIKING

Mount Akrafjall is the pride and joy of Akranes residents. Many locals have memories of foraging for gull eggs and playing on the mountain as children. It's known as a relatively easy climb, especially from the Akranes car park. You have two options. A shorter climb takes you to **Haihnukur** (555 meters), which has a nice view of the outskirts of town. It's about two hours and six kilometers round-trip. If you're up for a longer climb, the highest peak is **Geirmundartindur** (643 meters), a 6.4-kilometer round-trip hike. The views from the top are breathtaking, especially on clear days when you can see Snæfellsjökull. It's about five hours round-trip for a leisurely climb.

The mountain can be reached by Route 51 and is 11 kilometers east from the town.

Akranes and Snæfellsnes Peninsula

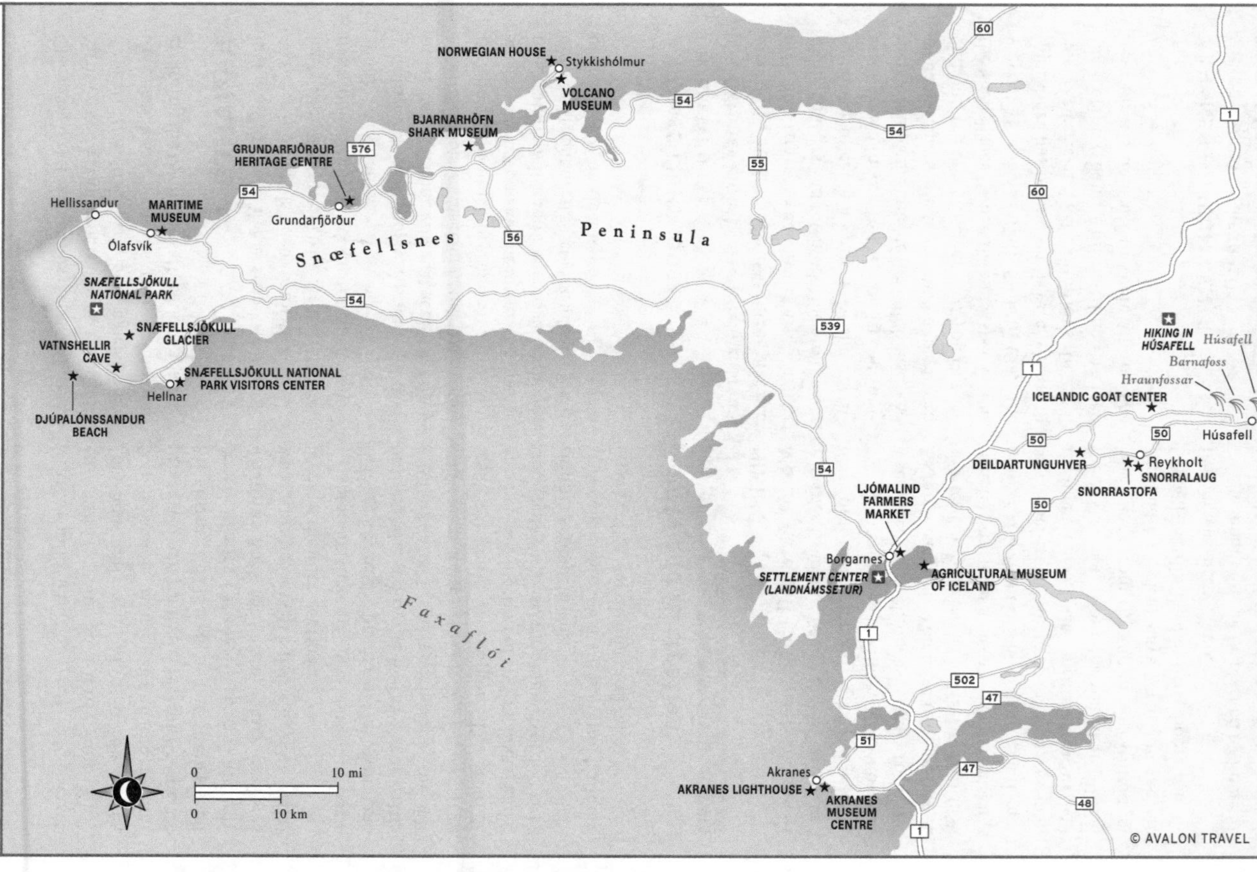

NORWEGIAN HOUSE
Stykkishólmur
VOLCANO MUSEUM
60
54
BJARNARHÖFN SHARK MUSEUM
GRUNDARFJÖRÐUR HERITAGE CENTRE
576
55
1
Hellissandur
MARITIME MUSEUM
Grundarfjörður
Ólafsvík
Snæfellsnes
56
Peninsula
SNÆFELLSJÖKULL NATIONAL PARK
SNÆFELLSJÖKULL GLACIER
VATNSHELLIR CAVE
SNÆFELLSJÖKULL NATIONAL PARK VISITORS CENTER
Hellnar
DJÚPALÓNSSANDUR BEACH
539
HIKING IN HÚSAFELL
Húsafell
Barnafoss
Hraunfossar
ICELANDIC GOAT CENTER
50
Húsafell
DEILDARTUNGUHVER
Reykholt
SNORRALAUG
SNORRASTOFA
LJÓMALIND FARMERS MARKET
Borgarnes
SETTLEMENT CENTER (LANDNÁMSSETUR)
AGRICULTURAL MUSEUM OF ICELAND
Faxaflói
502
47
51
0
10 mi
0
10 km
Akranes
AKRANES LIGHTHOUSE
AKRANES MUSEUM CENTRE
48
© AVALON TRAVEL

ship at the Akranes Museum Centre

SWIMMING

The **Jadarsbakkar Pool** (Innesvegur, tel. 354/433-1100, hkj@akranes.is, 6:15am-9pm Mon.-Fri., 9am-6pm Sat.-Sun., 600ISK) is a splendid outdoor pool with views of Mount Akrafjall. Take a dip in the geothermally heated waters or soak in one of the hot tubs.

GOLF

Garðavöllur (Garðar, tel. 354/431-2711, www.leynir.is, May 1-Sept. 30), in Akranes, is a challenging 18-hole course with several bunkers, scattered trees, and bodies of water. The scenery is beautiful, with Mount Akrafjall, sheep, and horses in the background. Clubs and golf carts are available to rent. Call ahead for a tee time. Hours are 8am-1pm Monday-Friday (greens fee 4,000ISK), 1pm-6pm Monday-Friday (6,000ISK), and 8am-6pm Saturday-Sunday (6,000ISK).

Food

★ **Galito Restaurant** (Stilholt 16-18, tel. 354/430-6767, www.galito.is, noon-10pm daily, entrées from 2,400ISK) is the most upscale restaurant in Akranes, but its prices are reasonable. Diners can choose from traditional options like shrimp soup and saltfish entrées, or hamburgers, pizza, sushi, and an array of sandwiches. The decor is modern and the staff is friendly.

Gamla Kaupfelagid (Kirkjubraut 11, tel. 354/431-4343, www.gamlakaupfelagid.com, 11:30am-10pm daily, entrées from 2,000ISK) is a cozy restaurant situated downtown, close to the tourist office. An eclectic menu ranges from fresh salads to Indian-inspired naan bread sandwiches, and the restaurant is not short on imagination. Icelandic staples include lamb and fish dishes, but hamburgers and tandoori oven-cooked pizzas are on the menu as well.

Café Kaja (Kirkjubraut 54, tel. 354/822-1669, matarburkaja@gmail.com, 1pm-5pm Mon.-Sat.) is Akranes's first and only organic café and market. Guests can enjoy sandwiches, cakes, juices, and coffee drinks as well as shop for local organic produce. The atmosphere is charming, with cozy furniture and a friendly staff.

Lesbókin Café (Kirkjubraut 2, tel. 354/864-1476, lesbokincafe@gmail.com, 9am-6pm Mon.-Fri., 10am-6pm Sat.-Sun.) is located in the heart of downtown Akranes and serves up delicious cakes, soups, and sandwiches. It's a casual eatery that's great for a coffee beverage, light meal, or beer.

Accommodations

Akra Guesthouse (Skagabraut 4, tel. 354/587-3901, www.akraguesthouse.com, rooms from 10,000ISK) is a small, family-run guesthouse with countryside charm. The five rooms are large and make you feel like you're staying with grandparents. Akra features wood floors, muted wallpaper, and a friendly staff. There's a common dining room for guests as well as an outdoor eating area and shared bathrooms.

Apotek Hostel & Guesthouse (Sudurgata 32, tel. 354/868-3332, www.stayakranes.is, rooms from 13,500ISK) offers single, double, triple, and family rooms as well as dormitory-style accommodations. Rooms are clean, bright, and cozy, and all have shared bathrooms. Apotek also has two fully equipped kitchens, a television lounge, free Wi-Fi, and laundry facilities.

Guesthouse Stay Akranes (Vogabraut 4, tel. 354/868-3332, www.stayakranes.is, rooms from 13,000ISK) offers dormitory accommodation in the summer (June-Aug). During the winter, the property houses students from the local high school. The guesthouse is no-frills, with double beds or sleeping bag accommodations, but the staff is friendly and helpful. Guests have access to private bathrooms with a shower, as well as a small fridge and a stove.

Kirkjuhvoll Guesthouse (Merkigerdi 7, tel. 354/868-3332, www.stayakranes.is, rooms from 14,000ISK) has doubles, triples, and family rooms. The rooms are clean and simple and include towels, linens, a garden view, and access to a shared bathroom. Free parking is provided and guests can use a shared lounge with a TV.

Teigur Guesthouse (Háteigur 1, tel. 354/431-2900, www.teigur-akranes.com, rooms from 11,000ISK) is a two-room guesthouse with the comforts of home. Guests have access to a full kitchen, washing machine, garden, and large terrace. A common living room has a TV, DVD player, and free Wi-Fi.

Information and Services

The **Akranes Information Center** is located in the Akranes Lighthouse (Breið 2). It is open 11am-6pm daily May 1-September 15; 11am-5pm Tuesday-Saturday September 16-April 30; and upon request for groups.

Transportation

Akranes, which is about a 40-minute, 48-kilometer drive from Reykjavík, is accessible from paved Route 51.

Many people make a stop in Akranes before making the 39-kilometer journey to Borgarnes, which takes about 30 minutes.

The **Strætó** 57 bus (www.straeto.is, 880ISK) runs from the bus station Mjodd in Reykjavík to Akranes in a little over an hour.

BORGARNES

About a 75-minute drive from Reykjavík, Borgarnes is a picturesque town that is home to about 2,000 people. Those traveling on the Ring Road will reach the town by one of the longest bridges on the island, considered an architectural feat for the country. Fans of the sagas will want to visit the town, as much of *Egil's Saga* takes place in the region. Film buffs may recognize Borgarnes from scenes in Ben Stiller's 2013 movie *The Secret Life of Walter Mitty*.

Sights

★ SETTLEMENT CENTER (Landnámssetur)

The **Settlement Center** (Brákarbraut 13-15, tel. 354/437-1600, www.landnam.is/eng, 10am-9pm daily, 2,500ISK adults, 1,900ISK students/seniors, free for children under 14) is the place to get a crash-course in the sagas and the earliest days of Icelanders during the settlement—including what everything on the newly discovered island was like, ranging from food to fashion. Interactive displays and re-created dwellings are on exhibit. Audio guides are available in 10 languages. A gift shop sells everything from gourmet salts to woolen goods, and a restaurant serves up lamb, fish, and sandwiches.

AGRICULTURAL MUSEUM OF ICELAND (Landbúnaðarsafn Íslands)

The **Agricultural Museum of Iceland** (Hvanneyri, tel. 354/844-7740, www.landbunadarsafn.is, noon-5pm daily June-Aug., 500ISK) is dedicated to the farming history of Iceland during the 19th and 20th centuries. The museum holds an extensive collection of farm artifacts, including the first plows and other horse-driven equipment used in Iceland. The museum also has the first tractors imported to Iceland, as well as farming equipment of the present day.

BORGARNES MUSEUM (Safnahús Borgarfjarðar)

The **Borgarnes Museum** (Bjarnarbraut 4-6, tel. 354/433-7200, www.safnahus.is, 1pm-6pm daily, 500ISK) is a nice spot to spend a couple of hours. It has two exhibitions: One features photography focusing on Iceland's 20th-century history, and the other is a collection of stuffed birds in a beautiful environment designed by the artist Snorri Freyr Hilmarsson. The museum is also home to the town's library and archives

LJÓMALIND FARMERS MARKET

Ljómalind Farmers Market (Brúartorg 4, tel. 354/437-1400, www.ljomalind.is, 11am-6pm daily) is a farmers market collective started by a group of 10 women in 2013. Situated on the main stretch of road in Borgarnes, the market sells fresh cream, eggs, jam, local meat, fresh produce, woolen goods, and souvenir trinkets. In the summer, you can find sunflowers and local tomatoes on offer.

Sports and Recreation

SWIMMING

The **Borgarnes Swimming Pool** (Þorsteinsgata 1, tel. 354/433-7140, 6:30am-10pm Mon.-Fri., 9am-6pm Sat.-Sun., 600ISK) is open year-round and has an outdoor swimming pool, a slide, hot tub, and gym.

GOLF

Borgarnes Golf Club (Golfklúbbur Borgarness) (Hamar, tel. 354/437-1663, May-Sept., greens fees 10,000ISK) is an 18-hole course situated on the property of Icelandair Hótel Hamar. The course, which is great for beginners, also has a driving range area and an 18-hole putting course. It's also easy to walk. Call ahead for a tee time.

Food

★ **Ok Bistro** (Digranesgötu 2, tel. 354/437-1200, www.okbistro.is, 11:30am-9pm Mon.-Fri., 5pm-9pm Sat.-Sun., entrées from 3,400ISK) is a fine-dining restaurant on the top floor of the Nordic Store building, around the corner from the town's information center. It's known for fish dishes, including roasted langoustines, pan-fried trout, and roasted cod. And carnivores won't be disappointed by the barbecue ribs, organic lamb, and beef burger quesadilla.

Búðarklettur (Brákarbraut 13-15, tel. 354/437-1600, 10am-9pm daily, entrées from 2,00ISK) is the restaurant housed above the Settlement Center. The menu is chock-full of Icelandic staples like fish soup, mashed fish, and Icelandic meat soup. Burgers and sandwiches are on the menu as well, and there are vegetarian options and a kids' menu. For a quick snack, the freshly baked cakes are delicious.

Geirabakari Kaffihus (Digranesgata 6, tel. 354/437-1920, geirabak@internet.is, 7am-5pm daily, entrées from 1,600ISK) offers light meals, including soups and sandwiches and an array of classic Icelandic cakes and pastries. The coffeehouse was used to film scenes from Ben Stiller's 2013 movie *The Secret Life of Walter Mitty*. Photos taken during filming are displayed throughout the space.

Kaffi Kyrrð (Skúlagata 13, tel. 354/437-1878, www.blomasetrid.is, 9am-9pm Mon.-Fri., 11am-7pm Sat.-Sun., entrées from 1,500ISK) is located inside Blómasetrið, a cute flower shop popular with locals. The café serves light meals like waffles, soups, and quiches, and well as coffee, tea, soft drinks, and beer.

La Colina (Hrafnaklettur 1b, tel. 354/437-0110, 5pm-9pm Mon.-Fri., noon-9pm Sat.-Sun., entrées from 2,100ISK) is a welcome addition to Borgarnes. Opening its doors in 2016, the pizzeria is warm and cozy and has delicious pies. Pizzas range from a classic Margherita to creative pies with shrimp, tuna, and lobster.

Accommodations

Borgarnes Hostel (Borgarbraut 9-13, tel. 354/695-3366, www.borgarneshostel.is, rooms from 18,000ISK) offers 20 rooms ranging from single rooms to triples. It has private room with private bathroom, private room with shared bathroom, and dorm accommodation with shared bathroom options. The hostel is centrally located, just a quick walk from the harbor and Settlement Center. Guests have access to two fully equipped kitchens, laundry facilities, a computer room, free Wi-Fi, and a common living room.

Hótel Borgarnes (Egilsgata 16, tel. 354/437-1119, www.hotelborgarnes.is, rooms from 25,000ISK) is a 75-room no-frills hotel perfect for short stays. It offers small, comfortable rooms with private bathrooms, and an in-house restaurant serves up a delicious breakfast buffet included in the price of the room.

Icelandair Hótel Hamar (Hamar, 310 Borgarnes, tel. 354/433-6600, www.icelandairhotels.com/en/hotels/hamar, rooms from 35,000ISK) was built on an 18-hole golf course and is in an especially scenic part of Borgarnes. Situated among waterfalls and lava fields, the 44-room hotel offers comfortable rooms with double beds and private bathrooms. There is an abundance of local art around the hotel, and it has a modern yet country atmosphere. The in-house restaurant is open 11am-10pm daily, serving everything from an Asian-inspired cod dish to lamb fillets.

Borgarnes Bed & Breakfast (Skúlagata 21, tel. 354/848-1129, www.borgarnesbb.is, rooms from 20,000ISK) is a lovely property that was built in 1947 by the same architect who designed the church of Borgarnes. Rooms range from singles with shared bathrooms to family rooms. Guests can enjoy a breakfast buffet, a shared dining area, free Wi-Fi, and a garden with a barbecue.

Ensku Húsin (Hótel við Langá, tel. 354/437-1826, www.enskuhusin.is, rooms from 19,000ISK) is a former fish lodge that has been transformed into a guesthouse and space for special events. There are 11 bedrooms that each accommodate two people, with a mix of private and shared bathroom facilities. Rooms are no-frills, but clean and comfortable, and the friendly staff makes you feel at home. The hotel is located along the river Langá.

Information and Services

Located in the Hyrnutorg shopping center, the **West Iceland Information Center** (Borgarbraut 58-60, tel. 354/437-2214, www.westiceland.is, 9am-5pm daily) has brochures, tour information, a gift shop, and free Internet access.

Transportation

Borgarnes is about a 1.25-hour (75-kilometer) drive north from Reykjavík on Route 1.

The **Strætó** 57 bus (www.straeto.is, 1,760ISK) runs from the bus station Mjodd in Reykjavík to Borgarnes. The trip takes about 1.5 hours each way.

REYKHOLT

Reykholt is a placid, sleepy town about an hour from Borgarnes. However, that laid-back, quiet atmosphere is part of the town's charm. A couple of sights are connected to Snorri Sturluson, one of the most famous and important figures in Icelandic literature. Snorri penned *Edda*, *Egil's Saga*, and *Heimskringla* before his death in 1241. Tourists might also want to take a look at Deildartunguhver, the largest hot spring in Europe.

Sights

ICELANDIC GOAT CENTER

(Íslenska Geitin)

The **Icelandic Goat Center** (Haafell, tel. 354/845-2331, www.geitur.is, 1pm-6pm daily June-Aug., 1,500ISK adults, 750ISK children 7-17, free for children under 7) was established to protect and maintain the goat stock in Iceland—believe it or not, the Icelandic goat is an endangered species. Tourists are welcome to visit the grounds and meet the goats as well as other animals on the farm, including sheep, horses, and chickens. Workers at the center show an enormous amount of care for the animals. It's an especially great place to visit if you're traveling with children. The local food store sells many goat products, including cheeses, as well as soaps and handicrafts.

DEILDARTUNGUHVER

Geology buffs will want to take a look at Deildartunguhver, which is considered Europe's most powerful hot spring. It provides 200 liters per second of 100°C (212°F) water. Most of the water used for central heating in the towns of Akranes and Borgarnes is taken from Deildartunguhver. The hot-water pipeline to Akranes stretches 64 kilometers, the longest in Iceland. The water is about 78-80°C when it reaches the town. Be sure to keep your distance, as there is a chance of getting splashed if you get too close. Visitors will see water bubbling up and splashing against moss and rock. Deildartunguhver is off of Route 50; the GPS coordinates are N 64.6631, W 21.4112.

SNORRASTOFA

Snorrastofa (tel. 354/433-8000, www.snorrastofa.is, 10am-6pm daily Apr. 1-Sept. 31, 10am-5pm Mon.-Fri. Oct. 1-March 31, 1,200ISK) is the cultural hub of Reykholt. It was established in 1995 as an independent research center to investigate and collect information on the medieval era in Iceland, with particular focus on the legendary saga writer and politician Snorri Sturluson, who lived in Reykholt until his death in 1241. The building also holds a tourist information center, an exhibition on Snorri Sturluson's sagas, and a public research library, and it hosts courses and lectures. A gift shop sells books, CDs, and handicrafts. The GPS coordinates are N 64.6648, W 21.2937.

SNORRALAUG

Snorralaug, or "Snorri's Pool," is a geothermally heated pool preserved from Iceland's medieval period and is one of Reykholt's oldest structures. The hot tub was built with hand-hewn lava from the 10th century, cut and shaped to exact measurements. The hot water in the pool comes from the Skrifla hot spring through a canal. The site is open to the public, but visitors cannot enter the pool to bathe. The GPS coordinates are N 64.664, W 21.2912.

Sports and Recreation

CAVE TOURS

Reykholt is home to **Víðgelmir**, the largest cave in Iceland. The cave is only accessible through a private guide: **The Cave** (Fljotstunga, tel. 354/783-3600, www.thecave.is, 9am-6pm June-Aug., 10am-4pm Mar.-Oct., 10am-3pm Dec.-Feb., 6,500ISK) can take you to explore the beautiful ice formations, including scores of stalactites and stalagmites.

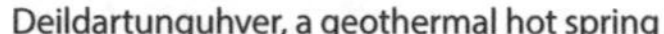

Deildartunguhver, a geothermal hot spring

Food and Accommodations

Hverinn Restaurant (Kleppjárnsreykir, tel. 354/571-4433, www.hverinn.is, 10am-9pm Sun.-Thurs. and 10am-11pm Fri.-Sat. May 1-Oct.1, entrées from 1,800ISK) is a quaint farm-style restaurant serving up comfort food. It uses organic ingredients from its farm and local meats in each dish, ranging from soups and salads to lamb and fish dishes. Sandwiches, hamburgers, and pizza are also on the menu.

Fosshotel Reykholt (Hálsasveitavegur, tel. 354/435-1260, www.fosshotel.is, rooms from 28,000ISK) used to be the only hotel in the region. The 53-room property has dated furniture, and some rooms with carpeting, which is not common in Iceland. However, the dreary decor is made up for with free Wi-Fi, private bathrooms, free parking, and outdoor hot tubs. The included breakfast is adequate, but nothing to write home about.

Hótel Á (Kirkjuból, tel. 354/435-1430, www.hotela.is, rooms from 23,000ISK) is a former farmhouse that was converted into a guesthouse with 14 double rooms and 1 family room. The decor is rustic and the staff friendly, and common rooms contribute to the laid-back vibe. Breakfast is included in the price of the room. The hotel also has an in-house **restaurant** (5pm-10pm daily) that offers meat (6,480ISK) and fish (5,480ISK) three-course dinners featuring local ingredients.

Information and Services

Housed in the Snorrastofa complex, the **Reykholt Information Office** (tel. 354/433-8000, www.snorrastofa.is, 10am-6pm daily Apr. 1-Sept. 30, 10am-5pm Mon.-Fri. Oct. 1-Mar. 31) offers tourist brochures and art exhibitions and hosts occasional lectures and concerts. The GPS coordinates are N 64.6648, W 21.2937.

Transportation

Reykholt is 41 kilometers northeast of Borgarnes on Route 518, which is paved.

The **Strætó** 81 bus (www.straeto.is, 880ISK) goes to Reykholt from Borgarnes.

HÚSAFELL

Húsafell is a tiny village surrounded by glaciers, ample hiking opportunities, and miles of lava fields. Most tourists make a stop to camp, visit two beautiful waterfalls, and check out some lava caves in nearby Reykholt or explore the Langjökull ice tunnel. Organized trips with a tour operator to Langjökull glacier are also available from Húsafell throughout the year.

Sights

HRAUNFOSSAR

Hraunfossar (Lava Waterfalls) is a series of waterfalls streaming over 900 meters out of a lava field. The lava flowed from an eruption from a volcano lying under the Langjökull glacier. The falls are beautiful to visit in any season, and rainbows are frequently seen near the falls on rainy/sunny days. Hraunfossar is 6.4 kilometers west of Húsafell on Route 518. The GPS coordinates are N 64.7028, W 20.9777.

BARNAFOSS

Barnafoss (Children's Falls) is a stunning waterfall, wide with water rushing over a rocky landscape, creating several cascades. It was named for children who disappeared from a nearby farm and drowned in the river, and lore has it that the mother of the disappeared children put a curse on the falls that people should not cross the river. Barnafoss is 6.2 kilometers west of Húsafell on Route 518. The GPS coordinates are N 64.7015, W 20.9727.

LANGJÖKULL ICE CAVE

For those looking for a little ice in Iceland, **Into the Glacier** (Viðarhöfði 1, tel. 354/578-2550, www.intotheglacier.is, tours from 19,500ISK) offers day tours to the world's largest man-made ice cave, Langjökull. A super truck picks up visitors close to Hotel Husafell for a breathtaking journey across the glacier to the base camp, which takes 25 minutes. The cave itself is an engineering feat where visitors are treated to views of crevices and the smooth ice walls. LED lighting embedded in the walls lights the ice nicely, and benches are scattered throughout the tunnel.

★ Hiking

Hikers have a number of options in Húsafell, ranging from easy walks to more challenging climbs. However, before you set out, be sure to check the weather forecast, bring the proper gear and plenty of drinking water, and let people know your whereabouts. The prime hiking season is June-August.

MOUNT STRÚTUR

While the climb to the summit of the 938-meter Mount Strútur, with an elevation gain of 469 meters, isn't very difficult, it is quite long. The hike takes several hours depending on the weather and your endurance. It is recommended you start from the low hill north of Kalmanstunga and follow a signposted track that leads up the mountain. The payoff for reaching the top is a spectacular view of mountains and the Borgarfjörður fjord. Kalmanstunga is 17 kilometers north of Húsafell and can be reached by Route 518.

ODDAR

The summerhouse settlement in the center of Húsafell is the starting point for wooded paths heading westward for an easy walk along Oddar, a group of brooks with diverse birdlife. From there it is just a short walk upriver to the meeting point of two rivers: the Norðlingafljót and Hvítá. Just below Hvítá is the waterfall Hundavaðsfoss, a great place to stop and marvel at the region's beauty. The route then leads southeast along the sands, to a path leading back to the summerhouse settlement. The walk is about 4 kilometers round-trip, takes about 1.5 hours, and is very easygoing.

Other Sports and Recreation

SWIMMING

The **Húsafell Swimming Pool** (Stórarjóður, tel. 354/435-1552, www.husafell.is, 10am-10pm daily June-Sept., 1pm-5pm Sat.-Sun. rest of year, 1,300ISK) has two pools, two hot tubs, and a big waterslide for kids.

GOLF

The **Húsafell Golf Course** (Stórarjóður, tel. 354/435-1552, www.husafell.is, 8am-6pm daily May-Sept., greens fees 4,650ISK) is a nine-hole course situated on a gorgeous patch

Hraunfossar waterfalls

of land overlooking mountains and lava fields. You must call ahead for a tee time. The GPS coordinates are N 64.6991, W 20.8709.

Food and Accommodations

Located at the Lava Waterfalls, **Hraunfossar Restaurant-Café** (Hraunás 4, tel. 354/862-7957, www.hraunfossar.is, 2,000ISK) has a good selection of light meals and snacks. Sit on the eatery's porch to enjoy coffee, cakes, ice cream, and sandwiches, along with a nice view.

★ **Hotel Husafell** (Borgarbyggd, tel. 354/435-1551, www.hotelhusafell.com, rooms from 38,000ISK) is a modern 48-room hotel that opened in 2015. The location is unbeatable, as it is nestled in a scenic spot with stunning views of the mountain landscape, close to lava caves and glaciers. Rooms feature comfortable beds, private bathrooms, and modern design accents, including wood furnishings and large windows. A breakfast buffet is included in the room price, and 24-hour room service is available. A pool and hot tubs are on-site, and the in-house **restaurant** (11:30am-10pm daily, entrées from 4,500ISK) is not to be missed. The menu features everything from tender lamb fillet to fresh fish.

The **Husafell Campground** (tel. 354/435-1556, 1,500ISK) is an open campground surrounded by trees, which cuts down on the wind a bit. Caravans and tents are welcome, and the facilities include restrooms, showers, hot and cold water, and laundry machines. The site is a short distance to the swimming pool, golf course, and hiking trails.

Transportation

Húsafell is 25 kilometers east from Reykholt on Route 518, which is paved. There are no direct buses to Húsafell.

Snæfellsnes Peninsula

Snæfellsnes is considered the jewel of the western coast. In part, it's because the region has a taste of everything. If you're looking for mountains, they're there. If you want to attempt a glacier walk, Snæfellsnesjökull is your place. If whale-watching is what you're after, this region has it. There's a reason why many locals refer to the area as "Iceland in miniature."

If you intend to visit Snæfellsnes while on the Ring Road, plan to spend some time here—at least two full days. The breathtaking landscape, with its long volcanic ridge spanning miles of rocky lava fields and towering mountains, demands more attention than a quick detour. The area is considered many an Icelander's favorite place on the island. Traveling to the region is not difficult, as there are numerous tours going to Snæfellsnes as well as buses. For a more leisurely visit, rent a car.

The western edge of the Snæfellsnes Peninsula is home to Snæfellsjökull National Park and small towns like Hellissandur, Ólafsvík, and Grundarfjörður. The Snæfellsjökull glacier, which lies on top of a volcano in the center of the national park, is the main event for many. You can book tours to walk on the glacier and explore some actual ice in Iceland. Charming fishing villages dot the peninsula and offer ample hiking routes and quirky museums.

TOP EXPERIENCE

★ SNÆFELLSJÖKULL NATIONAL PARK

The Snæfellsjökull glacier became world famous after author Jules Verne described it in *A Journey to the Center of the Earth* as the starting point of the titular journey. There is plenty to explore inside the park. Take some time, wear comfortable yet sturdy footwear, and bring your camera. Plan at least two days in the region.

Sights

SNÆFELLSJÖKULL GLACIER

The Snæfellsjökull glacier lies on top of a volcano, situated in the center of the national park. The glacier's peak reaches 1,446 meters, and it can be seen from Reykjavík on a clear day. The volcano is considered active, though the last eruption occurred 1,900 years ago.

It's about 190 kilometers from Reykjavík to the Snæfellsjökull glacier; the drive takes about 2.5 hours. From Reykjavík, take Route 1 north through the town of Borgarnes and then turn left onto Route 54. Head west on Route 54 across the peninsula for about 98 kilometers, connecting to Route 574. Continue west on Route 574 for about 35 kilometers. You'll find the road leading up to the volcano on the right-hand side, and signs are posted all the way up to a parking lot. Be sure to check the forecast before heading out and be advised that roads leading to the volcano are unpaved.

DJÚPALÓNSSANDUR BEACH

Djúpalónssandur beach, on the southwestern edge of the Snæfellsnes Peninsula, is one of the region's highlights. The vast beach is covered by small black stones that were shaped by the force of the tides and whipping of the wind. Visitors love to wander among the frozen lava landscapes and the interesting rock formations. A short paved road through lava fields leads directly from Route 574 to Djúpalónssandur beach. The GPS coordinates are N 64.7493, W 23.9122.

VATNSHELLIR LAVA CAVE

The Vatnshellir lava cave, a site made available to the public in 2011, is another highlight. Scientists believe the 200-meter-long cave was created in an eruption between 6,000-8,000 years ago. The cave has two main sections. The upper section showcases unique lava formations that are curved on the sides of the lava tube. The lower part, which can be reached by a long and narrow but well-maintained staircase, takes tourists deep (about 35 meters) underground to a place hidden from the outside world for thousands of years. The cave is accessible only through a guided tour from **Summit Guides** (tel. 354/787-0001, www.summitguides.is, 45-minute tours 3,250ISK adults, 2,600ISK students/seniors, free for children 3-11). Tourists are required to have hiking boots, gloves, and warm clothing. The tour guide provides helmets and flashlights. The Vatnshellir cave is located in the southern end of the park, near Route 574.

view of Snæfellsjökull

Hiking

Many Icelanders say the beauty of Snæfellsnes is unrivaled, calling the region their favorite place in the country. Why? Snæfellsnes has it all. There are mountains to climb, lava fields to explore, and glaciers to scale, all accessible by countless hiking trails with varying degrees of difficulty. Specific information on trails can be found at the park's visitors center.

Feel free to roam and take in the sights. Whether you head out alone, with a small group, or with a tour, always go out for a hike prepared: Check the weather forecast, bring proper gear and drinking water, and let people know your whereabouts.

Rauðhóll is a leisurely hike within the park where travelers can walk around a vast lava field with jagged earth and a treeless plain giving unobstructed views of the glacier looming in the distance. The 2.3-kilometer loop hike is easy, on relatively flat ground, and takes about 45 minutes. The landscape is filled with moss and lichen-covered lava stones and lava tubes, where lava once flowed out of the volcano. Coming from Hellissandur, you'll find the hiking path down an unnumbered road off of Route 570 (which is unpaved but no longer an F road); look for a sign that says "Eysteinsdalur Snæfellsjökull" and turn left. On the south side of the road is a signpost for the Rauðhóll trail, and red stakes along the path mark the way.

GLACIER HIKE

Snæfellsjökull, rising 1,446 meters from the western tip of the Snæfellsnes Peninsula, offers gorgeous views during a challenging trek, on which you can embark with a guided tour (this hike isn't recommended as an independent trek). The adventure starts and ends at the small fishing village of Arnarstapi, off Route 54 down Útnesvegur. **Arctic Adventures** (tel. 354/562-7000, www.adventures.is, Apr. 7.-Aug. 31, 34,990ISK) takes you to the Jökulháls pass, where you'll start your hike toward the summit of the glacier. The first part of the hike is over volcanic rock, but as you climb, snow and ice become dominant, and crampons will be necessary near the top of the glacier. The hike is about 7-8 kilometers, with a total elevation gain of 760 meters, and it takes about 3-5 hours, depending on the conditions and weather.

Remember to bring warm outdoor clothing, a waterproof jacket and pants, a hat, and gloves. Good hiking shoes are essential on this tour. Waterproof outerwear and sturdy hiking shoes can be rented from the tour company with advance notice.

Tours

If you're after other structured, guided tours, some companies offer excursions. Check out **Reykjavík Excursions** (tel. 354/580-5400, www.re.is) for a list. It offers a 12-hour "Wonders of Snæfellsnes" tour year-round from Reykjavík that includes visits to the glacier, sandy beaches, craters, and fishing villages (21,000ISK adults, 10,500ISK children 12-15, free for children under 11).

Food

Hótel Búðir Restaurant (Búðir, tel. 354/435-6700, www.hotelbudir.is, 4pm-10pm daily, entrées from 4,500ISK) features Icelandic staples like fresh cod and lamb dishes, but the chef likes to mix up the menu depending on the season. In the summer expect local puffin meat on the menu. The food is fresh, elegant, and memorable.

Fosshotel Hellnar Restaurant (Brekkubær, tel. 354/435-6820, www.fosshotel.is, 8am-9pm daily May-Oct., entrées from 2,500ISK) is open for breakfast, lunch, and dinner during the summer. The fresh fish options are tempting, and a few tasty vegetarian options are on the menu as well.

Accommodations

Guests at **Hótel Búðir** (Búðir, tel. 354/435-6700, www.hotelbudir.is, rooms from 40,000ISK) are treated to a comfortable stay with spectacular views of the Snæfellsjökull glacier. The 20-room boutique hotel features clean and cozy rooms with private bathrooms. The hotel's top-notch breakfast is included in the price. It frequently hosts weddings and conferences. The hotel is 27 kilometers southeast of Ólafsvík on Route 54.

Hótel Eldborg (Laugagerdisskola, tel. 354/435-6602, www.hoteleldborg.is, rooms from 18,000ISK) is a charming 26-room countryside hotel with very large rooms and one of the friendliest staffs you will find. They are happy to arrange for tours ranging from horse riding to glacier walking. Guests have access to shared bathroom facilities. An in-house restaurant serves breakfast, lunch, a dinner buffet, and light meals throughout the day.

★ **Fosshotel Hellnar** (Brekkubær, tel. 354/435-6820, www.fosshotel.is, May-Oct., rooms from 27,000ISK) is a beautiful 39-room country hotel that takes pride in the small things. Guests can find fresh flowers throughout the hotel, a warm staff, and a splendid in-house restaurant. Each room has a private bathroom, comfortable bed, and television. The restaurant uses fresh, organic ingredients with lots of fish and meat options.

Guesthouse Langaholt (Ytri-Garðar Staðarsveit, tel. 354/435-6789, www.langaholt.is, rooms from 27,000ISK) is a 20-room family-run guesthouse with spacious rooms, classic decor, free Wi-Fi, and a shared terrace. Amenities include an on-site restaurant, nearby golf course, plenty of free parking, and on-site camping facilities for budget travelers.

Information and Services

The **Snæfellsjökull National Park visitors center** (Malarrif, tel. 354/436-6888, 10am-5pm daily mid-May-mid-Sept., 11am-4pm daily mid-Sept.-mid-May) gives an overview of the history, flora, fauna, and geology of the park. The center also provides information on hiking paths and the wildlife that can be seen in the park.

Transportation

Snæfellsjökull can be reached by Route 574, which spans the perimeter of the park along the coastline. Please bear in mind that the road is unpaved and is not feasible for cyclists.

Tour companies such as **Reykjavík Excursions** (tel. 354/580-5400, www.re.is) include stops at Snæfellsjökull. The **Strætó** 57 and 58 buses (tel. 354/540-2700, www.straeto.is, 4,400ISK) to Snæfellsnes can be taken daily in the summer from the bus station Mjodd in Reykjavík. The ride takes about three hours.

HELLISSANDUR

Hellissandur is a blink-and-you'll-miss it kind of town, but it's home to an interesting fishing museum that's worth a stop if that strikes your fancy.

Sights

HELLISSANDUR MARITIME MUSEUM (Sjómannagarður)

Hellissandur Maritime Museum (Útnesvegur, tel. 354/436-6961, 10am-5pm daily June 1-Sept. 30, 500ISK) was established by the Council of Seamen of the towns of Hellissandur and neighboring Rif to preserve the history of fishers and fishing stations in the region. One-stroke engines, a fisherman's house (called Þorvaldarbúð), and Iceland's oldest preserved fishing boat, *Bliki,* are on display, showing the rich fishing history of the town. The well-curated museum is a must-see for those interested in fishing history.

INGJALDSHÓLSKIRKJA

The other big draw in Hellissandur is **Ingjaldshólskirkja** (tel. 354/436-6970), or Ingjaldshóls Church, which was, according to legend, the site where Italian explorer Christopher Columbus traveled in 1477 to meet with Icelanders. Columbus was interested in speaking with islanders whose ancestors had traveled to America. In the basement of the church is a mural of Columbus's meeting with the Icelanders. The church is a classic Icelandic structure built in 1903, and it has a white exterior and a red roof. However, the land has been a church site since the year 1317. The church is on Route 574, east of Hellissandur.

Sports and Recreation

HIKING

A great moderate five-hour day hike of around 20 kilometers total leads from Hellissandur village into the Eysteinsdalur valley. Hikers should take the unmarked gravel road between the campground and Hellissandur Maritime Museum, which leads toward Snæfellsjökull. The road becomes a hiking trail after about one kilometer and leads you to the **Prestahraun** lava field. Follow the trail to see a red scoria crater and rifts in lava and basalt rocks. The trail continues past waterfalls, the glacial river Ljósulækir, and breathtaking views of the glacier. Detailed hiking maps are available from the tourist information office in Hellnar.

Food and Accommodations

Kaffi Sif (Klettsbúð 3, tel. 354/577-3430, www.kaffisif.is, 11am-8pm Sun.-Thurs., 11am-11:30pm Fri.-Sat., entrées from 1,800ISK) is an adorable café that serves up comfort food and a dynamite cup of coffee. If you're stopping in for a meal, the fish soup is superb.

Hótel Hellissandur (Klettsbúð 9, tel. 354/430-8600, www.hotelhellissandur.is, rooms from 16,000ISK) is a 20-room hotel with standard double rooms featuring private bathrooms and free Wi-Fi. Rooms are big but sparsely decorated, and the in-house restaurant serves adequate meals.

The Freezer Hostel (Hafnargata16, tel. 354/865-9432, www.thefreezerhostel.com, beds from 4,700ISK), located in Rif, several kilometers east of Hellissandur off Útnesvegur, is a former fish factory that's been converted into one of the coolest spots in the region. It's a hostel that offers dorm beds, a culture center, and an artist residency. The space is stripped down yet comfortable and serves as a social spot for tourists and locals alike. The Freezer hosts theater performances and concerts throughout the year.

Transportation

Hellissandur is 9 kilometers northwest of Ólafsvík and 35 kilometers north of Hellnar. By car, take Route 574 to Hellissandur; this stretch is paved.

A couple of buses pass through the town. Check the bus schedule from **BSÍ** (www.bsi.is) to see departure times. Typically, buses depart from Reykjavík, Grundarfjörður, Ólafsvík, and Stykkishólmur.

ÓLAFSVÍK

Ólafsvík is a charming fishing village situated on the western end of the Snæfellsnes Peninsula. The small town has approximately 1,100 residents and is the main town of the Snæfellsbær municipality, which includes the villages of Hellissandur and Rif. Because of its proximity to the national park, Ólafsvík, which means "Olaf's bay," is often used as a base camp where travelers can get a bite to eat and gas up the car.

Sights

A former trading store built in 1844, the **Pakkhús Museum** (12 Ólafsbraut, tel. 354/433-6929, www.snb.is, noon-5pm daily June 5-Aug. 31, 800ISK) is a national monument. The 2nd and 3rd floors house the Snæfellsbær regional museum, where guests can see items from as early as the days of Iceland's settlement, including fishing equipment and household goods. The museum gives insight into how Icelanders lived in this region of the island, managing on very little. On the ground floor, you'll find a general store and handicraft shop.

Sports and Recreation

SWIMMING

The **Ólafsvík Swimming Pool** (Ennisbraut 11, tel. 354/433-9910, 8am-9pm daily, 600ISK) is popular among locals as well as tourists passing through. Amenities include an indoor 12.5-meter swimming pool, hot tubs, and an outdoor area for catching some sun (when it's out).

Accommodations

Hofðagata Guesthouse (Hofðagata 11, tel. 354/694-6569, www.hofdagata.is, rooms from 25,000ISK) is known as the oldest guesthouse in town. The concrete structure might not be much to look at from the outside, but inside it is warm and inviting. Rooms are decorated with great care, mixing warm hues with classic Scandinavian comfort. The four rooms include shared bathrooms, free Wi-Fi, and a hearty breakfast.

Holmur Inn (Skulagata 4, tel. 354/899-9144, www.holmur-inn.com, rooms from 18,000ISK) is a seven-room guesthouse on a quiet street in Stykkishólmur, just past the main road. Rooms are small but modern and comfortable. Guests have access to a common kitchen and shared bathroom facilities with showers. Breakfast is included.

The 11-room **Hótel Breiðafjörður** (Aðalgata 8, tel. 354/438-1417, www.hotel-breidafjordur.is, rooms from 16,000ISK) is a converted school that has been in business for more than 30 years. Rooms are sparsely decorated with a lot of wood throughout the house and vinyl flooring. The staff is accommodating, but the guesthouse is quite basic and not memorable.

Fosshotel Stykkishólmur (Borgarbraut 8, tel. 354/430-2100, www.fosshotel.is, rooms from 30,000ISK) is chic, stylish, and inviting. All 80 rooms have private bathrooms and large, comfortable beds. Guests have access to free Wi-Fi, free parking, an included breakfast buffet, and a hotel bar.

Information and Services

The **tourist information center** (Borgarbraut 4, tel. 354/433-8120, www.westiceland.is, 10am-5pm daily), located at the town's swimming pool complex, provides brochures on local sights as well as places to see in the surrounding area.

Transportation

Stykkishólmur is approximately a two-hour drive from Reykjavík, traveling north along Route 1 and then west along paved Route 54, 165 kilometers via the Hvalfjörður tunnel.

The **Strætó** 58 bus (tel. 354/540-2700, www.straeto.is, 3,960ISK) runs twice daily between Reykjavík and Stykkishólmur. The ride takes about 3.5 hours.

FLATEY

Flatey (Flat Island) is the largest of the western islands in Breiðafjörður, a bay that separates the Westfjords from the southern part of the country. It is reachable only by ferry. The small island, which is north of the Snæfellsnes Peninsula and about one kilometer wide and two kilometers long, is an ideal visit for those seeking a spot in Iceland that is as old world as it gets—as in, not much has changed on this island in centuries. The colorful wood houses and single road evoke a simpler time, one that has not been overcrowded with industry.

Flatey is very much a seasonal destination, ideal for leisurely walks, bird-watching, and taking a break from some of the more popular attractions in the Westfjords. Icelanders who own a second home here make regular trips in the summer, and only a handful of people remain during the winter months. The main hotel-restaurant on the island is open for business only during the summer, so plan accordingly if you want to venture out to the island in the winter.

Sights and Recreation

TOP EXPERIENCE

BIRD-WATCHING

The island offers unspoiled nature at its best, with hordes of migrating birds coming to nest and few human souls occupying the island. Flatey is a good place to spot **puffins** that migrate to the island in the summer (June-Aug.), as well as other species, including **Arctic terns, gulls,** and **oystercatchers.** However, note that part of the island is restricted from mid-May to mid-July to protect nesting birds from outside interference.

FLATEY CHURCH

Flatey church was erected in 1926. The exterior is classic minimalist Icelandic design, but the inside features works from Spanish painter Baltasar Samper, who captured scenes from the island in the 1960s. Baltasar is the father of renowned filmmaker Baltasar Kormakur, who directed movies like *101 Reykjavík* and *Contraband.* Across from the church is a small cemetery which includes graves that are several hundred years old.

Food and Accommodations

Hótel Flatey (tel. 354/555-7788, www.hotelflatey.is, rooms from 29,000ISK) is housed in a traditional timber house, a type that is prevalent on the island. The rooms are small yet tastefully decorated in a classic Scandinavian style—wood furniture, quaint white linens, and lots of minimalist charm. Each of the rooms is named after a different bird species that inhabits the island. The staff is accommodating and the house is centrally located. This place is a winner. It's open June-August. The in-house **restaurant** (9am-9pm daily in summer, entrées from 4,300ISK) is a favorite among tourists and locals, with a mouthwatering menu that includes lumpfish caviar, mussels, lamb fillets with blueberry salt, and a delicate pan-fried cod dish with lobster sauce.

CAMPING

The Flatey **Krákuvör** campsite (tel. 354/438-1451, 1,200ISK) is small and as basic as it gets. It's an open area with no shelter, and the weather can be unforgiving. Camping here isn't recommended unless you have top-notch equipment—including a waterproof tent that can withstand high winds.

Transportation

There is one way to get to Flatey—by ferry. The *Baldur* ferry is operated by **Seatours** (www.seatours.is, round-trip 7,840ISK) and departs from the harbor in Stykkishólmur, where you can buy round-trip tickets. In the summer there are daily departures. The schedule in the winter varies. Be sure to check the website for up-to-date timetables.

Flatey

The Westfjords

The Westfjords are simply beautiful. Endless coastlines, jaw-dropping cliffs, and gorgeous mountain landscapes await those who make the trip. Rent a car to explore the region because bus service is limited.

ÍSAFJÖRÐUR

Ísafjörður is the unofficial capital of the Westfjords, but don't let that "title" fool you; it's just a tiny town of about 4,000 people. It's easy to feel isolated in Ísafjörður, but it's a feeling many tourists relish. Ísafjörður is a good base for exploring the Westfjords. The town itself is quaint, with a small downtown area with shops and restaurants, and the surroundings are picturesque with mountains in the background and a bustling harbor. A short drive outside town, you'll find towering mountains, interesting rock formations, and more sheep than people.

Sights

WESTFJORDS HERITAGE MUSEUM (Byggðasafn Vestfjarða)

The **Westfjords Heritage Museum** (Neðstakaupstað, tel. 354/896-3291, www.nedsti.is, 9am-6pm daily May 15-Sept. 15, 900ISK, seniors 750ISK) pays homage to the traditional methods of fishing, with equipment and fishing boats used in the old days on exhibit. The museum is housed in an 18th-century building that sets the tone for the exhibits. There are also ship models on display, informative documentaries on view, and a special exhibition on the processing of sun-dried salted fish and its significance to the town.

CULTURE HOUSE (Gamla Sjúkrahúsið)

Ísafjörður's **Culture House** (Eyrartún, tel. 354/450-8220, www.safnis.is, 1pm-6pm Mon.-Fri., 1pm-4pm Sat., free) was originally built in 1925 as the town's hospital, but it has morphed into Ísafjörður's library, with an art collection and photo archives that have a regional focus. The building itself is striking, with a white exterior and bright green roof. The interior is warm and cozy and a great place to hide out in for a couple hours when the weather is particularly bad. There are several computers available for use with Internet connection for a small fee, and many treasures wait to be discovered in the archives.

Sports and Recreation

KAYAKING

Wild Westfjords (Hafnarstræti 9, tel. 354/456-3300, www.wildwestfjords.com) offers a year-round 2.5-hour kayak tour for 14,000ISK from Ísafjörður; it's perfect for an easy introduction to kayaking. Peacefully paddle and enjoy the stunning mountain surroundings, with a good chance to see birds and seals.

SWIMMING

If the weather is particularly challenging, it's great to escape to the local indoor **Ísafjörður Swimming Pool** (Austurvegur 9, tel. 354/456-3200, 7am-9pm Mon.-Fri., 10am-5pm Sat.-Sun., 600ISK) for a few hours.

TOURS

For those who would like to explore the rugged terrain of the Westfjords, local operator **IBC Travel** (Urdarvegur 27, tel. 354/861-2845, www.ibctravel.is) runs a year-round super-jeep tour from Ísafjörður. A two-hour tour (8,000ISK) takes you to Arnarnes, a cape on the outskirts of Ísafjörður, where it is possible to see Drangajökull glacier, the only glacier in the Westfjords; taking a tour is the only way to visit Drangajökull. The company also offers other sightseeing tours.

Food

★ **Tjoruhúsið** (Nedstikaupstadur, tel.

The Westfjords

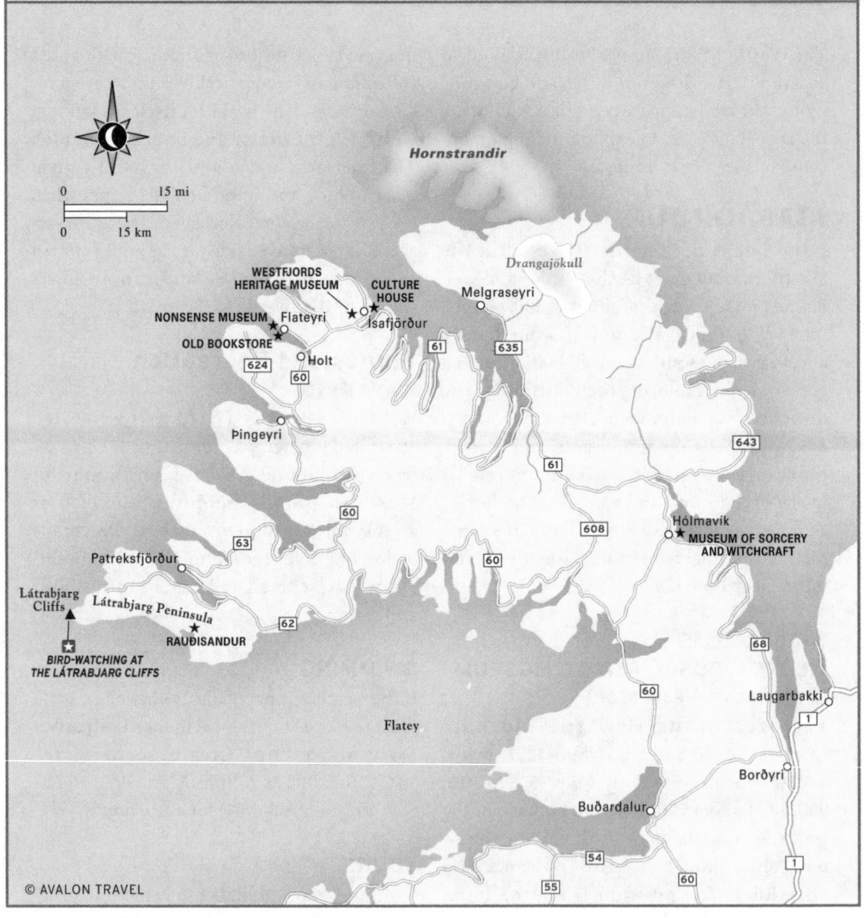

354/456-4419, noon-2pm and 7pm-10pm daily June-Sept., entrées from 2,500ISK) is a family-run restaurant that serves delicate, fresh fish in inventive ways. The rustic wood interior is cozy, the service top-notch, and the menu consists of the catch of the day. It could be haddock, cod, salmon, or other fish served with great care alongside fresh veggies. At night, there is an all-you-can-eat buffet for 6,000ISK per person, and it is well worth it.

Bræðraborg Café (Aðalstræti 22, tel. 354/456-3322, www.borea.is, 9am-6pm daily, entrées from 2,500ISK) is a cheerful, comfortable space and great hangout spot with bright blue tables, plush seating, rustic hardwood floors, and friendly staff. It serves delicious snacks and light meals. Locals frequent the café for a coffee and freshly baked bread and jam in the mornings and the soup of the day for lunch.

Við Pollinn (Silfurtorg 2, tel. 354/456-3360, www.isafjordurhotels.is, entrées from 4,300ISK) is located in Hótel Ísafjörður and offers locally sourced options including dishes ranging from lamb to fish to more adventurous fare like sautéed puffin, smoked minke whale, and horse tenderloin. The mussels in white wine sauce from nearby Drangsnes are divine. A kids menu is available.

Accommodations

Hótel Ísafjörður (Silfurtogr 2, tel. 354/456-4111, www.hotelisafjordur.is, rooms from 30,500ISK) is the nicest hotel in town, but you will pay for that stay. The 36-room hotel is decorated in standard Scandinavian simplicity and has private bathrooms, free Wi-Fi, free parking, and a staff that is happy to arrange tours and make recommendations. The hotel is centrally located, and all the main attractions are within walking distance.

Hótel Edda Ísafjörður (Torfnesi, tel. 354/444-4960, www.hoteledda.is, mid-June-mid-Aug., rooms from 24,000ISK) is a 40-room hotel operated only during the summer months to accommodate the high season. The hotel offers 20 rooms with private bathrooms and 20 rooms with a washbasin and shared bathroom facilities. Rooms are bright, clean, and sparsely decorated. Most rooms have hardwood floors and Ikea-type furniture. A breakfast buffet is available for a fee, and there is free Wi-Fi in the hotel's public areas.

Gamla Gisthúsið (Mánagata 5, tel. 354/456-4146, www.gistihus.is, rooms from 20,000ISK) is a standard nine-room guesthouse that offers the comforts of home. Rooms are small but clean and comfortable. The common lounge feels like you're visiting Icelandic relatives, with classic Scandinavian furniture and a reading corner with lots of books on the shelves. Guests have access to kitchen and laundry facilities.

Hotel Horn (Austurvegur 2, tel. 354/456-4611, www.hotelhorn.is, rooms from 28,000ISK) offers standard, deluxe, and family rooms year-round. All rooms have a private bathroom and free Wi-Fi, and family rooms also have a small kitchen. Rooms are tastefully decorated, and the lobby is bright and colorful. Breakfast is included in the rate of the room, and free parking is just outside the hotel.

Information and Services

The **tourist information center** (Aðalstræti 7, tel. 354/456-5121, www.westfjords.is, 8am-6pm Mon.-Fri., 8:30am-2pm Sat., 10am-2pm Sun. June 1-Aug. 31; 8am-4pm Mon.-Fri. Sept. 1-May 31) offers many services, including the option to rent camping equipment and bicycles. Brochures on the region are available,

view of Ísafjörður

and many tourists use the outpost as a place to join hiking groups.

Transportation

Ísafjörður is accessible by Route 61, which is paved. It's a little over five hours and 456 kilometers from Reykjavík.

There are buses to Ísafjörður by way of Reykjavík, Akureyri, Hólmavík, Patreksfjörður, Látrabjarg, and other towns throughout the year. The schedule changes often and can be viewed at www.isafjordur.is. The price from Reykjavík to Ísafjörður is 17,000ISK.

By plane, daily flights are available through **Air Iceland Connect** (www.airicelandconnect.is), which is operated at Reykjavík's domestic airport and Ísafjörður (tel. 354/570-3000). Depending on the weather, your 45-minute flight could be eventful due to wind conditions, but the view is amazing. A round-trip flight from Reykjavík is about 34,000ISK.

FLATEYRI

Flateyri was established as a trading post in 1792, and in the 19th century was a base of operations for whaling and shark-hunting. Most of the colorful houses on Flateyri's seafront street, Hafnarstræti, were built between 1880 and 1915. Over the years, the towns fishing industry waned due to a major fish company closing, and the town has since transformed itself to attract tourists in the summer months. Today, it's a popular with sea anglers and kayak enthusiasts. A couple of museums and a stunning landscape of mountains and endless ocean make the tiny town a worthwhile stop when traveling through the Westfjords.

Sights

OLD BOOKSTORE (Gamla Bókabúðin)

Visitors to the **Old Bookstore** (Hafnarstræti 3-5, tel. 354/865-6695, www.westfjords.is, 11am-5pm Tues.-Sat., 2pm-5pm Sun. June-Aug., open by arrangement Mon. and rest of year, donations accepted) can have a look at an exhibition of the old living quarters of the merchant family who made their home in the building. It's a unique take on what life was like in the town a couple of centuries ago. The nondescript building also has an exhibition about dried fish, which was a big part of the town's history before Flateyri's fishing industry ground to a halt. Used books are sold by the kilo in the store, which also sells souvenirs and toys.

NONSENSE MUSEUM (Dellusafnið)

The **Nonsense Museum** (Hafnarstræti 11, tel. 354/894-8836, 1pm-5pm daily June-Aug., Sept.-May by appointment only, 1,000ISK, 12 and under free) is one of those quirky museums that tend to pop up in the countryside of Iceland. This museum is a labor of love for the owner, and its wackiness is worth a visit. There's no rhyme or reason to the collections, but they are certainly fun and/or unexpected. For instance, there are more than 100 police hats on display, from forces around the world. There are also collections of ship models (including a huge replica of the *Titanic*), teaspoons and sugar packets, matchboxes, salt and pepper sets, and lighters. It's a fun place to peruse when the weather is bad, or if you have planned an extended stay in the region.

Sports and Recreation

FISHING

Flateyri is a beautiful place to fish, with the chance to spot whales while angling for cod, haddock, and catfish. **Iceland Pro Travel** (Hafnarstræti 9, tel. 354/456-6667, www.icelandprofishing.com) is a local tourism company that runs eight-day sea angling tours (207,000ISK) as well as day trips April-September. Contact the company for detailed itineraries and prices.

KAYAKING

Flateyri's fjord is a popular place for kayakers to visit, and local company **Grænhöfði**

(Hjallavegur 9, tel. 354/456-7762, jens@snerpa.is) offers half- and full-day trips around Önundarfjörður. Kayak enthusiasts are treated to calm waters amid stunning views of the fjord. The trips are run June-August, and prices start at 30,000ISK.

SWIMMING

The **Flateyri Swimming Pool** (Tjarnagata, tel. 354/456-7738, 10am-8pm Mon.-Fri., noon-4pm Sat.-Sun., 600ISK) is a central meeting place for locals, and tourists are more than welcome to take a dip and chat with the residents. The facility has a heated pool, hot tub, and sauna.

Food and Accommodations

Vagninn (Hafnarstræti 19, tel. 354/456-7751, www.vagninn.is, 4pm-11pm Sun.-Thurs., 4pm-3am Fri.-Sat., entrées from 2,000ISK) is your best bet for a bite to eat when in Flateyri—otherwise you will have to settle for fast food at the local gas station. Even though Vagninn is the only game in town, it still goes out of its way to please diners. The food is exceptional, including classic Icelandic fish and lamb dishes, and other menu options range from sandwiches and soups to hamburgers. The atmosphere is fun and easygoing, with live music on the weekends.

Grænhöfði (Hjallavegur 9, tel. 354/456-7762, jens@snerpa.is, rooms from 20,000ISK) offers three apartments that can accommodate up to six people. The rooms are huge, and guests have access to a fully equipped kitchen, private bathrooms, and plenty of parking. The owners also offer kayaking tours, so be sure to inquire if that's of interest.

Sima Hostel & Apartments (Ránargata 1, tel. 354/897-8700, www.icelandwestfjords.com, May 20-Sept. 5, rooms from 30,000ISK) offers rooms and apartments in the heart of Flateyri. Guests will find modern decor, luxury linens, and cozy common areas. Free Wi-Fi and free parking are available, and the property is close to local attractions.

Transportation

Flateyri is about 20 kilometers west of Ísafjörður and can be reached via a paved stretch of Route 60; after about 12 kilometers, turn right onto a road and follow it for about 7 kilometers.

There are three daily buses during weekdays between Ísafjörður and Flateyri (30 minutes, 1,500ISK).

ÞINGEYRI

Þingeyri is a tiny village of fewer than 300 residents that has scenic seaside views of the fjord Dýrafjörður. Tourism in the village isn't centered on museums or cultural exhibitions, but rather outdoor activities like hiking, swimming, and horse riding.

Sports and Recreation

HIKING

From Þingeyri, you can hike into the **Westfjords Alps**, a striking mountain range with pointed peaks unlike the usual flat-topped variety. Kaldbakur peak is the tallest mountain in the Westfjords Alps at 998 meters. A moderate out-and-back hike from Keldudalur, a farm, to Helgafell starts at the farmstead Hraun, which you can reach via Route 60 and then Route 622, which you'll drive down for 13 kilometers, turning left onto a gravel road where you'll be able to park your car. The trailhead is at the parking area, and you'll head west to climb the Helgafell hill. This trail is in a stretch of Iceland that doesn't get a lot of tourist traffic; it's possible to be alone on it, which can be very appealing for some hikers. Several peaks, including Kaldbakur, are visible from the well-maintained trail, along with sweeping valleys and lush green vegetation. The highlight is reaching the top of Helgafell, where you'll catch views of the western Westfjords Alps. The round-trip hike takes about five hours, is about 25 kilometers, and has an elevation gain of 549 meters. Be sure to check the weather forecast before attempting the hike. Bring waterproof outer layers, hiking shoes, water, and a charged mobile phone.

HORSE RIDING

Simbahöllin (Fjarðargötu 5, tel. 354/869-5654, www.westfjords-horseriding.com) offers horseback tours daily May 15-September 15. The two-hour tour (9,900ISK) takes travelers along the Sanda river, where you'll see lush vegetation along the calm riverbanks and take in stunning views of the Westfjords Alps. This is an easy tour, suitable for ages 6 and up.

SWIMMING

The **Þingeyri Swimming Pool** (Þingeyraroddi, tel. 354/456-8375, 8am-9pm Mon.-Fri., 10am-5pm Sat.-Sun., 600ISK) is conveniently located right next to Þingeyri's campsite.

Food and Accommodations

Simbahöllin (Fjarðargata 5, tel. 354/899-6659, www.simbahollin.is, noon-6pm daily June 1-June 15, 10am-10pm daily June 16-Aug. 15, noon-6pm daily Aug. 16-Aug. 31, snacks from 800ISK) is a charming countryside café located in a 1915 building that served as a grocery store. The old-fashioned atmosphere is adorable, the cakes and pastries fresh, and the staff makes you feel like family. The specialty is Belgian waffles with fresh rhubarb jam and cream. Your taste buds will thank you.

Núpur Guesthouse (Dýrafjörður, tel. 354/456-8235, www.hotelnupur.is, rooms from 22,000ISK) offers 40 rooms ranging from singles to triples. The block-style buildings were once part of a school complex. The rooms are clean and neat, but nothing special. Guests have access to shared bathroom facilities, a kitchenette, and free parking. The in-house **restaurant** serves Icelandic staples with an emphasis on lamb and fish. The menu includes oven-baked leg of lamb, seafood soup, shrimp and monkfish with salad, and pineapple pan-fried cod with tartar sauce. The fish of the day costs 4,800ISK and the meat of the day 5,500ISK.

Við Fjörðinn (Aðalstræti 26, tel. 354/847-0285, www.vidfjordinn.is, rooms from 20,000ISK) offers eight rooms with standard beds and simple furnishings for a clean, no-frills stay. Guests have access to shared kitchen and bathroom facilities. There are also apartments available for larger groups. Breakfast is available for an added charge of 1,000ISK.

CAMPING

The **Þingeyri Campground** (Þingeyraroddi, tel. 354/450-8470, 1,500ISK) is close to the swimming pool, so there's a lot of foot traffic in the area. It's a small campsite with an adequate cooking area, toilets, and room for tents and RVs. The campsite is in an open field with no shelter, but it has stunning views of the fjord. It's open mid-May to mid-September.

Information and Services

The **tourist information center** (Hafnarstræti 5, tel. 354/891-6832, www.thingeyri.is, 10am-6pm Mon.-Fri., 11am-5pm Sat.-Sun. June 1-Sept 1.) has brochures, suggestions for local tour operators, and Internet access.

Transportation

By car, Þingeyri is 49 kilometers southwest of Ísafjörður and is accessible via a paved stretch of Route 60.

While Þingeyri feels a bit off the beaten track, a bus operated by **Westfjords Adventures** (Aðalstræti 62, tel. 354/456-5006, www.westfjordsadventures.is) runs twice a day from Ísafjörður (1 hour, 4,000ISK) via Flateyri.

DYNJANDI

Dynjandi is likened to a bridal veil. The waterfall is 30 meters wide at its highest point and 60 meters wide at its lowest. It's the largest waterfall in the Westfjords, and visiting the chute makes for a beautiful little hike. From a parking area on Route 60, it's a 15-minute walk up to the base of the waterfall. Along the way you'll pass six other smaller falls, so plan on spending more time along the route for photo stops and to enjoy the surroundings.

Dynjandi is about 35 kilometers southeast of Þingeyri via an unpaved stretch of Route 60.

PATREKSFJÖRÐUR

Patreksfjörður is the kind of sleepy fishing town you will come to love and expect as you travel along the Westfjords. Many travelers use the town as a base while heading out on excursions and day trips. Spend some time in Patreksfjörður if you're a sea angler or if you want to check out sights like the harbor area.

Sports and Recreation

FISHING

Sea angling in the Westfjords is an unforgettable experience, and Patreksfjörður has especially rich fishing grounds. **West Tours** (tel. 354/456-5111, www.westtours.is) offers a two-hour tour with a guide. Gear is provided, and the fishing is for cod and haddock. The tour is offered May-November and costs 12,000ISK.

SWIMMING

The town has one of the nicest swimming pools in the region. **Patreksfjörður Swimming Pool** (Aðalstræti 55, tel. 354/456-1301, 9am-9pm Mon.-Fri., 10am-6pm Sat.-Sun., 600ISK) is an outdoor pool with hot tubs, a steam bath, and an indoor gym.

TOURS

The tour company **Westfjords Adventures** (Aðalstræti 62, tel. 354/456-5006, www.westfjordsadventures.com) offers bird-watching tours by bicycle to see gorgeous landscapes and seabirds including puffins. The eight-hour "Bird Cliffs and Biking Tour" (35,000ISK pp) is available Tuesday-Saturday May 1-September 15. Tourists are advised to wear layers and comfortable footwear. The company also offers all-day jeep tours on rocky terrain for action junkies (34,000ISK) as well as a leisurely three-hour hike around town (4,900ISK), with a guide pointing out the major sights, including the scenic harbor area and fish market.

Food and Accommodations

Stúkuhúsið Café/Restaurant (Aðalstræti 50, tel. 354/456-1404, www.stukuhusid.is, 11am-11pm daily June 1-Aug. 31, limited hours winter, entrées from 2,000ISK) is a cute café situated just off the water. The eatery consists of a simple room with an outdoor deck for enjoying good summer weather. The menu includes cakes and pastries, along with soups and sandwiches. For dinner, you can choose between fresh fish of the day and a lamb fillet with roasted potatoes, vegetables, and pepper sauce. For starters, there's a choice of salmon or soup of the day.

★ **Fosshotel Westfjords** (Aðalstræti 100, tel. 354/456-2004, www.fosshotel.is, rooms from 22,000ISK) is one of the nicest outposts of Iceland's Fosshotel chain. The lobby and rooms have an earthy, natural feel with warm hues and lots of wood accents. The beds are quite comfortable. Rooms are larger than average and have free Wi-Fi, private bathrooms, and flat-screen TVs. Meals are served in the cozy in-house **restaurant** (6pm-10pm daily Apr.-Oct., entrées from 2,600ISK), which specializes in fish. Entrées are light and fresh, and the chefs have a classic sensibility. Expect cod, salmon, lobster, and other fish, as well as meat and a couple of vegetarian options. The hotel is open April 1-October 31.

Hotel West (Aðalstræti 62, tel. 354/456-5020, www.hotelwest.is, rooms from 27,000ISK) offers single, double, and superior rooms, all with private bathrooms. Rooms are clean and sparsely decorated, but many have views over the fjord. The hotel is close to the grocery store and pharmacy, and is a short drive from the Látrabjarg cliffs, where you can go puffin-watching.

Stekkaból Guesthouse (Stekkar, tel. 354/864-9675, stekkabol@snerpa.is, rooms from 16,000ISK) is a cute countryside guesthouse run by a husband and wife who aim to make you feel at home. The rooms are on the small side, but tidy, and free Wi-Fi is included. The guesthouse is in a picturesque spot on the fjord, making it a perfect spot to spend the night. Breakfast is available for an added cost of 1,700ISK per person.

Information and Services

The **tourist information center** (Aðalstræti 62, tel. 354/456-5006, 10am-4pm) is in the Westfjords Adventures office in the center of town. You can book tours and pick up pamphlets and hiking maps for the region, and access the Internet.

Transportation

Patreksfjörður is a 2.5-hour, 130-kilometer drive southwest of Þingeyri via an unpaved stretch of Route 60 and unpaved Route 62. Dynjandi is about a 1.5-hour, 92-kilometer drive southwest on an unpaved stretch of Route 60 and Route 62, also unpaved.

LÁTRABJARG PENINSULA

The Látrabjarg Peninsula is in the northwest fjord region near Patreksfjörður and has dramatic sea cliffs and an abundance of bird species, making it a paradise for bird lovers. From June through August, the cliffs around the peninsula are home to numerous puffins, gulls, and kittiwakes.

Sights and Recreation

TOP EXPERIENCE

★ BIRD-WATCHING

Látrabjarg is one of the best bird-watching spots in the west, as millions of seabirds gather to nest here each season. Puffins are a common sight in the summer months—you can see the adorable, bright-beaked birds May-August. You can also see fulmars, razorbills, and guillemots along the cliffs May-August.

The colossal rock formations of the **Látrabjarg cliffs** jut out of the earth at interesting angles, and the layered basalt forms intricate crevices that host nests. Trails allow you to access the cliffs by foot; stay on marked paths. Always be respectful of the area and be mindful where you step to avoid nests. The height of the cliffs is humbling, with some reaching up to 441 meters. The cliffs offer some of the most scenic views on the peninsula.

If you trek the cliffs by foot, you will want to have a pair of binoculars on hand to get a closer look. It's best to park your vehicle at the end of Route 612 and walk east toward the cliffs.

Látrabjarg cliffs

RAUÐISANDUR

Rauðisandur is a secluded beach with golden-red sand and gorgeous views of the Látrabjarg area. Snæfellsjökull looms in the background. Take a walk along the shore, and be on the lookout for seals bobbing in the water. Route 614, an unpaved road, takes you to the beach.

Food and Accommodations

Hotel Breiðavík (Breiðavík/Látrabjarg, tel. 354/456-1575, www.breidavik.is, rooms from 21,500ISK) is conveniently close to the Látrabjarg cliffs and offers darling accommodations for your stay. Double rooms look a little dated, with bright carpet and old-fashioned linens, but the beds are comfortable, and some rooms with private bathrooms are available. All rooms have access to Wi-Fi, kitchen facilities, and a washing machine. The staff is warm and welcoming and the breakfast is hearty. For budget travelers, there are sleeping bag rooms as well as camping, but be sure to call ahead for availability. The in-house **restaurant** (5pm-10pm daily, entrées from 2,500ISK) specializes in fish and lamb, but has other options. The salmon is fresh, seasoned perfectly, and highly recommended.

Hótel Látrabjarg (Fagrihvammur, tel. 354/456-1500, www.latrabjarg.com, rooms from 34,500ISK) offers larger-than-average rooms with killer views from gigantic windows. Rooms are bright with standard beds (some are carpeted), and all rooms have simple furnishings ranging from two-seat couches to armchairs. Breakfast is included in the price of the room.

Transportation

You have one option to get to Látrabjarg: Route 612, which can be rough on your rental car because it's unpaved. Beware of steep drops and do not dream of exceeding the speed limit. Be safe. Látrabjarg is 59 kilometers southwest from Patreksfjörður.

HÓLMAVÍK

Hólmavík, while a small town, is the largest in the Strandir area, which makes up the easternmost tip of the Westfjords. It's a popular stop for those looking to check out the unique Museum of Sorcery and Witchcraft and the cute Sheep Farming Museum, along with the beautiful coastline. Many travelers use the town as a base for exploring nearby villages.

Hólmavík harbor

Sights

MUSEUM OF SORCERY AND WITCHCRAFT (Galdrasafnið á Hólmavík)

The **Museum of Sorcery and Witchcraft** (Höfðargata 8-10, tel. 354/897-6525, www.galdrasyning.is, 9am-7pm daily, 950ISK adults, 700ISK students, free for children under 15) has a name that grabs your attention, and the exhibits are truly unique. The exhibits tell the story of Iceland's infamous 17th-century witch hunts, and this is the only museum on the island that gives a comprehensive overview of the period. The two-story facility also features wax figures, an audio tour, and information about spells and runes. The museum may be a little unnerving to children under the age of 12, as there are depictions of death and violence. If you still have an appetite, there's a gift shop and museum café that serves coffee and snacks.

SHEEP FARMING MUSEUM (Sauðfjársetur á Ströndum)

The **Sheep Farming Museum** (Sævangur, tel. 354/451-3324, www.strandir.is, 10am-6pm daily June-Aug., free) is a region-specific museum that's great if you're traveling with children. The museum focuses on Icelandic sheep and sheep-farming methods that have been employed in the Strandir region for centuries. A favorite among kids is feeding young sheep milk from a bottle while learning about the breed. There's also a souvenir shop and small café, where you can grab a coffee or cocoa and a snack.

Sports and Recreation

SWIMMING

The **Hólmavík Swimming Pool** (Jakobínutún, tel. 354/451-3560, 9am-9pm daily, 600ISK) is quiet and gets a bit of traffic in the summer because it's close to the campsite. There are a few hot tubs and a steam bath to enjoy as well.

GOLF

Hólmavík Golf Club (Hafnarbraut 18, tel. 354/892-4687, www.golf.is, greens fees 7,000ISK) is a nine-hole course with sweeping views of the ocean, valleys, and mountains. Be sure to call ahead for a tee time. The facility is open year-round, but it's wise to confirm hours of operation because they're highly changeable.

Food and Accommodations

Café Riis (Hafnarbraut 39, tel. 354/451-3567, 11:30am-9pm daily, entrées from 3,400ISK) is the town's only place for a sit-down meal. The nondescript green building has a tourist-friendly menu ranging from traditional fish and lamb dishes to pizza, sandwiches, and snacks. On weekends, Café Riis serves as the town's main watering hole, where locals congregate to grab some drinks and let loose.

Finna Hotel (Borgabraut 4, tel. 354/451-3136, www.finnahotel.is, rooms from 16,000ISK) is a small guesthouse in a quaint yellow house on a quiet road in the center of town. Rooms are clean, smart, and furnished simply. If you have a choice, request a room on the 2nd floor—those rooms underwent a recent renovation. Amenities include free Wi-Fi, free parking, and shared bathrooms. Room rates with or without breakfast are available.

Hótel Laugarhóll (Bjarnarfjörður, tel. 354/451-3380, www.laugarholl.is, rooms from 25,000ISK) offers 16 rooms, 11 of which have private bathrooms. The rooms are bright and tidy, with Wi-Fi access and free parking. The hotel is in a large estate set within a rocky landscape. It's close to town (about 25 kilometers east of Hólmavík) but remote enough to maintain a countryside feel. The in-house **restaurant** (7am-9pm daily) offers a breakfast that's included in the room price, as well as a lunch and dinner menu. Entrées start at 2,400ISK and range from fish and lamb dishes to lighter items like soup, sandwiches, and vegetarian options.

CAMPING

The town has a centrally located, well-maintained campsite, **Hólmavík Campground** (Jakobínutún, tel. 354/451-3111, 1,400ISK), that is close to the swimming pool. There are adequate cooking facilities and hot showers. Tents and RVs are welcome, with hookups available. The site is in an open field with no shelter, so be prepared for the elements if you're camping in a tent.

Information and Services

The **tourist information office** (Höfðagata 8, tel. 354/451-3111, www.holmavik.is, 9am-6pm daily) is in the center of town and offers Internet access, pamphlets about the region, and information on local tours and horse rentals.

Transportation

By car, Hólmavík is a popular stop on the Westfjords for travelers coming from Ísafjörður, as Ring Roaders tend to need gas by this point. Route 61 is paved and connects Hólmavík, which is 223 kilometers southeast of Ísafjörður, to the Ring Road.

The **Strætó** 59 bus (tel. 354/540-2700, www.straeto.is, 4,800ISK) goes from Borgarnes to Hólmavík and takes about two hours.

DRANGSNES

Drangsnes is a small fishing village with fewer than 70 residents. It has an active harbor, a school, some summer houses, and a couple of popular hot pots. Boat tours leave from Drangsnes to Grímsey island, which is a prime spot for puffin-watching in the summer.

Sports and Recreation

GRÍMSEY TOURS

Just offshore from Drangsnes, the island of Grímsey is known for its **puffin colony** (about 80,000 nesting pairs) and a small lighthouse. No homes, buildings, or facilities are on the island—just birdlife and pristine nature. From Drangsnes, scheduled boat trips to the island take around 10 minutes, and tours last around four hours (8,000ISK 12 and over, 4000ISK children 6-11, free for children under 6). Visitors spend their time independently exploring the small island, stopping by the lighthouse for photos, and observing puffins nesting on the cliffs. Tours depart twice a week on Thursdays and Sundays at 2pm June 15-mid-August, weather permitting. Booking in advance is recommended (354/853-6520), but if there is space, walk-ups are taken. The fee can be paid at Malarhorn guesthouse.

SWIMMING

Drangsnes's three free **hot pots** are popular year-round with locals and visitors alike. They're great spots to relax and enjoy the scenery; from their location along the shoreline, you can see the harbor and Grímsey in the distance. They are visible from the road, Route 645, and there's a changing area across the street. Be sure to bring a towel.

The **Drangsnes Swimming Pool** (Grundargata 15, tel. 354/451-3201, sundlaug@drangsnes.is, 10am-9pm Mon.-Thurs. and 10am-6pm Fri.-Sun. June 15-Aug. 30, 4pm-7pm Tues.-Wed and Fri. and 3pm-5pm Sat.-Sun. Sept 1-June 14, 600ISK) is a small outdoor pool with a hot tub that's popular with locals. It's located close to Malarhorn, the town's only guesthouse.

Food and Accommodations

Malarhorn (Grundargata 17, tel. 354/853-6520, www.malarhorn.is, rooms from 28,000ISK) is the only game in town in Drangsnes. The guesthouse has three buildings with singles, doubles, family rooms, luxury rooms, and self-catering cottages. There are common areas and a mix of shared and private bathrooms. Rooms are comfortable and sparsely decorated with simple wood furniture and bare walls. Guests have access to porches and gas barbecues. Malarhorn's **restaurant,** Malarkaffi, is open from dusk till dawn in the summer, and open by request the rest of the year. Soups, sandwiches, and burgers are on the menu for lunch, and dinner includes pan-fried cod, fish stew, grilled wolffish, and grilled lamb.

Transportation

The only way to get to Drangsnes is by car. From Hólmavík, head north on Route 61 and then east on Route 643 and south on Route 645. The trip is about 33 kilometers on the paved routes and takes 40 minutes.

HORNSTRANDIR

The Hornstrandir Peninsula is the northernmost part of the Westfjords, and it is idyllically isolated. It's a perfect spot to explore by foot, enjoying hiking paths and observing the rich birdlife. Nature rules in this spot of the Westfjords—you won't find museums or cultural attractions, but who needs them when there are millions of seabirds and arctic fox sightings are common? It isn't just foreign travelers making their way to these parts, but also Icelanders in search of pure solitude and striking beauty. On bird cliffs, the subjects of postcard-perfect photos, you can see puffins, kittiwakes, fulmars, and guillemots. A long, sandy beach is the perfect place to roam while basking in the shadows of sharp mountains and the jagged landscape.

Sights and Recreation

HIKING THE HORNSTRANDIR NATURE RESERVE

The **Hornstrandir Nature Reserve,** which was established in 1975, lies on the north edge of the peninsula. Be mindful that this stretch of land is fiercely protected; cars are banned within the reserve limits and fishing is strictly prohibited. Enjoy the land, but be respectful and obey the rules.

The moderate hike between the small village of **Hesteyri** and **Aðalvík Bay** at the tip of Hornstrandir is the most popular option, and it's about an eight-hour hike at a leisurely pace, during which you can enjoy the cliffs, the rocky landscape, and unspoiled nature. It's about 12 kilometers round-trip with an elevation gain of about 300 meters.

There are also longer hiking trails, but you must monitor weather conditions and be prepared. Good maps are necessary and can be found in the online shop at www.galdrasyning.is.

The terrain could be treacherous depending on the weather, so it's not ideal for casual hikers, but rather for more experienced trekkers. Because of its northern locale, the winds can be fierce and the rain plentiful. Make sure you are prepared with a good pair of boots, waterproof gear, and lots of layers because it can get really cold. Use common sense—there are streams that need to be crossed, sections can be slippery with ice, and portions where crampons are necessary. Visitors must bring their own tents if the plan is to camp overnight. Weatherproof equipment is necessary, as snow can be expected at any time of the year and storms can break with little warning. Thick fog often occurs in the region, and it's a good idea to have GPS with you.

If you are a novice hiker or would like the structure of an organized tour, **West Tours** (tel. 354/456-5111, www.westtours.is) offers packages and excursions throughout the year.

Camping

The campground **Höfn in Hornvík** (free) has basic camping facilities, including restrooms, a cooking area, and hot and cold water. Be respectful of the surroundings, dispose of your trash, and leave no trace. The campsite is in an open space with little shelter. The GPS coordinates are N 66.4232, W 22.4882.

Transportation

Travel to Hornstrandir is very much seasonal, with the high season being from the middle of June to the end of August. Because of its northern locale, the weather can be especially cold, even in the summer, and very wet.

There are daily 45-minute flights from Reykjavík's domestic airport to Ísafjörður for 34,000ISK, and from Ísafjörður, you can catch a ferry operated by **Sjóferðir** (tel. 354/456-3879, www.sjoferdir.is) that stops at Aðalvík, Hornvík, Grunnavík, Hesteyri, and Vigur for 5,000ISK.

The easiest way to travel to the region is to book an excursion, as there are detailed logistics involved and it's best to have a local tour company handle them. There can be delays because of weather, and travelers can avoid headaches by booking a tour. Local tour companies include Ísafjörður-based **West Tours** (tel. 354/456-5111, www.westtours.is), **Arctic Adventures** (tel. 354/456-3322, www.adventures.is), and **Borea Adventures** (www.boreaadventures.com), also in Ísafjörður.

North Iceland

There's a lot to explore in North Iceland, and Akureyri is the center of it all.

Iceland's second most populous city, Akureyri has a thriving art scene, gorgeous gardens, and restaurants that rival Reykjavík's. The harbor serves as a port for large cruise ships, and visitors are treated to views of the country's highest peaks and longest fjord.

Akureyri is a perfect place to base yourself when exploring the north. The open terrain from Akureyri to Siglufjörður, the northernmost town in Iceland, treats visitors to traditional churches, wondrous waterfalls, and a dreamy seaside.

Farther west is Northwest Iceland. This region comprises sparsely populated farm country. In fact, depending on the time of year, you may see more seals, birds, horses, and whales than people in areas like Húnaflói and Skagafjörður.

Heading from Akureyri toward eastern Iceland, stops include Krafla's steamy lava fields, Lake Mývatn's lush lands, and the majestic Dettifoss waterfall. In the summer, birders and geology buffs will want to stretch the drive out an extra couple of days.

From waterfalls and hiking trails to the best skiing on the island, the north has plenty to keep you busy.

PLANNING YOUR TIME

North Iceland is a huge chunk of land (for Iceland), but it's quite easy to split into manageable sections, using a major town as a home base and doing day trips from there. Akureyri, Húsavík, and Mývatn are the largest and most frequented destinations for tourists, with museums, outdoor activities, and historical sites to visit.

If you're traveling the Ring Road, Northwest Iceland would be your first destination after visiting the Westfjords. The northwest offers some of the most exquisite scenery on the island in its small towns and counties, including Hvammstangi, Blönduós, and Skagafjörður. Akureyri is a great base while visiting this area.

Akureyri rivals Reykjavík for the center of artistic life in Iceland. Plan to spend as much time as possible up here, with at least one day each in Mývatn and Húsavík and two days in Akureyri—three days if you want to include a trip to Grímsey.

Previous: central Skagafjörður; traditional Icelandic farm with mossy roofs in Glaumbær. **Above:** Dettifoss.

Look for ★ to find recommended sights, activities, dining, and lodging.

Highlights

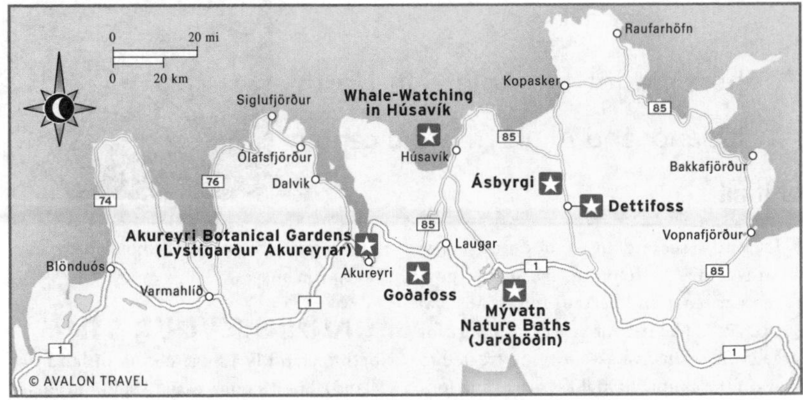

★ **Akureyri Botanical Gardens (Lystigarður Akureyrar):** The northernmost botanical garden in the world has an eclectic collection of native and international flora (page 176).

★ **Goðafoss:** Witness the thundering Waterfall of the Gods, a spectacular sight any time of year (page 188).

★ **Mývatn Nature Baths (Jarðböðin):** Just try to resist taking a dip in the soothing, heated waters of Mývatn (page 189).

★ **Whale-Watching in Húsavík:** The unofficial whale-watching capital of Iceland offers a chance to view as many as 12 species of these gentle giants (page 196).

★ **Ásbyrgi:** This gigantic canyon features cool rock formations, looping walking paths, lush greenery, birds—and tons of photo opportunities (page 199).

★ **Dettifoss:** The largest waterfall on the island, and the most powerful in Europe, is 100 meters wide and 45 meters high (page 200).

North Iceland

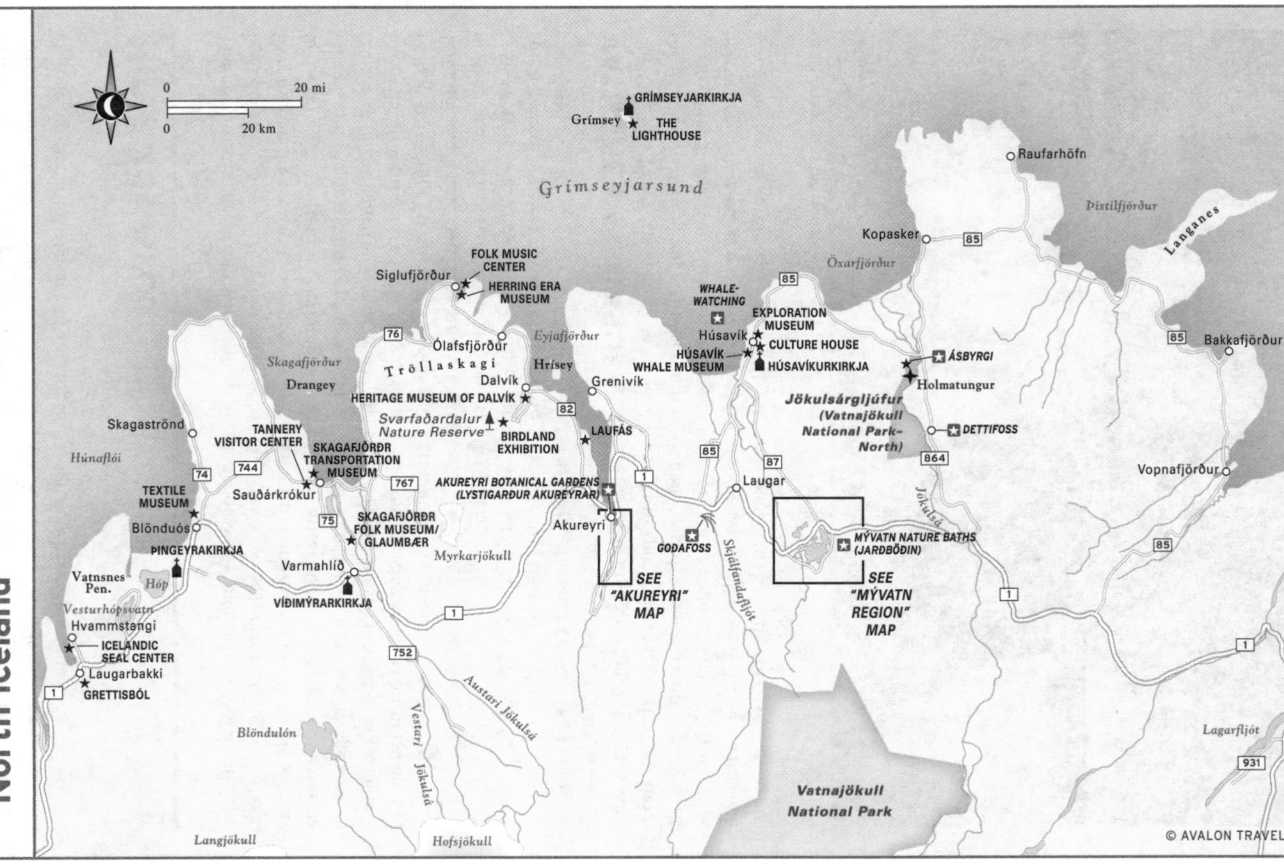

0 20 mi
0 20 km
GRÍMSEYJARKIRKJA
Grímsey
THE LIGHTHOUSE
Raufarhöfn
Grímseyjarsund
Þistilfjörður
Langanes
Kopasker
Öxarfjörður
FOLK MUSIC CENTER
Siglufjörður
HERRING ERA MUSEUM
WHALE-WATCHING
EXPLORATION MUSEUM
Húsavík
CULTURE HOUSE
HÚSAVÍK WHALE MUSEUM
HÚSAVÍKURKIRKJA
Bakkafjörður
Ólafsfjörður
Eyjafjörður
Skagafjörður
Tröllaskagi
Hrísey
ÁSBYRGI
Holmatungur
Drangey
Dalvík
Grenivík
HERITAGE MUSEUM OF DALVÍK
Jökulsárgljúfur (Vatnajökull National Park-North)
Svarfaðardalur Nature Reserve
BIRDLAND EXHIBITION
LAUFÁS
DETTIFOSS
Skagaströnd
TANNERY VISITOR CENTER
SKAGAFJÖRÐR TRANSPORTATION MUSEUM
Húnaflói
Vopnafjörður
TEXTILE MUSEUM
Sauðárkrókur
AKUREYRI BOTANICAL GARDENS (LYSTIGARÐUR AKUREYRAR)
Laugar
Blönduós
SKAGAFJÖRÐR FOLK MUSEUM/ GLAUMBÆR
Akureyri
MÝVATN NATURE BATHS (JARÐBÖÐIN)
ÞINGEYRAKIRKJA
GOÐAFOSS
Myrkarjökull
Jökulsá
Varmahlíð
Vatnsnes Pen.
Hóp
SEE "AKUREYRI" MAP
SEE "MÝVATN REGION" MAP
Vesturhópsvatn
VÍÐIMÝRARKIRKJA
Skjálfandafljót
Hvammstangi
ICELANDIC SEAL CENTER
Laugarbakki
GRETTISBÓL
Austari Jökulsá
Vestari Jökulsá
Blöndulón
Lagarfljót
Vatnajökull National Park
Langjökull
Hofsjökull
1
74
744
75
752
76
767
82
85
87
864
931
© AVALON TRAVEL

When driving in the north, it's important to take the weather into consideration. Some roads are impassable in the winter. It's possible to see much of North Iceland by sticking to the Ring Road, which is the best-maintained road in the region. However, always be sure to check the road conditions and weather forecast before heading out in a car.

Húnaflói Area

The northwest is steeped in saga history, as legendary hero Grettir the Strong was said to have lived in the area, but most people travel to the Húnaflói area for the charming fishing villages and the opportunity to spot whales, seals, and birds. Húnaflói is a large bay between the Strandir coast and the Skagaströnd region. It is about 50 kilometers wide and 100 kilometers long, with the small towns of Blönduós and Skagaströnd located on the bay's eastern side. The region is lush in the summer, with a majestic coastline similar to the Westfjords.

VATNSNES PENINSULA

The Vatnsnes Peninsula is home to some of the best seal-watching opportunities in the north (in the summer, you have a good chance of spotting harbor and gray seals), and there's a museum with lovely exhibitions at the Icelandic Seal Center, which does research on local seal species. **Hvammstangi** is the largest town on the peninsula and the site of many tourist attractions. The Vatnsnes Peninsula juts out into Húnaflói, marked by jagged rocks and bobbing hills. Visitors can access Route 711 from the Ring Road to Hvammstangi and around the peninsula.

Sights

ICELANDIC SEAL CENTER

(Selasetur Íslands)

The **Icelandic Seal Center** (Brekkugata 2, Hvammstangi, tel. 354/451-2345, www.selasetur.is, 10am-3pm Mon.-Fri. Oct. 1-Apr. 30, 9am-4pm daily May, 9am-7pm daily June 1-Aug. 31, 9am-4pm daily Sept., 950ISK adults, free for children under 12) is as cute as it sounds, if you like seals. There is a research component to the facility that is quite serious,

rock formation in the Húnaflói bay

but the museum section captures these lovable, adorable creatures perfectly. Most of the exhibitions are geared toward children, and topics include the seals of the North Atlantic and the Arctic, the importance of seals in Icelandic culture and tradition, seal biology (with skeletons on display), and the evolution of seal hunting on the island. There are also documentaries on Icelandic seals in English. The main seals the center works with are harbor, harp, bearded, gray, hooded, and ringed seals. (There's also the odd walrus that comes ashore in Iceland from Greenland—the seal center is contacted in that event.) The staff has information on the best sites for seal-watching opportunities, and a small shop (hours variable; check website) sells souvenirs and light meals. For independent travelers, it is possible to go to the popular seal-watching spots without a tour guide.

GRETTISBÓL

Grettisból (Laugarbakki, tel. 354/451-0050, www.grettistak.is), Grettir's Lair, is an outdoor area and cultural center dedicated to the great saga hero Grettir "the Strong" Ásmundsson from *Grettir's Saga*. One of the most infamous outlaws of the sagas, Grettir was born on the farm Bjarg, which is only seven kilometers south of this cultural center. There is a Viking garden at Grettisból, and from the road you will see a big Viking sword sculpture. In the summer months (June-Aug.), a market in the house sells Viking-related wares, such as figurines, artwork, and woolen goods. The center is open year-round, and if you're a fan of the sagas, this should be on your itinerary.

An annual festival held at Grettisból in August is called **Grettistak;** locals have a strongman competition in the spirit of Grettir.

MERCHANT MUSEUM (Bardúsa-Verslunarminjasafn)

The **Merchant Museum** (Brekkugata 4, Hvammstangi, tel. 354/451-2747, 10am-6pm Mon.-Fri., 11am-4pm Sat.-Sun. June-Aug., 1,000ISK) is a small museum in Hvammstangi housed in the remains of an early-20th-century shop. Today, the museum keeps all the old goods that were key to society in the town, such as fishing equipment, kitchen utensils, and other home goods. The museum also sells Icelandic-made handcrafts.

Food

Sjavarborg Restaurant (Strandgata 1, tel. 354/451-3131, http://www.sjavarborg-restaurant.is, 11am-10pm daily, entrées from 2,550ISK) is a popular eatery located close to the town harbor. The building was originally a slaughterhouse, and then a freezing plant, before becoming the restaurant it is today. Its interior is a modern mix of concrete and wood with rustic driftwood accents. The menu is simple with burgers, fish, and soup for lunch, and fish, steaks, burgers, sandwiches, pasta, and salads for dinner.

Accommodations

Guesthouse Hanna Sigga (Garðavegur 26, tel. 354/451-2407, gistihs@simnet.is, rooms from 15,000ISK) offers six rooms, a common kitchen for preparing meals, and an outdoor hot tub. It's close to whale- and seal-watching opportunities. Rooms are small but clean, and guests share bathroom facilities. Free Wi-Fi is also available.

Hotel Hvammstangi (Norðurbraut 1, tel. 354/855-1303, rooms from 22,000ISK) is a guesthouse about six kilometers from the highway and in the middle of some great seal-watching spots. Rooms are small but neat and tastefully decorated. Each room has a private bathroom, there is a shared TV lounge with complimentary coffee and tea, and guests have access to free Wi-Fi. The town's public swimming pool, with hot tub and steam bath, is across the street from the hotel, and admission is free for guests.

Dæli Holiday Farm (Viðidalur, tel. 354/451-2566, www.daeli.is, rooms from 26,100ISK) has larger-than-average rooms, some wood-paneled, that are simple and smart. The 14 rooms have private bathrooms, TVs, and free Wi-Fi, and guests have access to a sauna, hot tub, mini golf, a playground, and a café. A kitchen is available to prepare meals, and guests have access to a barbecue grill.

★ **Gauksmýri** (Þjóðvegur, tel. 354/451-2927, www.gauksmyri.is, rooms from 24,000ISK) is hands-down the area's best place to stay, especially if you love horses. The 24-room ranch offers cozy, comfortable rooms with adorably appropriate horse-print bedding. The beds are comfortable, the decor is rustic cool, and the amenities are superb. Most rooms have private bathroom facilities, and all guests have access to free Wi-Fi and huge windows overlooking the gorgeous landscape. The owners are obviously horse enthusiasts (they also operate a horse-rental business). There are short guided horse tours and demonstrations showing the various gaits Iceland's horses are known for, and training and teaching facilities are on-site. Breakfast is included in the room price.

Ósar Hostel (Vatnsnesvegur, tel. 354/451-2678, www.hostel.is, beds from 4,100ISK) is just 20 minutes from the Ring Road, making this a popular choice in the area for budget travelers making the trek around the island. Rooms are adequate but nothing to write home about. A few rooms have private bathrooms, but most share facilities. It's open May-September.

Transportation

By car, Hvammstangi is 190 kilometers north of Reykjavík on Route 1 and 200 kilometers west of Akureyri.

It's best to have a rental car to explore this region, but there is bus service from Akureyri. The **Strætó** 57 bus (tel. 354/540-2700, www.straeto.is) departs from Akureyri and travels roughly three hours to Hvammstangi for 3,960ISK.

BLÖNDUÓS

Blönduós is a tiny town that was built around a bridge over the Blanda River (Blönduós means "mouth of the river Blanda" in Icelandic). Home to just a few shops, private homes, and guesthouses, the town is a small spot that has a few attractions. If you are traveling on the Ring Road and have some time, think about visiting the Textile Museum and the local church, which is steeped in history.

Sights

TEXTILE MUSEUM (Heimilisiðnaðarsafnið)

The **Textile Museum** (Árbraut 29, tel. 354/452-4067, www.textile.is, 10am-5pm daily June 1-Aug. 31, 1,200ISK adults, free for children under 16) is a quaint museum for fiber enthusiasts. On display are local crafts, Icelandic national costumes, looms of different sizes, and wonderful woolen products. The gift shop has a collection of cute wares, including wool for knitting projects and classically patterned Icelandic sweaters.

ÞINGEYRAKIRKJA

Þingeyrakirkja (Austur-Húnavatnssýsla, tel. 354/895-4473, 10am-5pm daily June-Aug., open by request rest of year, free), Þingeyrar Church, offers one of the most beautiful panoramic views in all of North Iceland, overlooking Húnafjörður bay. Þingeyrakirkja was built out of stone in Romanesque style and was officially consecrated in 1877. The land surrounding the church was the site of Iceland's first monastery, which was founded in 1133. An important place from the time of early settlement, Þingeyrakirkja is mentioned in the saga literature as a regional assembly site. Next to the church is a large circular structure, which is believed to be a judgment circle; it is listed as a heritage site. In the summer, tourists can enter the church and have a look.

Sports and Recreation

HORSE RIDING

Galsi Horse Riding (Arnargerði 33, tel. 354/692-0118, www.galsi.is) is a small, family-run business that offers tours for beginners and experienced riders. For an introduction to the Icelandic horse, Galsi offers a 20-minute lesson on how to properly saddle and sit on one. The course costs 3,500ISK per person.

Galsi also offers an easy1.5-hour ride in the scenic surroundings of Blönduós for 8,000ISK, or advanced riders can opt for a 4-hour tour for 18,000ISK.

Food and Accommodations

B&S Restaurant (Nordurlandsvegur 4, tel. 354/453-5060, www.bogs.is, entrées from 2,190ISK) is housed in a bright orange building in the heart of town. The menu is full of comfort food like burgers, pizza, and sandwiches, as well as meat and fish dishes. The restaurant is also family friendly, with an extensive children's menu.

Gladheimar Guesthouse (Brautarhvammi, tel. 354/820-1300, www.gladheimar.is, cottages from 18,000ISK) offers 20 self-contained cottages year-round that include private bathrooms, a patio, hot tub, barbecue grill, and proximity to the town's swimming pool. The cottages aren't luxurious, but they're clean, convenient, and won't break the bank.

Hotel Blanda (Aðalgata 6, 354/452-4205, www.hotelblanda.is, rooms from 18,000ISK) is located in a quaint house in the heart of town. The family-run guesthouse offers rooms ranging from singles to family rooms. All rooms feature simple, modern decor with TVs and private bathrooms. Breakfast is included.

Transportation

Blönduós is 58 kilometers northeast of Hvammstangi on Route 1.

The **Strætó** 57 bus (tel. 354/540-2700, www.straeto.is) runs from Akureyri, takes 2.5 hours, and costs 2,640ISK. Be sure to check schedules, as they change frequently due to weather.

Skagafjörður

With sloping mountains, a beautiful coastline, and chunks of glacial ice dotting the fjord, Skagafjörður's landscape is heavenly. Skagafjörður is often described as horse country, and that's very true. Horse farms and horse tour operators abound in the region—and it's the only county in Iceland where horses outnumber humans.

Skagafjörður is just 40 kilometers long and 15 kilometers wide, with the towns of Sauðárkrókur and Varmahlíð the main areas for tourism. Here, farms reign supreme and all residents are involved in agriculture in one form or another. Tourism has picked up in recent years, and there are a few museums, some historical sites, and plenty of outdoor activities to keep visitors entertained.

VARMAHLÍÐ

Tourists don't typically travel to the town of Varmahlíð, but rather through it, as it's close to where Route 1 passes through the area. There's a historic church to check out, but those who stick around for a few hours usually have booked a river-rafting or horse tour. The town has defined itself as a place for adventure activities over the past few years.

Sights

VÍÐIMÝRARKIRKJA

Just outside Varmahlíð lies **Víðimýrarkirkja** (tel. 354/453-5095, 9am-6pm daily June-Aug., 750ISK), one of the last remaining preserved turf churches in Iceland. Turf houses are representative of a very old building method. Víðimýri Church, which features a frame made from driftwood, was built in 1834 and has turf walls but timber gables both back and front. At the beginning of the 20th century, the church's fate was uncertain, but the National Museum of Iceland became responsible for its renovation and maintenance. The church still holds Sunday services at 11am, and tourists are welcome to attend. The GPS coordinates are N 65.5389, W 19.4710.

Sports and Recreation

HORSE RIDING

Skagafjörður is horse country. **Hestasport** (Vegamót, tel. 354/453-8383, www.riding.is) offers riding tours year-round on scenic paths along the region. The staff clearly has a passion for horses, and guides are well informed, patient, and excited to take you to some hidden gems in the area. Options range from one-hour to full-day tours, and the staff has all the equipment you need for your excursion—helmets, rain clothes, and all other necessary gear. Tours start at 8,500ISK per person.

RIVER RAFTING

Bakkaflöt Rafting (560 Varmahlíð, tel. 354/453-8245, www.bakkaflot.is) has been offering river-rafting tours for more than 30 years on the Austari Jökulsá River and the Vestari Jökulsá River, which are fed by the Hofsjökull glacier. Five levels of rafting classes range from easy to very demanding, based on an individual's level of experience. Tours are available May-September, last three hours, and cost 14,900ISK.

Bakkaflöt is 37 kilometers from Sauðárkrókur, about 300 kilometers from Reykjavík, and about 100 kilometers from Akureyri. Once you arrive in Varmahlið along Route 1, take Route 752 and follow that for 10 kilometers.

SWIMMING

The **Varmahlíð Swimming Pool** (560 Varmahlíð, tel. 354/455-6020, 10:30am-9pm Mon.-Fri., 10:30am-6pm Sat.-Sun. June-Aug., 9am-8pm Mon.-Thurs., 8am-2pm Fri., 10am-3pm Sat. Sept.-May, 700ISK) has two sections—one that is 12.5 by 25 meters for adults and a children's pool that's 12.5 by 8 meters. The children's pool is extremely popular among local families, and the slide is a favorite with kids. For adults, there are hot tubs and a sauna in the sports hall that's connected to the pool area.

Accommodations and Food

Located near Route 1, **Hótel Varmahlíð** (tel. 354/453-8170, www.hotelvarmahlid.is, rooms from 24,000ISK) is the only hotel in the area, and it's a lovely place to stay. The 19 rooms are cozy and modern with private bathrooms, TVs, free Wi-Fi, and gorgeous photographs of the area by locals adorning the walls. It is a comfortable spot with hospitable employees and an in-house restaurant serving yummy dishes. A breakfast buffet is included in the price of the room, and lunch and dinner

Skagafjörður harbor

menus focus on local ingredients found in the region, such as lightly salted cod heads, horse fillets, and tasty rhubarb cobbler made from local farm products. The **restaurant** is open 7:30am-10pm daily, and entrées start at 3,800ISK.

Information and Services

In the center of the village, the Skagafjörður **tourist information office** (tel. 354/455-6161, www.visitskagafjordur.is, 9am-6pm daily June-Aug., noon-6pm Mon.-Fri., 1pm-6pm Sat.-Sun. Sept.-May) has pamphlets about the region, Internet access, maps, and the ability to book tours.

Transportation

Varmahlíð is 286 kilometers northeast of Reykjavík on Route 1 and 93 kilometers west of Akureyri on Route 1.

Varmahlíð is well connected with buses to and from Akureyri. The **Strætó** 57 bus (tel. 354/540-2700, www.straeto.is) has daily departures from Akureyri. Trips take a little over an hour and cost 2,200ISK.

SAUÐÁRKRÓKUR

Sauðárkrókur is Skagafjörður's largest town, but don't let that fool you—this is a village of fewer than 3,000 people. The name means "sheep's corner" in Icelandic, but that's a bit misleading, as this remains more of a fishing town than a sheep-farming town.

Sights

SKAGAFJÖRÐUR FOLK MUSEUM (Byggðasafn Skagfirðinga)

The **Skagafjörður Folk Museum** (tel. 354/453-6173, www.glaumbaer.is, 9am-6pm daily mid-May-mid-Sept., 10am-4pm daily mid-Sept.-Oct., open by request rest of year, 1,700ISK adults, free for children under 17) is an extensive exhibition that includes several buildings. The main event is the farmhouse, **Glaumbær,** which was built circa 1879. It was constructed from stones, turf, and timber, and the structure has been maintained incredibly well. Builders made do with what they had, as the estate provided little rock suitable for building purposes, but there was plenty of good turf, so the walls of the farmhouse contain relatively little rock. The property consists of 13 buildings, each of which had its own function, ranging from a kitchen to a sleeping room. According to the sagas, the first known inhabitants of the Glaumbær farm lived there in the 11th century.

Also on the museum grounds at Glaumbær

Glaumbær

are two 19th-century timber houses, **Áshús** and **Gilsstofa,** that are typical of the homes built in the area at that time. Áshús contains exhibitions about the region and houses the museum's administrative offices. **Áskaffi** is a café housed in a timber house that serves traditional light Icelandic cuisine, including soup and sandwiches. In Gilsstofa, there are offices, an information center, and a souvenir shop.

Also on the property is the **Glaumbær church,** which was built in 1926. Earlier churches at Glaumbær had been built of wood, and most of them were covered with turf for protection against the elements. However, the last wooden church was blown down in a storm. The church that currently stands is a more modern structure with a concrete base and wood over it.

The **Heritage House** showcases exhibitions that highlight four 20th-century tradesmen's workshops. Also on permanent display are objects from the private collections of novelist Guðrún from Lundur (1887-1975), composer Eyþór Stefánsson (1901-1999), and artist Jóhannes Geir Jónsson (1927-2003). Guðrún's books are still read widely today in Iceland, and Eyþór's songs are sung regularly around the country. Jóhannes Geir's paintings, on display, show saga scenes depicting life in the 13th century.

From the Ring Road, head north on Route 75 to reach the Folk Museum. The GPS coordinates are N 65.6104, W 19.5036.

SKAGAFJÖRÐUR TRANSPORTATION MUSEUM (Samgönguminjasafn Skagafjarðar)

The **Skagafjörður Transportation Museum** (Storagerdi, tel. 354/455-6161, www.visitskagafjordur.is, 11am-6pm daily mid-June-Aug., 800ISK) is a great place to spend a little time inside if the weather is bad, admiring the large collection of classic cars under one roof. The makes and models of automobiles vary widely, and there's also some farm machinery on display dating back to the middle of the last century. Car fans will be pleased.

TANNERY VISITOR CENTER

Tannery Visitor Center (Borgarmýri 5, tel. 354/512-8025, gestastofa@sutarinn.is, Mon.-Fri. 8am-4pm and Sat.-Sun. 8am-noon May 15-Sept. 15, 11am-4pm Mon.-Fri. Sept. 16-May 14) is an interesting place for a stop. The center is the only tannery in Europe that focuses solely on fish leather, which is used for handbags, shoes, clothing, and a variety of high-end crafts. Here you can learn about the tannery process and purchase goods made from fish leather. Tours are available twice a day May-September and cost 500ISK.

Sports and Recreation

SWIMMING

The **Sauðárkrókur Swimming Pool** (Skagfirðingabraut, tel. 354/453-5226, 7am-9pm Mon.-Fri., 10am-5pm Sat.-Sun. June-Aug., 7am-8:30pm Mon.-Fri., 10am-4pm Sat.-Sun. Sept.-May, 600ISK) is a 25-meter outdoor pool with hot tubs, a sauna, and sun beds.

GOLF

The **Hlíðarendi Golf Course** (Rte. 75, tel. 354/453-5075, www.gss.is, greens fees 4,500ISK) is the longest nine-hole golf course in Iceland. It is located in picturesque country surroundings backdropped by mountains. Reserve a tee time in advance. The facility is open year-round, but call ahead for opening hours because they change frequently.

Food

Hard Wok Café (Aðalgata 8, tel. 354/453-5355, 11:30am-9:30pm daily, entrées from 1,800ISK) is an interesting Asian/pizza fusion restaurant that seems out of place in a small town in Iceland, but it works. The food is surprising, with choices including fish-and-chips, stir-fry dishes, hamburgers, pizza, and Asian-inspired sandwiches. The restaurant is a favorite among locals.

Ólafshús (Aðalgata 15, tel. 354/453-6454, 11am-10:30pm daily, entrées from 2,800ISK) offers the most elegant dining experience in town. The bright blue exterior looks cool and

inviting, and the interior doesn't disappoint. The feel is rustic and homey. The menu mixes fresh and local ingredients with flavors you may not expect. For instance, the pan-fried catfish with scallops, leeks, and sweet peppers is surprisingly delicious, and the lamb fillet with mushrooms and berry puree is splendid. Other options on the menu range from barbecue ribs to pizza and pasta dishes. There's something for everyone, and the prices won't break the bank.

KK Restaurant (Aðalgata 16, tel. 354/453-6299, www.kkrestaurant.is, 11am-10pm daily, entrées from 2,990ISK) is in an attractive building on the main street of town that dates back to 1887. Today, it's a modern, comfortable restaurant that serves casual food like burgers, pizza, and appetizers like mozzarella sticks and onion rings. It also serves meat and fish dishes, including pan-fried Arctic char, roasted lobster tails, and lamb fillet. The dinner buffet (5,800ISK) is quite popular and features appetizers, pizza, and fish entrées.

Accommodations

Hótel Mikligarður (Skagfirðingabraut 24, tel. 354/453-6330, www.arctichotels.is, rooms from 25,000ISK) offers 65 small rooms with private bathrooms, and not much else. There aren't a lot of amenities, but the location is convenient and it makes for an adequate short stay. Free Wi-Fi is available, and breakfast is included.

Mikligarður Guesthouse (Kirkjutorg 3, tel. 354/453-6880, www.arctichotels.is, rooms from 20,000ISK) does not get points for style—the decor is dated and the rooms are small and a tad depressing—but the rooms are clean and the staff is accommodating. Guests have access to shared bathroom facilities, free Wi-Fi, free parking, and a tasty breakfast included in the room price.

Hótel Tindastóll (Lindargata 3, tel. 354/453-5002, www.arctichotels.is, rooms from 30,000ISK) occupies two adjacent buildings. The original, a green house with a traditional look, has the distinction of being the oldest hotel in Iceland. It opened in 1884 and has undergone a number of renovations. The rooms are cozy, tastefully decorated, and have the feeling of home. In 2012, the second building opened, and its rooms are spacious, bright, and modern with flat-screen TVs, free Wi-Fi, and private bathrooms. Breakfast is included.

Transportation

By car, take Route 75, which is paved, from the Ring Road. Sauðárkrókur is 25 kilometers north of Varmahlíð.

The **Strætó** 57 bus (tel. 354/540-2700, www.straeto.is) has daily departures from Akureyri. The trip takes a little over an hour and costs 2,200ISK.

DRANGEY

Drangey is a small, rocky island, dotted with moss and grass, in the middle of Skagafjörður. It juts almost 200 meters out of the sea. The cliffs are steep. The island is home to pure natural beauty and thriving birdlife. Drangey is a favorite nesting spot for puffins and guillemots, along with razor-billed auks, ravens, gyrfalcons, and other seabirds.

Other than the secluded beauty and birdlife, Drangey is known for its inclusion in several sagas. Grettir Ásmundarson was said to have lived on the island for nearly three years with his brother Illugi. Grettir swam to Reykir (a farm) from Drangey to get equipment to make a fire, and his journey was pretty daring because the water temperature was so cold. However, in the year 1031, Grettir, his brother, and a slave were killed in his hut on the island.

During the summer months you can reach the island by boat from Reykir. **Drangey Tours** (tel. 354/821-0090, www.drangey.net) operates daily boat trips (11am June-mid-Aug., 12,500ISK adults, 6,900ISK children 7-14, free for children 6 and under). The excursion takes about four hours, and it's a wonderful way to spend the day. Be sure to check the schedule, as it may change due to weather. It is not necessary to book in advance.

Tröllaskagi

Tröllaskagi (Troll Peninsula), which lies between the fjords Skagafjörður and Eyjafjorður, has a gorgeous mountainous landscape, with some peaks reaching more than 1,400 meters above sea level. Several deep valleys throughout the peninsula were created by glaciers and rivers. Tröllaskagi offers opportunities for outdoor activities, including hiking and whale-watching.

DALVÍK

Dalvík is a small fishing town perhaps best known to tourists as the gateway to Grímsey and Hrísey islands, as the ferry to those places departs from the Dalvík harbor. But it's also a great spot for hikers up for the challenge of navigating the hilly and mountainous landscape around the town. Every year in late June or early July, there is a "hiking week" in Dalvík, during which groups get together and hike with a guide.

Sights

BIRDLAND EXHIBITION (Friðland Fuglanna)

Just outside Dalvík is the **Birdland Exhibition** (Húsabakki, tel. 354/466-1551, www.birdland.is, noon-5pm daily June-Aug., open by request rest of year, 800ISK adults, 400ISK children), a charming museum that is a great place to take children. The family-friendly spot allows kids to conduct experiments, learn about bird species, and check out an artistic bird egg display. It's a cute little museum, but not a must-see unless you're a real bird enthusiast. It's just a few kilometers south of downtown Dalvík.

SVARFAÐARDALUR NATURE RESERVE

The **Svarfaðardalur Nature Reserve**, in a valley just west of town, is about eight square kilometers of wetlands on the banks of the Svarfaðardalsá. The unspoiled environment is a perfect breeding ground for a number of bird species, including great northern divers and harlequin ducks. Be sure to watch where you walk to avoid nests. Wear rubber boots in wet weather. A popular trail begins from the Húsabakki campsite.

Dalvík

HERITAGE MUSEUM OF DALVÍK (Byggðasafnið Dalvík)

The **Heritage Museum of Dalvík** (Hvoli við Karlsrauðatorg, tel. 354/460-4928, www.dalvikurbyggd.is, 11am-6pm daily June-Aug., 2pm-5pm Sat. Sept.-May, 700ISK, seniors 500ISK) has an extensive collection of photographs and objects, including tools and home furnishings, that relate to the life and work of Dalvík's residents over the years. A natural history collection contains mounts of Icelandic mammals and birds, along with eggs, rocks, shells, and grass/moss. Other exhibits relate to renowned individuals that hail from the area, ranging from politicians to artists. The collection is vast and a bit quirky.

THE BEER SPA

The Beer Spa (Bjórböðin) (Ægisgata 31, tel. 354/414-2828, www.bjorbodin.com, 11am-9pm daily, 6,900ISK) is an exciting development in North Iceland, owned and operated by local brewery Kaldi. It features seven spa tubs (maximum two people) made from kambala wood that are full of beer for a relaxing soak. Once you arrive at the facility, a staff member welcomes you, explains the soaking process, provides you with a towel, and shows you to the locker room. After you secure your belongings and change into a bathing suit, you'll be shown to your bath in a private room. Guests have 25 minutes to soak in the beer bath, and then you head to a relaxation room for another 25 minutes. There are also two outside hot tubs requiring a separate entry fee (2,000ISK) that can hold 8-10 people. It's recommended you not shower for at least four hours afterward so your skin reaps the benefits of the therapeutic bath. It's also recommended you book your reservation in advance online. The Beer Spa is located about 12 kilometers southeast of Dalvík via Routes 82 and 808, both of which are paved.

Sports and Recreation

TOP EXPERIENCE

WHALE-WATCHING

Arctic Sea Tours (tel. 354/771-7600, www.arcticseatours.is) operates a three-hour whale-watching tour where you have a 98 percent chance to see whales or dolphins, according to the company. You might get to see white-beaked dolphins, minke whales, harbor porpoises, and, if you're lucky, a humpback whale or an enormous blue whale. At the end of the tour, you will have an opportunity to do some fishing, and the fresh catches (most likely cod) will be grilled back on land for all to enjoy. The tours leave from Dalvík harbor year-round and cost 9,900ISK per person.

HIKING

Dalvík is quite hilly, and locals love to hike. Every summer (late June/early July) locals and tourists gather for a **"hiking week,"** which features nine different guided hikes over nine days on which hikers explore the mountains along Tröllaskagi. Hikes range 2-10 hours and vary in difficulty from leisurely walks along the Dalvík harbor to steep mountain climbs. Shorter hikes cost 1,500ISK and longer hikes are 3,000ISK. For more information, visit www.dalvikurbyggd.is.

SWIMMING

The **Dalvík Swimming Pool** (Svarfaðarbraut 34, tel. 354/466-3233, 7am-8pm Mon.-Fri., 9am-5pm Sat.-Sun., 550ISK) is close to the town's campsite, so expect a crowd in the summer months. The facility has an outdoor pool, hot tubs, a children's pool, waterslide, sauna, and gym.

GOLF

Just seven kilometers outside Dalvík is the **Arnarholt Golf Course** (Arnarholt Svarfaðardal, tel. 354/466-1204, year-round, greens fees 5,000ISK), a nine-hole course said to have been built on a 9th-century burial ground. If that doesn't spook you away, you'll find a course that is well maintained, and carts, clubs, and equipment are available to rent. Be sure to call ahead for a tee time. An on-site restaurant is open 1pm-9pm daily.

Food

Gregor's Pub (Goðabraut 3, tel. 354/847-8846, noon-1:30am Mon.-Thurs., 9pm-3am

Fri.-Sat., 6pm-11pm Sun., entrées from 1,800ISK) offers a great casual dining experience ranging from soup to tender lamb fillets. The menu also includes hamburgers, sandwiches, and pizza. At night the place transforms into a bar where locals gather to grab a pint and catch up.

The Beer Spa (Bjórböðin) Restaurant (Ægisgata 31, tel. 354/414-2828, www.bjorbodin.com, 11am-9pm daily, entrées from 2,280ISK) is the Beer Spa's 75-seat restaurant. Enjoy a meal or a beer—selections are from local brewery Kaldi, which owns The Beer Spa—inside or, if the weather is nice, outside on a lovely patio that overlooks the mountainous landscape. It's a casual eatery with a friendly staff, and the menu includes nachos, french fries, sandwiches, and a soup of the day. The Kaldi Burger is the winner, topped with bacon, cheese, caramelized onions, and tomatoes. There's a kids' menu as well.

Accommodations

Fosshotel Dalvík (Skiðabraut 18, tel. 354/466-3395, www.fosshotel.is, rooms from 24,000ISK) is your standard chain hotel in Iceland. The 30 clean and average-sized rooms have standard beds, private bathrooms, and free Wi-Fi. The rooms have a bit of a 1980s feel to them with red carpeting and gold accents. An on-site restaurant serves breakfast (included in the price of the room), and guests have access to free parking.

Ytri-Vík Lodge (Árskógsströnd, tel. 354/466-1982, www.sporttours.is, cottages from 26,000ISK) offers cottages that range from accommodations for two people up to a three-story house for a large group. The cottages are made from wood and have fully equipped kitchens, roomy sleeping spaces, and all the comforts of home. The cottages all have decks, which have glorious views of the sea with mountains looming in the background. It's a gorgeous scene to enjoy while sipping your morning coffee.

CAMPING

The **Dalvík Campground** (Sundlaug Dalvíkur, tel. 354/460-4940, 2,200ISK) is close to the town's swimming pool. The facility is pretty basic, with an adequate cooking area and warm showers. The campground, which accommodates tents and RVs (with hookups), is open June-August. In addition to the pool, there is a nice playground nearby, as well as a football pitch and a basketball court.

Information and Services

The tourist information center is based inside the **Berg Menningarhus Cultural Center** (Goðabraut, tel. 354/846-4908, info@dalvikurbyggd.is, 9am-6pm Mon.-Fri., 1pm-5pm Sat.) and offers Internet access, pamphlets about the region, maps, and information about local sights.

Transportation

By car, Dalvík is 34 kilometers southeast of Siglufjörður on Route 82, which is paved; 18 kilometers south of Ólafsfjörður on Route 82; and 42 kilometers south of Akureyri, also on Route 82.

The **Strætó** 78 bus (tel. 354/540-2700, www.straeto.is) travels to and from Ólafsfjörður (440ISK), about 15 minutes away; Akureyri (1,320ISK), about 35 minutes away; and Siglufjörður (880ISK), also about 35 minutes away.

Most notably, the ferry **Sæfari** (www.saefari.is) provides daily trips from Dalvík to the islands of Grímsey (about 3.5 hours away) and Hrísey (a short 30 minutes away). Check the website for the latest timetable, as it tends to change.

HRÍSEY

Hrísey was established as a herring station and today is a major tourist draw for visitors exploring the north. Known as the "pearl of Eyjafjörður," the island, which is 35 kilometers north of Akureyri, has a lot of appeal for bird-watching enthusiasts. Hrísey is 7.5 kilometers long and 2.4 kilometers wide, and about 200 people call it home. Its population soars during the summer months when ferries full of tourists come to shore.

The attractions are minimal, but tractor rides on a hay wagon are quite popular, and there's a small exhibition on shark hunting. The **tractor rides** are about 40 minutes long and take visitors around the island. The rides can be arranged by calling 354/695-0077 and cost 1,300ISK; children are free. **The House of Shark-Jörundur (Jörundur Hus)** (Norðurvegur 3, 354/695-0077, www.hrisey.net, 1pm-5pm daily June-Aug.) is a small museum that houses objects related to shark hunting. The house was owned and built by Jörundur Jónsson, called Shark-Jörundur, in 1885, using timber from Norwegian ships that had run ashore on Hrísey. In 1917 the house was moved down the hill to its current site, but a statue of Jörundur is erected where the house originally stood.

The main reason tourists come to Hrísey is for the nature, and it's wise to budget one full day for the island.

Sports and Recreation

BIRD-WATCHING

About 40 bird species nest in Hrísey, and its populations thrive because hunting and egg collection are strictly prohibited and there are no predators on the island (such as mice, mink, or foxes). Hrísey is known for having the densest population of ptarmigans in Iceland during the nesting season. The southern part of the island has the best bird-watching opportunities.

Food and Accommodations

Verbúðin 66 (Sjávargata 2, tel. 354/467-1166, 4pm-10pm Fri.-Sat., entrées from 2,000ISK) has the distinction of being the only restaurant on the island. Most tourists choose to dine in Akureyri after a day trip, but if you're spending the night and want to go out for a meal, this is your chance. The menu is simple with choices like fish-and-chips, cheeseburgers, and soups.

Lodging options on the island are very limited. Many visitors opt to spend the day at Hrísey and sleep in Akureyri or Dalvík. If you would like to spend the night on Hrísey, **Wave Guesthouse** (Austurvegi 9, www.waveguesthouse.com, rooms from 12,000) is your chance. The guesthouse has four rooms—three doubles and a single—and the warm hosts make you feel like you're staying with relatives. It's cozy, with comfy quilts in each room. Rooms are bright with simple IKEA furnishings, and guests have access to a common lounge, a shared kitchen, shared bathrooms, and a gas grill.

CAMPING

The **Hrísey Campground** (tel. 354/461-2255, June-Aug., 1,400ISK) is small with adequate facilities. It's conveniently located next to the swimming pool. The campsite, which is in an open field, has showers, hot and cold water, and restrooms. The location in the center of town and close to the sea is lovely, but it can get quite chilly. Be sure to have appropriate gear for cold temperatures.

Information and Services

The **tourist information office** (Norðurvegur 3, tel. 354/695-0077, hrisey@hrisey.net) is open daily June-August, and you can book tours, buy tickets for the ferry, and get maps and information about the island.

Transportation

The ferry **Sævar** (tel. 354/695-5544, www.hrisey.net) sails between the island and the nearby village of Árskógssandur, just a few kilometers east of Dalvík. Sævar sails nine times daily June 1-August 31, and a round-trip fare costs 3,000ISK for adults or 1,500ISK for children 12-15. The ferry trip takes less than 30 minutes and is subject to weather conditions. Be sure to call ahead for current departure times, as they tend to change often due to stormy weather.

ÓLAFSFJÖRÐUR

Between Dalvík and Siglufjörður is Ólafsfjörður, a small and sleepy fishing village of fewer than 900 residents nestled under towering mountains and next to an active harbor. Ólafsfjörður comes alive during the summer months because tourists tend to pass through the town or stop to gas up before continuing onto Siglufjörður or Dalvík.

Food and Accommodations

Hótel Brimnes (Bylgjubyggð 2, tel. 354/466-2400, www.brimnes.is, cabins from 26,000ISK, doubles in guesthouse start at 18,000ISK) is the only hotel in Ólafsfjörður, and it's truly a lovely place to stay. The facility includes 11 rooms in a guesthouse and 8 self-contained Finnish-style cabins. The cabins are wood-paneled and comfortable with private bathrooms, a cooking area, and cozy sleeping quarters. Also, each cabin has a hot tub on the patio area that's great to enjoy in any season. Fresh linens and towels are included free of charge in the cabins; however, breakfast and laundry services incur an extra fee. The hotel rooms are much more modern, with bright white walls, neutral bedding, and pops of color in pillows and design accents. The surroundings are secluded, with mountains as your closest neighbors. The cabins and hotel have beautiful views. As for dining, **Brimnes's restaurant** (6:30pm-9:30pm daily June 1-Aug. 31, entrées from 3,000ISK) offers classic Icelandic staples, including fresh fish, lamb, beef, and chicken options. The food is not very inventive, but it's hearty and tasty. Breakfast is included in the rate of hotel rooms, but not cabins.

Transportation

Getting to Ólafsfjörður is pretty straightforward, as Route 82 (paved) connects with the town from the west and exits on the east as the central road that leads to Dalvík. From the north, Route 76 (paved) heads toward Siglufjörður. Be sure to check the weather forecast before heading out, as the winds and snow can be punishing in the winter. Ólafsfjörður is 17 kilometers southeast of Siglufjörður and 18 kilometers south of Dalvík.

The **Strætó** 78 bus (tel. 354/540-2700, www.straeto.is) goes from Akureyri to Ólafsfjörður, takes about an hour, and costs 1,760ISK. The same bus goes between Ólafsfjörður and Siglufjörður in about 20 minutes and costs 440ISK.

SIGLUFJÖRÐUR

Just a one-hour drive from Akureyri, secluded Siglufjörður is the northernmost town in all of Iceland. It's easy to fall in love with this beautiful harbor town. Siglufjörður's marina is home to much of the activity in the village, with bustling restaurants and a few town-specific museums focusing on the herring industry and the local music scene. For much of the year, the town of less than 2,000 is quiet, as it endures a sometimes-punishing winter with wind that feels like it's cutting right through you. That said, skiers are attracted to the region, and there are a couple of trails to enjoy. In the summer, however, the town comes alive with exhibitions, concerts, and packed coffeehouses and restaurants.

Sights

HERRING ERA MUSEUM (Síldarminjasafn Íslands)

The **Herring Era Museum** (Snorragata 10, tel. 354/467-1604, www.sild.is, 10am-6pm daily June-Aug., 1pm-5pm daily May and Sept., by appointment rest of the year, 1,800ISK) is one of the most well-presented museums in Iceland. Yes, it's educational and it's about fish, but it's anything but boring. The main exhibition is based in a large red building named Róaldsbrakki, a former Norwegian salting station that was built in 1907. Inside are interactive exhibits of photographs and film clips showing how fish was processed and salted, which was the source of the town's livelihood for generations. There's a boat inside, along with a lot of fishing gear and equipment. It's clear that great care went into creating this museum. If you're in town, this is definitely worth a visit.

Buying a ticket for this museum also grants you entry into the **Folk Music Center;** the **Icelandic Poetry Center** (Túngötu 5, tel.

354/865-6543, noon-4pm daily), which houses numerous books of poetry and hosts events in Icelandic; and the **Old Slipway** (Snorragata 10, tel. 354/467-1604, 10am-6pm daily), a boatyard that includes an exhibition on the 200-year history of boatbuilding in the town. There are displays of woodworking hand tools and of machinery—some nearly 100 years old.

FOLK MUSIC CENTER (Þjóðlagasetrið Siglufjörður)

The **Folk Music Center** (Norðurgata 1, tel. 354/467-2300, www.folkmusik.is, noon-6pm daily June-Aug., by request rest of year, 800ISK) is a charming two-floor museum set in what once was the private home of folklorist Reverend Bjarni Þorsteinsson (1861-1938). The museum showcases Bjarni's collection of classic Icelandic folk songs, along with interesting instruments, photographs, and film clips. You have the opportunity to listen to music that includes genres like hymns, the traditional chanting style called *rimur,* and nursery rhymes.

Sports and Recreation

SKIING

Iceland is not known for its skiing opportunities, but there are a few ski areas in the north, with the **Siglufjörður Skiing Center** (Tjarnargata 14, tel. 354/467-2120, 10am-4pm Mon. and Thurs.-Sun., 3pm-7pm Tues.-Wed. in winter, lift ticket 1,500ISK) being the best. Three lifts carry skiers up to the slopes, with the highest lift measuring 530 meters in length with a vertical rise of about 180 meters. The top of the lift is over 650 meters. The scenery is breathtaking. All the equipment you need is available to rent, and there are instructors on-site. Snowboarding and cross-country skiing are also possible. It's typically open November-April, but that can change due to weather; be sure to call ahead.

SWIMMING

The **Siglufjörður Swimming Pool** (Hvanneyrarbraut 52, tel. 354/467-1352, 7am-8pm Mon.-Fri., 10am-5pm Sat.-Sun, 600ISK) is a delightful place to spend a couple of hours when the weather is frightful. You will find a lot of locals and their children enjoying the pool. The facility includes a 10-by-25-meter indoor pool and a large hot tub outside.

Food

★ **Restaurant Hannes Boy** (Gránugata 23, tel. 354/461-7730, 5pm-10pm daily, entrées from 3,900ISK) cannot be missed. Literally. It's a bright yellow structure on the harbor that doesn't give much of a hint to what's inside. The interior is chic with roomy wood tables, antique furnishings, and a menu that rivals restaurants in much larger cities. The small courses, using fresh ingredients including mackerel, herring, and cod, are a great way to start the meal, and the main courses are hard to choose from because they all sound so delicious. The pan-fried salted cod with mashed potatoes and fresh tomatoes is exquisite.

Kaffi Rauðka (Gránugata 19, tel. 354/467-1550, www.raudka.is, 11am-10pm daily, snacks from 800ISK) is hands down the town's best place to hang out in the summer. The outdoor seating area is filled with tourists and locals sipping coffee drinks or cocktails or enjoying light meals. Inside, the two levels are decorated in a rustic theme with lots of wood and loads of comfort. The bright red building is hard to miss, and it's owned and operated by the same folks who own Hannes Boy next door.

Harbor House Café (Gránugata 5b, tel. 354/659-1394, www.harborhouse.is, 10am-1am Mon.-Thurs., 10am-3am Fri.-Sat., 10am-1am Sun., entrées from 1,800ISK) is a small harborside café that sells light meals and coffee for lunch and delectable seafood dishes for dinner. The seafood soup with mussels, shrimp, and lobster is memorable. The café is small and cozy, and the staff is very friendly. You will see a local or two with their laptop and a cup of coffee or tourists curling up with a book to get in out of the rain.

Torgið (Aðalgata 32, tel. 354/467-2323, 5pm-9pm Sun.-Thurs., 5pm-1am Fri.-Sat., entrées from 1,990ISK) is the best family-friendly option as well as the best place to grab a quick bite to eat before heading out to explore the surroundings. Tourist-friendly fare on the menu includes hamburgers, sandwiches, and pizza, as well as some seafood options.

Accommodations

★ **Siglunes Guesthouse** (Laekjargata 10, tel. 354/467-1222, www.hotelsiglunes.is, rooms from 18,000ISK) is the hippest place to stay in the north, and it attracts a lot of young travelers. The interior is darling, with vintage wood furniture and cool rugs, art, and wallpaper. Ten rooms have private bathrooms. It's a mixture of vintage and retro furniture that works well. An old-fashioned piano and fireplace is in the lobby area, and it's a great place to relax after a day of exploring the sights. Rooms are larger than average, with comfy beds and an antique flavor to the decor. Breakfast is included in the room price, and the in-house restaurant and bar is quite popular.

Sigló Hótel (Snorragata 3, tel. 354/461-7730, www.siglohotel.is, rooms from 36,000ISK) is a beautiful property along the harbor and close to major town attractions. Rooms, ranging from doubles to suites, are all bright and airy with private bathrooms. All rooms have a window seat overlooking the town, free Wi-Fi, a TV, and comfortable furniture. Breakfast is included in the price.

CAMPING

The **Siglufjörður Campground** (Gránugötu 24, tel. 354/460-5600, mid-May-mid-Sept., 1,200ISK) is near the center of town, close to the harbor and with beautiful mountain views. It has a cooking area and hot showers. The campsite is in an open field with little shelter and welcomes tent campers as well as RVs. The main museums and restaurants are all within walking distance.

Transportation

Getting to Siglufjörður is a trying exercise at times. By car, a tunnel links Siglufjörður, Olafsfjörður, and Dalvík. Driving through the one-lane, two-way tunnel can be heart-stopping, with cars turning into pockets on the side to let the driver going the opposite way pass by. Route 82 connects to Route 76, both paved, to Siglufjörður from Akureyri if the weather is cooperating. Akureyri is 76 kilometers southeast of Siglufjörður. Ólafsfjörður is 17 kilometers southeast of Siglufjörður on Route 76.

The **Strætó** 78 bus (tel. 354/540-2700, www.straeto.is) goes between Ólafsfjörður and Siglufjörður, takes about 20 minutes, and costs 440ISK.

Grímsey

About 40 kilometers off the coast of Iceland, Grímsey is a windswept and secluded island, about five square kilometers in area, that is as striking in beauty as it is difficult to reach.

Just 100 people reside in Grímsey, and those who remain come from hardy stock, battling arctic temperatures and isolation. Fishers brave the elements, including frost and storms and waves that could reach 15 meters high. It's not an easy life.

Tourists come to explore the tiny island, bird-watch, and experience 24 hours of daylight in the height of the summer. Night does not reach Grímsey until late July, when the sun sets around midnight, only to rise a short time later. The island can be explored in one day.

SIGHTS

Grímseyjarkirkja

Grímseyjarkirkja, the Grímsey Church, was built in 1867 from driftwood that washed ashore. The building was renovated and enlarged in 1932. The exterior is white with a reddish-brown roof. The highlight of the church is the altar painting, a copy of a Leonardo da Vinci piece, that was done by a local artist in 1878.

The history of the church site is interesting; one of Iceland's early Catholic bishops, Jón Ögmundsson, consecrated a church on Grímsey in the 11th century, dedicated to St. Olaf, the patron saint of Norway. At the time, it was said that there should always be two priests at the church who should lead a daily mass (two a day on special occasions). Today a vicar from the mainland visits Grímsey to serve in the church approximately four times a year.

The Cliffs

The cliffs on the east side of the island tower 60 to 100 meters. In the old days, the basalt cliffs served as a major source of food, as locals collected eggs along the rifts. It was a tenuous task: a rope would be lowered 60 meters down from the edge of the cliff while the individual collected eggs. There was a great risk that the rope would break or a large rock could break off, hitting and killing the climber. Today, the egg collection practice is safer and more modern, but the cliffs are a reminder of the past and their importance to the island's sustenance. They're also interesting formations and serve as a great backdrop when photographing birds.

The Lighthouse

Bright yellow and close to the cliff's edge, Grímsey's lighthouse is one of the most significant buildings on the island. It was built in 1937 and is situated on the southeast corner of the island. It was originally operated manually with a gas lamp that had to be turned on and off by hand. Today, the lighthouse is automatic and still plays an important role in directing boat traffic along the coast. Although the lighthouse itself is closed to the public, it's a popular place for photos, capturing birdlife and the cliffs in the background.

SPORTS AND RECREATION

Bird-Watching

Grímsey is one of the best spots in North Iceland for bird-watchers interested in seabirds. The high season for birding is from April, when birds migrate to the island to nest, to August, when birds depart the island for warmer weather. Bird-watchers will have

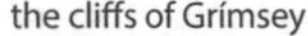
the cliffs of Grímsey

Crossing the Arctic Circle

Want to witness the **midnight sun?** That's when the sun remains above the horizon for a full 24 hours during the summer solstice on June 21. There's only one place you can experience this phenomenon in Iceland: where the Arctic Circle crosses the country's northernmost point, on Grímsey. (If you'd prefer nearly 24 hours of darkness, there's always **polar night,** on December 21.)

A small **symbolic bridge** crossing the Arctic Circle can be found at 66°33'N, north of Grímsey's airport terminal and next to Guesthouse Básar. Beside the bridge is a pole showing the distance to many well-known cities in the world, including London and New York.

Tourists who make the pilgrimage can buy evidence of their trip in the form of a **diploma** in the local gift store **Gallerí Sól** (Sólberg 611, tel. 354/467-3190, gullsol@visir.is), which is open Monday, Wednesday, and Friday during the summer months (June-Aug.). You can also reserve your diploma at Gallerí Sól by phone or email. Diplomas cost 1,000ISK. Those who come to Grímsey on a tour receive a diploma free of charge.

a chance to see arctic terns, black-legged kittiwakes, northern fulmars, razorbills, common guillemots, black guillemots, and murres. You can also see white wagtails, northern wheatears, and snow buntings.

The main attractions, however, are the adorable Atlantic puffins, as Grímsey is home to one of the largest colonies in Iceland. The birds, with their bright beaks and big personalities, are a delight to watch nesting and gliding along the cliffs. Please be aware of eggs and be careful not to disturb nesting areas.

Swimming

The **Grímsey Island Thermal Pool** (tel. 354/461-3155, 8pm-9:30pm Mon.-Wed., 2pm-4pm Sat., 750ISK) is situated near the airport and is a quiet spot to take a dip. You likely won't find crowds here, and the hours change often. For current hours, inquire at the tourist information office or at your guesthouse.

FESTIVALS AND EVENTS

Grímsey Day

Grímsey Day is an annual festival that takes place at the beginning of June each year over three days. It focuses on old traditions from Grímsey, like collecting eggs from the cliffs, as well as enjoying seasonal local food, music, and art. Visit www.grimsey.is for information and a schedule of events.

FOOD

Restaurant Krian (Hafnargata 3, tel. 354/467-3112, www.grimsey.is, noon-midnight daily summer, entrées from 2,400ISK) is only open during the summer, but it will open to accommodate large groups on request. The menu focuses on local fare and is chock-full of fresh fish and meat from seabirds, like pan-fried puffin. Standard options include sandwiches and hamburgers.

ACCOMMODATIONS

Guesthouse Básar (tel. 354/467-3103, www.gistiheimilibasar.is, rooms from 18,000ISK), next to the small airport, is an eight-room guesthouse just steps from the Arctic Circle. Literally. Rooms are simple and neat, and amenities include a common TV lounge and a fully equipped kitchen. Breakfast is available for an added fee of 1,500ISK, and lunch and dinner can be requested as well. The guesthouse is open year-round.

Guesthouse Gullsól (Sólbergi, 354/467-3190, www.grimsey.is, rooms from 5,000ISK) offers four single rooms and two doubles in a charming wood house, one of the oldest structures on the island. Rooms are small, but clean and neat, and it's the closest guesthouse to the main population area. Guests share bathroom facilities and have access to a fully equipped kitchen to prepare meals. It's open year-round.

INFORMATION AND SERVICES

In 2009, the towns of Grímsey, Hrísey, and Akureyri voted to become a municipality overseen by Akureyri. Tourist information and ferry fares schedules for all three towns can be found at the **tourist information center** at Hof concert hall by the harbor in Akureyri (tel. 354/460-1199, www.visitakureyri.is).

Safety

Weather can be your greatest enemy on the island, with unexpected wind gusts and horizontal rain. All children under the age of 14 must wear a life jacket when in the harbor area, whether they are playing, walking, or about to board a ferry. It is island law. The ferry staff provides life jackets at the harbor.

TRANSPORTATION

Sea

Sæfari (tel. 354/458-8970, www.samskip.is) operates ferry service between Dalvík and Grímsey five times a week in the summer and three times a week in the winter. It takes about three hours each way, and the ferry holds 108 people. Book in advance in the summer months; tickets can be purchased at the **tourist information office** at Hof concert hall in Akureyri (tel. 354/450-1050, info@visitakureyri.is). A round-trip fare is about 9,660ISK. Departure times from Dalvík in the summer are Monday, Tuesday, Wednesday, Friday, and Sunday at 9am; the ferry returns from Grímsey at 8pm. Check the website for up-to-date departure information. Schedules can vary due to weather.

Air

The flight from Akureyri to Grímsey is one of the most beautiful 30-minute airplane rides you will ever take. The jaw-dropping views of the landscape make the trip feel a tad too short. The landing is not for the faint of heart, as the small plane has to land on a miniscule strip of grass on an island that looks like a rock in the middle of the ocean. During the summer (June-August), **Air Iceland Connect** (www.airicelandconnect.com) provides daily flights to Grímsey from Akureyri for 27,000ISK round-trip. For current departure timetables and precise ticket prices, check Air Iceland's website. There are four flights a week September-May.

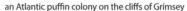

an Atlantic puffin colony on the cliffs of Grímsey

Akureyri

Akureyri is commonly referred to as Iceland's "second city," a moniker many of the town's 18,000 residents find amusing given its size. Akureyri has its own personality, and it looks and feels quite different from Reykjavík. Some might say Akureyri feels more low-key, more relaxed than the capital city. There are gorgeous gardens to explore, charming museums, paddleboats littering the fjord in the summer months, and a booming art scene. Akureyri has a tighter community than Reykjavík, and there is a lot support for local artists. Akureyri also boasts delicious restaurants and first-rate hotels, and its concert hall, Hof, is a must-see for architecture enthusiasts. Akureyri is a perfect place to base yourself while exploring Eyjafjörður, Iceland's longest fjord (60 kilometers).

Many tourists choose Akureyri as their home base when exploring the north, opting to spend nights in the town while booking day tours or putting some miles on their rental car to places like Húsavík and Mývatn.

Akureyri has gotten more traffic in recent years because it's becoming a popular stop for cruise ships, and word of mouth is spreading about what a charming and beautiful town this is. It's also surprisingly easy to get to. If you have the time, spend at least a couple of days here.

SIGHTS

★ Akureyri Botanical Gardens (Lystigarður Akureyrar)

The **Akureyri Botanical Gardens** (Eyrarlandsholt, tel. 354/462-7487, www.lystigardur.akureyri.is, 8am-10pm Mon.-Fri., 9am-10pm Sat.-Sun. June-Sept., free) are gorgeous and well kept; it's hard to find a better place in the city to take a stroll. The attraction is treasured by locals, and they're thrilled to share the beauty and tranquility with tourists. Known as one of the northernmost botanical gardens in the world, the public park opened in 1912, and flowers and plants made their debut in the park in 1957. Thousands of types of native and international flora can be found in the garden beds and nursery. While roaming the gardens during the summer, you'll see arctic poppy flowers, northern

a view of Akureyri

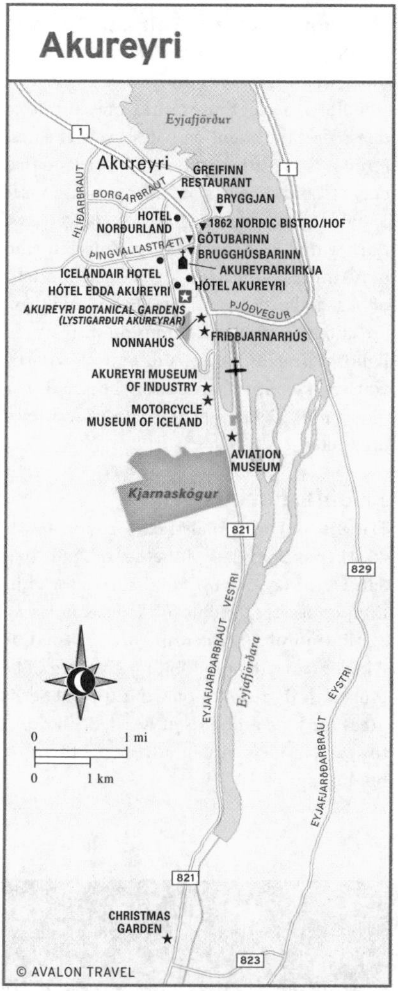

Akureyri

marsh violets, bilberry bushes, frog orchids, and hundreds of other species. The caretakers are always introducing new species to keep the collection fresh and eclectic. You'll also find walking paths, bridges, and a fountain in the gardens.

Akureyrarkirkja

The **Akureyrarkirkja** (Eyrarlandsvegur, tel. 354/462-7700, www.akureyrarkirkja.is, 10am-4pm Mon.-Sat., 4pm-7pm Sun. June 15-Aug. 15, free), the Akureyri Church, is in the center of the city, rising above it on a hill. The steep steps up to the grounds, with the church towering above, make for a great photo opportunity. The church was designed by state architect Guðjón Samúelsson, who delivered a design that is unique and Icelandic with stark white walls, wood pews, and a lot of windows. While the outside is beautiful, the interior is exquisite, complete with a 3,200-pipe organ and a large central window that once belonged to Coventry Cathedral in England. The church, which was completed in 1940, is open to the public in the summer. The Sunday service is at 11am year-round, and tourists are more than welcome to join. Please note that the church is closed to tourists when there are funerals or other ceremonies.

Nonnahús

Nonnahús (Aðalstræti 54, tel. 354/462-3555, www.nonni.is, 10am-5pm daily June 1-Sept. 1, 1,200ISK adults, free for children 17 and under), or Nonni's House, is a museum in the childhood home of Jesuit priest and children's author Jón Sveinsson (1857-1944). The house was built in 1850, and it looks like a nondescript black wooden house from the outside. Inside, however, you get a sense of the life and work of one of Akureyri's most treasured sons. On the ground floor, there is a collection of Jón's books, from about 40 different countries where his works were published. Upstairs, which is a little cramped, you can get a look at his bedroom and some personal artifacts. The house gets its name from Jón's nickname, Nonni, and it's one of the oldest structures in the town. A little gift shop sells his books in various languages.

Art Museums

Akureyri boasts a thriving art scene that rivals Reykjavík's. Painters, sculptors, and craftspeople occupy numerous private studios. The museums reflect the rich cultural landscape of the town, displaying varied works from some of the region's most important artists.

CENTER FOR VISUAL ARTS (Sjónlistamiðstöðin)

The **Center for Visual Arts** (Kaupvangsstræti 12, tel. 354/461-2610, www.listasafn.akureyri.is) comprises three art museums in three separate buildings. The first, the **Akureyri Art Museum (Listasafnið á Akureyri)** (1pm-5pm Wed.-Sun., 500ISK) hosts exhibitions in a variety of media, including landscape and portrait paintings, sculpture, photography, and other visual arts. The exhibitions focus on contemporary art. New exhibitions are revealed every eight weeks or so. The second building is the gallery **Kettle House (Ketilhús),** which serves as a space for local concerts and meetings, as well as art- and design-related events. Exhibitions in Kettle House are by invitation only and can include everything from painting exhibitions to performance art. The third building, **Melting Pot (Deiglan),** across the street from the Akureyri Art Museum, is devoted to young artists, giving them a platform to express and show their work.

MUSEUM OF ICELANDIC FOLK AND OUTSIDER ART (Safnasafnið)

For something a little different, try the **Museum of Icelandic Folk and Outsider Art** (Svalbarðsstrond, tel. 354/461-4066, www.folkart.is, 10am-5pm daily May 13-Sept. 3, 1,000ISK), one of those quirky museums that doesn't get the attention it deserves. The museum is the only institution on the island that collects and displays outsider art. It houses 5,000 works from local artists, as well as a library and research facility. You will find paintings, sculptures, drawings, models, books, dolls, tools, and toys. Every year there are about 15 new exhibitions on display, delighting locals and surprising tourists with art you won't see anywhere else on the island. The museum is 12 kilometers north of Akureyri on Route 1.

Friðbjarnarhús

Friðbjarnarhús (Aðalstræti 46, tel. 354/863-4531, 1pm-5pm daily June-Sept., 2pm-4pm Sat. Oct.-May, 800ISK adults, free for children under 15), Friðbjörn's House, holds an exhibition of 20th-century toys owned by Akureyri resident Guðbjörg Ringsted. The museum, in an old house built in 1856, is great for kids and kids at heart, with dolls, toy cars, models, and hundreds of other toys on display.

the Akureyri Botanical Gardens

Akureyrarkirkja

Aviation Museum
(Flugsafn Íslands)

The **Aviation Museum** (Akureyri Airport, tel. 354/461-4400, www.flugsafn.is, 1pm-5pm daily June-Aug., 1pm-5pm Sat. Sept.-May, 1,500ISK) is a small museum located at a hangar at the airport, dedicated to the planes and pilots who have flown the windy skies over Iceland. On display are a flying ambulance and Iceland's first gliders, as well as some relics from World War II, when U.S. and British troops occupied Iceland. There are lots of photographs and some accounts from pilots.

Akureyri Museum
(Minjasafnið á Akureyri)

The **Akureyri Museum** (Aðalstræti 58, tel. 354/462-4162, www.minjasafnid.is, 10am-5pm daily June-mid-Sept., 2pm-4pm Sat. mid-Sept.-May, 1,400ISK) has historical exhibitions including displays that feature nautical maps, 19th-century photography, and artifacts from everyday life in the settlement era. The exhibits also detail the region's geological background and its role in saga stories. The museum grounds have a beautiful garden.

Akureyri Museum of Industry
(Iðnaðarsafnið á Akureyri)

The **Akureyri Museum of Industry** (Krókeyri, tel. 354/462-3600, www.idnadarsafnid.is, 10am-5pm daily June-mid-Sept., 2pm-4pm Sat. mid-Sept.-May, 1,000ISK) displays relics from Iceland's industries, such as agriculture, fishing, and construction, throughout the years. Exhibitions include products, machinery, and photos of people hard at work in the region. It's a quaint museum with a passionate curator, but you can skip this if time is an issue.

Motorcycle Museum of Iceland
(Mótorhjólasafnið)

The **Motorcycle Museum of Iceland** (Krókeyri 2, tel. 354/866-3500, www.motorhjolasafn.is, 10am-5pm daily June-Aug., 1,000ISK adults, free for children 13 and under) is a small museum founded in the memory of local biker Heidar Johannsson. The museum has about 50 bikes on display, as well as photographs, objects, and gear related to Iceland's 100-year history of motorbikes.

Christmas Garden
(Jólagarðurinn)

If you're a fan of Christmas, do not miss the **Christmas Garden** (tel. 354/463-1433, 10am-9pm daily June-Aug., 2pm-9pm daily Sept.-Dec., 2pm-9pm daily Jan.-May, free), just a 10-minute drive from downtown Akureyri. The bright red house, which resembles a gingerbread house, has an astounding number of Christmas decorations, ranging from traditional to Icelandic-themed wares featuring the Yule Lads (Christmas elves). You can pick up a locally made trinket and buy some Christmas-themed candy or just enjoy the jolly atmosphere. A garden outside offers benches, local art, and a tiny place to buy waffles and coffee. It's a cute space.

The Christmas Garden is about 10

kilometers south of downtown Akureyri on Route 821.

SPORTS AND RECREATION

Fishing

Iceland Fishing Guide (tel. 354/660-1642, www.icelandfishingguide.com, tours 40,000ISK) provides guided fishing tours to lakes and rivers around Akureyri. You'll have a chance at reeling in salmon, trout, and arctic char, among other fish. The tours, available April-September, are suitable for beginners as well as experienced anglers, and you can choose from day tours or longer trips. The licenses needed for the tour are arranged in advance.

Hiking

While Akureyri is known as more of an urban playground, similar to Reykjavík, there are some hiking opportunities on the outskirts of town, namely around Eyjafjarðardalur, a wide valley surrounding the Eyjafjarðará River. To get information on trails and pick up maps, visit the tourist information center at Hof. Most hikes are moderate in difficulty.

Ice-Skating

Skautahollin (Naustavegi 1, tel. 354/461-2440, 1pm-4pm and 7pm-9pm Fri., 1pm-5pm Sat., 1pm-4pm Sun. Sept.-May, 1,000ISK) is a delightful skating hall chock-full of local families. If the weather is bad outside, visit the hall, rent a pair of skates, and join the fun.

Skiing

The **Hlíðarfjall** ski area (tel. 354/462-2280, www.hlidarfjall.is, day pass 4,900ISK adults, 1,400ISK children 6-17) is just a few minutes outside of town and offers more than a dozen well-kept trails. If you're dying to ski on a glacier, this is your chance. Bear in mind that the trails are 1,000 meters at the highest, so don't expect major vertical drops. A shuttle bus can pick you up at the tourist information office for 1,500ISK round-trip if you don't have a rental car. Other activities include snowboarding and cross-country skiing. You can rent all the equipment you need at the ski area. The season is November-April. Check the website for hours, as they tend to change due to weather.

Swimming

If you're going to visit one swimming pool in North Iceland, the **Akureyri Swimming Pool** (Þingvallastræti, tel. 354/461-4455, 7am-9pm Mon.-Fri., 8am-7:30pm Sat.-Sun., 900ISK) should be it. The fantastic facilities include two outdoor pools, children's pools and play areas, waterslides, a sauna, and a steam room. The pool is in the center of town and well-maintained, drawing both locals and tourists. Rain or shine, this is a great spot to relax and spend some time.

Golf

Akureyri Golf Course (Jadar, tel. 354/462-2974, greens fees 6,150ISK) is a wildly popular 18-hole facility that has the distinction of being the northernmost course in the world. The par-71 course loops around broad ridges and is quite scenic, with towering mountains in the background. Club and gear rentals are available on-site. Be sure to call ahead for a tee time. The course also plays host to the Arctic Open, held during the summer solstice. It's open year-round, but call ahead for opening hours because the schedule is changeable.

Bowling

You won't find many bowling alleys in Iceland, and that's what makes **Keilan Akureyri** (Hafnarstræti 26, tel. 354/461-1126, www.keilan.is, 11am-11:30pm Mon.-Sat., 11am-10pm Sun.) so special. It has eight lanes, a restaurant serving snacks and light meals, and several arcade games. It has an old-fashioned feel and is a local hangout spot for teenagers. A game costs 850ISK on weekdays, 1,000ISK on nights and weekends.

Tours

Saga Travel (Kaupvangsstræti 4, tel. 354/558-8888, www.sagatravel.is) is an Akureyri-based company that offers day tours from Akureyri and Mývatn, including horse-riding, lava cave visits, super-jeep tours, sight-seeing by bus, and hiking excursions. Day tours start from 19,900ISK.

Another Akureyri-based tour company is **Nonni Travel** (Brekkugata 5, tel. 354/461-1841, www.nonnitravel.is), which offers day tours in North Iceland to sites like Goðafoss, Dettifoss, Grímsey, and Lake Mývatn. Tours start at 9,900ISK.

ENTERTAINMENT AND EVENTS

Nightlife

Brugghúsbarinn (Kaupvangsstræti 23, tel. 354/896-6782, www.brugghusbarinn.is, 6pm-1am Sun.-Thurs., 6pm-4am Fri.-Sat.) is a small, hip bar in the city center that focuses on beer produced at the local brewery Kaldi. It serves light and dark beers, including seasonal beers around Christmas, Easter, and Þorrablót (the annual midwinter festival). Cocktails and coffee drinks are also on offer.

Götubarinn (Hafnarstræti 96, tel. 354/462-4747, 5pm-1am Sun.-Thurs., 5pm-4am Fri.-Sat.) is a wildly popular bar that has a great selection of beers and wines. It's situated in the city center in a nondescript green building, but the inside is warm, friendly, and crowded.

Græni Hatturinn (Hafnarstræti 96, tel. 354/461-4646), which means "The Green Hat," is a centrally located bar that features live music and DJs. The crowd tends to be on the younger side, and it can get very loud and very crowded on weekends. The opening hours vary depending on special events, but it's usually open 8pm-3am Friday-Saturday. Check local listings for concerts and events during the week.

Performing Arts

Hof (Strandgata 12, tel. 354/450-1000, www.menningarhus.is) is the striking building by the harbor that is home to Akureyri's big concert performances, including rock concerts, symphonies, and everything in between. Hof, which opened in 2010, also houses the restaurant 1862 Nordic Bistro and the main tourist information office. Even if you're not going to attend a concert, or pick up brochures at the tourist office, architecture buffs will want to visit this building for its unique round concrete design. The interior is amazing, with modern curved wood accents intertwined with metal. It's open 8am-10pm daily, or later when there is a performance.

Festivals and Events

Dedicated to winter extreme sports, **AK-Extreme** (www.akx.is) is an annual snowboard and music festival held in Akureyri over four days in mid-April. There's skiing, snowboarding, live music, and lots of fun.

FOOD

Icelandic

★ **1862 Nordic Bistro** (Strandgata 12, tel. 354/466-1862, www.1862.is, 11:30am-9pm Mon.-Sat., 11am-9pm Sun. summer, 11:30am-6pm Mon.-Sat., 11am-6pm Sun. winter, entrées from 2,500ISK) is housed in Hof, the main concert hall in Akureyri right next to the harbor, and the views from the restaurant's huge windows are stunning—you'll see the town, harbor, and mountains in the distance. If you're visiting during the winter and the forecast is favorable, it would be a lovely spot to view the northern lights. The restaurant is known for its brunch buffet, which features Icelandic delicacies including traditional fish gratin, smoked lamb, and marinated herring. There are also Danish style open-face sandwiches with a variety of toppings.

Kaffi Ilmur (Hafnarstræti, tel. 354/571-6444, www.kaffiilmur.is, daily 8am-11pm, entrées from 1,200ISK) is a delightful little café off the main street in town. You'll find soups, sandwiches, salads, snacks, and fresh pastries, along with a great cup of coffee. Situated in a two-story house perched on a small hill, it's a lovely, quiet spot to have a light meal in the heart of downtown Akureyri. The lunch buffet is very popular with locals and costs 2,290ISK. The buffet includes hot dishes, a salad bar, soup of the day, and fresh homemade bread. Kaffi Ilmur is especially great to visit during the summer when the large patio is filled with people enjoying meals and drinks, overlooking the town.

Seafood

Rub 23 (Kaupvangsstræti 6, tel. 354/462-2223, www.rub23.is, 11:30am-10pm Mon.-Fri., 5:30pm-10pm Sat.-Sun., entrées from 4,290ISK) is your best bet if you're looking for fresh and eclectic fish dishes. The restaurant, which also serves scrumptious sushi, specializes in cod, arctic char, blue ling, and salmon with a choice of "rubs," including citrus rosemary, Indian, sweet mango chili, Texas barbecue, and Asian fusion, among others. Meat dishes include lamb, chicken, beef, and minke whale with your choice of rub. Dinner for two, with drinks, can be pricey, but if you want a taste, the lunch menu (available on weekdays from 11am-2pm) is glorious as well.

Casual

Icelandic Hamburger Factory (Íslenska Hamborgarafabrikkan) (Hafnarstræti 87-89, tel. 354/460-2000, www.fabrikkan.is, 11:30am-11pm daily, from 2,195ISK) is the best spot to grab a hamburger in Akureyri. The family-friendly joint offers 120-gram hamburgers on a square bun, ranging from traditional beef burgers to more exotic whale-meat burgers. There's something for every meat eater here. The "surf and turf burger" is a sight to behold, with a beef patty, tiger prawns, Japanese seaweed, cheese, red onions, lettuce, tomatoes, and a garlic-cheese sauce. Other combinations include a barbecue burger, a lamb burger, and a Mexican-inspired salsa burger.

Bautinn (Hafnarstræti 92, tel. 354/462-1818, www.bautinn.is, 9am-11pm daily June-Aug., 9am-9pm Sun.-Thurs. and 9am-10pm Fri.-Sat. Sept.-May, entrées from 1,850ISK) is a typical casual eatery with plenty of tourist-friendly fare. You will find hamburgers, pasta, pizza, sandwiches, and soup on the menu, as well as more traditional Icelandic cuisine such as lamb, horse, whale, and beef steaks and an array of fish dishes. This is a popular place for locals as well as large tourist groups. The service is friendly and accommodating.

Nætursalan (Strandgata 6, tel. 354/462-4020, 8am-10:30pm Mon.-Wed., 8am-2am Thurs., 8am-5am Fri.-Sat., 11am-8pm Sun., entrées from 1,700ISK) attracts locals and tourists with its no-frills fast food. Stop by here for some decent fried chicken, sandwiches, and hamburgers. Because of its late

Hof concert hall

hours, the place attracts Akureyri's bar/club crowd on weekends, and it's usually packed with teenagers during the day in the summer months.

Greifinn Restaurant (Gléragata 20, tel. 354/460-1600, www.greifinn.is, 11:30am-10pm daily, entrées from 1,500ISK) feels like the Icelandic version of TGI Friday's. There are mozzarella sticks, hamburgers, nachos, soups, sandwiches, burritos, and even pizza. It's casual, family friendly, and quick with no surprises.

Strikið (Skipagata 14, tel. 354/462-7100, www.strikid.is, 11:30am-10:30pm daily, entrées from 3,500ISK) does a nice job with lamb and fish dishes, some more traditional, others with a Middle Eastern and Italian flair. The restaurant occupies one of the highest buildings in Akureyri, allowing fantastic views of the town. There's a lovely four-course menu (8,900ISK) available that really hits the spot—ginger and lemongrass shellfish soup, fresh fish of the day, and warm chocolate cake with ice cream for dessert. If you're after some fine dining that doesn't break the bank (by Iceland standards), this is a good option.

Asian

Indian Curry Hut (Hafnarstræti 100b, tel. 354/461-4242, www.curryhut.is, 11:30am-1:30pm and 5:30pm-9pm Mon.-Fri., 5:30pm-9pm Sat.-Sun., entrées from 1,895ISK) is a surprisingly wonderful Indian takeaway restaurant housed in a small shack-like structure on the main street. Don't be fooled, though; this is a great spot to get a tasty, affordable meal. The food is fantastic, with cooks specializing in perfectly spiced chicken and lamb dishes.

Krua Siam (Strandgata 13, tel. 354/466-3800, www.kruasiam.is, 11:30am-1:30pm and 5pm-9:30pm Mon.-Fri., 5pm-9:30pm Sat.-Sun., entrées from 2,050ISK) has all the main dishes you'd expect at a Thai restaurant, without many surprises. The mainstays are here, including spring rolls, pad thai, and beef and curry with coconut milk. But the lamb and fish are fresh, local, and divine.

Mediterranean

Bryggjan (Strandgata 49, tel. 354/440-6600, www.bryggjan.is, 11:30am-9pm Sun.-Thurs., 11:30am-10pm Fri.-Sat., entrées from 2,290ISK) is known for its perfect pizzas in just about any combination of ingredients you could imagine. You can go the traditional route with a ham and pepperoni pizza, or more exotic with a shrimp, tuna, onion, and tomato pie. If you're not up for pizza, there are soups, sandwiches, and starters, such as mozzarella sticks and nachos.

La Vita é Bella Ristorante (Hafnarstræti 92, tel. 354/461-5858, www.lavitaebella.is, 6pm-10pm daily, entrées from 2,940ISK) is a delightful Italian restaurant that serves all the traditional favorites: lasagna, spaghetti Bolognese, and even pizza and calzones. It's a cute, family-style restaurant with a friendly staff and casual atmosphere.

Cafés

Bláa Kannan Café (Hafnarstræti 96, tel. 354/461-4600, 8:30am-11:30pm daily summer, 9am-11:30pm Mon.-Fri., 10am-11:30pm Sat.-Sun. winter, 1,800ISK) is a charming café housed in a bright blue building on the main street, one of the oldest structures in the city. The interior is quaint and cozy, and the friendly staff serves freshly baked bread, pastries, soups, and sandwiches. The café tends to get crowded during lunchtime, when fresh soup is served with bread and butter. During the summer, locals and tourists sip drinks and soak up the sun at the outdoor tables. The central location and simple, good food make this place a winner.

Te og Kaffi (Hafnarstræti 91-93, tel. 354/540-2180, www.teogkaffi.is, 1,000ISK) is housed in the front of the Eymundsson bookstore on the main street. There's a decent selection of teas, coffee drinks, and fresh pastries on offer from this popular chain shop. You'll see locals perusing magazines while sipping on lattes.

Kaffi Kú (Café Cow) (Garður farm, tel. 354/867-3826, www.kaffiku.is, 10am-6pm daily, 2,000ISK) is a fun experience for everyone from solo travelers to families. The café is housed in a cowshed, and guests can order light meals, coffee, and cakes while overlooking the cows from a glass partition. It's located on a farm just 10 kilometers south of Akureyri, about a 10-minute drive via Routes 1 and 829.

Ice Cream

Ice cream is serious business in Iceland, and the holy grail is **Brynja** (Aðalstræti 3, tel. 354/462-4478, noon-11:30pm daily, from 400ISK). Icelanders are known to enjoy ice cream in any type of weather, and Brynja has been supplying locals with delicious creamy concoctions since 1942. In the summer, it's common to see a line outside the shop. In short, the ice cream is fantastic. Try a scoop or two.

ACCOMMODATIONS

Hotels

★ **Icelandair Hótel Akureyri** (Þingvallastræti 23, tel. 354/518-1000, www.icelandairhotels.com, rooms from 37,800ISK) is one of Icelandair Hótels' latest additions and one of the loveliest hotels in the north. The 99-room hotel is beautiful, with art and design accents touching every corner of the property. The lobby is rustic and Nordic chic with sheep and reindeer skins adorning gorgeous wood furniture. Rooms range from standard twins to family rooms and suites, and the clientele ranges from business travelers in town for a night to families staying multiple days. The hotel restaurant also doesn't disappoint; fresh and local ingredients go beyond traditional lamb and fish dishes. Breakfast is included in the room price.

Hótel Akureyri (Hafnarstræti 67, tel. 354/462-5600, www.hotelakureyri.is, rooms from 25,000ISK) is a posh boutique hotel close to the city center. The exterior looks quaint and old-fashioned, but the inside reveals modern and tastefully decorated rooms with standard beds, private bathrooms, free Wi-Fi, and free parking. For an extra fee, you can request a room with a beautiful ocean view. A standard breakfast buffet is included in the room price.

Hótel Edda Akureyri (Þórunnarstræti, tel. 354/444-4900, www.hoteledda.is, mid-June-mid-Aug., rooms from 16,380ISK) offers 204 rooms during the summer. The rest of the year, the hotel serves as accommodations for university students. For hotel guests, the digs are comfortable, with private bathrooms for 132 of the rooms (the rest have shared facilities), free Wi-Fi, and clean, minimalist decor. The rooms with private bathrooms are large with comfortable beds. The remaining no-frills rooms are small but clean and comfortable. A breakfast buffet is also available (2,300ISK adults, 1,150ISK children 6-12, free for children 5 and under).

Hótel Kea (Hafnarstræti 87-89, tel. 354/460-2000, www.keahotels.is, rooms from 29,600ISK) has modern amenities and first-class service. The 104-room hotel, which is a stone's throw from the Akureyri Church, features an elegant interior. Spacious rooms offer hardwood floors, big, comfortable beds, free Wi-Fi, satellite television, and private bathrooms. Some of the luxury stems from 24-hour room service and same-day dry-cleaning services. The hotel restaurant serves a hearty breakfast that's included in the room price.

Hótel Norðurland (Geislagata 7, tel. 354/462-2600, www.keahotels.is, rooms from 24,000ISK) is a 41-room hotel owned by the same folks as the nearby Hótel Kea. It's a more simple and affordable option, and the décor is dated, but the location is good, the staff is friendly, and the rooms are clean and adequate. All rooms have private bathrooms, free Wi-Fi, and satellite television. Breakfast is included in the room price.

Apartments

Hótel Íbúðir (Geislagata 10, tel. 354/892-9838, www.hotelibudir.is, apartments from 27,000ISK) offers seven self-catering apartments ranging from studios to three-bedrooms. Apartments are chic and modern with all the comforts of home. Guests get fully equipped kitchens and comfortable beds, plus balconies to enjoy views of the city and mountains.

Guesthouses and Hostels

Akureyri Backpackers (Hafnarstræti 98, tel. 354/571-9050, www.akureyribackpackers.com, private rooms from 16,300ISK) caters to the twentysomething traveler looking for a fun atmosphere and a clean place to stay. Rooms range from privates to dormitory-style accommodations. However, tourists tend to stay here for the facilities and the opportunity to meet fellow travelers. The hostel's bar tends to get packed, its restaurant frequented by young guests. Tourist information services are top-notch; there's a desk for booking tours, buying bus and flight tickets, and renting cars. A common cooking area allows you to prepare your own meals, and laundry facilities are available. Recommended for young travelers.

Guesthouse Brekkusel (Byggðavegur 97, tel. 354/461-2660, www.brekkusel.is, rooms from 14,900ISK) is a charming, family-run guesthouse that offers bright, minimalist rooms for solo travelers, couples, or families. There are singles, doubles, triples, and family rooms, some with private bathrooms. Guests have access to a fully equipped kitchen, free Wi-Fi, and a beautiful common garden where it's nice to drink your morning coffee or read a good book. Breakfast is included.

Apotek Guesthouse (Hafnarstræti 104, tel. 354/469-4104, www.apotekguesthouse.is, rooms from 20,000ISK) is located on the main street in Akureyri and is conveniently close to everything. The property offers single rooms with a shared bathroom, double rooms with shared and private bathrooms, and a 110-square-meter apartment dubbed "the penthouse." Rooms are clean, sparsely decorated, and ideal for a city-break stay. All guests have access to free Wi-Fi, a shared kitchen on the top floor with a dining area, and a lounge with a TV.

Camping

There are two main campsites in town. The first, **Thórunnarstræti Camping** (Hafnarstræti 49, tel. 354/462-3379, 1,400ISK), is in an ideal location right next to the town's swimming pool and a stone's throw from shops, restaurants, and museums. The facilities are good, with hot showers and a decent cooking area. The second campsite, **Hamrar Camping** (Kjarnaskógur, tel. 354/461-2264, 1,400ISK), is a little outside the city center, but it's larger and slightly less crowded. The facilities are similar, with hot showers and an adequate cooking area. Both campsites are open May-September, and both welcome tent and RV campers; hookups are available.

INFORMATION AND SERVICES

Tourist Information

The **tourist information office** (Strandgata 12, tel. 354/450-1050, www.visitakureyri.is, 8am-6:30pm daily June 1-Sept. 20, 8am-4pm daily Sept. 21-May 31) is based in Akureyri's main concert hall, Hof, by the harbor. It has pamphlets on tours and seasonal events, along with a gift shop that sells unique Icelandic wares. Just a few steps from the information center is the restaurant 1862 Nordic Bistro.

Medical Services

Akureyri Hospital (Eyrarlandsvegi, tel. 354/463-0100, www.sak.is) is North Iceland's largest hospital. The hospital provides general and specialized health care services and emergency care.

Akureyri Pharmacy (Akureyrarapótek) (Kaupangur, tel. 354/460-9999, www.akureyrarapotek.is, 9am-6pm Mon.-Fri., 10am-4pm Sat., noon-4pm Sun.) is close to the swimming pool and camping area.

If you have a medical emergency, dial 112 for help.

TRANSPORTATION

Getting There

AIR

Air Iceland Connect operates daily flights from Reykjavík City Airport, which take about 45 minutes. The flight offers spectacular views of the landscape when the weather is clear. **Akureyri Airport** sits at the base of Eyjafjörður, just three kilometers from the city center, and is a quite small commuter airport. It's a 30-minute walk or a 5-minute drive from downtown. Taxis can be hired at Hof, along the harbor, or arranged by your hotel or guesthouse. Check flight schedules and book tickets at **Air Iceland Connect** (tel. 354/460-7000, www.airicelandconnect.com, starts at 10,000ISK each way).

CAR

By car, Akureyri is 391 kilometers from Reykjavík on Route 1. In good weather, it will take you about five hours.

BUS

Bus travelers have a few options. In the summer, **Sterna Travel** bus service (tel. 354/551-1166, www.sternatravel.com) leaves from Harpa concert hall in Reykjavík Monday-Friday, bringing you to the Akureyri campground in about eight hours for 9,500ISK. The schedule changes often, so make sure you check the website for departures. The **Strætó** 57 bus (www.straeto.is) leaves the Mjodd bus station in Reykjavík a couple of times a week, reaching downtown Akureyri in about eight hours for 9,680ISK. Check the website for details.

SEA

Arriving to Akureyri by sea is becoming more common, as cruise ships are increasingly adding Akureyri as a port of call. Most cruise ships dock at Strandgata, a few steps from downtown Akureyri.

Getting Around

BUS

Akureyri is small and walkable, but if you want to hop on a local town bus, they are free of charge. The yellow buses run 6:25am-11pm on weekdays and noon-6pm on weekends and holidays. The schedule can be obtained from your hotel or guesthouse or from www.straeto.is.

TAXI

BSO (Strandgata, tel. 354/461-1010, www.bso.is) is the only cab company in Akureyri, and it provides service 24 hours a day. It's possible to get taxis that can take up to eight people, as well as special cars for people with disabilities.

Laufás

CAR

Parking in Akureyri is considered a sport by some. If you are a local with a personal parking space, you're in the clear. Tourists, however, must be mindful of where they park and how long they have left the car. To deal with the limited parking spaces, the town has instituted a system where you must retrieve a small cardboard clock that has movable hands from the tourist information center or local gas stations. Before you leave your car in a designated parking area, move the hands of the clock to show the current time and display it clearly on the dashboard. Most spaces allow for two-hour parking, but make sure. Also, parking attendants closely monitor the clocks, and if you are past the time, or the attendant cannot see the clock, you will be issued a fine of 15,000ISK.

OUTSIDE AKUREYRI

Laufás

Laufás (tel. 354/463-3196, www.visitakureyri.is, 9am-5pm daily June 1-Aug. 31, 1,200ISK) is an ancient farm estate that gives a peek inside what life was like in the region as far back as the settlement era, complete with turf-covered houses that you can enter. The farm is even mentioned in historical records soon after the settlement of Iceland (874-930). The church on the property was built in 1865 and contains a pulpit dating from 1698, and the rectory dates from 1853. There have been numerous churches built, and then rebuilt, at the site over the centuries. It's a lovely place to spend a couple of hours, soak in the scenery, and reflect on what farm living looked like in the 19th century. There's a café in the service center, along with a small souvenir shop.

The farm is 30 kilometers north of Akureyri and can be reached by Route 83.

Grenivík

Fewer than 400 people call Grenivík home, but the small, close-knit village is a popular place to stop to take some photos of the stunning fjord and mountainous landscape or to climb **Mount Kaldbakur,** which stands at 1,167 meters. Hikers rave about the view from the top, where on clear days you can get a glimpse of Hrísey Island. For hiking routes, stop by the tourist information office at Hof by the harbor in Akureyri (tel. 354/460-1199, www.visitakureyri.is). **Kaldbakur Tours** (tel. 354/837-3770, www.kaldbaksferdir.com) offers snowcat and sledding tours January-May, starting at 7,500ISK.

Goðafoss waterfall

Grenivík is 38 kilometers north of Akureyri via Route 83.

BETWEEN AKUREYRI AND MÝVATN

The stretch between Akureyri and Mývatn is a beautiful drive that includes the must-see Goðafoss waterfall.

TOP EXPERIENCE

★ Goðafoss

In a country full of spectacular waterfalls, what sets Goðafoss apart is the sheer width of the tumbling falls. White water surges over the rim, thundering down and crashing into rocks and water. The water of the Skjálfandafljót River falls from a height of 12 meters over a width of 30 meters. It's quite a show. Plan to spend some time here, walking along the perimeter, snapping photos, and taking in the beauty.

Goðafoss, which means "waterfall of the gods," derives its name from Iceland's long history with Christianity. In AD 1000, lawyer Þorgeir Þorkelsson made Christianity the official religion of Iceland. After his conversion, Þorgeir threw his statues of the Norse gods into the waterfall. The name Goðafoss was born.

FOOD AND ACCOMMODATIONS

Guesthouse Fosshóll (tel. 354/464-3108, www.godafoss.is, rooms from 22,000ISK) is just 500 meters from Goðafoss. The charming yellow house offers 21 rooms, including singles, doubles, and triples. Rooms are simple, bright, and cozy, with standard beds. Some rooms have private bathrooms, and guests have access to free Wi-Fi and free parking. It's also near a gas station and a grocery store, which is a plus. The guesthouse is only open mid-May to mid-September; book early, as rooms tend to sell out. **Restaurant Fosshóll** (tel. 354/464-3108, 7:30am-10pm daily mid-May-mid-Sept., entrées from 2,200ISK) is the restaurant on the ground floor of the guesthouse. It provides tourists with a good meal in an isolated spot. The cooks do a nice job with Icelandic staples like salmon, cod, and lamb fillets.

TRANSPORTATION

Goðafoss is located just off Route 1, 50 kilometers east of Akureyri and 49 kilometers west of Reykjahlíð. It's 46 kilometers from Húsavík via Route 85 and then Route 845.

Laugar

Laugar is a tiny stretch of land that is the closest town to Goðafoss. Granted, there isn't a lot to do or see in Laugar, but its proximity to Húsavík and Mývatn makes it a place to gas up the car and pick up supplies.

ACCOMMODATIONS

North Aurora Guesthouse (Lautavegur 8, tel. 354/860-2206, www.auroraguesthouse.is, rooms from 20,000ISK) is a five-room guesthouse that includes single and double rooms. Guests have access to a kitchen, free coffee, three shared bathrooms, a common living room area, and access to laundry facilities. Rooms are colorful, have large windows, and are minimalist. It's nothing fancy, but it's comfortable and close to nearby attractions.

TRANSPORTATION

Laugar is located on Route 1, about 65 kilometers east of Akureyri and about 35 kilometers west of Reykjahlíð. It's about 40 kilometers from Húsavík following Route 85 and then Route 845, both paved roads.

Mývatn Region

Mývatn is one of the fastest-growing tourist destinations in the northeast. Visitors are lured by gorgeous hiking trails, rich birdlife, activities along Lake Mývatn, and the soothing Mývatn Nature Baths. The region has been shaped over time by punishing volcanic eruptions. It's a place to soak in the rugged landscape, with its vast lava fields, gigantic craters, soaring mountains, and, of course, the 36.5-square-kilometer lake that is home to scores of bird and fish species.

The Mývatn region is perfect for independent travelers who prefers to roam on their own time. Jump into a rental car and discover everything from the charming town of **Reykjahlíð,** on the northeastern shore of Lake Mývatn, to roaring waterfalls, volcanic craters, and black lava rock pillars. Alternatively, tours in the region include birdwatching, whale-watching, and jeep tours.

SIGHTS

TOP EXPERIENCE

★ Mývatn Nature Baths (Jarðböðin)

Despite obvious comparisons to the Blue Lagoon, the **Mývatn Nature Baths** (tel. 354/464-4411, www.myvatnnaturebaths.is, 9am-midnight daily May 15-Sept. 30, noon-10pm daily Oct. 1-May 14, 4,300ISK), three kilometers east of Reykjahlíð, have their own unique personality and atmosphere. There's more room to wade and fewer people in the locker rooms, and the steam baths are far from full.

The bathing experience is heavenly, soothing your skin and relaxing every inch of your body. The views of the landscape are striking, with the volcanic crater of Hverfjall and the edge of Lake Mývatn in the background.

The milky-blue water, which stands at 36°C (96.8°F), comes from the National Power Company's borehole in Bjarnaflag. The water temperature reaches a scorching 130°C (266°F) when it arrives to the basin next to the lagoon, but it cools significantly before filtering into the glorious man-made hot spring. Overall, the basin and lagoon hold about 2.5 million liters of water.

The bottom of the lagoon is covered by gravel and sand, and it contains a large amount of minerals. Because of its chemical composition, vegetation and bacteria are not a problem. There is some sulfur in the water, which is beneficial for skin problems such as eczema and psoriasis, as well as respiratory issues. However, it's not a good idea to wear silver or brass jewelry in the water, as the pieces can be damaged by the sulfur.

Kaffi Kvika (11am-9pm daily June-Aug., noon-8pm daily Sept.-May) serves light, healthy meals overlooking the lagoon including soup, sandwiches, pastries, and a salad bar. Beer and wine are available for purchase, and you're allowed to bring drinks to the lagoon, provided you have a wristband.

Dimmuborgir

Dimmuborgir, which means "dark cities" or "dark castles," comprises interesting rock formations jutting out of the ground, resembling a fort guarding an ancient city. The black lava pillars were born from a collapsed lava tube created by a large volcanic eruption more than 2,000 years ago. Scientists say that lava pooled over a small lake in the region, and as it crossed wet land the water started to boil; the vapor emitting from the lava then formed pillars, some of which reach several meters in height. There's a popular photo opportunity in the structure known as Kirkjan (the Church), which is a curved lava tube resembling a steeple. While it's tempting to scale many of the structures, climbing is strictly prohibited.

To get there, head south from Húsavík, turning onto Route 87; keep straight once you reach the first junction at Lake Mývatn and then follow it around the eastern edge. It is about a 45-minute drive from Húsavík.

Hverfjall

Hverfjall (or Hverfell, depending on which Icelander you ask) is the largest tephra crater in the Mývatn region. Tephra craters are created from volcanic debris. The crater is striking because it's almost a perfect circle, and considering its size (140 meters deep and 1 kilometer across), it's quite impressive. Scientists have said that the crater was formed after repeated eruptions over 2,500 years ago. There are two walking paths around the rim, one on the north side and one on the south, and it takes about 15 minutes to climb. It gives you a good view of the landscape.

Take Route 1 to get to Hverfjall. It's 15 kilometers east of Mývatn off of Route 848, about a 20-minute drive. The GPS coordinates are N 65.6061, W 16.8751.

Krafla

The Krafla lava fields are home to **Víti** (Hell), one of the best-known craters in Iceland. Víti is huge, about 300 meters in diameter, exposing interesting formations that resulted from lava flows and hydrologic forces. The crater was formed during a massive volcanic eruption in 1724. The eruption continued for five years, and Víti's bubbling cauldron of mud boiled for more than a century after that. The area is another reminder of how active this island has been, and continues to be, with spectacular eruptions continually reshaping of land. Today you can visit this region to get a glimpse of the crater, hike around the area, and take in the very-much-alive hot springs and mud pools.

Krafla is 24 kilometers northeast of Mývatn off of Route 1, about a 25-minute drive. Víti is situated near Krafla, and a paved road leads up to it from Route 1. The car park area is right next to the rim; you should spend at least an hour walking around the rim.

Námaskarð

Námaskarð is a big draw for tourists because of its sheer otherworldly atmosphere. The yellow and brown colors of the clay, along with the gray mud pools, make it look like a movie scene from another planet. A path loops around the region; be sure to stay on it for safety reasons, as the mud pools can reach temperatures of 100°C (212°F). The area is secluded and the smell of sulfur can be a bit much for some, but it's worth a visit.

Mývatn Nature Baths

Mývatn Region

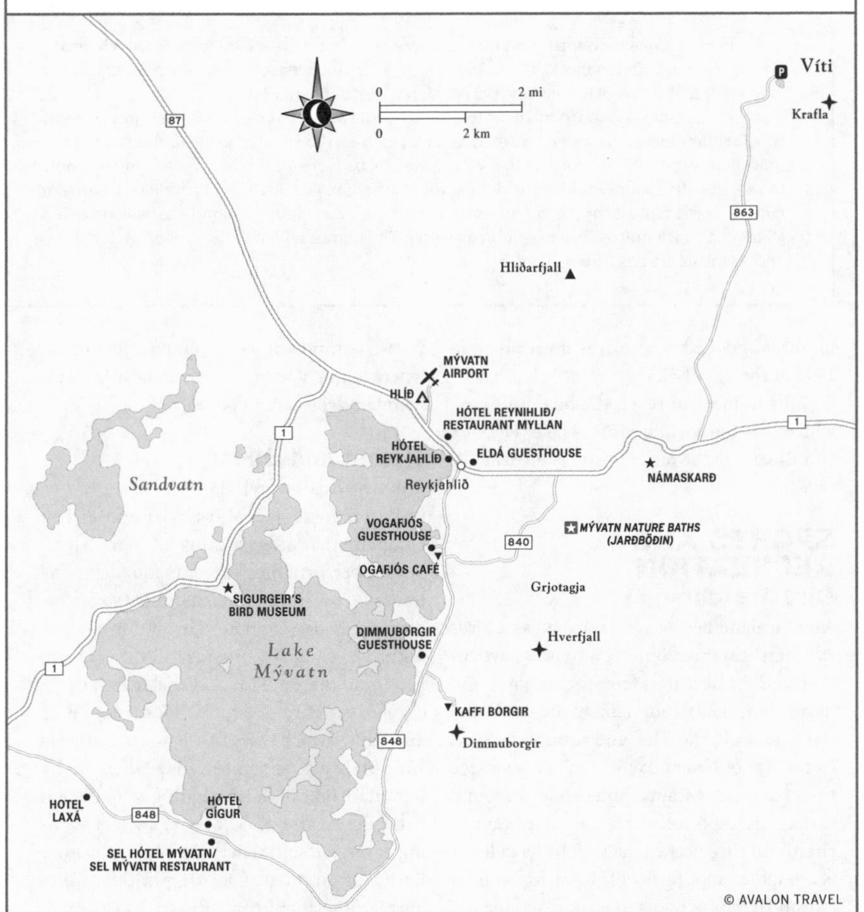

Námaskarð is 15 kilometers northeast of Lake Mývatn on Route 1.

Sigurgeir's Bird Museum (Fuglasafn Sigurgeirs)

Sigurgeir's Bird Museum (Ytri-Neslond, tel. 354/464-4477, www.fuglasafn.is, noon-5pm daily mid-late May, 9am-6pm daily June-late Aug., noon-5pm daily late Aug.-Oct., 2pm-4pm daily Nov.-mid-May, 1,200ISK adults, 600ISK children 7-14, free for children 6 and under) is Iceland's largest privately owned mounted bird collection. It is at the farm Ytri-Neslond near Lake Mývatn. The museum features about 180 species of birds and more than 300 birds in total, ranging from goldeneye ducks to puffins. The birds are in glass displays, and they are labeled with information about the species. An on-site café serves coffee and snacks. Binoculars are available to use for bird-watching outside the museum. The museum was created in honor of Mývatn resident Sigurgeir Stefansson, who had a passion

The Mysterious *Marimo* of Mývatn

A rare form of algae is disappearing from Lake Mývatn. The algae, called *marimo* (which means "water plant ball" in Japanese), is a round spongy moss that collects on the bottom of lakes. It exists only in this part of Iceland and parts of Japan, Scotland, and Estonia.

Iceland's *marimo* can be found in water that is about two meters deep, and they grow at most to 12 centimeters in diameter. The *marimo* in Mývatn was discovered in 1978. You can see the moss gently roll back and forth in the waves. The lake balls are a curiosity, as they can grow only in very specific conditions with the right amount of sediment, certain light conditions, and lake current. Perhaps most curious, for non-scientists, is the Icelandic translation: Lake balls are called *kúluskítur,* which means "ball of shit" in Icelandic. The numbers of *marimo* have been declining, and scientists are unsure why.

for birds and died tragically in an accident in 1999 at the age of 37.

Take Route 1 to reach the bird museum, which is on the north side of the lake. The GPS coordinates of the museum are N 65.6288, W 16.9951.

SPORTS AND RECREATION

Bird-Watching

All of Iceland has been established as a bird-watchers' paradise, but Mývatn gets particular props for hosting a few species not found in much of the island, namely the duck species—gadwall, shoveler, and common scoter. In the bay of Neslandavík, you can see large flocks of greater scaup, Eurasian wigeon, and tufted duck species, as well as common pochard and ring-necked ducks. The Laxa River is a popular spot for locals to bring binoculars and a pair of boots to walk along the perimeter in search of harlequin ducks. Other waterbirds that are common to the area include the red-breasted merganser, whooper swan, and great northern diver. Short-eared owls are seen rarely. Keep your eyes peeled.

The best season for bird-watching is from the beginning of May to the middle of August, as that's the high nesting season, but some species, such as geese, remain in the autumn. Remember that the lake is a protected area, and some regions are off-limits to cars. Stop by the **tourist information office** in Reykjahlíð (Hraunvegi 8, tel. 354/464-4390, www.visitmyvatn.is) for maps and tips on where to catch certain species, and always remember to be careful of nests.

Hiking and Biking

Hike and Bike (tel. 354/899-4845, www.hikeandbike.is) is a Mývatn-based tourism company that offers a range of tours April-September, including three- to four-hour day tours and overnight tours that allow you to explore the region by mountain bike, by foot, or both. The company provides all the gear you need, and there are tours available for all levels of experience. A popular tour is the "Bike and Bath," which is about 4-5 hours and costs 18,990ISK per person. A guide takes you by mountain bike to sites including an old steam bath, the fissure of Grjotagja, ancient bathing caves, and ultimately the Mývatn Nature Baths for an hour of soaking in the milky-blue, geothermally heated water.

Jeep Tours

Sel Hótel Mývatn (tel. 354/464-4164, www.myvatn.is) offers action-packed super-jeep tours year-round. They range from riding on mountain tracks in the summer to navigating on top of fresh winter snow. Tours take you to the rock formations of Dimmuborgir, the crater at Hverfjall, and some hidden places that the local tour guide knows well. It's a great option to get out and explore nature with an experienced guide who has all the safety equipment needed to handle any difficult weather conditions. Tours are about three hours and cost 23,000ISK per person.

Swimming

If you aren't up for a dip in the Mývatn Nature Baths, but want to swim, the **Mývatn Swimming Pool** (Mývatnssveit, tel. 354/464-4225, 8am-8pm Mon.-Fri., 10am-7pm Sat.-Sun., 600ISK) is just outside Reykjahlíð. The GPS coordinates are N 65.6431, W 16.8932.

FOOD

Restaurant Myllan (Kísilvegur, Reykjahlíð, tel. 354/464-4170, 6:30pm-9pm daily, www.reynihlid.is, entrées from 4,000ISK), located in Hótel Reynihlíð, is the fanciest restaurant in Mývatn. The food is fresh and hearty, with dishes like lamb shoulder with oven-baked vegetables, Icelandic fish stew, and fried char with almonds, grapes, and hollandaise sauce.

Gamli Bistro (Gamli Baerinn) (Mývatnssveit, tel. 354/464-4170, www.myvatnhotel.is, 10am-11pm daily, entrées from 1,900ISK) is a cozy countryside café that offers soups, sandwiches, burgers, coffee, and cakes. Its Icelandic meat soup is hearty and hits the spot.

Sel Mývatn Restaurant (Skútustaðir, Mývatn, tel. 354/464-4164, www.myvatn.is, noon-2pm and 6pm-9pm daily summer, 6pm-9pm daily winter, entrées from 2,590ISK), at Sel Hótel Mývatn, is your best bet for a traditional Icelandic dinner buffet featuring island delicacies, such as smoked trout and marinated salmon, and more exotic dishes, such as shark, blood pudding, smoked lamb, liver pudding, and sheep's head jelly. But if you're not after something so exotic, don't fret, because there are plenty of fish and lamb dishes on the menu.

Kaffi Borgir (tel. 354/464-1144, www.kaffiborgir.is, entrées from 2,100ISK) is conveniently situated near the Mývatn Nature Baths and Dimmuborgir, which means this place can get crowded in the summer months. It's a cafeteria-style café that serves hot meals like lamb or fish, coffee, and pastries. It's good for a quick bite to eat. It's open daily 10am-9:30pm from April until September and is closed the remainder of the year.

Vogafjós Café (Vogar, tel. 354/464-4303, www.vogafjos.is, 11am-10pm daily summer, 10am-9:30pm daily winter, entrées from 2,600ISK) is a cute and quirky café based in a dairy barn on a family farm. While enjoying your meal of sandwiches, salads, or hot food, you can watch dairy cows get milked from the other side of a glass partition (milkings are at 7am and 6pm). Many of the ingredients are locally sourced, including the beef; the hamburger you order will literally be farm-to-table. And try the fresh mozzarella. The entire experience is worthwhile, from the cows to the quality food to the beautiful landscapes you see from the café's huge windows.

ACCOMMODATIONS

Hotels

Fosshotel Mývatn (Grímsstaðir, tel. 354/453-0000, www.fosshotel.is, rooms from 30,000ISK) opened its doors in July 2017, adding 92 rooms to the popular region. The exterior blends into the surrounding nature thanks to its turf roof, muted colors, and wood design. Rooms are bright and spacious with modern furnishings and wood floors. Options range from standard doubles to suites with access to an outdoor hot tub. Breakfast is included in the rate of the room.

Hótel Reynihlíð (Kísilvegur, Reykjahlíð, tel. 354/464-4170, www.myvatnhotel.is, rooms from 32,000ISK) is a smart and modern hotel with spacious rooms, killer views, and an accommodating staff. Rooms have big, comfy beds and huge windows overlooking gorgeous scenery. The hotel restaurant serves up a delicious breakfast that is included in the room price. And the dinner menu has all the lamb and fish dishes you'd expect.

Hótel Reykjahlíð (Kísilvegur, Reykjahlíð, tel. 354/464-4142, www.myvatnhotel.is, rooms from 26,000ISK) offers nine rooms on two floors. The four rooms on the top floor are larger and slightly nicer than the five on the ground floor, but overall, this is a great place to stay in town. Rooms are neat and clean, furnished in a tasteful manner, and overlooking the lake. Breakfast is included, and guests are invited to have coffee or tea any time of day in the restaurant, free of charge.

Sel Hótel Mývatn (Skútustaðir, Mývatn, tel. 354/464-4164, www.myvatn.is, rooms from 39,000ISK) is halfway between modern and quaint. The hotel's exterior is a gray block structure that looks fairly new, while the rooms boast vintage furniture, dainty linens, and all the comforts of home. The in-house restaurant does a fantastic Icelandic dinner buffet.

Hótel Gígur-Kea Hotels (Skútustaðir, tel. 354/464-4455, www.keahotels.is, rooms from 29,000ISK, mid-May-Sept.) is in a dynamite location near the southern shore of Lake Mývatn. The 37 rooms, mostly doubles, have private bathrooms, free Wi-Fi, free parking, and an in-house restaurant. The hotel feels a bit dated, especially the restaurant, but it's clean, centrally located, and a convenient place to spend a couple of nights. The staff is friendly, and breakfast is included in the room price.

★ **Hotel Laxá** (Olnbogaás, tel. 354/464-1900, www.hotellaxa.is, rooms from 39,000ISK) is a stylish addition to Myvatn. The 80-room hotel is modern, convenient to the major attractions in the region, and gets high points for service. During the winter months, guests can request northern lights "wake-up calls" if the natural phenomenon makes an appearance. Rooms are spacious, with large windows, wood furnishings, and modern accents. There is also an in-house restaurant and bistro bar for lighter fare.

Guesthouses

Dimmuborgir Guesthouse (Geiteyjarströnd 1, Mývatn, tel. 354/464-4210, www.dimmuborgir.is, rooms from 25,000ISK) offers eight double rooms with private bathrooms, as well as nine cottages. Rooms are bright and clean with simple furnishings and free Wi-Fi. A living room has a television. Cottages are roomy and wood-paneled, and half have private bathrooms. The owners are warm and friendly and have a long tradition of smoking trout in a nearby smokehouse that they love to show guests. Breakfast is included.

Eldá Guesthouse (Helluhraun 15, Mývatn, tel. 354/464-4200, www.elda.is, rooms from 28,000ISK) offers rooms in several small houses with a breakfast buffet included in the room price. It's possible to rent an entire house that has a fully equipped kitchen, private bathrooms, and all the comforts of home.

Vogafjós Guesthouse (Vogafjós Vegur, Mývatn, tel. 354/464-4303, www.vogafjos.is, rooms from 26,000ISK) has been owned and operated by the same family for more than a century. With spectacular views of mountains and lava fields, the guesthouse offers 26 rooms. All have private bathrooms, and breakfast is included.

Camping

There are a couple of camping opportunities around Mývatn, but it's important to note that they become quite full during the summer months.

The **Bjarg** campsite (tel. 354/464-4240, May-Sept., 1,700ISK) is situated perfectly, right next to the lakeshore of Lake Mývatn near Reykjahlíð. It's close to shops, the tourist information office, and excellent hiking trails. The facilities are top-notch, with laundry facilities, a cooking area to prepare meals, hot showers, and a place to rent bicycles. It's in an open field with no shelter. Tents and RVs are welcome.

Hlíð (tel. 354/464-4103, www.myvatnaccommodations.is, 1,700ISK) is a campsite that includes cottages for rent. The camping section is on the northern shore of Lake Mývatn, and it's a short five-minute walk to the grocery store and tourist information office. It's in an open field with no shelter, in a pretty space close to the lake. It has an adequate cooking area, warm showers, and an area for tents and caravans. There are laundry facilities on-site. Two-bedroom cottages cost 40,000ISK per night and are available June-early September.

INFORMATION AND SERVICES

Mývatn's **tourist information center** (Hraunvegi 8, Reykjahlíð, tel. 354/464-4390, www.visitmyvatn.is, 9am-4pm daily May, 7:30am-6pm daily June-Aug., 9am-4pm daily Sept., 9am-noon Mon.-Fri. Oct.-Apr.) offers Internet access, pamphlets about the region, and the chance to book tours in the area.

TRANSPORTATION

It's best to have a car to explore the region or to book a tour from Akureyri.

By car, Lake Mývatn is 92 kilometers east of Akureyri on Route 1. The town of Reykjahlíð connects to paved Route 848, which follows Lake Mývatn's northern edge. The lake's perimeter is about 40 kilometers.

Strætó (www.straeto.is) has departures on the 56 bus from Akureyri and Egilsstaðir in the east. It's about one hour from Akureyri and two hours from Egilsstaðir. Be sure to check the website for current timetables. Buses stop in Reykjahlíð and cost 2,640ISK.

Húsavík

Húsavík has transformed itself from a placid small town with little appeal to the outside world to a must-see destination for tourists interested in some of the best whale-watching opportunities on the island. Húsavík is home to fewer than 3,000 full-time residents, but in the summer the numbers spike dramatically as Icelanders from other towns, tourists coming in on bus tours, and independent travelers converge on Húsavík's harbor. The main draw for tourists is, of course, whale-watching tours, but the charm of the small town, with its tasty restaurants and classic Icelandic hospitality, makes this a destination to consider even if you're not up for a boat tour.

SIGHTS

Húsavík Whale Museum (Hvalasafnið á Húsavík)

The **Húsavík Whale Museum** (Hafnarstétt 1, tel. 354/414-2800, www.whalemuseum.is, 8:30am-6:30pm daily June-Aug., 9am-6pm daily May and Sept., 10am-4pm daily Oct., 10am-4pm Mon.-Fri. Nov.-Apr., 1,900ISK adults, 500ISK children) is a comprehensive museum on Iceland's most famous marine mammals. The exhibits have been developed and maintained with great care, and the curator clearly has a passion for whales. The museum, which is housed in a huge building that used to be a slaughterhouse, provides information on the whale species that inhabit the waters off Iceland's coasts as well as whale ecology and conservation. There are 10 different whale skeletons to check out, as well as a sperm whale jawbone that is the size of a car. It's incredible to stand next to it. Short films available in English teach about whales, and a library has a large selection of marine books. If you visit only one museum in Húsavík, this should be it.

Exploration Museum (Könnunarsögusafnið)

The **Exploration Museum** (Héðisbraut 3, tel. 354/848-7600, www.explorationmuseum.com, 2pm-7pm daily June 1-Aug. 31, 11am-4pm Sun.-Fri. Sept., open by appointment Oct.-May, pay what you wish) is a great spot to see something a little different in Iceland. The museum focuses on various types of exploration, from Vikings coming to Iceland to Americans landing on the moon. Maps and photographs are on display, and documentaries about Apollo astronauts training in Húsavík before missions are available in English. It may not sound like it makes sense, but the exhibits work, doing a nice job of tying Viking captains, arctic explorers, and astronauts together.

Culture House at Húsavík (Safnahúsið á Húsavík)

The **Culture House at Húsavík** (Stóragarði 17, tel. 354/464-1860, www.husmus.is, 10am-6pm daily June-Aug., 10am-4pm Mon.-Fri. Sept.-May, 800ISK) features two fantastic exhibitions that provide a window into life in Húsavík over the ages. The first exhibit has a maritime theme and includes a number of boats, many of which were built in Húsavík. Other displays include fishing equipment, tools used for seal and shark hunting, and photos and documentaries in English. The second exhibit focuses on daily life and natural history in the region. Here you can view homemade objects and crafts and learn about subsistence farming. Regional archives and a library are on-site.

Húsavíkurkirkja

Located close to the harbor, the **Húsavíkurkirkja** (9am-11am and 3pm-5pm daily June-Aug., free) is one of the most significant landmarks in the town. Built in 1907, the Húsavík Church stands 26 meters high and has a white exterior with reddish-brown trim and a dark green steeple/roof. The interior features strong wood beams, beautiful windows, and red-cushioned pews. Icelandic state architect Rögnvaldur Ólafsson designed the church, and all of the wood used to construct it was imported from Norway. The painting behind the altar is revered by town locals. Icelandic artist Sveinn Thórarinsson was commissioned to portray the resurrection of Lazarus for the church. His work incorporated Iceland's landscape, including the mountains and mist of Dettifoss.

Húsavíkurkirkja

SPORTS AND RECREATION

TOP EXPERIENCE

★ Whale-Watching

If you leave Húsavík without getting on a whale-watching boat to view the gentle giants up close, you're missing out. The main whale-watching season runs from the middle of May to the end of October, but the high season is June and July. That time frame is your best chance to see as many as 12 species of whales, with the most common being minke and humpback whales. If you're lucky, you'll spot fin whales, orcas, and blue whales. You can always count on sighting dolphins, as they love to hang out close to the bay. Many of the guides are passionate about whales and love sharing stories about up-close-and-personal encounters.

Three main companies offer whale-watching tours. Each company operates boats of different sizes and all have stellar reputations for ethical environmental practices. The tours are about three hours and depart daily.

- **Gentle Giants** (tel. 354/464-1500, www.gentlegiants.is, 10,300ISK adults, 4,200ISK children 7-15, free for children 6 and under), April 1-November 30
- **North Sailing** (tel. 354/464-7272, www.northsailing.is, 10,500ISK adults, 4,500ISK

children 7-15, free for children 6 and under), March 1-October 14

- **Salka** (tel. 354/464-3999, www.salkawhalewatching.is, 9,950ISK adults, 4,200ISK children 7-15, free for children 6 and under), mid-May-mid-September

Bring your camera, plus a pair of binoculars if you're inclined, and dress warmly, even in the summer. The tours do venture out into the open ocean and sea conditions vary according to the weather; it can get very wet and windy. Bring a hat, gloves, scarf, and layers, including a waterproof layer.

Swimming

The **Húsavík Swimming Pool** (Héðinsbraut, tel. 354/464-1144, 6:45am-9pm Mon.-Fri., 10am-6pm Sat.-Sun., 600ISK) is close to the campsite, which means it can get pretty crowded. Besides the pool, a couple of hot tubs also draw a crowd.

FOOD

Gamlí Baukur (Hafnarstett 9, tel. 354/464-2442, www.gamlibaukur.is, 9am-9pm daily, entrées from 2,260ISK) is a unique restaurant built from driftwood found along the coastline of Húsavík. The rustic vibe continues inside, with large tables and photos of the town's fishing history adorning the walls. The food is hearty, and the fish and lamb dishes hit the spot. The meat soup is also divine. The casual ambience of the restaurant carries over to the evening, when it transforms into a concert venue for local and visiting Icelandic acts. The combination of good music and good beer is hard to beat.

Salka Restaurant (Garðarsbraut 4, tel. 354/464-2551, 11:30am-10pm daily, entrées from 2,800ISK) is a harborside restaurant that is owned by a whale-watching company. The food is good, but predictable, though the pizzas are quite nice. There are also soups, sandwiches, hamburgers, and fish and lamb dishes on the menu. The restaurant is proudly whale friendly, so whale meat is not an option.

★ **Naustið** (Naustagarður 2, tel. 354/464-1520, noon-10pm daily, entrées from 2,800ISK) is known for its seafood. The restaurant uses fresh ingredients and local fish including cod, salmon, and blue ling. An outdoor eating area is delightful in good weather, and local musicians often play concerts. The interior is rustic, with wood-paneled walls and seafaring-related artwork.

Fish and Chips (Hafnarstett 19, tel. 354/464-2099, flokiehf@simnet.is, 11:30am-8pm daily June-Aug., entrées from 1,600ISK)

a whale in Húsavík

serves quick and fresh fried cod and french fries from a harborside hut. It's the best fast-food option in Húsavík by far.

ACCOMMODATIONS

Hotels

Fosshotel Húsavík (Ketilsbraut 22, tel. 354/464-1220, www.fosshotel.is, rooms from 27,000ISK) is a 70-room hotel, with 44 standard rooms and 26 superior rooms with king-sized beds, satellite TV, and private bathrooms. The hotel is decorated in nautical accents, and superior rooms have a fun and fresh whale theme to the decor. The hotel's bar is appropriately called Moby Dick, and the restaurant, Terian, serves fresh fish and other traditional Icelandic cuisine. Guests have access to free Wi-Fi and free parking, and breakfast is included.

Húsavík Cape Hotel (Laugarbrekka 26, tel. 354/463-3399, www.husavikhotel.com, rooms from 35,500ISK) is housed in a historic 1950 building that was owned by the Húsavík Fishing Company. In 2012 it was transformed into a smart and rustic hotel, complete with standard beds, hardwood floors, and simple furnishings. Guests have access to free Wi-Fi, and breakfast is included.

Guesthouses

Árból Guesthouse (Ásgarðsvegur 2, tel. 354/464-2220, www.arbol.is, rooms from 20,900ISK) is a quaint guesthouse close to the center of town. Some of the rooms have the look of a wood-paneled hunting lodge, while others look like you're staying at your grandmother's house. The rooms (singles, doubles, triples, and family rooms) are clean and comfortable and a bit larger than average. All rooms share bathroom facilities, and breakfast is included.

Húsavík Guesthouse (Laugarbrekka 16, tel. 354/463-3399, www.husavikguesthouse.is, rooms from 13,000ISK) is a family-run guesthouse with options ranging from singles to family rooms. The atmosphere looks and feels very much like you're staying in a comfortable, well-loved home. There's art on the walls, jam-packed bookshelves with everything from novels to travel guides, and comfortable guest rooms. Guests share bathroom facilities, and breakfast is included.

Guesthouse Sigtun (Tungata 13, tel. 354/846-9364, www.guesthouse-sigtun.com, rooms from 22,900ISK) also has options from singles to family rooms, just minutes from the harbor. Rooms are cozy and the amenities are great, with free Wi-Fi, access to a fully equipped kitchen, a public computer, a washing machine to use free of charge, and a grill.

Camping

The **Húsavík Campground** (Héðinsbraut, tel. 354/845-0705, May 15-Sept. 30, 1,400ISK) regularly receives kudos. It's a well-maintained, large, and efficient facility that is wildly popular in June and July. The kitchen area is great and the showers are steaming hot. The campground, which is close to the center of town, is situated in an open field with no shelter. Tents and RVs are welcome.

INFORMATION AND SERVICES

The **tourist information office** (Hafnarstett 1, tel. 354/464-4300, www.visithusavik.is, 10am-4pm daily June-Sept.) is close to the harbor and offers Internet access, pamphlets about the region, and tour bookings.

TRANSPORTATION

Eagle Air (tel. 354/562-4200, www.eagleair.is) offers 10 flights a week from Reykjavík. It's about a 45-minute flight and costs 19,000ISK each way. Húsavík Airport is 10 kilometers south of the center of Húsavík.

By car, Húsavík is 90 kilometers northeast of Akureyri via paved Route 85, and it's 56 kilometers north of Mývatn on Route 87, which is also paved.

Strætó (tel. 354/540-2700, www.straeto.is) offers year-round bus service from Akureyri to Húsavík on the 79 bus, which takes about two hours (2,640ISK). Check the website for recent timetables.

Jökulsárgljúfur (Vatnajökull National Park–North)

TOP EXPERIENCE

Jökulsárgljúfur National Park was established in 1973 and became part of Vatnajökull National Park in 2008, forming the largest national park in Europe. Jökulsárgljúfur is the northern division of Vatnajökull National Park. Within it are some of North Iceland's most visited sites, including Dettifoss and Ásbyrgi. Several well-maintained hiking trails travel along the perimeter of waterfalls, rivers, and canyons. Many tourists stop at Dettifoss to photograph the powerful waterfall, but the park has other treasures that are worthy of a longer visit; the mountainous landscape is breathtaking. Try to spend at least one day in this area.

Note that hikers must register with the park office at Ásbyrgi before they set out on their journey. Safety first.

SIGHTS

★ Ásbyrgi

Ásbyrgi (Shelter of the Gods) is an enormous canyon full of interesting rock formations, lush grass, well-maintained walking paths, thriving birdlife, and several bodies of water, including rivers and waterfalls. The horseshoe-shaped canyon measures roughly 3.5 kilometers in length and 1.1 kilometers across.

Scientists have said that Ásbyrgi was most likely formed by glacial flooding of the Jökulsá á Fjöllum River after the last ice age, and additional flooding some 3,000 years ago. However, Icelandic folklore has a different explanation for the unique shape of the canyon. The canyon has been nicknamed Sleipnir's Footprint, as folklorists have said that the canyon was formed when Odin's eight-legged horse, Sleipnir, touched one of its feet to the ground, creating the depressions. Folklore also stipulates that the canyon is the central meeting point of the *huldufólk* (hidden people) who live among the cliffs.

Tourists make the trek to Ásbyrgi to take in the steep rock formations and enjoy a hike.

the rock formations of Ásbyrgi

In some spots hikers have to be careful in navigating the rocks. Be sure to wear proper footwear and take caution over any slippery-looking patches. One easy hike, which is about one kilometer and takes 30-60 minutes, starts at the car park at Ásbyrgi and leads to a platform at a small pond named Botnstjörn. Along the way are lots of trees, shrubbery, and rock formations. A lovely view over the pond takes in ducks and other birds and offers vistas of the western side of the canyon.

Ásbyrgi is 65 kilometers south of Húsavík. To reach the visitors center in Ásbyrgi from Húsavík, take paved Route 85.

Hólmatungur

Hólmatungur is an area on the western side of the canyon of the glacial Jökulsá river that has breathtaking basalt column formations, along with choppy streams and the wondrous waterfall Rettarfoss. It's a beautiful spot that offers scenic views and wonderful photo ops.

To reach Hólmatungur from Ásbyrgi and Route 85, head south on Route 862, which is on the west side of the Jökulsá. Route 862 is a gravel road between Route 85 and Dettifoss. Hólmantungur lies along this unpaved stretch. (Heading south of Dettifoss to Route 1, the road is paved.) The gravel road is passable for normal vehicles, but it's closed during wintertime and does not open until late May or early June.

TOP EXPERIENCE

★ Dettifoss

Dettifoss, which means "tumble falls," is the largest waterfall on the island, and the most powerful in Europe, with an average flow of 200 cubic meters of water per second. During an especially rainy day, the flow can reach 500 cubic meters per second. This force is not because of the fall's height, but its width. Spanning 100 meters wide and 45 meters high, Dettifoss is gigantic. The grayish color of the water comes from sand and rocks that get picked up along the way.

Because of the waterfall's size and sheer beauty, plan to spend at least a couple of hours here to take it all in. There are several viewing platforms. This is an open, slippery spot with lots of steps and minimal guardrails; be careful. If you're visiting on a windy day, expect to get hit with spray—but that's part of the fun, to really experience the falls. It's also common to see a rainbow or two depending on the weather

Tour companies include Dettifoss as part of the "Diamond Circle," a popular route around the Mývatn region and Húsavík, based in Akureyri. For a day tour, check out **Reykjavík Excursions** (tel. 354/580-5400, www.re.is).

Dettifoss is 28 kilometers south of Ásbyrgi. From Ásbyrgi and Route 85, head south on Route 862 on the west side of the river Jökulsá. Route 862 is a gravel road between Route 85 and Dettifoss. (Heading south of Dettifoss to Route 1, the road is paved.) The gravel road is passable for normal vehicles, but it's closed during wintertime and does not open until late May or early June.

ACCOMMODATIONS

You won't find any hotels or guesthouses within the park limits; the only option for overnight guests is the **Ásbyrgi campground** (tel. 354/470-7100, 1,700ISK). The site, which is situated in an open field, is open from mid-May through September and allows for 350 tents as well as caravans (with hookups). There are adequate cooking facilities, hot showers, and a small shop that sells some food and hiking gear. Bring all the food, water, and supplies you need with you.

INFORMATION AND SERVICES

The national park's **tourist information center** (tel. 354/465-2195, www.ust.is, 11am-3pm daily) is based at Ásbyrgi and open year-round.

TRANSPORTATION

It's best to have a car to explore the park. Keep in mind that while Jökulsárgljúfur is

Visiting Vatnajökull National Park

Vatnajökull National Park

Vatnajökull National Park (www.vatnajokulsthjodgardur.is) is huge, covering 13 percent of the island and 13,700 square kilometers, and is the largest national park in western Europe.

Jökulsárgljúfur National Park and **Skaftafell National Park** were combined with **Vatnajökull glacier** in 2008 to form Vatnajökull National Park. Jökulsárgljúfur and Skaftafell are now considered the northern and southern divisions of the park.

Vatnajökull National Park has visitors centers in the north (Jökulsárgljúfur visitors center at Ásbyrgi), south (Skaftafell visitors center), and east (Snæfellsstofa visitors center at Egilsstaðir).

There are no roads in the national park except for the tracks leading up to private farms. Wardens operate in the park, assisted by park rangers during the summer months (June-Aug.). Visitors are encouraged to seek information and advice from park staff. Hiking trips led by park rangers give visitors the opportunity to get to know the area and find out about its history, ecology, and geology, in the company of a well-informed guide. The hikes follow a variety of routes, and everyone should be able to find a suitable outing.

open year-round, the roads beyond Ásbyrgi, including Route 862, are closed during wintertime and do not open until late May or early June.

If you don't have a car, a tour could be a great option. Akureyri-based **SBA** (tel. 354/550-0700, www.sba.is) offers a Dettifoss Grand Tour (21,700ISK) from mid-June to mid-September. The tour departs from the Reykjahlíð information center and takes you from Mývatn to Dettifoss, Ásbyrgi, Húsavík, and back to Mývatn.

The Northeastern Corner

The northeastern corner is one of the least populated, most desolate regions of Iceland. There is no mad tourist rush here. Þórshöfn is a small fishing village in the area, located on the northern coast of the Langanes Peninsula on the Þistilfjörður bay. Fewer than 400 people live on the peninsula.

LANGANES

Langanes (Long Peak) is a narrow, 40-kilometer-long peninsula situated between two bays (Þistilfjörður and Bakkaflói) that is shaped like a goose with a very large head. Some may be quick to dismiss the area, but the sloping coastal landscape is ideal for birdwatching and photographing steep sea cliffs. If you are driving through, it's worth a stop to take some photos of gannets, terns, gulls, and guillemots.

Be aware that the main road on Langanes is challenging to drive on, as it's unpaved and extremely rocky in some spots. This is something to consider if you rented a compact car; four-wheel drives fare much better in this region. For those who do make the journey, at the end of the peninsula there is a charming lighthouse that was erected in 1950. If you are passing through in the winter, the lighthouse is a perfect place to catch a glimpse of northern lights (if the forecast is favorable).

Accommodations

Ytra-Lón Hostel (tel. 354/846-6448, www.ytralonhostel.com, apartments from 22,000ISK) offers nine self-catering apartments for 2-3 people with private bathrooms and a fully equipped kitchenette. The overall facility has beds for 50 people with some dormitory-style rooms. The hostel is remote, with the nearest grocery store and restaurants about 14 kilometers away, so bring food and supplies with you, or shop early because stores in this region tend to have irregular hours. Ytra-Lón is on Route 869, which is 14 kilometers northeast of Þórshöfn.

TRANSPORTATION

Langanes is 252 kilometers northeast of Akureyri via Route 85, which is paved, and 69 kilometers north of Vopnafjörður (in East Iceland) on Route 85.

East Iceland and the Eastfjords

Look for ★ to find recommended sights, activities, dining, and lodging.

Highlights

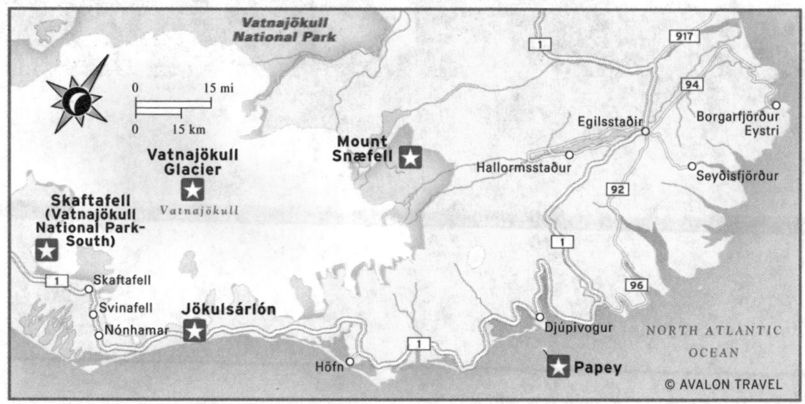

★ **Mount Snæfell:** It's only a moderate hike to the top of Iceland's highest mountain, where views span from the highlands to Vatnajökull and all the way out to sea (page 213).

★ **Papey:** Affectionately called "Bird Island," Papey hosts 30,000 pairs of puffins during the summer (page 224).

★ **Vatnajökull Glacier:** Covering about 8 percent of the country, this is the biggest glacier in Europe—and under the ice cap are still-active volcanoes (page 231).

★ **Jökulsárlón:** At the Glacier Lagoon, the deepest lake in Iceland, huge blocks of ice constantly break off a glacier and float on the surface (page 231).

★ **Skaftafell (Vatnajökull National Park—South):** One of East Iceland's most beautiful places has striking white glaciers set against a backdrop of green fields and black sands (page 232).

East Iceland is where you find the actual "ice," including Vatnajökull glacier, a giant white spot on the map that is truly breathtaking in person. You can drive or hike right up to the glacier's edge in Skaftafell.

In the summer, the only practical time to tour this region, it can be crowded with fellow travelers, but there are plenty of detours to take to avoid the hordes. Lacking infrastructure and people, the east is the most remote part of the island, and travel is difficult in winter.

One of the least visited destinations in Iceland is one you should keep on your radar: the Eastfjords. If you're looking for remote, unspoiled beauty, it's here. The Ring Road weaves through the fjords, where you will see gorgeous mountains, charming fishing villages, and thriving wildlife. It's not easy to get around the region (you need a car), but it's worth the costs and trouble.

The east is also home to one of the most active volcanic areas on the island, and Vatnajökull National Park deserves at least one day of its own. Navigating the glacier (with a guide and proper equipment) is one of those unforgettable, bucket-list excursions.

East Iceland is often overlooked but has some of the most pristine, untouched nature in Iceland. If you can spare a couple of days, spend some time hiking and photographing the Eastfjords. Even during the high season, there's a good chance you won't bump into many other tourists. The east can be your own private treasure.

PLANNING YOUR TIME

East Iceland is not conducive to tight schedules, as weather can be unpredictable and winds punishing. It's best to visit in summer. Winter travel to and around the area is challenging. The wind and snow can make travel difficult at best, dangerous at worst. Monitor weather conditions closely and check to see if roads have been closed.

The Ring Road (Route 1) takes you through the east, and most people choose either Egilsstaðir and/or Seyðisfjörður as a base. Both towns are complete with guesthouses,

Previous: a sheep pauses on a rocky hillside; traditional turf houses at a farm near Skaftafell. **Above:** Jökulsárlón Glacier Lagoon.

East Iceland and the Eastfjords

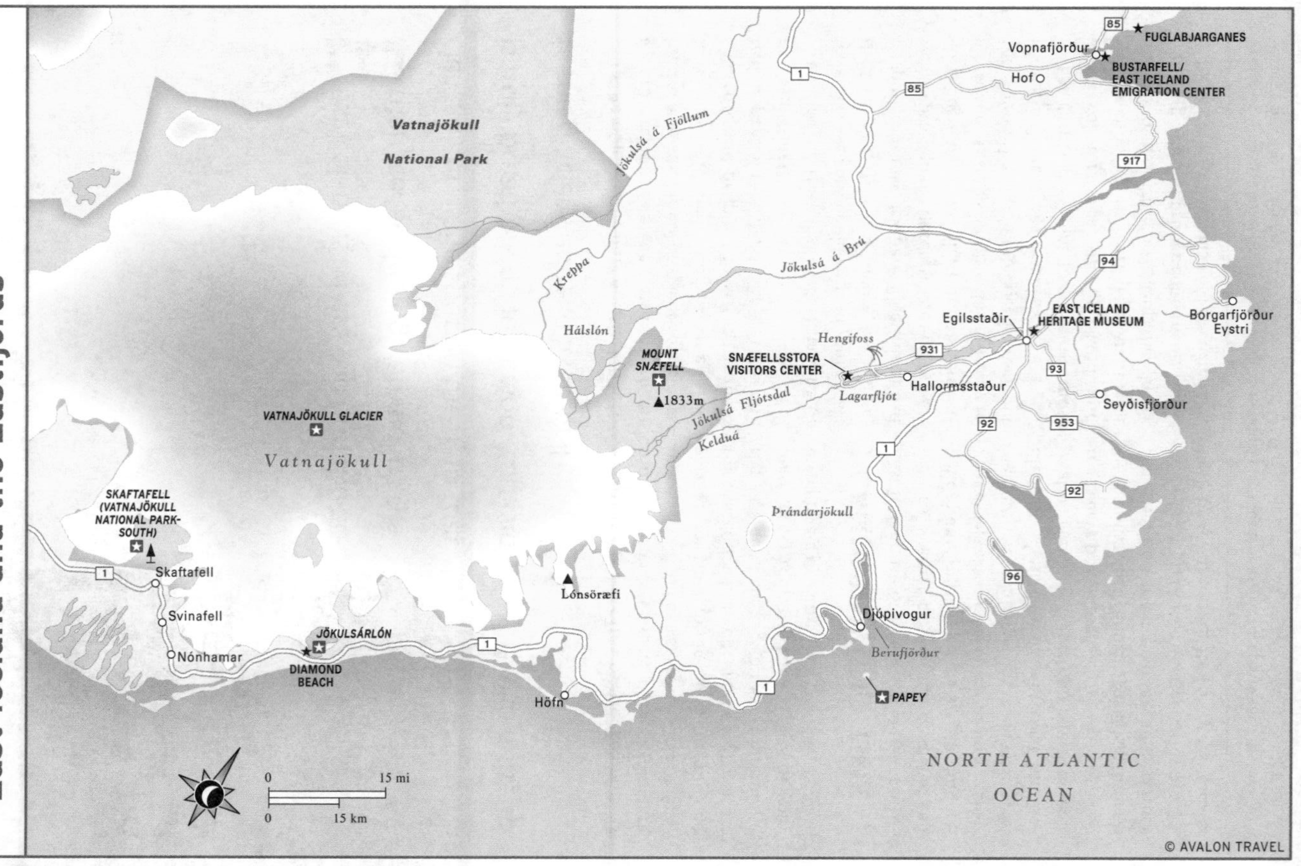

FUGLABJARGANES
Vopnafjörður
BUSTARFELL/ EAST ICELAND EMIGRATION CENTER
Hof
Vatnajökull National Park
Jökulsá á Fjöllum
Krepa
Jökulsá á Brú
Hálslón
MOUNT SNÆFELL
1833m
Hengifoss
SNÆFELLSSTOFA VISITORS CENTER
Egilsstaðir
EAST ICELAND HERITAGE MUSEUM
Borgarfjörður Eystri
Hallormsstaður
Lagarfljót
Jökulsá Fljótsdal
Kelduá
Seyðisfjörður
VATNAJÖKULL GLACIER
Vatnajökull
SKAFTAFELL (VATNAJÖKULL NATIONAL PARK-SOUTH)
Skaftafell
Svinafell
Nónhamar
JÖKULSÁRLÓN
DIAMOND BEACH
Lónsöræfi
Þrándarjökull
Djúpivogur
Berufjörður
Höfn
PAPEY
NORTH ATLANTIC OCEAN
0
15 mi
0
15 km
1
85
917
94
931
93
953
92
96

bus stations, and airports. Some guesthouses and restaurants operate only June-August. Seyðisfjörður is the best option for an extended stay in the Eastfjords.

Vopnafjörður

Vopnafjörður (Weapon Fjord) is full of picturesque mountains, pure waterfalls, and historic farms. It's one of the best spots to get a glimpse of killer whales. It's pretty, steeped in medieval history, and home to gorgeous wildlife.

The history of the town, also called Vopnafjörður, dates back 1,100 years. The bay was first settled by Viking seafarers from Norway. Foreign merchants frequently sailed to Vopnafjörður in the early modern age, and a settlement gradually formed on a peninsula where the village of Vopnafjörður now stands. It became one of Iceland's major commercial harbors in the 18th and 19th centuries. In the last half century, the fishing industry has grown considerably, and is today the largest business sector in the area.

The town has also had an impact on literature: *Independent People,* the epic Icelandic novel by Nobel Prize winner Halldór Laxness, was said to have been inspired by life in the highlands around Vopnafjörður.

SIGHTS

Bustarfell

The old farm of **Bustarfell** (off Rte. 85 about 20 km south of Vopnafjörður, tel. 354/471-2211, www.bustarfell.is, 10am-5pm daily June 1-Sept. 20, entrance 1,100ISK) is one of the best-preserved of the traditional Icelandic turf houses. The museum offers a great opportunity to see how people's ways of living have changed through the centuries. The rooms are furnished in the style of centuries past, giving an authentic look into what homes were like. The foundations of the current house are from 1770, but the house has undergone alterations over the years. The museum covers life from the 18th century to the mid-20th century. A café within the museum is a good spot to enjoy coffee, light meals, and yummy pastries as well as exhibitions from local artists.

East Iceland Emigration Center (Vesturfaramiðstöð Austurlands)

The **East Iceland Emigration Center** (Kaupvangur 2, tel. 354/473-1200, www.vesturfarinn.is, 1pm-6pm Mon.-Wed. and Sat. June-Aug., open by request Sept.-May, free) is dedicated to the period of 1875-1914, when many residents emigrated from the region after the great Askja eruption of 1875 displaced hundreds. The center is focused on the history of the region and renewing contact with emigrants' descendants. There are documents and photos on display.

Fuglabjarganes

Fuglabjarganes is a prominent cliff that juts out on the northern coast of the town. You can get a good look at it from a marked walking path from the unpaved Strandhafnarvegur road, which is along the Fugla River. The scenery is beautiful, with white beaches, stone walls, towering cliffs, and impressive rock caverns and pillars.

SPORTS AND RECREATION

Bird-Watching

Vopnafjörður is a bird-watcher's dream. You can see a mix of seabirds, waterfowl, waders, passerines, and raptors. The Tangi Peninsula north of Vopnafjörður is a beautiful and remote spot to watch seabirds, and the area around the Nypslon estuary provides habitat for various duck species.

Fishing

The **Hofsa River** is just a 15-minute drive

east from Vopnafjörður, and the stretch of the river open to angling encompasses 19 miles in a wide valley. Salmon season runs July 1-September 20. Permits are needed and must be secured in advance. For details on permits, visit the region's website (www.vopnafjordur.com/activities/angling). The **Sela River** is a 10-minute drive north from Vopnafjörður and has long been one of the most popular of Icelandic salmon rivers. Fishing is fly only, and the river has a catch-and-release system in place. Guides are available. The **Vesturdalsa River** is a 15-minute drive south from Vopnafjörður. It originates from the runoff of Lake Arnarvatn in the highlands above Vopnafjörður, flows 34 kilometers to the lowlands, and empties into Nypslon estuary. The fishing area reaches 27 kilometers up to a waterfall not accessible to salmon. A catch-and-release policy is in effect.

Hiking

Vopnafjörður offers several hiking routes that vary from easy to challenging. Beginners will find a wide range of mapped routes and marked trails that offer scenic views of the whole of Vopnafjörður—the bay, the Tangi Peninsula, inland areas, and mountains. An easy route that is popular among locals is around Drangsnes Peninsula and to the towering waterfalls at the Gljufursa River. The out-and-back hike takes about three hours round-trip and is six kilometers total. It's accessible via Routes 85 and 917, about three kilometers south of town.

More experienced hikers looking for a challenging trail should hike to the top of Krossavik mountain, which reaches 1,080 meters. The mountain stands opposite the village on the other side of the bay, and the trailhead is accessible via Route 917.

For maps and detailed trail information, visit the **tourist information center** (Hafnarbyggd 6, tel. 354/473-1341, www.vopnafjordur.is), and always be sure to check the weather forecast and report your itinerary.

Swimming

The local swimming pool is called **Selárlaug** (3.5 km from Rte. 85, tel. 354/473-1499, 10am-7pm daily, 600ISK), where you will find locals taking a dip and socializing with friends and family.

FOOD

Cafe Hjaleigan (tel. 354/471-2211, www.bustarfell.is, 10am-5pm daily mid-June-mid-Sept., entrées from 2,000ISK) is the café at Bustarfell museum (off Rte. 85 about 20 km south from Vopnafjörður). It serves coffee, soft drinks, and light meals such as sandwiches, as well as pastries.

Ollasjoppa (Kolbeinsgata 35, tel. 354/473-1803, 9am-11pm Mon.-Sat., 10am-11pm Sun., entrées from 2,200ISK) is a tiny café that offers quick fare including pizza, hamburgers, sandwiches, and pitas, along with hot dishes with lamb, fish, and chicken.

ACCOMMODATIONS

Hotel Tangi (Hafnarbyggd 17, tel. 354/473-1840, hoteltangi@simnet.is, rooms from 18,000ISK) is a standard countryside hotel with 17 rooms, a restaurant, and a bar. The exterior of the blue block building isn't much to look at, but the inside is comfortable, with standard beds and IKEA-like furniture. There are single and double rooms, some with shared bathroom facilities.

Sireksstadir Farm Cottages (Sireksstadir, tel. 354/473-1458, www.sireksstadir.is, rooms from 16,000ISK) offers two cottages for families or groups that can accommodate 4-6 people, as well as seven double guest rooms. The cottages are cozy and have a large deck and a barbecue grill. Guests are invited to observe farm activities, and the rooms are available year-round. The staff is friendly, welcoming, and inclusive.

Syðri-Vík (tel. 354/473-1199, www.farmholidays.is, early Mar.-late Oct., rooms from 18,000ISK) is a six-room guesthouse based on a working farm. Guests have access to a fully equipped kitchen, common dining and living rooms, and shared bathroom and laundry

Fljótsdalur Valley

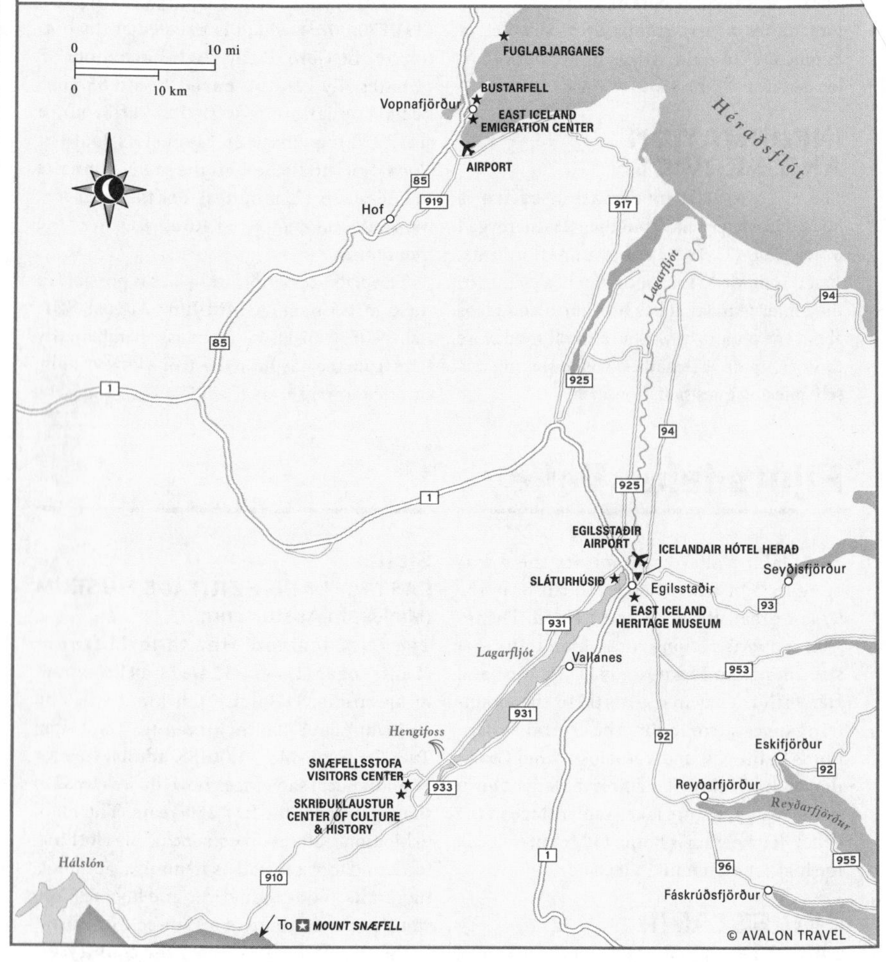

daily June-Aug., 11am-5pm May and Sept., noon-4pm Apr., open by request Oct.-Mar., 1,100ISK) is an impressive historical site that includes the ruins of a 16th-century monastery as well as the home of the celebrated novelist Gunnar Gunnarsson, the author of *Af Borgslægtens Historie (Guest the One-Eyed)*, the first Icelandic book made into a movie. Gunnar's home was built in 1939 and was donated to the state by the writer in 1948. You can view photographs and objects that belonged to Gunnar Gunnarsson, and the building also serves as a cultural center where various events and exhibitions are held throughout the year.

SLÁTURHÚSIÐ

The **Sláturhúsið** (Kaupvangur 7, tel. 354/471-1479, www.slaturhusid.is) has injected some much-needed culture into Egilsstaðir. Founded in 2005, the Slaughterhouse Culture Center is home to theater and dance facilities. The owners are very friendly, and it's a lot of fun to stay in such an active farm. The owners also rent out two summer cottages for families or large groups. Syðri-Vík is eight kilometers from the village of Vopnafjörður, located near Route 85.

INFORMATION AND SERVICES

The main **tourist information office** is housed in a huge yellow building (Hafnarbyggd 6, tel. 354/473-1341, www.vopnafjordur.is, 10am-5pm Mon.-Fri., noon-4pm Sat.-Sun.) in the center of town. It has brochures and maps about the region, as well as a small food store to stock up on essentials if you're staying at a self-catering guesthouse or farm.

TRANSPORTATION

There are flights from the northern town of Akureyri to **Vopnafjörður Airport** (354/570-3075), which is situated at the bottom of the fjord. Daily flights are about 45 minutes. By car, the paved Route 85 connects Vopnafjörður with Bakkafjörður, a small fishing village 34 kilometers south of Vopnafjörður. Route 1, in the south, connects to Egilsstaðir (75 minutes). For the most scenic route, take unpaved Route 917 over the mountains.

Travel to Vopnafjörður by bus is possible in the summer months. Mid-June-August, **SBA** (tel. 354/550-0700, www.sba.is) operates daily trips from the northern town of Akureyri. The three-hour trip costs 6,900ISK each way.

Fljótsdalur Valley

Fljótsdalur Valley encompasses the towns of Egilsstaðir and Fellabær, which form the largest urban center in East Iceland. The region supports a strong rural community that stretches from Biskupsháls in the west and Héraðsflói, a bay in the north, to the mountain ranges surrounding the central eastern fjords in the east and Vatnajökull and Öxi in the south. While Egilsstaðir is the largest town in the region, nature takes center stage in the valley: The region is home to Mount Snæfell, the highest mountain in Iceland.

EGILSSTAÐIR

Egilsstaðir is considered the unofficial capital of East Iceland, but don't let that fool you; it's a "capital" with fewer than 3,000 residents. The quaint town earned its name based on a reference to the nearby farm Egil's stead, which appears in saga stories. The community developed and grew after Iceland gained independence from Denmark in 1944. That said, the town today remains sparsely populated, but the harbor welcomes thousands of visitors who come to Iceland via ferry from mainland Europe.

Sights

EAST ICELAND HERITAGE MUSEUM (Minjasafn Austurlands)

The **East Iceland Heritage Museum** (Laufskógar 1, tel. 354/471-1412, www.minjasafn.is, 11:30am-7pm Mon.-Fri. and 10:30am-6pm Sat.-Sun. June-Aug., 11am-4pm Tue.-Fri. Sept.-May, 1,00ISK adults, free for 17 and under) showcases how life was lived in the region over the last 200 years. The main exhibition features objects including clothing, food, and tools, as well as items used for hunting, crafts, food production, and hobbies. You can also enter a room of a 19th-century farmhouse that was moved from the countryside into the museum. The display depicts a small bedroom/living room, with sparse furnishings. It's an interesting view into what life was like in this remote part of Iceland—a hardscrabble, difficult existence.

SKRIÐUKLAUSTUR CENTER OF CULTURE & HISTORY

The **Skriðuklaustur Center of Culture & History** (Skriðuklaustur, tel. 354/471-2990, www.skriduklaustur.is, 10am-6pm

Hengifoss

productions as well as workshops, performances, lectures, and exhibitions. An artist residency available to locals and visitors provides studio space in exchange for tuition. The concrete building is cold and nondescript, but one might expect that from an old slaughterhouse.

SNÆFELLSSTOFA VISITORS CENTER

The **Snæfellsstofa visitors center** (Skriðuklaustur, tel. 354/470-0840, 10am-4pm Mon.-Fri., 10am-6pm Sat.-Sun. May-Sept., open by request in winter) is the information center for the east area of Vatnajökull National Park. The visitors center houses a fascinating exhibition on the area, the glacier, and local flora and fauna. Snæfell is one of the most visited destinations within the national park, and the center gives you a preview into the vast region. The center's souvenir shop focuses on local products, including woolen goods and food products.

HALLORMSSTAÐUR

In surveying the landscape, you've certainly noticed that trees are a rare sight in Iceland. Hallormsstaður has the distinction of being the largest forest in the country, though it would be considered small by other standards. It stretches along a 35-kilometer-long glacial lake called **Lagarfljót** and by a small cove; it's beautiful to roam among native birch trees that have survived inclement weather and found a way to thrive. There are also scores of imported species, including willow and rowan. It's possible to rent horses from **Riding Iceland** (tel. 354/859-3560, www.riding-iceland.com) for a leisurely ride in the forest. Hallormsstaður is 23 kilometers southwest of Egilsstaðir on Route 1 and Route 931, which is unpaved, about a 20-minute drive.

HENGIFOSS

After roaming Iceland's largest forest, take a walk to the opposite side of the lake and look at the towering 120-meter waterfall Hengifoss. The landscape reveals a layer of basalt above ancient tree trunks. Have your camera ready. Hengifoss is 34 kilometers from Egilsstaðir on Route 931, a gravel road. The walk to Hengifoss from Hallormsstaður is 12 kilometers. For a closer look by car, you can stop at the designated car park off of Route 931 and walk uphill about 2.5 kilometers to the waterfall.

LAGARFLJÓTSORMUR

Scotland has the Loch Ness monster and Iceland has Lagarfljótsormur, a huge worm-like monster said to call Lagarfljót home. People have reported spotting the monster inside the freshwater, glacier-fed lake, which is about 30 kilometers long, as well as outside the body of water. It is said to have many humps and slither in a slow fashion. The tale is part of Icelandic folklore, and locals have a sense of humor about "sightings." If you do happen to see the monster, make sure you report it to the local heritage museum in Egilsstaðir.

Sports and Recreation

HORSE RIDING

Those interested in a horse-riding tour have a great option with the travel service at **Sandfellsskógur** (17 km south of Egilsstaðir on Rte. 1, tel. 354/471-2420), which also offers horse rentals. Beautiful trails wind through the forest and traverse hills and valleys. You can rent a horse for 1-4 hours, and there's even a midnight summer tour available. Horse tours are available June through mid-September and cost 7,000ISK for a one-hour rental.

SWIMMING

The **Egilsstaðir Swimming Pool** (Tjarnarbraut 26, tel. 354/470-0777, 6:30am-8:30pm Mon.-Fri., 10am-6pm Sat.-Sun., 550ISK) is one of the nicest in the region, with a 50-meter heated pool, waterslides for kids, hot tubs, and a fitness center.

GOLF

The **Ekkjufell Golf Course** (Fellabær, tel. 354/894-0604, greens fees 2,500ISK) is the sole course in the town. It's open year-round and is frequented by locals, so be sure to call ahead for a tee time.

Food

★ **Icelandair Hótel Herað** (Miðvangur 5-7, tel. 354/471-1500, www.icelandairhotels.is, 8am-10:30pm daily, entrées from 3,950ISK) is the most upscale dining you'll find in the town, and the chefs don't disappoint. The hotel restaurant serves dishes with fresh ingredients you'd expect, like fish and lamb, but includes some surprises as well, like a reindeer steak. If you're not game for reindeer, I recommend the arctic char with baby potatoes. You'll also find burgers and pâté on the menu.

Café Nielsen (Tjarnarbraut 1, tel. 354/471-2626, www.cafenielsen.is, 11:30am-11:30pm Mon.-Fri., 1pm-11pm Sat.-Sun., entrées from 3,100ISK) is a small café serving flavorful dishes ranging from reindeer steaks to fresh mussels in a tomato-garlic sauce. The food is surprising and very tasty, with an interesting mix of ingredients. The pan-fried salted cod with garlic, chorizo, and olives is recommended.

Accommodations

★ **Icelandair Hótel Herað** (Miðvangur 5-7, tel. 354/471-1500, www.icelandairhotels.is, rooms from 27,000ISK) is the town's most upscale lodging option. The 60-room hotel, which is huge for the location, is chic, modern, and has that classic Nordic style you'd expect to see in Reykjavík. But, this is an Icelandair Hótel, so the sleek interior and rooms are to be expected. The decor is heavy on wood, with gorgeous hardwood floors throughout the building, classic Scandinavian wood furnishings, and even modern wood art. The restaurant offers an eclectic menu featuring local ingredients.

Hótel Eyvindará (Eyvindará 2, tel. 354/471-1200, www.eyvindara.is, rooms from 23,000ISK) is a ranch-style guesthouse that offers 28 rooms and seven cottages. Rooms are tastefully decorated with cozy country accents and large windows that overlook a gorgeous view. Most of the rooms have private bathrooms, but a handful have shared facilities. The hotel's restaurant serves breakfast daily, and dinner is available late May through early September. The dinner menu emphasizes fish and lamb dishes but has a few vegetarian options.

Hótel Edda Egilsstaðir (Tjarnarbraut 25, tel. 354/444-4880, www.hoteledda.is, June-mid-Aug., rooms from 22,000ISK) is an adequate 52-room hotel just outside of town. What it lacks in luxury is made up for with the location, especially for those who want to be close to nature. The hotel is close to a 25-meter outdoor swimming pool, a nine-hole golf course, and a scenic stretch in the fjord where you can spot seals and take woodland walks. Rooms have standard beds and basic furniture, but all rooms have private bathrooms and there is free Wi-Fi in the common areas. The hotel restaurant serves a breakfast buffet 7am-10am that includes waffles, fresh fruit, and oatmeal, and a dinner buffet is available 6:30pm-9pm.

Húsey (Hróastunga, tel. 354/471-3010,

husey@simnet.is, beds from 20,000ISK) is a 20-bed youth hostel that was converted from an old farmhouse. It's in an isolated part of the village, and there are great opportunities to spot seals and hike remote paths. The hostel has a common kitchen available for preparing your own meals. Sheets are available for a fee, and there is a barbecue available.

Lake Hotel Egilsstaðir (Egilsstöðum 1-2, tel. 354/471-1114, www.english.lakehotel.is, rooms from 25,000ISK) is a comfortable 50-room guesthouse with a country farmhouse theme. Rooms are large and range from singles to triples. While all have wooden floors, a TV, and free Wi-Fi, some rooms also boast sweeping mountain views. There is also an in-house restaurant and a spa.

CAMPING

The **Egilsstaðir Campsite** (Kaupvangur 10, tel. 354/471-2320, June-Aug 31, 1,500ISK per adult, free for children under 12) can be quite busy in the summer. The campsite is close to town, and amenities include hot showers and adequate cooking facilities. There are areas for tents and RVs with hookups. The campsite is situated in an open field with trees along the perimeter. You must pay at the tourist information center (Kaupvangur 10, tel. 354/471-2320, www.east.is, 8am-10pm daily summer, 9am-6pm Mon.-Fri., noon-4pm Sat.-Sun. winter).

Information and Services

Egilsstaðir's **tourist information center** (Kaupvangur 17, tel. 354/470-0750, www.east.is, 8am-10pm daily June-Aug., 9am-6pm Mon.-Fri., noon-4pm Sat.-Sun. Sept.-May) is the largest and most comprehensive in the region, and one of the largest in the country. You will find hiking maps, basic travel supplies, a café and souvenir shop, Internet access, and a booking center for an array of tours. The site is also home to the bus station and the local campsite.

Transportation

By car, Route 1 connects Egilsstaðir with the North Iceland town Akureyri, which is 3.5 hours and 266 kilometers away.

The **Strætó** 56 bus (tel. 354/540-2700, www.straeto.is) operates from Egilsstaðir to Akureyri all year. It takes about four hours from Akureyri and costs 7,920ISK each way.

Egilsstaðir Airport (354/424-4040) is in the heart of town, and there are daily flights by **Air Iceland Connect** (www.airicelandconnect.com) from Reykjavík's domestic airport. Flights take about one hour and cost around 17,000ISK each way.

★ MOUNT SNÆFELL

Mount Snæfell (Snow Mountain) is the highest mountain, excluding glaciers, in Iceland. Despite towering 1,833 meters, it's fairly easy to scale. The dormant volcano offers spectacular views over the highlands, down Fljótsdalur valley, and of Vatnajökull glacier. You can see rivers, canyons, and valleys—and you may even catch a glimpse of a reindeer herd. Climbing doesn't get better.

To get to the base, take unpaved Route 910 to Route F909. Getting here requires a rugged four-wheel drive, as the roads are at best challenging and at worst treacherous. Don't try to make it in a compact rental car or you'll wind up stranded. Don't be foolish.

A well-kept trail begins at the base station and continues to the top. Hiking groups start at the mountain hut **Snæfellsskáli** (tel. 354/575-8400); the GPS coordinates are N 64.8042, W 15.6418. The mountain hut offers basic amenities including beds, bathrooms, and cooking facilities. The cost is 5,800ISK per night. The whole area is open only in the summer.

The moderate hike is about eight kilometers and takes about 8-9 hours. The top of the mountain is snowcapped all year long. Bring good boots and waterproof gear, alert people of your travel plans, and monitor the weather closely. If conditions are not good, do not attempt a climb.

There is also a challenging trek from Mount Snæfell to **Lónsöræfi** that is about 55 kilometers and takes about four days. Hikers experience steep hills, glaciers, and waterfalls amid the rocky landscape.

The Eastfjords

The Eastfjords are some of the most remote and unspoiled parts of Iceland. In all, there are 14 fjords, each with its own charm and tiny population. There are waterfalls among small fishing villages, and unique museums lure tourists off the Ring Road. If you're on an extended trip to Iceland, you should make time to explore this wonderful land where wildlife greatly outnumbers humans.

BORGARFJÖRÐUR EYSTRI

This fjord is a prime destination for hiking, as there are numerous well-maintained trails, gorgeous mountains, and deserted bays. The big draw is the spectacular scenery that you don't have to share with hordes of tourists, unlike in other parts of the country.

Sights

KJARVALSSTOFA

Kjarvalsstofa (Fjarðarborg, tel. 354/472-9950, www.dyrfjoll.is, noon-6pm daily June-Aug., open by request Sept.-May, 1,00ISK) is a small museum dedicated to the work of celebrated artist Jóhannes Kjarval (1885-1972), who is known for his haunting landscape paintings as well as works that depict saga stories and Iceland's folklore.

ÁLFABORG

Álfaborg, or "fjord of Borg," is a 30-meter rocky hill known in folklore as the home of the queen of Iceland's hidden people. Many locals are amused by this history and happily relay stories of elves that have been passed down through the years. Álfaborg is a legally protected natural site, and a fun "elf rock" to photograph and climb upon. It can be found off of Route 94, a few kilometers south of town. GPS coordinates are N 65.3119, W 13.4832.

Sports and Recreation

TOP EXPERIENCE

BIRD-WATCHING

Birdlife thrives in the area. About 8,000 pairs of puffins nest every summer in Borgarfjörður Eystri from mid-April to mid-August. Other common bird species nesting there are

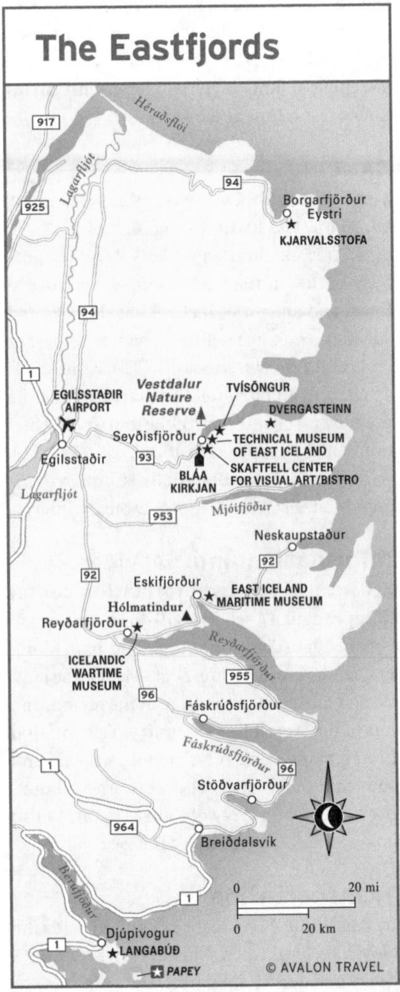

The Eastfjords

fulmars, kittiwakes, and eider ducks. An observation platform at the marina connects to a small islet that puffins love, giving you a close-up view from about two meters away. The islet is a photographer's dream; the birds are plentiful and the scenery breathtaking.

HIKING

Borgarfjörður Eystri is home to numerous well-maintained hiking trails and has earned the nickname "Paradise of the Hiker." There are 27 day routes in the region where hikers can see black-sand beaches, towering mountains, ancient farm ruins, and colorful hills and valleys. The region is also known for its exceptional hiking facilities, including lodges and restrooms at certain points. A hiking map is for sale at local tourism businesses as well as the information center in Egilsstaðir. The hikes vary in degree of difficulty and length, so be sure to consult the maps closely.

Food and Accommodations

Álfacafé (Iðngarðar, tel. 354/472-9884, alfacafe@simnet.is, 10am-8pm daily mid-May-mid-Sept., limited hours mid-Sept.-mid-May, entrées from 2,00ISK) is a charming café that serves delicious fish soup, salted cod snacks, and fresh pastries and breads.

Alfheimar Guesthouse (Brekkubær, tel. 354/861-3677, www.alfheimar.com, rooms from 16,00ISK) is a remote 30-room guesthouse situated near a puffin colony. The hosts, a husband and wife, are inviting, making you feel like you're staying with friends. Rooms are spacious and have the comforts of home. The free Wi-Fi is surprisingly strong for the region, and the in-house **restaurant** (7am-8pm daily, entrées from 2,800ISK) has some delicious options. A breakfast buffet is included in the price of the room.

Blábjörg Guesthouse (Gamla Frystihusid, tel. 354/861-1792, www.blabjorg.com, rooms from 18,000ISK) offers 11 rooms in an unexpected building: a renovated fish processing factory. Rooms are bright and cozy, and six rooms have beautiful seaside views. Amenities include a common kitchen and dining room, shared bathroom facilities, and free Wi-Fi throughout the building. The ground floor features a spa and wellness center with hot tubs and saunas.

Transportation

Borgarfjörður Eystri is 70 kilometers north of Egilsstaðir. Route 94, a paved road, connects to Egilsstaðir, which is about an hour away from the fjord.

horses grazing in the Eastfjords

SEYÐISFJÖRÐUR

Seyðisfjörður gets a lot of traffic for a tiny town of fewer than 1,000 residents. This is due to the harbor acting as the main ferry terminal that shuffles passengers to and from continental Europe. You may be arriving as a point of necessity, but the darling town has lots of reasons to stay a couple of days and explore.

Sights

BLAA KIRKJAN

The **Blaa Kirkjan** (Hafnargata 44, tel. 354/470-2308, www.blaakirkjan.is), or Blue Church, is a quaint wooden structure built in 1922 that hosts a series of concerts during the summer months. Genres range from classical music to choral to jazz. Concerts are held in July and August and cost 2,500ISK. Check the website for the summer schedule. If you like traditional churches, be sure to check it out, but if you're not seeing a concert here, you can skip it.

TECHNICAL MUSEUM OF EAST ICELAND (Tækniminjasafn Austurlands)

The **Technical Museum of East Iceland** (Hafnargata 44, tel. 354/472-1596, www.tekmus.is, 11am-5pm Mon.-Fri. June-mid-Sept., by appointment mid-Sept.-May, 1,000ISK) is home to the first telegraph station in Iceland, along with exhibitions that depict technical innovations from 1880 to 1950. There are tools on display, a letterpress machine and type, and equipment used in the fishing industry. It's an unexpected museum due to the remote surroundings, and it's worth the trip. A couple of exhibitions are geared toward children.

TVÍSÖNGUR

Tvísöngur is sound sculpture by German artist Lukas Kühne that is situated on a mountainside in Seyðisfjörður. The concrete structure consists of five interconnected domes of different sizes ranging 2-4 meters. Each dome has its own unique resonance that corresponds to a tone in the Icelandic musical tradition of five-tone harmony, and the dome works as a natural amplifier to that tone. Guests can experience an acoustic sensation that can be explored and experimented with. The site's remoteness and serenity offer a perfect setting for playing music or singing—alone, in harmony, or even for an audience. Tvísöngur is accessed by a gravel walking path that starts across from the Brimberg Fish Factory (Hafnargata 47). It takes 15-20

the Blaa Kirkjan

minutes and is a moderately difficult walk. Make sure you have good shoes.

SKAFTFELL CENTER FOR VISUAL ART (Myndlistarmiðstöð Austurlands)

The **Skaftfell Center for Visual Art** (Austurvegur 42, tel. 354/472-1632, www.skaftfell.is, noon-6pm daily, free) works hard to bring contemporary art exhibitions to a predominantly rural area—and it succeeds. The center hosts exhibitions by local and visiting artists as well as a permanent exhibition of contemporary art featuring Icelandic and international artists. You can take a private tour for 2,500ISK.

VESTDALSEYRI NATURE RESERVE

The Vestdalseyri Nature Reserve, about one kilometer north of town, is a valley known for its many waterfalls and rich birdlife. It's a beautiful place to roam and take in the mountain scenery. It contains an easy hike that is one of the most popular trails in Seyðisfjörður. You can start at the Vestdalseyri entrance and follow the trail. After passing a few glorious waterfalls, you will arrive at a small lake, Vestdalsvatn, which remains frozen most of the year. The hike is about four kilometers and takes about 2.5 hours.

DVERGASTEINN

Dvergasteinn (Vesturgata 12), or Dwarf Boulder, was once the site of a church, with the namesake boulder behind it. The church moved, but the boulder remained, and folklore enthusiasts say the stone is inhabited by dwarves, or "hidden people."

Sports and Recreation

FISHING

Sea Angling Seyðisfjörður (at the marina, tel. 354/471-3060) is a company operated by local fisherman Haraldur Arnason, who will take you out to fish, observe bird settlements, and enjoy the open sea. You can have your catch prepared at Hótel Aldan's restaurant for a fee. The tour is available all year but is dependent on the weather conditions. Call for the schedule and rates, as they vary depending on the time of year.

HIKING

Seyðisfjörður has quite a few trails to choose from, ranging from easy to more challenging. Hiking maps are available at the town's tourist information center.

For an easy lowland hike, start from the parking area by the Austdalsa River and head to the nature reserve **Skalanes,** where there is a guesthouse and museum. This hike includes views of the gorgeous Skalanesbjarg bird cliffs, where you can see nesting eider ducks May-July. Please be mindful of nests and eggs and be careful where you step along the way. It's about a 90-minute hike, a distance of 4.5 kilometers.

A more challenging trail starts from Skalanes and goes up along the edge of the cliffs to the Skollaskard pass, which is steep. You continue on into a valley, **Afrettadalur.** The landscape is breathtaking, but be careful to monitor weather conditions. The hike is about eight hours out-and-back, with an elevation gain of 643 meters, and the total distance is 17 kilometers.

The hike through **Brimnes** is another gem of a trek. Brimnes is on the north shore of Seyðisfjörður and was for centuries one of the major fishing villages in East Iceland. Start at the Selsstadir farm, which is signposted, 10 kilometers from the center of town, where you'll find ruins of old buildings and a small orange lighthouse. A walk out to Brimnes in good weather with good visibility is memorable. Be sure to have your camera ready. The moderately difficult hike is about two hours round-trip and covers a total distance of 5.5 kilometers.

Experienced climbers with endurance should check out the historical trail that leads from the Austdalsa parking area and up past the abandoned farmstead Austdalur. It's extremely important to follow the trail posts down into the Brekkugja opening, as well as to be careful when crossing the snowbanks above it, before continuing down the Brekkudalur valley to the **Brekka settlement,** a historic village. The out-and-back hike takes a total of about 14 hours and covers about 24 kilometers. The highest elevation reached is 781 meters, and the trail has some steep climbs. This is typically done as a long day hike in the summer, strictly in June-August while monitoring weather conditions.

SKIING

The **Stafdalur Ski Area** (tel. 354/898-2798, stafdalu@stafdalur.is, Dec.-May) is nine kilometers southwest from Seyðisfjörður and has a 1,000-meter ski lift, as well as a lift for children. Cross-country skiing and snowmobiling are possible from the ski area; there is excellent access for snowmobiles from the ski area to magnificent mountains, deserted fjords, and the famous Dyrfjoll mountains. Lift tickets are 2,500ISK for adults, 1,000ISK for children.

SWIMMING

The town swimming pool, **Sundhöll Seyðisfjarðar** (Suðurgata 5, tel. 354/472-1414, 6:30am-9am and 3pm-8pm Mon.-Fri., 1pm-4pm Sat., 550ISK), is small, but it's frequented by locals and their children. If the weather is bad, a dip in one of the hot tubs is divine.

Food

Skaftfell Bistro (Austurvegur 42, tel. 354/472-1633, www.skaftfell.is, noon-10pm daily, entrées from 2,00ISK) is a cool spot to grab a bite to eat. It's decorated with works by the artist Dieter Roth, and has shelves of art books to check out while you dine. Sandwiches, pizza, pastries, and soup are on offer.

Cafe Lára El Grillo Bar (Norðugata 3, tel. 354/472-1703, 11:30am-1:30am Mon.-Thurs., 11:30am-3:30am Fri.-Sat., 12:30pm-1:30am Sun.) is a relaxed café in town where you can have a cup of coffee, watch a football game, and dine outside when the weather is nice. You can buy coffee, cakes, soups, sandwiches, and other light meals. At night, the place turns into the local bar, and locals gather to drink a few pints and listen to music.

Accommodations

★ **Hótel Aldan** (Norðurgata 2, tel. 354/472-1277, www.hotelaldan.is, rooms from 26,000ISK) is an adorable guesthouse that features seven double rooms and two triples with vintage furniture, antique lamps, and modern amenities, including Wi-Fi, minibars, private bathrooms with showers, TV and DVD players, and laundry service. Rooms are tasteful, charming, and Icelandic chic, with wood furnishings, muted colors, and minimalist design. Breakfast is included in the room rate, and the hotel is open year-round.

Hótel Snæfell (Austurvegur 3, tel. 354/472-1277, www.hotelaldan.com, rooms from 18,000ISK) is operated by the same owners as Hótel Aldan. This guesthouse is based in a large three-story wooden house and offers 12 rooms. The rooms are bright and spacious and feature comfortable beds, but they lack the charm of rooms at Hótel Aldan. Guests have access to free Wi-Fi, a private bathroom with a shower, a small television, and laundry service. Breakfast is included.

Skalanes Mountain Lodge (Skalanes, tel. 354/861-7008, www.skalanes.com, May-Sept., rooms from 19,000ISK) is a 1927 farmhouse that now includes a comfortable library, sauna and hot tub, and a lounge with a classic wood-burning stove. Rooms are small but clean and orderly, and common areas are equipped with Wi-Fi. The deck, which overlooks the sea, has an outdoor fireplace and is a perfect place to curl up with a book when the weather is pleasant. Skalanes's restaurant serves baked cod, lamb fillets, and vegetarian options like veggie burgers.

Hafaldan Seyðisfjörður Hostel (Suðurgata 8, tel. 354/611-4410, www.hafaldan.is, rooms from 12,200ISK) offers rooms in two buildings. Halfaldan Harbor Hostel is on the north side of the fjord, just two minutes from the town center, offering twin, double, and four-bed rooms, all with shared bathroom and kitchen facilities. The second location, Hafaldan Hospital Hostel, occupies a historic former hospital building. It offers private double rooms as well as double, twin, and dormitory rooms with shared facilities. In both locations, the dining and living rooms are lively and great places to meet fellow travelers. Rooms aren't pretty, but they are clean and adequate. The guests tend to be young budget travelers.

CAMPING

You have the option to camp close to the town center at the **Seyðisfjörður Campsite** (Ranargata 5, tel. 354/472-1521, May 1-Sept. 30, 1,600ISK per adult, free for children under 14), in a facility that has showers, hot and cold running water, and shared kitchen facilities. There's also a free Internet connection. The campsite accommodates tents and RVs, and hookups are available.

Information and Services

The **tourist information center** (Hafnargata 44, tel. 354/470-2308, 9am-4pm Mon.-Fri.) is at the ferry terminal by the harbor. You can find brochures about the region, ferry timetables and rates, hiking maps, road maps, and stamps. There's also free Wi-Fi, and a small café serves coffee, soft drinks, and snacks.

Transportation

Seyðisfjörður is 27 kilometers east of Egilsstaðir, the nearest hub. By car, Route 93, which is paved, is your only option to get to Seyðisfjörður.

FAS (tel. 354/893-2669) operates a year-round daily bus connecting Egilsstaðir's airport to Seyðisfjörður. Each way costs 1,080ISK, and the trip takes about one hour. For information on schedules, visit www.visitseydisfjordur.com/project/local-bus-schedule.

Smyril Line (tel. 298/345900, www.smyrilline.com) operates a ferry from Denmark to the Faroe Islands to Iceland, with weekly departures from Hirtshals, Denmark. The trip from Denmark to Iceland is approximately 47 hours and costs about 120,000ISK each way with a vehicle. For more information, check the rates and schedule online.

REYÐARFJÖRÐUR

Reyðarfjörður's population hovers around 1,000, and locals are amused by the attention their tiny town has been getting of late. The longest and widest of the eastern fjords, Reyðarfjörður has the charm you'd expect from a small town with quaint accommodations and scenic mountain walks.

Sights

ICELANDIC WARTIME MUSEUM

The **Icelandic Wartime Museum** (Spitalakampur, tel. 354/470-9063, 1pm-5pm daily June-Aug., rest of year by request, 1,000ISK) may seem like an odd museum to be based in one of the most peaceful countries in the world. Iceland has never had its own military, but British and American troops were based in Iceland for decades leading up to and following World War II. This museum is dedicated to the days when Allied troops were stationed in the region. You can find photos, models, weapons, uniforms, and information on how troops passed their time in the small fishing village.

Sports and Recreation

HIKING

Reyðarfjörður is the perfect town for taking leisurely strolls. The lovely slopes above the village include a trail beginning along the southern part of the Búðará River. Above the residential area, you will find delightful areas to explore. Grab hiking maps in the **Reyðarfjörður tourist information office** (Heiðarvegur 37, tel. 354/470-9000, 1pm-5pm daily June-Aug.).

Food and Accommodations

Hotel Austur (Búðareyri 6, tel. 354/474-1600, rooms from 21,000ISK) looks and feels like a hunting lodge with dim lighting, lots of wood furnishings, and a remote location. Rooms are average-sized and sparsely decorated, and Wi-Fi is available. It's close to a host of activities, including horse riding, golf, skiing, and fishing. The room price includes a breakfast buffet, and the **restaurant** (6pm-10pm daily, entrées from 2,500ISK) serves classic Icelandic food for dinner with lots of fish and lamb on the menu.

Hjá Marlín Guesthouse (Vallargerdi 9, tel. 354/474-1220, www.bakkagerdi.net, rooms from 16,000ISK) is a cozy guesthouse that features singles, doubles, and dorm accommodations. Rooms are small and no-frills, but some rooms have private bathrooms. Guests have access to a fully equipped kitchen, TV lounge, sauna, and laundry facilities. The **restaurant** (5pm-8pm daily, entrées from 2,800ISK) serves lots of lamb dishes as well as fresh fish, including lobster, scallops, cod, and salmon.

Tærgesen Guesthouse (Buðargata 4, tel. 354/4704444, www.taergesen.com, rooms from 13,000ISK) is an old-fashioned guesthouse that features rooms with standard beds, free Wi-Fi, and wood furnishings. Some rooms have spectacular views of the landscape. The in-house **restaurant** (5pm-10pm daily, entrées from 3,500ISK) offers classic Icelandic cuisine, such as smoked leg of lamb and salted cod, but also tourist-friendly fare like hamburgers and pizza.

Transportation

Reyðarfjörður is 58 kilometers south of Seyðisfjörður on Route 92, the only way to the town. Be sure to check the weather forecast before you head out as the road, though paved, can be challenging—even dangerous—during wet weather.

ESKIFJÖRÐUR

Eskifjörður is a small, single-road village that was established as a base of operations for Norwegian fishermen. Today, it's a quiet town of about 1,000 residents with a couple of guesthouses that draw tourists in the summer months. A few scenic hiking paths offer splendid views of the landscape and local birdlife.

Sights

EAST ICELAND MARITIME MUSEUM (Sjóminjasafn Austurlands)

The **East Iceland Maritime Museum** (Strandgata 39b, tel. 354/470-9063, 1pm-5pm daily June-Aug., open by request Sept.-May, 1,000ISK) pays tribute to the town's rich fishing history with exhibits of items relating to fishing and seafaring, as well as artifacts of local trade, industry, and medicine from times past. The collection is housed in a black wooden building that was built in 1816, called **Gamlabúð.**

Sports and Recreation

HIKING

Mount Holmatindur, which stands 985 meters high, towers over the fjord opposite the town. Locals take great pride in the peak. The trek to the top, which has fantastic views of the east, can be challenging, but those who make it can sign a logbook declaring their achievement. Because the trailhead is situated near paved Route 92 just 3.5 kilometers east from the center of town, it's quite easy to get to the mountain. The 10-kilometer round-trip is moderately difficult and takes about eight hours total to hike. Check the weather forecast before you head out, bring the proper gear, and alert your hotel of your plans.

SWIMMING

The **Eskifjörður Swimming Pool** (tel. 354/476-1218, 6am-9pm Mon.-Fri., 10am-6pm Sat.-Sun. June-Aug., 6am-8pm Mon.-Fri., 1pm-6pm Sat.-Sun. Apr.-May and Sept.-Oct., 650ISK) features an outdoor 25-meter pool, a children's pool with three waterslides, and two hot tubs, a sauna, and a fitness center.

GOLF

The **Byggðarholt** golf course (Strandgata 71a, tel. 354/892-4622, year-round, greens fees 3,000ISK) is a nine-hole course with yardage markers, a putting green, chipping green, and practice bunker area.

Food and Accommodations

The **Seahouse Restaurant** (Strandgata 120, tel. 354/477-1247, lunch and dinner daily in summer, entrées from 3,500ISK) offers local delicacies like shark meat, dried fish, pickled herring, and reindeer steaks as well as fresh fish from the fjord.

Hotel Apartments in Eskifjörður (Strandgata 26, tel. 354/892-8657, www.hotelibudir.net, apartments from 16,000ISK) has four self-catering apartments for rent. The apartments are 60 square meters with one bedroom (two beds, extra beds and mattresses available), a living room with a dining area, a fully equipped kitchen, a laundry room, and a bathroom. The apartments have all the comforts of home, including free Wi-Fi. The location is perfect, in the center of town and close to the harbor.

Mjoeyri Guesthouse (Strandgata 120, tel. 354/477-1247, www.mjoeyri.is) offers two types of accommodations: standard rooms at the guesthouse (from 19,400ISK) and five self-catering cottages (from 31,900ISK). Cottages are equipped with a kitchen, dining room, one bedroom, and a balcony with a beautiful view of the landscape. Rooms are no-frills with standard beds and basic furnishings. The owners are friendly and accommodating. A breakfast buffet costs 2,100ISK per person.

Transportation

Eskifjörður is 73 kilometers south of Seyðisfjörður on Route 92. Be sure to check the weather forecast before you head out; the road, though paved, can be challenging—even dangerous—during wet weather.

NESKAUPSTAÐUR

Fifty years ago, Neskaupstaður was only accessible by sea, making it the most remote and untouched spot in the Eastfjords. However, a tunnel was built that connected the town with Eskifjörður via paved Route 92. There still isn't a lot to do here, but there is a trio of museums to visit if you want to make a quick stop before continuing on the Ring Road.

Sights

The **Museum House (Safnahúsið)** (Miðstræti 1, tel. 354/ 477-1446, www.fjardabyggd.is, 1pm-5pm daily June-Aug., 1,000ISK) is home to three museums. The **Museum of Natural History** will be a winner if you're traveling with children, as a special exhibition allows them to touch different animals. There are also displays of Icelandic

Mount Holmatindur

mammals, birds, insects, and shellfish, as well as exhibitions on stones and flora found in East Iceland. The **Josafat Hinriksson Maritime Museum** showcases relics relating to ironwork, fishing, boatbuilding, and the way in which people lived in East Iceland in the old days. The town's art museum, the **Tryggvi Olafsson Art Collection,** is dedicated to the works of local artist Tryggvi, who was born in the town in 1940. He is one of East Iceland's most revered contemporary artists. Tryggvi's bright, colorful paintings mix abstract art with wildlife and landscape themes.

Rauðubjörg, which means "red cliffs," is a great example of the varied landscape of East Iceland. While the cliffs are predominantly red, you can see hues ranging from brown to white, and it's a striking sight against the bright blue sea. You'll find a lookout point where you can safely pull off the road just south of Neskaupstaður via paved Route 92.

Food and Accommodations

Located in the center of town, **Nesbær** (Egilsbraut 5, tel. 354/477-1115, 9am-6pm Mon.-Sat., 1pm-5pm Sun., entrées from 1,990ISK) is a cozy coffeehouse popular among locals and tourists for lunch. The menu features crepes, sandwiches, salads, and soup.

Hótel Edda Neskaupstaður (Nesgata 40, tel. 354/444-4860, www.hoteledda.is, mid-June-mid-Aug., rooms from 21,000ISK) offers 29 rooms with private bathrooms and free Wi-Fi. Rooms are average-sized with bright white walls and bedding, and a huge window overlooking the mountainous landscape. A breakfast buffet is available for 1,750ISK per person, and the hotel's dinner menu consists of straightforward fish and lamb choices.

Hildibrand Hotel (Hafnarbraut 2, tel. 354/477-1950, www.hildibrandhotel.com, rooms from 15,000ISK, apartments from 21,000ISK) is a guesthouse offering 9 double rooms and 15 self-catering apartments. While the guesthouse rooms are a little on the Spartan side, the apartments are spacious with full-size kitchens, large sofas, flat-screen TVs, and ocean views.

Transportation

Neskaupstaður is 72 kilometers southeast of Egilsstaðir on Route 92. Check the weather forecast before you head out, as the road, though paved, can be challenging—even dangerous—during wet weather.

FÁSKRÚÐSFJÖRÐUR

Fáskrúðsfjörður is a small village of fewer than 500 people nestled on a long fjord of the same name. It's the most "French" part of Iceland. The village was originally a base for more than 5,000 French fishermen who came every year to fish the Icelandic waters. Some settled here in the late 19th century. The village had a hospital, chapel, and cemetery that were built by the Frenchmen, and both the buildings and the history remain, as the streets of Fáskrúðsfjörður are marked in both Icelandic and French. If you visit during the last weekend in July, you can join in with the **French Days** festival, which celebrates the town's history with French-inspired food and flags. A museum aptly named **French Fishermen in Iceland** (Hafnargata 12, tel. 354/475-1170, 10am-6pm daily June-Aug., 1,00ISK) does a great job of describing the history of the town and the importance of the impact of the French, and it even has a delightful and popular little café that sells coffee, cakes, and light meals.

Food and Accommodations

Café Sumarlína (Búðavegur 59, tel. 354/475-1575, www.sumarlina.is, 11am-10pm Mon-Fri., 1pm-10pm Sat.-Sun., entrées from 2,050ISK) occupies a cute white house in the center of town. The atmosphere is warm and inviting, and the staff is the same. The menu features pizzas, burgers, lamb and fish entrées, and quite a few French-inspired dishes, like crepes and baguette sandwiches.

Fosshotel Eastfjords (Hafnargata 11-14, tel. 354/470-4070, www.fosshotel.is, rooms from 27,000ISK) is a 47-room hotel with

French-inspired decor, paying homage to the history of the town. It offers standard, superior, single, and triple rooms with hardwood floors, muted wallpaper, quality linens, and simple furniture. It has an in-house **bar and restaurant** (6:30am-9pm daily, dinner entrées from 3,900ISK), free parking, and free Wi-Fi. Breakfast is included in the price of the room.

Transportation

Fáskrúðsfjörður is 50 kilometers south of Egilsstaðir on Route 92. Be sure to check the weather forecast before you head out because the road, though paved, can be challenging and dangerous during wet weather.

STÖDVARFJÖRÐUR

Stöðvarfjörður is another minuscule village in the Eastfjords that has strikingly beautiful nature to explore, including rocky terrain, mountains, and a gorgeous shoreline.

Sights

PETRA'S STONE & MINERAL COLLECTION

(Steinasafn Petru Stöðvarfirði)

Petra's Stone & Mineral Collection (Fjarðarbraut 21, tel. 354/475-8834, www.steinapetra.is, 9am-6pm daily May-Sept., 9am-3pm daily Oct.-Nov. and Feb.-Apr., 1,500ISK, free for children 13 and under) is a stunning private collection of more than 1,000 stones that are cut and polished, revealing crystals and other beautiful facets. The owner started amassing stones in 1976, and the collection includes lava, crystals, basalt, pearls, granite, opals, and amethysts.

SAXA

Saxa, a sea geyser, is an interesting natural phenomenon where the waves crash into a rocky crevice and shoot high into the air, creating water "eruptions." The name Saxa is derived from the kelp and seaweed that are *saxað* (chopped) inside the crevices and then hurled into the air with the waves. The sea geyser is a cool sight and unique to the area.

Food and Accommodations

SAXA Guesthouse (Fjarðarbraut 41, tel. 354/511-3055, saxa@saxa.is, rooms from 14,000ISK) is close to the harbor in the heart of the town. Its 14 rooms are bright and minimalist. A common lounge has a TV and a terrace to enjoy in good weather. Breakfast is included. The in-house **café** (7am-9pm daily, entrées from 2,800ISK) is open for breakfast, lunch, and dinner and offers soups, salads, sandwiches, and lamb and fish meals.

Transportation

Stöðvarfjörður is 73 kilometers southeast of Egilsstaðir on Route 92. Be sure to check the weather forecast before you head out; the road, though paved, can be dangerous during wet weather.

BREIÐDALSVÍK

Breiðdalsvík is a blip of a town with fewer than 200 residents. There's not much going on here, but a couple of guesthouses serve those who need a break from the Ring Road.

Food and Accommodations

The Old General Store (Sólvellir 25, tel. 354/475-6670, 7am-10pm daily) is a quaint café and shop that retains the charm of its history. Built in 1956, has its original wood shelves and displays some old product tins of brands that were popular in Iceland during the 1950s and 1960s. It's also a great spot to grab a cup of coffee and slice of cake or pick up some necessities for your journey.

Hótel Bláfell (Solvellir 14, tel. 354/475-6770, www.hotelblafell.is, rooms from 18,000ISK) is a darling 34-room country hotel offering singles, doubles, and family rooms that range from simple modern decor to wood-paneled, rustic chic. All rooms have private bathrooms, free Wi-Fi, and standard beds. The hotel also has a sauna, lounge with fireplace, and library with interesting books and even board games. The **restaurant** (7am-9pm daily, entrées from 3,900ISK) does a nice take on classic fish and lamb dishes, but the menu doesn't have any surprises.

Hótel Staðarborg (tel. 354/475-6760, www.stadarborg.is, rooms from 19,000ISK) offers 30 rooms ranging from singles with shared bathrooms to family rooms. Rooms are small but adequate, with minimal furnishings. There's a hot tub out back, but that's where the amenities end. The **restaurant** (6pm-9pm daily) is pricey, as it costs 3,000ISK for breakfast and almost 6,000ISK for a meat or fish dinner. The hotel is located on Route 1, about seven kilometers from Breiðdalsvík. It's a fine spot to spend a night while navigating the Ring Road, but you'll pay quite a bit.

Café Margrét (Heimaleiti, tel. 354/475-6625, cafemargret@simnet.is, rooms from 20,000ISK) is a small four-room guesthouse right off Route 1. The guesthouse has standard rooms with shared bathroom facilities. Its **restaurant** (5:30pm-10pm daily, entrées from 3,800ISK) serves up classic Icelandic cuisine (lamb and fish) as well as soups, salads, and sandwiches.

Eyjar Fishing Lodge (Eyjar, tel. 354/567-5204, rooms from 24,000ISK) has the look and feel of an authentic fishing lodge, with some luxury amenities. Its eight rooms come with heated floors and free Wi-Fi, and are decorated with lots of wood and fish-inspired art. The lodge also has a common lounge, hot tub, and sauna.

Transportation

Breiðdalsvík is 83 kilometers southeast of Egilsstaðir on Route 1. Check the weather forecast before you head out because wet weather could make the road challenging—even dangerous.

DJÚPIVOGUR

Djúpivogur, a town of fewer than 500 people, has a history of fishing and trading dating to 1589. A picturesque landscape is the backdrop to countless hiking trails, where are free to roam and explore. The 1,069-meter **Mount Búlandstindur** looms over the town, dominating the terrain. A few museums are aimed at tourists looking to spend time indoors.

Sights

LANGABÚÐ

Langabúð (Búð 1, tel. 354/478-8220, www.langabud.is, 11am-6pm daily mid-May-mid-Sept., open by appointment mid-Sept.-mid-May, 500ISK) is the oldest building in the town, dating back to 1790, and it houses a heritage museum as well as an exhibition dedicated to a local sculptor. The folk museum contains an eclectic collection of pieces integral to the town's history, including fishing equipment such as whale harpoons as well as antique parts that belonged to early wagons. The collection may seem like there isn't a strong theme, but that's part of the charm, a mishmash of town history. As for the art portion of the building, artist **Ríkarður Jónsson** (1888-1974) was known as the founder of a national folk-art movement in Iceland. Classic themes of work and family are depicted in his portraiture and wood sculpture, and the museum houses many of his wood carvings and the tools he used in his work.

BIRD AND MINERAL MUSEUM (Fuglavefur Djupavogs)

The **Bird and Mineral Museum** (Bakka 1, tel. 354/478-89288, www.djupivogur.is, 10am-6pm daily in summer, open by appointment in winter, 500ISK) holds about 130 species of stuffed birds, along with nests and eggs. There are also photos and books about birdlife and Icelandic minerals. The focus may seem random, but the curators have taken great care to unify the bird and mineral collections under one roof.

★ PAPEY

The small island of Papey, south of Djúpivogur, is about two square kilometers and teems with birdlife and basking seals. It's affectionately called "Bird Island" by many due to the 30,000 pairs of puffins that occupy the island during the summer. Eider ducks and black-legged kittiwakes typically nest on Papey as well.

Papey is also home to the smallest and oldest wooden church in the country, which was built in 1807. North of the church is a beautiful little hill called Einbúi (The Loner), where the church of the fairies is supposed to be located, according to Icelandic lore.

Irish monks are believed to have lived on the island before Viking settlement; the monks left when the Vikings arrived, as they didn't want to share the land with such unsavory fellows. The island is named after these monks, called Papar. Other local names, like Papatættur and Írsku Hólar (Irish Hills), also reflect their presence.

Papeyjarferðir (tel. 354/478-8119, www.djupivogur.is/papey) runs guided tours—your only opportunity to get a peek at the island—at 1pm daily June-August from Djúpivogur marina. During the 50-minute boat trip, you might see seals hanging out in the surf and on the rocks. Have your camera ready! The trip is four hours long total and includes a guided hike on the island. It costs 12,000ISK for adults and 6,000ISK for children aged 5-11 but is free for children under 5.

Sports and Recreation

HIKING AND BIRD-WATCHING

Hiking the serene and well-kept trails around the flat **Bulandsnes Peninsula** is a must for bird-watchers. Most of the birds nesting in Iceland can be seen on or around Bulandsnes during the migration period in the summer, with the places of greatest interest being the lakes Breidivogur and Fyluvogur. In this area, you can see tufted ducks and pintails, as well as less common species like red-throated divers and black-tailed godwits.

Two different routes begin and end at the cairn Bondavarða east of Djúpivogur. The longer route is about 10 kilometers, a moderate four-hour hike, and the shorter one is easier and approximately 5 kilometers, which takes about two hours.

If you opt for the shorter route, you must turn on Ulfseyjarsund (a fork) and continue to the airstrip, then continue to the lakes Breidivogur and Fyluvogur and back to where you started.

If you choose the longer route, you have to turn near Ulfseyjarsund, go to the airstrip, and from there hike to Ulfsey. At the southwest tip of Ulfsey, there is a sign, and from there you can choose whether to view Ulfsey, Hvaley, or Sandey, a trio of islets that are now connected to the mainland. Then you go back the same way from the sign in Ulfsey, to the airstrip and then to the lakes Breidivogur and Fyluvogur and back to Bondavarða.

church in Papey

SWIMMING

On a rainy day, the **Djúpivogur Swimming Pool** (Varða 6, tel. 354/478-8999, 7am-8:30pm Mon.-Fri., 10am-6pm Sat.-Sun, 600ISK) is a great option. In the winter, you will see locals and their children taking a dip in the heated pool or one of the hot tubs, but the summer sees a lot of tourist traffic.

Food and Accommodations

Langabúð (Búð 1, tel. 354/478-8220, 10am-6pm daily May 15-Sept. 15, meals from 2,000ISK) is a tiny café that serves pastries, coffee, and light meals that hit the spot. The cakes are hard to resist, and the ingredients for the soups and sandwiches are local and fresh.

★ **Hótel Framtíð** (Vogalandi 4, tel. 354/478-8887, www.hotelframtid.com, rooms from 28,000ISK) is the place to go if you want to stay in town. This is the only close option. The 42-room hotel has wood-paneled rooms that remind you of a hunting lodge, standard beds, and simple furnishings. Its **Framtíð Restaurant** (call ahead because opening hours vary, entrées from 4,650ISK) features entrées including baked fish with white butter sauce, chicken breast with salad and potatoes, and lamb fillets with fresh vegetables and potatoes. Desserts are scrumptious, including whipped *skyr* with cream and mixed berries and apple cake with fresh cream. Group menus are available for parties of 10 or more.

Berunes Hostel (Berufjörður, tel. 354/478-8988, www.berunes.is, open only Apr.-Sept., rooms from 13,800ISK) is a charming converted farmhouse just outside of Djúpivogur. The hostel offers rooms that accommodate 1-4 people as well as five self-contained cottages that can house 2-5 people. Rooms are small but comfortable, and some of them remind you of a guesthouse out of the 1970s. Berunes serves meals in a building next to the hostel. **Gestastofa Café** serves breakfast year-round (7am-10am daily), and a three-course dinner is served in July and August (6pm-9pm daily).

Havarí (Karlsstaðir, tel. 354/663-5520, www.havari.is) is an organic farm, hostel, café, and music venue operated by Svavar Eysteinsson, of the band Prins Póló, and his wife Berglind Häsler. The couple serves up their own vegan sausages as well as soup, cakes, sandwiches, and waffles at the café (9am-9pm Mon.-Sat., 11am-9pm Sun.). The hostel offers double and family rooms as well as dorm accommodations; hostel accommodations start from 5,000ISK and rooms start from 15,000ISK. In the summer, the farm hosts concerts from some of the most popular musicians and bands in the country. Havarí is 42 kilometers north of Djúpivogur on Route 1.

CAMPING

The **Djúpivogur Campground** (tel. 354/478-8887, May 1-Sept. 30, 1,600ISK per person) is conveniently situated close to Hótel Framtíð, which is where you pay the camping fees. At the height of the summer season (July), the site is littered with vans and campers, but it can feel like a little community and it's fun to meet fellow travelers. The facilities are decent, with an indoor cooking area and steaming-hot showers. The campground is in an open field, and there is room for tents and RVs, with hookups available.

Information and Services

The **tourist information center** (Bakka 3, tel. 354/478-8204, www.djupivogur.is, 9am-5pm Mon.-Fri., noon-4pm Sat.-Sun. mid-May-mid-Sept.) offers hiking maps, brochures about the region, and Internet access.

Transportation

Djúpivogur is 86 kilometers south of Egilsstaðir on Route 1.

SBA (tel. 354/550-0700, www.sba.is) operates daily bus trips from Egilsstaðir to Djúpivogur mid-June-August. The three-hour trip costs 6,000ISK each way.

The Vatnajökull Region

In the Vatnajökull region, Iceland earns its "fire and ice" reputation. You'll see the glacier descend into black sands and hot streams erupt from frozen banks of ice.

The region is easy to access, as there are frequent flights and buses between Reykjavík and Höfn. For flights, check out **Eagle Air** (www.eagleair.is), and for buses, try **Strætó** (www.straeto.is) and **Reykjavík Excursions** (www.re.is). Höfn is the best gateway to the region and the perfect town in which to base yourself.

HÖFN

Höfn, which means harbor, is the gateway to Vatnajökull glacier, and guesthouses and cafés accommodate the growing number of tourists to the region. There are roughly 2,000 residents of Höfn, which makes it quite a sleepy town, but it comes alive in the summer, when legions of tourists from around the world gear up to scale the glacier. The town has a few small museums, including a spectacular one dedicated to the looming Vatnajökull.

Sights

FOLK MUSEUM
(Gamlabúð)

The **Folk Museum** (Hafnarbraut, tel. 354/478-1833, 9am-4pm daily year-round, free) has a small collection of artifacts that shows what life was like in one of the most isolated parts of the country from the 19th century on. You will find objects related to the old ways of farming, including antique tractors and cars. The museum is small, and free, but don't feel bad if you miss it.

HORNAFJÖRÐUR ART MUSEUM
(Listasafn Hornafjarðar)

The **Hornafjörður Art Museum** (Hafnarbraut 27, tel. 354/470-8000, 9am-4pm Mon.-Fri., 11am-4pm Sat.-Sun. May-Sept., 9am-4pm Mon.-Fri. and by request rest of year, free) displays the work of celebrated local artist Svavar Gudnason, who had a strong connection to his hometown of Höfn and the Vatnajökull region. Svavar was born in Höfn in 1909 and spent his youth there before moving to Reykjavík in 1928. He had been introduced to landscape painting at an early age, and his work depicts the natural surroundings in southeast Iceland, portraying the sea, glaciers, lakes, and mountains. In the winter months, works from other artists are displayed alongside those of Svavar.

Sports and Recreation

BIRD-WATCHING

Bird-watchers must head to **Ósland,** a conservation area in the south of Höfn that was once an island but is now connected to the mainland (you can reach it by walking from the harbor in Höfn). Arctic terns are a common sight during their nesting season, which takes place early in the summer, and there are walking trails along the perimeter of a pond they frequent. Located on the hill Óslandshæð is a memorial to fishermen lost at sea and an information board about the surrounding natural area, including details on the flora and fauna.

SWIMMING

The local **Höfn Swimming Pool** (Víkurbraut 9, tel. 354/470-8477, 6:45am-9pm Mon.-Fri., 10am-7pm Sat.-Sun. mid-May-Sept., 6:45am-9pm Mon.-Fri., 10am-5pm Sat.-Sun. Oct.-mid-May, 600ISK) isn't as spectacular as some of the other pools in the region, but it's a nice spot for a dip when taking a break from hiking and touring.

GOLF

The **Silfurnesvöllur** golf course (Dalbraut, tel. 354/478-2197, greens fees 4,000ISK) is on the outskirts of Höfn. It is a well-kept nine-hole course open year-round that stretches

The Vatnajökull Region

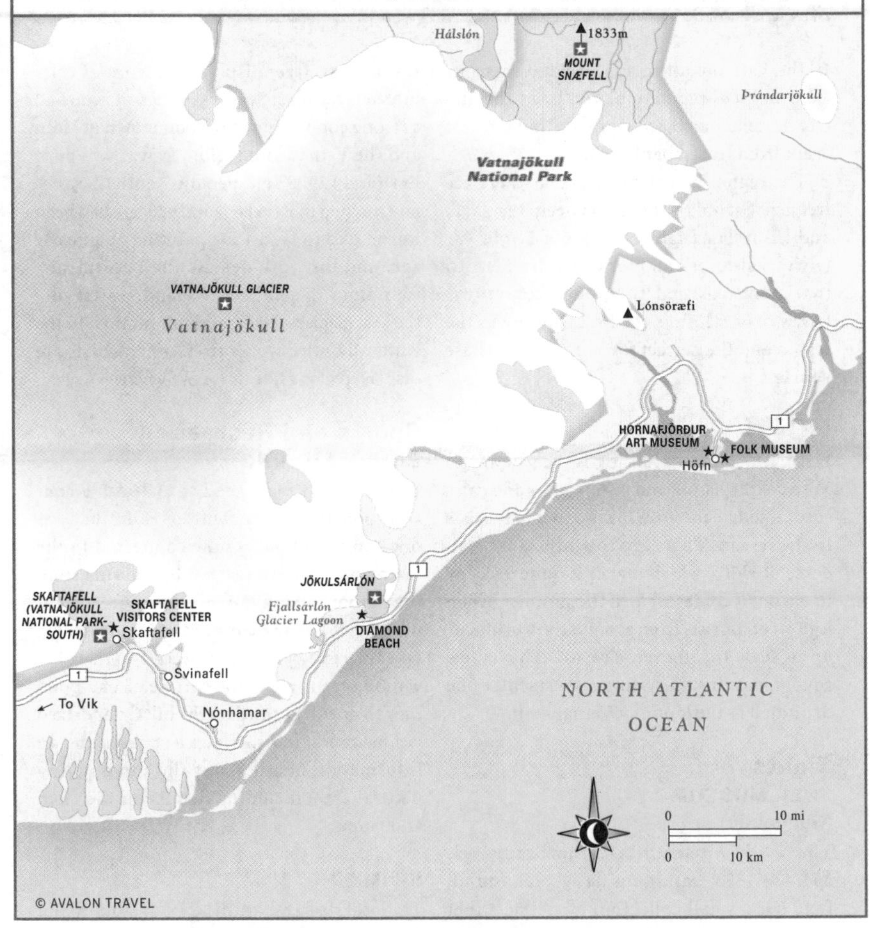

along the shore with a breathtaking view over Vatnajökull glacier and its mountain ridge.

Food

★ **Humarhofnin** (Hafnarbraut 4, tel. 354/478-1200, www.humarhofnin.is, entrées from 6,900ISK) is a quaint but can't-miss restaurant for those who want a taste of fresh Icelandic lobster; it focuses on local langoustines. Located close to the harbor where the daily catch comes in, guests are treated to some of the freshest food on the island. If you're traveling with a non-seafood eater, there are some other options on the menu, including Icelandic lamb and veggie courses.

Hótel Höfn (Víkurbraut 20, tel. 354/478-1240, www.hotelhofn.is, 6pm-10pm daily, 3,950ISK) has an eclectic menu for a hotel restaurant. It offers a few lobster dishes, and you can't go wrong with any—though the chili-and-garlic-roasted lobster tails in particular are divine. Other menu options include "tapas for two," featuring cod, lamb, beef, and shrimp options; pizza; vegetarian entrées; and pasta.

Accommodations

Hótel Edda Höfn (Ranarslod 3, tel. 354/444-4850, www.hoteledda.is, mid-May-Oct. 1., rooms from 24,000ISK) is a chain hotel offering 36 rooms that are spacious and bright, but devoid of character. But the amenities are good, and each room has a private bathroom. Guests have access to free Wi-Fi and parking, and a yummy breakfast buffet is available for 2,300ISK per person and free for children five and under.

Hótel Höfn (Víkurbraut 20, tel. 354/478-1240, www.hotelhofn.is, rooms from 22,000ISK) is a 68-room hotel that looks and feels like a chain hotel designed for business travelers. The rooms are sparsely furnished with standard beds, hardwood floors, flat-screen TVs, and free Wi-Fi. The in-house restaurant serves classic Icelandic cuisine ranging from fresh fish to lamb dishes. There are a couple of vegetarian options.

Nýibær Guesthouse (Hafnarbraut 8, tel. 354/478-1736, www.hostel.is, rooms from 20,000ISK) is in a pretty location, just a two-minute walk to the harbor. Rooms are small but brightly decorated, and guests have access to free Wi-Fi and free parking. Bathrooms are shared, and guests can use a common coffee area. Breakfast is included.

CAMPING

The **Höfn Campground** (Hafnarbraut 52, tel. 354/478-1606, June-Aug., 1,100ISK per person) is one of the nicer ones in the region and gets quite a bit of traffic when it's open in summer. Campers have access to steaming-hot showers and a nice cooking area, along with washing machines and the Internet. The site accommodates tents and RVs, with hook-ups available.

Information and Services

The **tourist information center** (Heppuvegur 1, tel. 354/470-8330, www.visitvatnajokull.is, 8am-8pm daily June-Aug., 10am-6pm daily May and Sept., 9am-1pm daily Oct.-Apr.) has tourist brochures about the region and hiking maps as well as Internet access and booking information for day tours.

Transportation

Höfn is on Route 1, 187 kilometers south of Egilsstaðir and 451 kilometers east of Reykjavík.

Höfn harbor

Höfn is challenging to get to if you aren't renting a car. **Strætó** (tel. 354/540-2700, www.straeto.is) operates one bus (bus 51) that leaves from the bus station Mjodd in Reykjavík every day, and it's about a seven-hour ride. The trip costs 12,760ISK each way.

Eagle Air (tel. 354/562-4200, www.eagleair.is) operates daily flights from Reykjavík for around 22,000ISK each way. The flight takes about one hour.

LÓNSÖRÆFI

Lónsöræfi is an isolated wildlife preserve in a raw part of the east, with birds outnumbering humans by the thousands. Bird enthusiasts looking for a glimpse of whimbrels will love Lónsöræfi. The brown and white waders with curved bills can be seen year-round.

The landscape is striking, but unforgiving, with strong winds and remnants of sub-glacial eruptions of the past. It's a beautiful patch of land, but be sure to monitor the weather closely before you head out for a hike, and keep in mind that there are not a lot of guesthouses or eateries nearby. You will feel like you're on your own, because in much of the area, you are. For accommodations, base yourself in Höfn.

Hiking from Mount Snæfell to Lónsöræfi

The trek from Mount Snæfell to Lónsöræfi is growing in popularity. The landscape is rocky and angular, with sweeping hills and vast valleys. Colors are muted, and the atmosphere is serene. Along the trek, hikers see glaciers, waterfalls, and cliffs. The hike, which starts at the **Snæfellsskáli mountain hut** (GPS coordinates N 64.8042, W 15.6418; tel. 354/575-8400), is about 55 kilometers and takes four days, with 6-8 hours of walking per day. The maximum elevation is 250 meters. It's challenging and for experienced hikers only—recent years have seen many search-and-rescue operations deployed in this isolated region in the name of stranded hikers. It's strongly recommended you explore the region as part of a tour. **Icelandic Mountain Guides** (tel. 354/587-9999, www.mountainguides.is) offers a fully guided tour, departing from Reykjavík with air transfers, an experienced guide, food for four days, and mountain hut accommodation for 145,000ISK. Departures are in July and August. Make sure you have proper gear like waterproof clothing for rain and wind.

Transportation

The only road into the Lónsöræfi reserve is

an arctic tern during nesting season

the F980, a rough gravel road off of Route 1 that ends after 25 kilometers at Illikambur. As it's only drivable for super jeeps (which are huge and outfitted for rugged terrain) and experienced drivers, please do not attempt to take a compact car or SUV on the trip. There is a river crossing along the way, and you will get stuck.

★ VATNAJÖKULL GLACIER

Vatnajökull (Water Glacier) is a cool spot to visit—quite literally, as it's Iceland's remaining piece of the last ice age. Vatnajökull features miles of white, pure ice, intertwined with blue and smoky hues in interesting shapes formed by compression. It's a wide-open space, sitting on top of active volcanoes. You will experience whipping winds, sky-high elevations, and cold temperatures.

Vatnajökull has the distinction of being the largest glacier in Europe and the third largest in the world (after glaciers in Greenland and Antarctica). It spans 8,805 square kilometers, which covers about 8 percent of the country, and the average thickness is 400 meters.

Of the volcanoes, the most active is the system near **Mount Grímsfjall** (1,719 meters) at **Grímsvötn** (1,725 meters). **Mount Barðarbunga** (2,009 meters), which awakened in 2014, is another volcanic fissure. **Mount Kverkfjöll** (1,929 meters) and **Mount Hvannadalshnjúkur** (2,110 meters) also lie beneath the glacier.

Vatnajökull's vast, rugged terrain is a large draw for hikers and climbers from around the world, but be sure you come prepared. Bring the necessary gear, monitor weather conditions, and alert people of your whereabouts.

Sports and Recreation

You can explore the glacier on a tour or with a private guide.

If you'd like to explore the glacier by snowmobile and jeep, **Vatnajökull Travel** (Bugðuleira 2, Höfn, tel. 354/894-1616, www.vatnajokull.is) offers tours all year. An 11-hour tour includes pickup at your hotel, jeep and snowmobile rides, and a boat ride on Jökulsárlón, which features large pieces of glacial ice that languish offshore. It's a spectacular sight. It's a fantastic way to spend the day and explore the region. The tour costs 45,000ISK.

Atlantsflug (tel. 354/854-4105, www.flightseeing.is) offers flights May-September from Skaftafell Airport, its private airport near Vatnajökull National Park, to various locations around Vatnajökull glacier, including Grímsvötn (volcano), Katla (volcano), Eyjafjallajökull (volcano), Langisjór (lake), Laki (crater), and Lakagigar (crater). You'll get a spectacular aerial view of volcanoes, mountains, glaciers, lakes, and rivers. Flight tours start at 40,500ISK for 45 minutes.

TOP EXPERIENCE

★ JÖKULSÁRLÓN

Jökulsárlón (Glacier Lagoon) is a spectacular sight that begs to be photographed. Chunks of ice are scattered about, walls of ice jut from the sea, and icebergs of various sizes float on the water. Huge blocks of ice constantly break off the Breiðamerkurjökull glacier into the lagoon which, though not very wide, is up to 250 meters deep—the deepest lake in Iceland—and then slowly move toward a river mouth and the Atlantic Ocean.

If you'd like a closer look at the icebergs, **Glacier Lagoon** (Jökulsárlón Ehf, tel. 354/478-2222, www.icelagoon.is, 9am-7pm daily June-Aug., 10am-5pm daily Apr.-May and Sept.-Oct., 4,000ISK) offers tours on amphibious boats April-October. During the excursion, you sail among the huge icebergs, get to taste the 1,000-year-old ice, and, if you're lucky, see seals bobbing in the lagoon. The tour lasts about 40 minutes and includes an English-speaking guide who explains the geology of the lagoon. Tours are weather-dependent, so be sure to call ahead.

You can also venture to the river mouth and nearby **Diamond Beach.** Chunks of ice sometimes wash ashore, and are scattered about like giant diamonds against a backdrop of black sand. The scene is spectacular any time of year, but truly magical when the sun is shining.

Jökulsárlón is a popular destination throughout the year, but it's quite crowded during the height of the summer season (July-Aug.). Even without a tour, plan to spend a couple of hours here to wander around and take in the beauty. It's close to Route 1, 80 kilometers west of Höfn and 377 kilometers east of Reykjavík.

TOP EXPERIENCE

★ SKAFTAFELL (VATNAJÖKULL NATIONAL PARK–SOUTH)

Skaftafell is one of East Iceland's most beautiful places, where visitors are treated to striking white glaciers against a backdrop of green fields and black sands. Skaftafell and Jökulsárgljúfur National Parks, along with Vatnajökull glacier, combined in 2008 to become Vatnajökull National Park. Skaftafell is the southern division of the park.

A common draw for many tourists is the black-sand beaches, which are a result of glaciers grinding down the bedrock. They're particularly striking on clear days with the snowcapped mountains and blue skies in the background. Much of the black sand is carried to the sea by glacial rivers, the waves and winds shaping the sand into complex formations. In the westernmost part of the Vatnajökull region is 1,000-square-kilometer **Skeiðarársandur,** which is the largest black glacier sand area in the world. It can be accessed by Route 1.

Tourism companies offer everything from ice walks to jeep tours. **Icelandic Mountain Guides** (tel. 354/587-9999, www.mountainguides.is) offers a year-round guided walking tour on the **Svínafellsjökull** glacier tongue in Skaftafell. The two-hour tour costs 11,900ISK.

Visitors Center

Whether you're just passing through, or planning a long hike, it makes sense to stop at the **Skaftafell visitors center** (Skaftafellsvegur, tel. 354/470-8300, www.vatnajokulsthjodgardur.is), which distributes maps and also has an exhibition on the geology and ecology found in the national park. The center is open 10am-4pm daily January, 10am-5pm daily February-April and October-November, 9am-7pm daily May-September, and 11am-5pm daily December.

Waterfalls

Hundafoss (Hound Falls) was named after the many dogs that were swept over the edge during floods. Be prepared to take a lot of pictures here. The falls are gorgeous in all seasons. In the summer, the rocky terrain behind the falls is surrounded by beautiful greenery. The drop is steep and the roar is soothing. **Þjófafoss** (Thieves' Falls) is a smaller waterfall set against a backdrop of lava fields. Ahead is the more spectacular **Svartifoss** (Black Falls) waterfall, where thundering white water cascades over striking black basalt rock columns. Svartifoss cannot be seen from the road, but it is just 1.5 kilometers from the Skaftafell visitors center, and the trail is clearly marked. The hike is easy, and it may be a surprise that you're going uphill; the view from above will alert you. The hike is about 90 minutes round-trip at a leisurely pace.

You can either return the same way or cross the river by Svartifoss and return from there. That route gives you a closer look at Þjófafoss.

Hiking from Núpsstaðarskógar to Skaftafell

Hiking from Núpsstaðarskógar, a valley rich with birch trees and rivers, to Skaftafell is an ideal five-day backpack that gives you a great slice of the beautiful east. The hike is a challenging one, clocking in at 60 kilometers (38 miles), and reaching an altitude of 800 meters (2,625 feet) with an ascent of 450 meters (1,475 feet). Most people start the hike at the bottom of the valley of Núpsstaðarskógar, and

Glacial Floods

When Grímsvötn volcano erupted underneath Vatnajökull in 1996, the world watched in fascination as lava flowed from fissures and ash launched thousands of feet into the air. But another phenomenon captured the attention of millions—***jökulhlaup,*** which is Icelandic for glacial floods. A glacial flood occurs when water dammed by a sub-glacial lake is released, triggered by volcanic eruptions. Glacial lakes can hold millions to hundreds of millions of cubic meters of water and can wreak havoc on surrounding areas when released.

Locals still talk about the 1996 eruption, and you have a chance to relive it through a film shown at the Skaftafell visitors center.

average 6-7 hours of walking a day. Along the way, hikers are rewarded with numerous waterfalls, steep canyons, a glacier lagoon, towering mountains, and a glorious birch forest. The hike is strenuous and only safe in the summer, but it's worth it. For those interested, **Icelandic Mountain Guides** (tel. 354/587-9999, www.mountainguides.is) offers a guided trek in July and August for 125,000ISK. The tour includes an experienced guide, transportation from and to Reykjavík, food for five days, and camping gear.

Food

If you're not bringing your own food (which is a huge mistake), your only close option is the restaurant at **Hótel Skaftafell** (Skaftafelli 2 Freysnesi, tel. 354/478-1945, www.hotelskaftafell.is, 8am-9pm daily), which serves traditional lamb and fish dishes as well as a few vegetarian options. The restaurant has a huge banquet room that tends to fill up with busloads of tourists.

Accommodations

Hótel Skaftafell (Skaftafelli 2 Freysnesi, tel. 354/478-1945, www.hotelskaftafell.is, rooms from 30,000ISK) is a 63-room hotel that looks a bit rustic, but it's comfortable and close to the national park. Rooms are standard with private bathrooms and classic countryside decor. A standard breakfast is included.

Hof 1 Hotel (Austurhus, tel. 354/478-2260, www.hof1.is, rooms from 26,000ISK) offers

Svartifoss

37 rooms and a few self-catered cottages. The ranch-style countryside hotel has spacious, surprisingly modern rooms, a friendly staff, and a great breakfast buffet included in the room price. The hotel is about a 15-minute drive from Skaftafell.

CAMPING

If you want to stay inside the park, the **Skaftafell Campground** (tel. 354/470-8300, May-Sept., 1,700ISK per night adults, 800ISK children 13-16, free for children under 12) is your only option. The campground is next to the entrance gate to the park; vehicle entry is allowed 7:30am-11pm. Visitors should register prior to camping. The facilities are great, but keep in mind that there is a distance between the facilities and where you set up camp. The campground offers hot showers and bathrooms (bring flip-flops; it can get pretty dirty during the height of camping season). Visitors can stock up on food and basic supplies at the visitors center, but it is advisable to bring what you need with you. The visitors center is also where you pay the camping fees. The open field accommodates about 400 tents, and there is a section for RVs with the option to pay for electricity.

Information and Services

The **national park office** (tel. 354/478-1627, 11am-4pm daily Jan.-Feb. and Nov.-Dec., 10am-5pm daily Mar.-Apr. and Oct., 8am-9pm daily June-Aug., 9am-7pm daily Sept.), which is near the entrance to the park, also serves as the visitors center. Here, you will find information, maps, and someone on hand to answer all your questions about the history and geology of the region.

Transportation

Skaftafell is on the Ring Road, Route 1, about 330 kilometers east of Reykjavík and 130 kilometers west of Höfn.

Strætó (tel. 354/540-2700, www.straeto.is) operates a daily bus (bus 51) from the Mjodd bus station in Reykjavík. The trip takes about five hours and costs 9,680ISK each way.

ÖRÆFI

Öræfi is farm country. Comprising about 24 farms, the region is known for livestock operations and overcoming harsh weather, fallout from volcanic eruptions, and glacial floods. The area is known as "the land between the sands" for its striking black-sand beaches, and its residents come from hardy stock, as it has never been an easy place to live or make a living. Thanks to the looming mountains and glaciers, locals are always reminded of the region's history, especially the 1362 eruption of **Öræfajökull,** which was one of the most destructive eruptions in Iceland's history thanks to devastating floods. The land was covered in ash, driving residents from their farms to rebuild and start anew. To give you an idea of the desolation of the area, the *öræfi* means "wasteland" in Icelandic.

Transportation

Öræfi is about 20 kilometers southeast of Skaftafell on Route 1.

The Highlands

Look for ★ to find recommended sights, activities, dining, and lodging.

Highlights

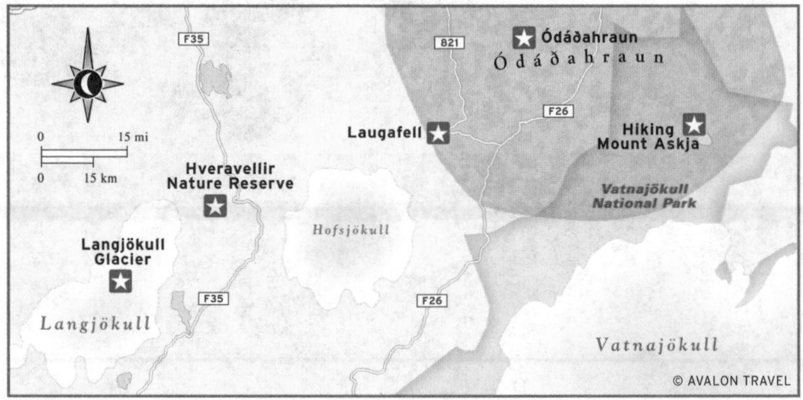

★ **Ódáðahraun:** See unusual lava and sand formations shaped by eruptions on the largest lava field in Iceland—which is actually considered an arctic desert. (page 240).

★ **Laugafell:** This popular geothermal hot spot is a desert oasis in an isolated stretch of the highlands (page 240).

★ **Hiking Mount Askja:** Hiking this volcano offers sensational views—and a can't-miss adventure (page 241).

★ **Langjökull Glacier:** Iceland's second-largest glacier, this mammoth ice cap beckons (page 244).

★ **Hveravellir Nature Reserve:** Soak in a hot spring and camp overnight in one of Europe's last great wilderness spots (page 245).

Iceland's uninhabited interior is home to an otherworldly landscape that must be seen to be believed.

It's full of dramatic and wild scenery, cut by endless wind and marked by vast expanses of ice and desert. It's the most distinctive and unforgiving landscape on the island, complete with lava and volcanoes. The country's largest glaciers—Vatnajökull, Langjökull, and Hofsjökull—form the region's backdrop.

The isolation seems romantic to some, especially travelers seeking an area relatively free of fellow tourists. But the highlands are not for those seeking lush greenery and gorgeous fjords in the background. Largely devoid of plant life, the highlands are essentially a desert, dry but starkly beautiful. If you are an avid hiker, are informed and prepared, and looking to explore something different in Iceland, this destination may be for you.

PLANNING YOUR TIME

Planning a trip to the highlands depends very much on what you want to see and do. If you want a peek at the interior without the burden of driving, take a day tour to see glaciers, volcanoes, and the landscape. Most companies offering tours to the highlands are based in Reykjavík. Other travelers like to plan five-day hikes throughout the interior. If you are keen on a lengthy hike, be sure to plan thoroughly, bring adequate gear and supplies, and take proper safety precautions.

Travelers have fewer choices for accommodations (mainly huts) and food, and they must stay abreast of the weather forecast every day. Be prepared for anything in the highlands, and make sure to book your accommodations ahead of time.

SAFETY

Navigating the highlands should not be taken lightly. The roads are rough, the wind punishing, and the weather can be unpredictable—it can snow any day of the year. Pay close attention to road closures, and if a road calls for a super jeep (a huge jeep with gigantic tires outfitted to handle rough terrain), don't attempt the ride in a smaller car; you will likely damage your vehicle. The best plan is to discuss your itinerary with the rental company and see if a super jeep is necessary. Do not guess; a mistake will be costly. Also, be mindful of filling up your tank before heading out, because there are no gas stations in the highlands.

Previous: a super jeep at Langjökull glacier; the volcanic landscape of the highlands. **Above:** flowers growing in Askja's lava field.

If you are planning a hike, be sure to wear appropriate windproof clothing, bring an adequate amount of water and food, and alert people of your trip itinerary. You can, and should, register your trip at www.safetravel.is. Bring maps and a GPS device and a compass, and know where all the emergency huts are located on your route. Be prepared for anything, and don't underestimate Iceland's weather; always check for weather alerts before setting off on any hike. If you find yourself in an emergency, dial the emergency number 112.

GETTING AROUND

The highlands are a seasonal destination, and that season is short. Snow could fall at any time of year. If you are planning a trip in the summer, there still might be road closures due to a late snowfall or possible volcanic activity. Roads to the interior are typically open June-August, but check for closures before you head out. For up-to-date conditions, visit the Icelandic Road and Coastal Administration website at www.road.is.

When it comes to car rentals, don't skimp on your vehicle choice if you are planning to drive to the region. You're required to drive an F-road-approved four-wheel-drive vehicle in the highlands, which have many unpaved roads and other challenges. A lot of different insurance options are offered on car rentals, and be mindful that Reykjavík driving is very different from driving in the highlands. There can be sandstorms and wind damage, so pick the right insurance for the region you plan to travel to. Fill up with gas before you leave and take gas cans.

TOURS

If you don't want to worry about renting a car and navigating the highlands on your own, tour companies offer everything from day trips to multiday tours. These companies are recommended.

Reykjavik Excursions (tel. 354/580-5400, www.re.is) offers a 12-hour day tour through Landmannalaugar in the highlands, and also includes sights such as Mount Hekla and Þjórsárdalur in the south. Tours run July 1-September 30 and are 19,900ISK per person. Guests are picked up in Reykjavík.

Extreme Iceland (tel. 354/588-1300, www.extremeiceland.is) is a Reykjavík-based company that operates a year-round two-day tour where you start off by exploring the Golden Circle (Þingvellir National Park, Geysir, and Gullfoss) and then continue to the geothermal area of Hveravellir in the Kjölur highlands. The tour (50,000ISK) includes hiking, sightseeing, and bathing in geothermal pools. Guests are picked up in Reykjavík. The company also runs an eight-hour tour November-April during which you can explore a manmade ice cave and go snowmobiling on Langjökull glacier (34,990ISK). Pickup is in Reykjavík.

Icelandic Mountain Guides (tel. 354/587-9999, www.mountainguides.is) runs a 10-day tour in July and August that hits all the hot spots in the highlands. Super jeeps will take you through the Kjölur and Sprengisandur routes, where you will see the Vatnajökull glacier, the Askja volcano, and the geothermal mountains of Kerlingarfjöll and Landmannalaugar. The package will run you 345,000ISK. Guests are picked up in Reykjavík.

The Highlands

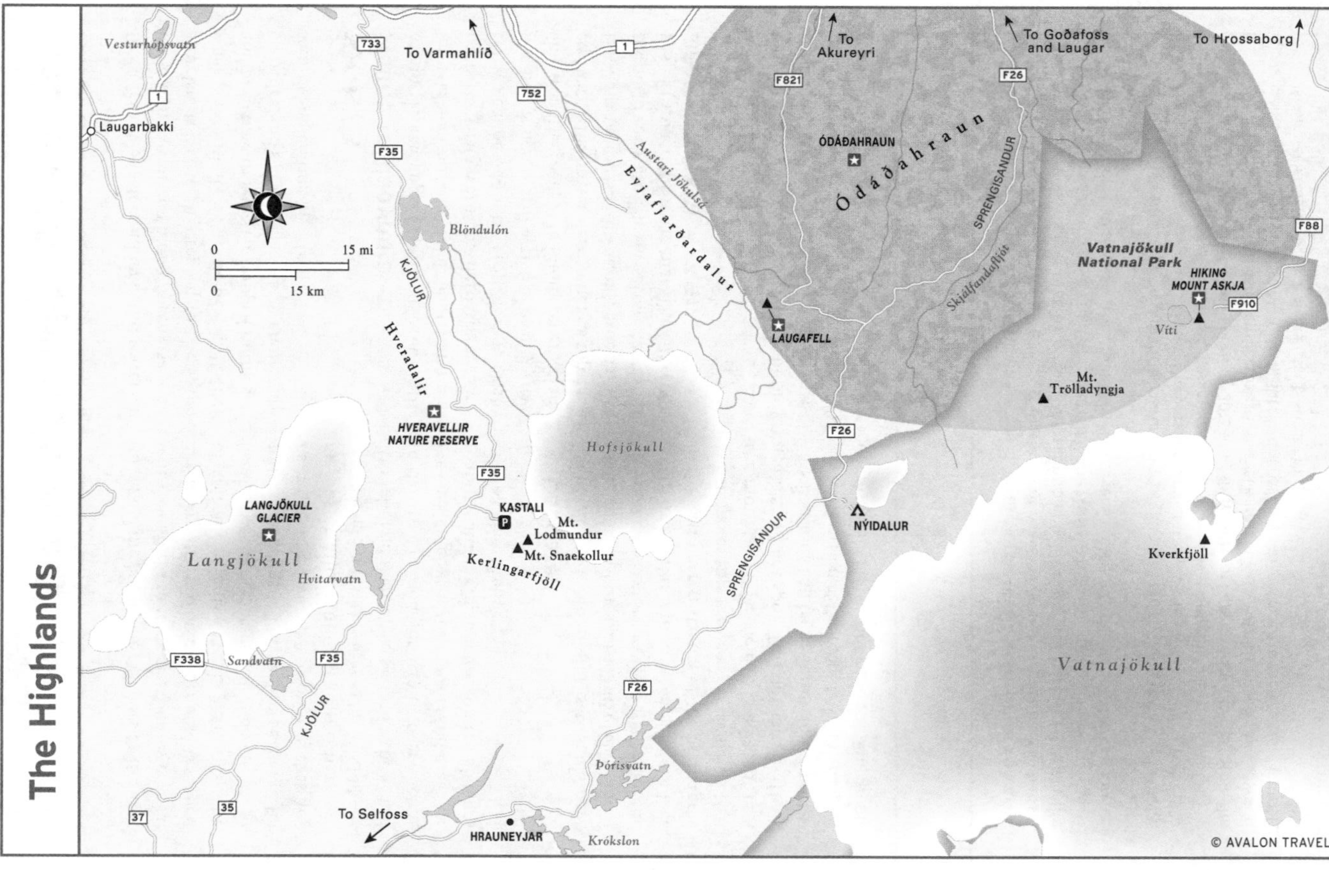

Route F26 (Sprengisandur)

Black lava, gigantic boulders, and towering mountains await you along Sprengisandur. Tourists travel to this region to check out what is essentially an arctic desert. It's dry and barren, with its water trapped in the glaciers. Iceland's summer is warm enough for significant melting.

SIGHTS

Mount Trölladyngja

Mount Trölladyngja (Troll's Volcano) is the largest shield volcano in the country and connects the Grimsvotn and Bárðarbunga central volcanoes. Mount Trölladyngja (1,468 meters), which is still active and only viewable from the road, is 10 kilometers in diameter with a 100-meter-deep crater on top. Lava flowed from it in all directions, especially to the north and west. The Gaesavotn Route F910 passes through the north of it. The GPS coordinates are N 64.8931, W 17.2547.

★ Ódáðahraun

Ódáðahraun (Crime Lava Field) is not only the largest lava field in Iceland, it's the largest desert in Europe, spanning more than 6,000 square kilometers. Black, brown, and gray dominate the landscape. Visitors to the area will see endless sand, vast expanses of lava, and interesting geological formations shaped by volcanic activity over the centuries. The lava shapes range from flat and smooth to rough and jagged. The region garnered its name, "crime lava," based on lore that numerous criminals hid out in the area trying to elude the authorities. The wind blows strongly, and there always seems to be a chill in the air. The isolation can be overwhelming—it's an eerie place to visit, and great for roaming and taking photos. Route F88 takes you to Ódáðahraun.

★ Laugafell

Laugafell (Bath Mountain) is situated near the northeast of the Hofsjökull glacier, about 20 kilometers southwest from the end of the Eyjafjarðardalur valley. It's a special place in the vast barren stretch of the highlands. What makes this area so spectacular is that the mountain (879 meters) is adjacent to a geothermal hot spot. Two hot springs (free), which visitors can bathe in, are in the northwestern portion of the mountain, and patches of grass and plants among the bubbling pools

Bárðarbunga Blows!

Iceland's most recent volcanic eruption began in August 2014 in the **Bárðarbunga volcanic system.** After a swarm of thousands of earthquakes over several weeks, the eruption began, emitting huge volumes of sulfur dioxide, impacting air quality in parts of Iceland, especially the east. The so-called fissure eruption occurred in the **Holuhraun** lava field, which is northeast of the Bárðarbunga caldera. Lava fountains shot several meters into the air from the crack in the earth.

The Holuhraun eruption did not occur underneath the ice cap, so there wasn't ash fallout. However, the airspace was closed three nautical miles around the eruption area up to 1,524 meters—meaning it did not affect commercial flights flying over Iceland.

The eruption ended in late February 2015 after six months of fiery lava shooting up from the earth. Locally, the event was referred to as a "tourist eruption," as tourists from around the world clamored to get a glimpse of the lava. But the only people allowed close to the site were journalists and scientists. Today, however, tours survey the area.

make it a desert oasis. Three mountain huts (rooms from 17,000ISK) are open during the summer; they have cooking facilities and guests can access a geothermal nature pool. Laugafell's GPS coordinates are N 65.0278, W 18.3319, and the region is accessible by Route F821.

Askja

Askja is a caldera in the surrounding Dyngjufjöll Mountains. Calderas are dramatic volcanic features that were formed by collapsing land after a volcanic eruption. They are essentially huge volcanic craters. The area is remote and awe-inspiring. Askja (1,510 meters) emerges from the Ódáðahraun lava field, and the terrain is quite rocky. **Víti** is a tremendous pale blue lake-filled crater that emerged after the great eruption of the Askja volcano in 1875. It's possible to take a dip in the water, which reaches a temperature of about 30°C (86°F).

Askja is one of the most popular destinations in the highlands. There are two mountain huts (the Dreki huts) on Route F88, about 100 kilometers from the Ring Road. From there, it's an eight-kilometer drive up into the Askja caldera. It is a walk of about 2.5 kilometers from the car park to Víti. Keep in mind that the roads are usually only open for about three months, from late June until September, depending on the weather. The open period could be longer or shorter.

Kverkfjöll

The Kverkfjöll volcano (1,764 meters) includes two calderas that are filled with ice. The area is striking for its range of colors. The deep black background gives way to gorgeous blues and icy white. The main event is ice caves that were created by hot springs slowly melting the ice into interesting shapes. However, please observe the caves from the outside; you never know when the ice mass could give way. Stay safe. The GPS coordinates for Kverkfjöll are N 64.7475, W 16.6315. To get to Kverkfjöll, take Route F910 southeast to Route F902.

SPORTS AND RECREATION

TOP EXPERIENCE

★ Hiking Mount Askja

Passionate hikers will want to walk the rim of Askja. It offers some slopes and ultra-rocky terrain along with spectacular views of lava fields, mountains, and the mighty Víti crater. It's about a 30-minute moderate

Sprengisandur's designated parking area

hike, 2.5 kilometers one-way, from the car park up to the caldera. The highest point in Askja is 1,516 meters. The rim is about 6.5 kilometers around, which takes about an hour to walk. If you are not planning to hike the rim, you can just explore near the car park. To reach the car park, take Route 1 to Route F88. The GPS coordinates are N 65.0140, W 16.4500.

While the trail is well maintained, the main challenge is weather. If the forecast calls for wind, it's best to skip the planned hike. Do not underestimate the power of Iceland's wind, especially in the highlands.

FOOD AND ACCOMMODATIONS

Make sure to book your accommodation ahead of time.

The Highland Center Hrauneyjar (Route F26, tel. 354/487-7782, www.thehighlandcenter.is, open year-round, 38,000ISK) offers 99 rooms ranging from doubles with shared bathroom facilities to double rooms with private bathrooms and free Wi-Fi. The GPS coordinates are N 64.1964, W 19.2655. Rooms are sparsely decorated with a bed, desk, and small table. It's not luxury, but it's the only option other than mountain huts. Along with the guesthouse, Hrauneyjar has a **restaurant** (7am-8pm daily) open year-round, a **gas station,** and a tourist shop that offers food, maps, and fishing permits. It's a good idea to stop here to pick up essentials (like food, water, and gas) even if you don't plan to stay at the guesthouse.

There are mountain huts along the valley **Nýidalur** (tel. 354/860-3334, www.fi.is) that sleep 79 people; the GPS coordinates are N 64.7355, W 18.0725. The area can be reached by Route F26. The huts have cooking facilities, toilets, and hot showers. It costs 8,000ISK per night to stay inside the huts, and it costs 2,000ISK for tent camping outside in an open field. The shower costs 500ISK to use. The huts are open July-August.

The **Laugafell huts** (tel. 354/462-2720, www.ffa.is) are located about 15 kilometers northeast of Hofsjökull glacier and 20 kilometers southwest from the end of the Eyjafjarðardalur valley; the GPS coordinates are N 65.0269, W 18.3321. The huts can be reached by Route F752 or F881 from Route F26 or by F821. The accommodations are basic, with gas available for cooking and restrooms near the swimming pool. It costs 8,000ISK to

the Víti crater

Navigating the Arctic Desert Safely

Safety needs to be your top priority. Every year tourists arrive in the highlands looking for a once-in-a-lifetime adventure but find themselves unprepared. Some tourists need to be rescued, and a few, unfortunately, don't make it out alive. Do not underestimate the weather in Iceland, even in the summer. Keep these things in mind—some may seem like common sense, but they're still important to note.

- Have an appropriate **rental car.** A **four-wheel drive approved for F roads** is required in the highlands, and if the trail calls for or a **super jeep,** take heed.
- **Have enough gas for your trip.** Gas stations are few and far between in the highlands.
- **Dress the part.** Make sure you have layers, warm clothing, and sturdy footwear.
- **Bring adequate food and water.** Don't count on buying food along the journey.
- Have **maps,** a **compass,** and a **charged mobile phone** on hand.
- If you find yourself in trouble, the **emergency number** in Iceland is **112.**

stay the night. The huts are open only during the summer.

The mountain huts closest to Askja are at Drekagil gorge. The **Dreki huts** (tel. 354/822-5190, www.ffa.is, www.nat.is) can be reached by Route F88 from the Ring Road east of Lake Mývatn or by Route F910 from Route F26; the GPS coordinates are N 65.0417, W 16.5948. There are two residential huts on the site that can accommodate 60 people. The huts have gas available for cooking and there are toilets and shower facilities. The Dreki huts are an ideal base for those interested in exploring the Askja caldera, which is an eight-kilometer drive from the huts. It costs 8,000ISK to stay the night. Showers cost an additional 500ISK. The huts are open only during the summer.

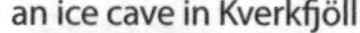
an ice cave in Kverkfjöll

TRANSPORTATION

Route F26 is not for the faint of heart. It cannot be emphasized enough that you must have a proper vehicle to navigate this road—an F-road-approved four-wheel drive. Weather is cruel to this road, and there are rivers to ford, large uneven sections, gravel, and potholes. The 200-kilometer route roams from Mount Hekla in the south to the glorious waterfall Goðafoss in the north. The route is not a year-round destination, and the road typically opens at the end of June. It could open later if the region had a particularly harsh winter with a lot of snowfall. To check road closures and the opening date, visit the **Icelandic Road and Coastal Administration** website (www.road.is).

Another important detail to keep in mind is that the only gas station along Route F26 is at Hrauneyjar. Be prepared and fill up before your journey. Also make sure you have all food, water, and supplies that you need.

To get to the region by bus, check out the schedule of **Reykjavik Excursions** (tel. 354/562-1011, www.re.is), which offers trips early July-late August. The 10-hour trip costs 8,400ISK each way and the tour departs from Reykjavík. You can purchase a bus pass that allows you to hop off and on the bus. It is necessary to book in advance.

Route F35 (Kjölur)

For a less treacherous route to the highlands, Route F35 is your best bet. The majority of the route is flat and can be accessible up until October (depending on the weather, of course). As elsewhere in the highlands, an F-road-approved four-wheel drive vehicle is required. Be safe, monitor weather reports, and be aware of road conditions.

SIGHTS

★ Langjökull Glacier

At 952 square kilometers, Langjökull (Long Glacier) is the second-largest ice cap in Iceland after Vatnajökull. Its volume is 195 cubic kilometers and the ice is quite thick, up to 580 meters deep. The highest point of the ice cap is about 1,450 meters above sea level.

Langjökull glacier

The rocky terrain and snowy patches are vast and haunting. Route F35 runs along the east side of Langjökull, between it and Hofsjökull. From Reykjavík, you head east on Route 1. Before you reach the town of Selfoss, take a left turn on F35 and continue past Gullfoss for about 37 kilometers.

★ Hveravellir Nature Reserve

Situated in the western highlands, the **Hveravellir Nature Reserve** (Route F35, tel. 354/452-4200, www.hveravellir.is) is one of the last great wilderness spots in Europe. It's about 90 kilometers north of Gullfoss on Route F35. Hveravellir is a natural geothermal hot spot with smoking fumaroles and bubbling water holes, and it's a special experience to see geothermal energy at work. There are private rooms in one of two huts (28,500ISK per room, linens and breakfast included), dormitories (7,500ISK pp), and a campsite (1,800ISK pp) available within the reserve. One bathing-friendly, waist-deep pool is situated close to the mountain huts, and it's a safe place to take a dip.

Kerlingarfjöll

The mountain range Kerlingarfjöll (Women's Mountains) shows all the characteristics of a matured caldera, including volcanic formations and geothermal hot spots. In short, this is a geology buff's dream. The towering peaks were created by eruptions from a large caldera lying under the mountains; while the caldera is still considered active, it has been silent for tens of thousands of years. Visitors will see steep slopes and pointy peaks dotted with ice, leading into a hotbed of geothermal activity. While the earth steams below, aboveground it's quiet and desolate. Accommodations are available at **Kerlingarfjöll** (tel. 354/664-7000, www.kerlingarfjoll.is), which has double (26,000ISK), triple (35,000ISK), and quadruple (41,000ISK) rooms, a campsite for tents (2,00ISK), and 10 cabins (54,000ISK). The breakfast buffet is 2,200ISK per person. To get to Kerlingarfjöll from Gullfoss, drive north on F35. For 15 kilometers the road is asphalt, and the remaining 38-kilometer section is gravel. The GPS coordinates are N 64.6834, W 19.2999.

Hofsjökull Glacier

Hofsjökull (Temple Glacier) is the third-largest glacier in Iceland after Vatnajökull and Langjökull. It is situated in the western highlands, north of the mountain range Kerlingarfjöll. The glacier covers an area of

Hveravellir Nature Reserve

925 square kilometers, reaching 1,765 meters at the top. It's vast and can be quite windy. Also, visitors will have to be careful of huge crevasses in the ice. The GPS coordinates are N 64.8167, W 18.8167.

SPORTS AND RECREATION

Hiking

Hikers have many choices for roaming the interior. These popular options vary in scenery and degree of difficulty.

TOP EXPERIENCE

HVERADALIR

Hiking the geothermal area Hveradalir (Hot Springs Valley) is wildly popular, and for good reason. The valley offers views of mountains, vast expanses of desert-like earth marked by steam vents (reminding visitors that the land is very much alive), and hot springs. Hveradalir is accessible off Route 1. The GPS coordinates are N 64.6453, W 19.2825.

A moderate hike begins at the car park by Neðri-Hveradalir (Lower Hveradalir) and takes you through the geothermal area Hveradalir, where ice and fire meet. The route is a three-kilometer loop and takes about three hours. Hikers will view the stark white glacial landscape and see the steam rise out of the ground near the numerous hot springs. Muted colors of brown and black in a desert-like landscape give way to pockets of stark white snow in some regions and lush green vegetation in others. Every few meters you'll want to stop and take in the views, and everything seems to warrant a photo.

For a longer, more demanding hike, start at the car park called Keis, toward the bottom of Hveradalir, where you follow the Ásgarðsá River for 4.5 kilometers. The hike is an 11.2-kilometer loop. Being so close to the river, you will see vegetation, which is a rare sight in much of the highlands. During the hike, there will be points where you have to cross water, so dress accordingly. Hikers will pass hills and geothermal hot spots as the river twists and turns. Overall, it's a five-hour hike and moderately difficult.

KERLINGARFJÖLL

For a more difficult walk, start at the car park called Kastali and continue to Mount Lodmundur (1,432 meters), then to the highest peak of Kerlingarfjöll, Mount Snaekollur (1,460 meters). The trail is rocky and there are quite a few slopes, but the payoff is the gorgeous views of the barren landscape below and

Hofsjökull glacier

mountains in the distance. It's one of the best overviews of the highlands. This is a seven-kilometer hike, in a loop, which takes about six hours.

TRANSPORTATION

The 200-kilometer Kjölur route (Route F35) begins near the picturesque waterfall Gullfoss in the south and extends to Blönduós in the northwest. This route is not a year-round destination: The road typically opens the middle of June, but it could be later if the winter was harsh. The road closes in September, but how early in September depends on the weather. You need an F-road-approved four-wheel-drive vehicle for the journey. Be sure to gas up before you head to the highlands, as there are no gas stations in the region. Depending on the duration of your trip, it might be necessary to bring gas cans.

SBA (tel. 354/550-0700, www.sba.is) operates summer buses between Akureyri in the north and Reykjavík along the Kjölur route. The 10-hour, one-way trip, which is only available late June through early September, costs 17,000ISK. You can purchase a bus pass that allows you to make stops along the route. Be sure to have a copy of the most recent bus schedule. It tends to change.

Background

The Landscape

GEOGRAPHY

Iceland is the westernmost European country, situated in the North Atlantic between North America and Europe. Iceland is east of Greenland and south of the Arctic Circle, atop the northern Mid-Atlantic Ridge. It lies 859 kilometers from Scotland and 4,200 kilometers from New York City. The area of Iceland is 103,022 square kilometers, and a frequent comparison among Icelandic tour guides is that Iceland is roughly the size of the U.S. state Kentucky.

Climate

Iceland isn't as cold as you may think. The Gulf Stream swirls along the western and southern coasts and works to moderate Iceland's climate. But "moderate" doesn't mean "calm," as the Gulf Stream is responsible for the frequent weather changes—as in lots of wind and rain. The biggest climate challenge is the unpredictability of it. The "summer" tourist season runs from the end of May to the beginning of September, and during that time, the climate ranges from rainy May days to the midnight sun in July to the possibility of snow in September. The winter climate brings colder temperatures, dark days, whipping winds, and the possibility of seeing northern lights flicker and dance on clear nights.

Weather

Weather in Iceland is not casual conversation, but serious business. Weather forecasts are frequent but largely hit or miss. The weather can change rapidly, from calm winds and sunny skies to rain, snow, sleet and back to calm wind and sunny skies, all in the same hour. It's unpredictable, frustrating, exhilarating, and confusing for many tourists, but Icelanders have learned to adapt and go with the flow. As a result, plans tend to be loose, whether it's for meeting friends for coffee or a going for a job interview. If the weather acts up, locals understand.

Some of the most extreme weather you could experience on this island is wind—the type of wind in winter that could knock you off your feet. If the weather forecast is showing strong winds, especially in the countryside, alter your plans accordingly. Do not underestimate the wind, and be sure to heed any storm advisories. Be safe, smart, and prepared. The changing conditions are part of the experience of traveling to Iceland, and the key is being prepared with layers of clothing, proper footwear, and waterproof outerwear.

Geology

Iceland is a volcanic island constantly in flux, with magma breaking through fissures and periodic eruptions that redesign the rocky landscape. Iceland's land is made up of igneous rock, most of which is basalt, which forms from cooling magma. Most of Iceland's mountains were formed with basalt that has been carved by water and ice erosion. Earthquakes are a common occurrence, but large tremors are rarely felt.

VOLCANOES

Volcanic eruptions are a growing source of tourism for the country. Local travel companies offer helicopter, jeep, and airplane tours when an eruption occurs. Most of Iceland's volcanic eruptions, such as the 2014-2015 Holuhraun eruption, are fissure vents, where lava seeps out of the cracks in the earth's

Previous: horses grazing in southern Iceland; Skógafoss.

crust. Holuhraun produced fountains of lava shooting out of the earth, delighting photographers and keeping volcanologists busy trying to determine if the nearby Bárðarbunga volcano would erupt. The three most active volcanoes on the island are Katla, Hekla, and Eyjafjallajökull. Eyjafjallajökull erupted in 2010, grounding air travel in Europe for days thanks to a large ash cloud.

Residents have learned to adapt to eruptions, and most volcanoes are away from residential areas. In the case of the 2014-2015 Holuhraun eruption, the region near Vatnajökull was evacuated of locals, and tourists and animals were moved from the area. There were no deaths or major injuries. The main threat was from toxins in the air, and those close to the region were asked to stay indoors and turn up their heating if they were sensitive to air quality.

Air

When there isn't an eruption, Iceland's air is some of the cleanest and purest you will experience, as pollution is low and the Gulf Stream produces a strong, steady wind that blows toxins away. The main source of pollution on the island is from industry, mainly aluminum smelters.

Water

Like the air, Iceland's water is perfectly pure. There's clean, tasty drinking water on tap and geothermally heated water that fills swimming pools and provides hot water in homes. Snow can fall in any month of the year, but large snowfalls are uncommon in the Reykjavík area, at least during the last couple of decades. Ice covers about 11 percent of the country, mostly in the form of Iceland's largest glaciers: Vatnajökull, Hofsjökull, Langjökull, and Mýrdalsjökull. Melting ice from the glaciers and snowmelt form the rivers.

Iceland's water is at the center of some of the country's tourist attractions. The manmade Blue Lagoon near Grindavík allows visitors to bathe in geothermally heated water, which soothes and heals the skin. Locals and tourists enjoy hot springs throughout the country, and spectacular waterfalls with roaring water tumble over basalt rock and earth. The largest and most visited waterfalls in Iceland are Gullfoss, Dettifoss, Goðafoss, and Skógafoss.

Northern Lights

The biggest winter attraction in Iceland is the aurora borealis (northern lights). People travel from around the world to catch a glimpse of

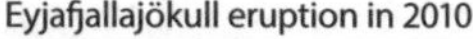
Eyjafjallajökull eruption in 2010

the green, white, blue, and red lights dancing in the night sky. There's something very special about bundling up in your warmest winter gear, trekking outside main towns to avoid bright lights, and hunting for the aurora borealis. The phenomenon is caused by solar winds, which push electronic particles to collide with molecules of atmospheric gases, causing an emission of bright light. The best time to see northern lights is from September to March, and there are forecasts predicting visibility on the **national weather website** (www.vedur.is). When the forecast is favorable, it's best to drive (or take a tour bus) to a dark area and look up. Northern lights tours are offered by **Reykjavík Excursions** (www.re.is).

PLANTS

Don't be fooled by photos of the vast, barren lava fields; there is in fact life thriving on Iceland's land. The most common plants in Iceland are the hundreds of species of moss found throughout the country, clinging to rocks, basalt columns, and the earth. It's common to find Icelandic moss, maritime sunburst lichen, dulse, rockweed, and several species of algae in Iceland.

Iceland has an abundance of rhubarb plants and bilberry shrubs (which Icelanders refer to as blueberries). Berry-picking season runs from late July to early August, but the season can be delayed if the winter was particularly bad.

As for flowers, the pale-pink glacier poppy is the country's national flower, and other common flowers are sea mayweed, alpine bartsia, meadow buttercup, and arctic poppy. Others include wood cranesbill, oysterplant, purple lupine, and bluegrass.

ANIMALS

Iceland may not be known for its land mammals—other than sheep, cows, horses, reindeer, and the arctic fox—but animals in the ocean and sky are varied and ample.

Fish

Fish are the lifeblood of Iceland: They sustain its inhabitants and serve as the country's biggest trade resource. In the waters surrounding Iceland, you will find cod, haddock, catfish, mussels, halibut, plaice, lumpfish, monkfish, skate, and Greenland shark. Native to Icelandic river waters are salmon, trout, and arctic char.

the northern lights above a lighthouse on the Reykjanes Peninsula

Seals

Several species of seals call Iceland home, with harbor seals and gray seals being the most common. There are seal-watching sites in the north of Iceland, and at Hvammstangi is a seal center that serves as a museum, information center, and seal-watching enterprise. Harbor seals are more common to spot because they spend more time on land, whereas gray seals prefer the ocean. Harp, ringed, hooded, and bearded seals are also spotted in Iceland, but seeing one is a long shot.

Whales

Whale-watching is a spectacular way to spend an afternoon in Iceland, and there are several species to see, depending on where in Iceland you set out on your excursion. High season for whales around Iceland is May to October, and 14 species of cetaceans have been seen off the coasts of the island. The species in Iceland are: blue, fin, minke, pilot, humpback, sei, orca, sperm, bottlenose, beluga, and narwhal whales, as well as white-beaked dolphins, white-sided dolphins, and harbor porpoises.

Birds

Bird-watchers are delighted when they visit, as there are more than 300 species of birds in Iceland. The island serves as a stopover for birds migrating between North America and Europe, and common species are ravens, eider ducks, arctic terns, Iceland gulls, white gulls, black-headed gulls, skuas, white-tailed eagles, gannets, fulmars, kittiwakes, and oystercatchers.

The bird that has become synonymous with Iceland is the adorable puffin, with its black and white body, bright orange feet, and colorful red, blue, and orange beak. Puffins are remarkable swimmers and divers, able to stay underwater for up to a minute and surface with as many as 10 small fish in their beaks. While exceptional in water, puffins are clumsy in flight and are known for their uneven landings on land. It's part of their charm. Millions of puffins call Iceland home, although their numbers have dwindled over the years. It's possible to see puffins during the summer in areas including the Westman Islands, Grímsey, and the Látrabjarg cliffs in the Westfjords.

a puffin in North Iceland

History

SETTLEMENT

Iceland has the distinction of being the last country in Europe to be settled. The country is known for impeccable record-keeping, and for that reason, it's known that the first permanent resident in Iceland was Ingólfur Arnarson, who built a farm in Reykjavík in the year 874. The earliest settlers were emigrants from Norway who opposed the king, Harald, due to a blood feud, and they wanted to make a new life in a new land. The Norwegians brought along their slaves from Ireland and Scotland, which means Icelanders are a blend of Norse and Celtic stock.

As word got out about the new land, within a few decades most of the coastline was claimed, with farms and fishing stations popping up. A government wasn't formed until 930, when the Alþing (parliament) was created, but in the meantime the new settlers determined that each farmstead should have a self-appointed chief. Once the Alþing was established in Þingvellir, a legislative body was elected.

CONVERSION TO CHRISTIANITY

Christianity came to Iceland, some say, by force. By the 10th century, the island faced mounting political pressure from the king of Norway to convert to Christianity or face the consequences, meaning war. As the end of the first millennium grew near, many prominent Icelanders had accepted the new faith.

By the year 1000, the Alþing was divided into two religious groups: modern Christians and pagans. The two groups were steadfast in their beliefs, and a civil war seemed likely. The law speaker, Þorgeir Þorkelsson, was called upon for a decision. (The law speaker was appointed to office and was required to recite the law during parliamentary meetings.) Þorgeir decided that Iceland would be a Christian country, but that pagans could still celebrate their rituals in the privacy of their farms. Þorgeir was baptized in Þingvellir, and Christianity became the law of the land. Christian churches were built, a bishop was established in 1056, and the majority of today's Icelanders are Christian.

DANISH RULE

Iceland remained under Norwegian kingship rule until 1380, when the death of Olav IV put an end to the Norwegian male royal line. Norway (and by extension, Iceland) became part of the Kalmar Union, along with Denmark and Sweden, with Denmark as the dominant nation. At this time, Iceland effectively became a colony of Denmark, with the king owning the land and the church's money. Iceland's government now answered to Denmark and did so for the next several hundred years.

Iceland was still very much centered on fishing and farming, and it was quite isolated from the dealings in mainland Europe. In 1602, the Danish government, which was pursuing mercantilist policies, ordered that Iceland was forbidden to trade with countries other than Denmark. The Danish trade monopoly would remain in effect until 1786.

INDEPENDENCE

Iceland began inching toward independence when it was granted a Minister of Icelandic Affairs in 1904, who would be based in Reykjavík. Hannes Hafstein was the first to serve in the minister position, and his place in Iceland's history is prominent. During this time, Iceland became more autonomous, building up Reykjavík's harbor, founding the University of Iceland, and eventually creating its own flag in 1915.

Over the next couple of decades, Iceland was taking more control of its affairs, and when World War II started, there was an economic opportunity for the island. Iceland was invited to join the Allied war effort by Great

Britain, but Iceland's government refused, declaring its neutrality. Britain pushed for Iceland's cooperation, but ultimately British naval forces arrived in Iceland, began building a base near Keflavík, and occupied the country for its proximity to North America. In all, 25,000 British soldiers occupied Iceland, which created a significant number of jobs for Icelanders. The British left in 1941, but more than 40,000 American troops replaced them, continuing the economic win for Iceland. There were jobs, opportunity, an American radio station, and lots of money flowing into the tiny island nation.

Denmark took a step back from Iceland's affairs during World War II, and Icelanders eventually held a referendum on its independence. Almost 99 percent of the population voted in the referendum, 97 percent of which voted for independence. On June 17, 1944, Iceland became totally independent of Denmark. American troops maintained the Keflavík NATO base until 2006.

stained glass window in Hallgrímskirkja

MODERN-DAY ICELAND

An independent Iceland plodded along, building up its fishing resources, investing in infrastructure, and looking toward the future. During years of rule by the center-right Independence Party, banks were deregulated in the early 2000s and Iceland's financial sector began taking off at a rapid pace. Iceland was being lauded for its financial acumen, but it all imploded in 2008, when the country's three major banks failed, sending Iceland into one of the deepest financial crises seen in modern Europe. Iceland is still rebuilding and recovering today.

One of the most divisive issues in Iceland has been whether to join the European Union (EU). Polls indicate that the majority of Icelanders are against joining, and the Independence/Progressive coalition that was elected in 2013 halted EU talks altogether. The debate continues as Icelanders demand a referendum on the matter, which was promised by the parties in power.

Iceland today is reaping the benefits of increased tourism. People from around the world have become aware of and infatuated with Iceland for its raw nature, volcanic eruptions, and culture.

Government and Economy

GOVERNMENT

Iceland's government dates back to the year 930, when the Alþing (parliament) was formed, but its constitution was signed on June 17, 1944, when Iceland achieved independence from Denmark. The Alþing, which consists of 63 seats, meets four days a week near Austurvöllur in the center of Reykjavík. Nine judges make up the High Court of Iceland and are appointed by the president. Iceland's president serves more of a ceremonial role, while the prime minister holds most of the executive powers. Other high-level cabinet positions are the Minister of Finance and Minister of Foreign Affairs.

Political Parties

Iceland's political parties number in double digits, with 12 parties running for seats in the 2016 election. However, in the Alþing, seven parties hold seats: Independence Party, Progressive Party, Social Democratic Alliance, Left-Green Movement, Bright Future, Pirate Party, and the Reform Party.

The Independence Party (Sjálfstæðisflokkurinn) is a center-right party that was formed in 1929 after a merger of the Conservative and Liberal parties. The current prime minister, Bjarni Benediktsson, a former lawyer, has served as leader of the party since 2009. The Independence Party was in power in the years leading up to the economic collapse of 2008. It was voted out of the majority in 2009 but regained seats, and power, in 2013. The Social Democratic Alliance, Bright Future, Left-Green Movement, and Pirate Party are the more liberal political parties on the island. Iceland's sitting president, Guðni Th. Jóhannesson, who took office in 2016, is a historian and former docent at the University of Iceland. Guðni is unaffiliated with any political party. He replaced Ólafur Ragnar Grímsson, who served five terms.

Defense

Iceland does not have a military, but it hosted British and American troops in Keflavík during and after World War II. American troops remained in Iceland, on the NATO base, until 2006, at the height of the U.S. military involvement in Iraq and Afghanistan. Iceland's Coast Guard oversees crisis management and protection along the coasts of Iceland and has been known to participate in daring rescues at sea. The Icelandic police force consists of fewer than 1,000 officers, who maintain the peace. The crime rate is exceptionally low in Iceland, and police officers do not carry handguns.

ECONOMY

Iceland's economy is best known to tourists for taking a dive during the 2008 financial crisis. The island has rebounded from the collapse, with tourism playing a significant role in this recovery, along with alternative energy.

Banking Crisis

In early 2008, Iceland's currency began floundering compared to the euro, and that was the first international signal that there was deep trouble lurking in Iceland's financial sector. By the autumn, all three of Iceland's major banks had failed, lifting the veil on Iceland's house of cards. Following the collapse, unemployment soared, pension funds shrank, and inflation skyrocketed to more than 70 percent. Loans taken out in foreign currency became unmanageable to thousands of Icelanders, credit lines were cut off, and capital controls were put in place that restricted how much money Icelanders could move out of the country. It was dire. The IMF made an emergency loan of $2.1 billion in November 2008.

Tourism

An increase in tourism helped Iceland recover from its 2008 economic collapse. In fact, tourism is now the country's second-biggest revenue source after fish. Tourism comprises 10 percent of Iceland's GDP, and it's estimated that more than two million tourists will visit Iceland in 2017. Most of Iceland's tourists come from the United States, Great Britain, the Nordic countries, Germany, France, and Switzerland. Tourism from Asian countries is also increasing. The issue going forward is how to keep tourism sustainable and protect Iceland's land from too much traffic.

Fishing

It's no secret that fish are the lifeblood of Iceland. They nourish its residents and are Iceland's number one export. Iceland's biggest trading partners are within the European Union, which is interesting because the reason to oppose joining the EU, for many, is for Iceland to maintain complete control of its fishing stock. Cod is the most common fish export.

Energy

One of the perks of living on a volcanic island is having a hotbed of geothermal energy. About 98 percent of the island's energy comes from geothermal and hydroelectric sources, which means low costs and low pollution. The pollution that does inhabit Iceland's airspace stems from an increasing number of aluminum smelters that have popped up in the last couple of decades. Foreign aluminum providers look to Iceland for its cheap energy and vast open land. The smelters do create jobs and revenue for the country, but it's a trade-off that many Icelanders remain unhappy about. As of this writing, Iceland was in talks with the United Kingdom on how to export geothermal energy there.

Currency

Iceland maintains its own currency, as it is not a member of the European Union. The Icelandic króna has a small circulation and is pegged to the euro. Following the financial crisis, inflation soared more than 70 percent, and Iceland's currency took a hit. The uncertainty was a maddening time for many Icelanders. Inflation is still high, and exchange rates rise and fall. Capital controls were created in 2008 that limit how much money Icelanders can move out of the country, but they started being lifted in 2017.

People and Culture

POPULATION

Nearly 340,000 people call Iceland home, and more than two-thirds live in the capital city, Reykjavík, and its suburbs. Outside of Reykjavík, Hafnarfjörður, and Kopavogur, the most populated towns in Iceland include Keflavík and Selfoss in the south, Akureyri in the north, Akranes and Borgarnes in the west, and Höfn and Egilsstaðir in the east. About 90 percent of the island population is composed of native Icelanders, but the foreign-born population continues to grow with the inflow of migrant workers and refugees. Iceland is as multicultural today as it has ever been.

Native Icelanders have a genetic makeup that combines Gaelic and Norse heritage, and many Icelanders consider themselves Nordic instead of Scandinavian. Social lives center on family, as Icelanders tend to be a close-knit bunch. People often either know one another or have friends in common.

LANGUAGE

The official language of Iceland is Icelandic, which is considered a Germanic language. Icelanders like to think of their language as poetic and musical, and maintaining their tongue is an important part of Icelandic culture. Most Icelanders speak English and are happy to converse with tourists in English, but they are proud of their mother tongue and enjoy when foreign tourists give the language a go, even just a few words. The closest language to Icelandic is Faroese, which roughly 50,000 people speak, and the other close language spoken by a larger group is Norwegian. Many Icelanders can understand Norwegian, Swedish, and Danish due to some similarities. Learning Icelandic is a challenge for many foreigners because of the complex grammar and accent.

Alphabet

The Icelandic alphabet has 32 letters, including letters not known in the English language, such as Ð and Þ. The letter Ð represents the sound "th" as in "this," while Þ represents "th" as in "thin."

ICELANDIC NAMES

Iceland has a strident naming committee that must approve names parents wish to give their newborns, in the spirit of maintaining Icelandic culture. For that reason, you will find a lot of common first names, including Bjorn, Jón, Ólafur, Guðmundur, and Magnús for males, and Guðrun, Sara, and Anna for females. Very few Icelanders have surnames; instead, Iceland follows a patronymic system in which children are given their father's first name followed by -son or -dottir. If a man named Einar has a son named Johannes and a daughter named Anna, their names will be Johannes Einarsson and Anna Einarsdottir.

RELIGION

Icelanders have an interesting relationship with religion. Most of the country identifies as Lutheran (about 70 percent), but most Icelanders aren't known to attend church regularly or be very vocal about their religious beliefs. While the majority of the country identifies as Christian, Iceland is considered a progressive nation. There is no separation of church and state in Iceland; the National Church of Iceland is subsidized by Icelanders through a church tax. However, non-Lutherans can choose to have their church tax donated to designated charities.

Of Iceland's religious minorities, Catholics are the largest group at about 4 percent, and there are about 1,000 Muslims estimated to call Iceland home, as well as about 100 Jews. There is not a single synagogue in Iceland, as the Jewish population has not requested one, but a mosque was approved by Reykjavík in 2014, and construction is ongoing as of 2017. The pagan Norse religion Ásatrúarfélagið has grown in membership in recent years to nearly 4,000.

According to legend, if you make a pyramid out of stones it will change into a troll and bring luck.

Best Festivals in Iceland

There's always something going on in Iceland—and whether it's the Viking Festival in June celebrating the country's roots, or the huge Iceland Airwaves music festival in the autumn, there's something for everyone.

FEBRUARY

Sónar Reykjavík (Reykjavík): This three-day music festival in mid-February features local and international rock, pop, and electronic bands.

Reykjavík Food & Fun Festival (Reykjavík): During this three-day festival at the end of February, world-renowned chefs occupy kitchens at trendy Reykjavík restaurants, using fresh local ingredients and lots of imagination.

MARCH

DesignMarch (HönnunarMars) (Reykjavík): Typically held in early March over four days, DesignMarch showcases the newest and best Icelandic design in pop-up shops, lectures, and fun events around the city.

APRIL

Reykjavík Blues Festival (Blúshátíð í Reykjavík) (Reykjavík): For a week in early April, blues music enthusiasts from around the world descend on Reykjavík for this annual festival that features international musicians and local artists.

AK-Extreme (Akureyri): Dedicated to winter extreme sports, AK-Extreme is an annual snowboard and music festival held in the northern city of Akureyri over four days in mid-April.

MAY

Reykjavík Arts Festival (Listahátíð í Reykjavík) (Reykjavík): For two weeks over late

FOLKLORE

Icelanders have a spiritual connection to nature, which has been depicted through literature, paintings, and stories about the *huldufólk* or "hidden people." It's easy to understand why stories of *huldufólk* are prevalent once you experience the otherworldly nature of Iceland, including northern lights, crazy rock formations, howling wind, and desolate lava fields where it feels that anything can happen. Many of the hidden people stories originate in the lava fields, where unexplained phenomena, like broken farm equipment, could be explained away by saying "it must be the *huldufólk*." Indeed, Iceland's hidden people live among the rocks, and certain rocks are deemed "*huldufólk* churches." It's easy to dismiss the idea of hidden people, especially when the term is loosely translated as elves, but many Icelanders are not willing to deny the existence of *huldufólk*. Does that mean that all Icelanders believe that elves physically walk among their human neighbors? Of course not. But it is part of their history and culture, and many Icelanders have a sense of humor about the foreign notion of *huldufólk*.

ARTS

Music

Music plays an important role in Icelandic society. There's still an emphasis on children learning to play instruments, and there are music schools around the country. It seems that everyone in Iceland is in at least one band. The earliest Icelandic music is called *rímur*, which is a sort of chanting style of singing that could include lyrics ranging from religious themes to descriptions of nature. Choirs are also very common in Iceland, and there are frequent performances in schools and

May and early June, Reykjavík is treated to exhibitions and outdoor installations of local and international artists.

JUNE

Viking Festival (Hafnarfjörður): Just outside Reykjavík, the annual Viking Festival in mid-June has fun reenactments of fights with traditional dress and weaponry, as well as food, music, and a market. The weeklong festival is great for kids.

AUGUST

Reykjavík Jazz Festival (Jazzhátíð Reykjavíkur) (Reykjavík): It may seem unexpected, but Icelanders have an affinity for jazz music, and they put on a great annual festival over five days in mid-August that features local and international musicians.

Culture Night (Menningarnótt) (Reykjavík): Held at the end of August, this daylong event is the biggest and most popular festival in Iceland, with more than 100,000 people participating. There's live music, food, and art to celebrate the end of the summer and Iceland's rich culture.

SEPTEMBER

Reykjavík International Film Festival (Reykjavík): Beginning at the end of September, this 11-day festival showcases short films, documentaries, and features from more than 40 countries.

NOVEMBER

Iceland Airwaves (Reykjavík): The largest music festival of the year hits Iceland in late October and early November. More than 200 local and international artists perform at the five-day festival, which has attracted bands including Kraftwerk, Flaming Lips, and local band Of Monsters and Men.

churches that are usually well attended by the community.

As for modern music, Iceland boasts quite a few acts that have gained a following abroad. Of course, there's Björk, who put Iceland on the musical map back in the 1980s with her band, the Sugarcubes, and later her solo career. Icelanders tend to be quite proud of Björk, as both an artist and an environmentalist. Sigur Rós became an indie favorite, and the band has been recording since 1994. Of Monsters and Men, Kaleo, Ólafur Arnalds, Amiina, Samaris, and GusGus are taking the world by storm. Reykjavík has cool venues in which to check out local bands and DJs, and some great record shops to pick up the newest and latest Icelandic releases.

Literature

Iceland has a rich literary history. The sagas, considered the best-known examples of Icelandic literature, are stories in prose describing events that took place in Iceland in the 10th and 11th centuries, during the so-called Saga Age. Focused on history, especially genealogical and family history, the sagas reflect the conflicts that arose within the societies of the second and third generations of Icelandic settlers. The authors of the sagas are unknown; *Egil's Saga* is believed to have been written by Snorri Sturluson, a 13th-century descendant of the saga's hero, but this remains uncertain. Widely read in school, the sagas are celebrated as an important part of Iceland's history.

Icelanders are voracious readers and love to write novels, prose, and poetry. The nation's most celebrated author is Halldór Laxness, who won a Nobel Prize for Literature in 1951 for his cherished novel

Independent People. His tales have been translated into several languages and center on themes near and dear to Icelanders—nature, love, travel, and adventure. Other authors who have been translated into English (and other languages) include Sjón, Arnaldur Indriðason, and Einar Már Guðmundsson, among scores of others.

Crafts (Knitting)

Icelanders have been knitting for centuries, and it remains a common hobby today. Icelandic sheep have been the source of wool that's been keeping Icelanders warm for generations, and a traditional, modern sweater design emerged in the 1950s or so in the form of the *lopapeysa*. A *lopapeysa* has a distinctive yoke design around the neck opening, and the sweater comes in a variety of colors, with the most common being brown, gray, black, and off-white. Icelanders knit with *lopi* yarn, which contains both hairs and fleece of Icelandic sheep. The yarn is not spun, making it more difficult to work with than spun yarn, but the texture and insulation are unmistakable.

Essentials

Transportation

GETTING THERE

Air

Keflavík International Airport (KEF, tel. 354/425-6000, www.kefairport.is), about 50 minutes west of Reykjavík, frequently gets kudos for being one of the best airports in Europe, and the plaudits are well deserved. Flying into Iceland is a pretty seamless experience. The country's main carrier, **Icelandair** (www.icelandair.com), serves more than 30 destinations in the United States, Canada, and Europe. Iceland's accessibility has been the country's main selling point as a travel destination because it is just five hours from New York City and about three hours from London. Icelandair cleverly introduced an option years ago that allows North American travelers going on to Europe to stop over in Iceland for no extra cost. You can spend a couple of days or more exploring Iceland, and then continue on to your destination in Europe. The summer season is obviously the most expensive, with round-trip tickets that could exceed $1,000 from North America. Icelandair offers great deals during the winter months, when you can grab a round-trip ticket for around $500. **WOW Air** (www.wowair.com) expanded to the U.S. market in 2016, offering low-cost flights to Iceland. In addition to Europe and Canada, the airline flies from Boston, Chicago, Cincinnati, Cleveland, Detroit, Los Angeles, Miami, New York, San Francisco, St. Louis, and Washington DC. One-way fares can be as cheap as $99.

Sea

For those traveling from mainland Europe, a ferry can be a great option, especially if you want to bring a car, camper, or bicycle for the trip. **Smyril Line** (www.smyril-line.fo) is a Faroese company that runs the ferry *Norröna*, which goes to Iceland from Denmark, Norway, and the Faroe Islands. The ferry drops you off in Seyðisfjörður, in East Iceland, which is convenient for those traveling with cars and who want to spend time in the countryside. But, if you want to stay in the south, where Reykjavík and Golden Circle attractions are, a ferry may not be the best option. The timetable tends to change frequently, so check the website for the latest information.

GETTING AROUND

Air

Iceland is surprisingly easy to get around by plane—if the weather is cooperating, that is. **Reykjavík City Airport** (tel. 354/569-4100, www.isavia.is) connects travelers to Akureyri, Egilsstaðir, Isafjörður, Vopnafjörður, Grímsey, and Þórshöfn. **Air Iceland Connect** (tel. 354/570-3000, www.airicelandconnect.com) and **Eagle Air** (tel. 354/562-4200, www.eagleair.is) fly year-round.

Car

Having access to a car gives you the ultimate freedom in seeing the island on your own schedule. However, if you plan to stay in Reykjavík for most of your trip or want to do short day trips in the southern or western parts of the country, it's not necessary to rent a car; you can book tours and travel by bus. But if you want a rental car and the freedom that comes with it, expect to pay dearly, especially in the summer months. Icelanders drive on the right side of the road.

ROAD CONDITIONS

Road conditions in Iceland can change quite quickly, as the weather is unpredictable. As a

Previous: a herd of sheep crossing the Ring Road in southern Iceland; traditional Icelandic sweaters for sale.

rule, always check road conditions before you head out on a trip. The best way to get information about road conditions and the weather is to call 1777 (or tel. 354/522-1100). The line is open 8am-4pm in the summer and 6:30am-10pm in the winter.

The **Ring Road (Route 1)** is the most accessible and popular route around Iceland. It runs 1,332 kilometers and connects many of the country's most popular tourist attractions. The Ring Road is paved for most of its length, but there are still stretches in East Iceland with an unpaved gravel surface.

F roads are unpaved tracks that may only be driven in vehicles with four-wheel drive. Some F roads have river crossings, so trying to navigate them with a compact car is dangerous. In recent years, the Icelandic government has made a commitment to improving some gravel roads. You can check on road conditions at **www.road.is.**

GPS NAVIGATION

GPS coordinates are a popular way to navigate Iceland. You can input coordinates into navigational apps or GPS units to obtain directions. However, it's important to keep in mind that sometimes roads are closed, so do some research on the route you plan to take, and don't just rely on the shortest-distance option. You don't want to wind up stranded. Carry physical maps in addition to a GPS device.

CAR RENTAL

Car rental prices remind you that you are very much on an island with very little price competition. In short, it's wildly expensive to rent a car (depending on the model of the car and season, it can be $200 per day with insurance) and pay for insurance, and gas prices are sky high (approximately $6.50 per gallon).

You can rent a car in advance or at the rental office at Keflavík International Airport, at BSÍ bus station, or within Reykjavík once you're settled. In the busy summer tourist season, it is recommended to arrange your rental in advance because some dealers sell out early.

Choosing the right car for your trip depends on what you want to see and where you plan to go. If you plan on staying close to Reykjavík and traveling on well-paved roads, such as the Ring Road, a compact car is the best and cheapest option. However, if you plan on going out to the countryside or to the highlands, don't try to get away with renting the cheap option. If you try to bring a compact car into a region that requires four-wheel drive, expect damage to the car at best, and being stranded and needing to be rescued at worst. Be smart and be prepared.

For insurance, car rental companies provide "full insurance" for each rental, which is the basic third-party insurance option. For an additional fee, drivers have access to "extra insurance" that includes a collision damage waiver. However, be aware that you will *not* be covered for damage caused by rocks, snow, wind, ice, and all the other elements that could damage a vehicle. If you have any damage to a car, you will be charged...*a lot.* Be sure to choose the right insurance for the region you plan to travel to. Gravel insurance is extra, and commonly purchased; if you're planning to travel on unpaved roads, it's recommended.

CAMPERVAN RENTAL

Traveling around Iceland by campervan is a popular option in season. This lets you explore at your own pace and frees you from worry over hotel reservations. However, there are important things to consider when traveling by campervan. Note that wild camping is strictly prohibited in Iceland and carries steep fines. Travelers must stay at campsites, where you will have access to facilities like toilets, showers, and cooking areas. Another important issue to consider is that traveling by campervan only makes sense during the summer months when campsites are open; many begin closing in early September. Additionally, campervans do not fare well in Iceland's windy winter conditions on icy roads. High winds can blow campervans off the road, leading to serious accidents. Be aware that campervan companies that rent during the winter months are trying to take advantage of tourists. Here are a couple of reputable options:

- **Happy Campers** (Stapabraut 21, Keflavik 260, tel. 354/578-7860, www.happycampers.is, from 30,000ISK/day for two including insurance)
- **CampEasy** (Smiðjuvegur 72, Kópavogur, tel. 354/571-1310, www.campeasy.com, from 28,000ISK/day for two including insurance)

RULES OF THE ROAD

Always drive with headlights on (day and night). Do not drive off-road (expect heavy fines). Always wear your seat belt, and watch out for sheep and birds in the countryside.

Do not drink and drive. The law forbids any driving under the influence of alcohol, and police aggressively monitor drunk driving.

Do not speed. Always remember that roads are unpredictable and car accidents involving foreign drivers are quite common. You can be traveling on a quiet, scenic paved road that suddenly turns into an unpaved, rough section. You can lose control of the car quite easily. The maximum speed limit for the entire island is 90 kph (55 mph), but in towns and residential areas, it can be much less. Always respect the limit. If you do speed and are caught by a police officer, expect a huge fine and a stern talking to. Don't risk it.

Monitor the weather forecast. Driving in Iceland can range from peaceful to harrowing, depending on the weather. To check road conditions, visit the **Icelandic Road and Coastal Administration** website (www.vegagerdin.is). If there is an advisory due to wind, rain, snow, or a volcanic eruption (it happens), stay off the road. Such advisories are to be taken seriously.

Bus

The bus system in Iceland is surprisingly adequate, especially in Reykjavík.

BSÍ (Vatnsmýrarvegi 10, tel. 354/580-5400, www.bsi.is) is the main bus station in Reykjavík and serves as the first destination for many visitors to the city, as BSÍ is the initial stop on the **Fly Bus** (tel. 354/580-5400, www.flybus.is) from Keflavík International Airport. One-way tickets on the Fly Bus cost 2,500ISK. (For an extra fee, the Fly Bus can connect to several locations in downtown Reykjavík close to hotels and guesthouses.) BSÍ also serves as a main departure site for many day-tour bus trips, such as those to the Blue Lagoon and Golden Circle, offered by companies such as **Reykjavík Excursions** (tel. 354/580-5400, www.re.is).

Strætó (tel. 354/540-2700, www.straeto.is) operates the city bus system in Reykjavík, with bright yellow buses running on numbered routes. The routes are quite comprehensive, linking downtown Reykjavík to outlying neighborhoods. Tourists can pay exact change for one-way trips (440ISK) or purchase a book of nine tickets for 3,000ISK. Hlemmur station is Strætó's central downtown bus station, where you can catch or connect to just about any bus line. Strætó's blue long-distance buses depart from Mjódd station, traveling to several regions around the country.

SBA-Norðurleið (tel. 354/550-0700, www.sba.is) is another bus company that offers day tours and bus service throughout the country.

There is a "bus passport" available through **Reykjavík Excursions** (tel. 354/580-5400, www.re.is) that allows unlimited travel on buses throughout the country for a specific period of time (7-15 days). The bus passport is available from June to September and starts at 65,000ISK. It's quite convenient for those traveling the Ring Road without a rental car, and many tourists love that it allows you to meet fellow travelers along the way.

Cycling

Cycling in Iceland is a favorite pastime among locals and tourists. While seeing Iceland by bicycle can be exhilarating and budget friendly, the downside is that the weather is unpredictable, even in the summer. There are summers that are relatively dry and sunny, but realistically, you need to be prepared for rain, and lots of it. Some cyclists are lured by gorgeous landscape photos and the thrill of long summer days, but are challenged by keeping themselves dry and motivated. Also, bike theft is rampant on the island, so you must be vigilant in keeping your bicycle and gear under lock and key. The plus side, however, is that you get to see the country powered by your own two feet, and you have the freedom to control how long you stay at sites without being tied to a tour bus. There are numerous well-kept bike paths throughout the country, and brochures with trail information are available at tourist information offices. The best advice is to plan, plan, and plan some more for challenging roads and unpredictable weather.

Hitchhiking

Hitchhiking is common practice, and legal, in Iceland, as it's a safe country with lots of drivers. If you are attempting to hitch along busier routes such as along the Reykjanes Peninsula, you will likely have more luck; however, in more remote destinations, it can be hit or miss. It's not advisable to be dependent on hitching in the winter months, because roads are less frequently traveled and the weather can be punishing. If you do score a ride, make sure you offer some cash for gas, as it's just good form.

Visas and Officialdom

VISAS AND PASSPORTS

Visitors to Iceland must have a valid passport that will not expire within three months of your scheduled departure. Tourists from the United States, Canada, Australia, and New Zealand do not need a visa if they are traveling to Iceland for fewer than 90 days. If you want to stay longer, you need to apply for a residence permit at the Icelandic immigration office (www.utl.is). For Europeans, Iceland is part of the Schengen Agreement, which allows free travel between Iceland and European Economic Area (EEA) and European Union (EU) countries; visas are not necessary.

EMBASSIES

Icelandic Embassies

Iceland has embassies in a number of countries, including:

- **Canada:** 360 Albert St., Suite 710, Ottawa, ON K1R 7X7, tel. 613/482-1944, www.iceland.is/ca
- **United Kingdom:** 2A Hans St, London SW1X 0JE, tel. 20/7259-3999, www.iceland.is/uk
- **United States:** 2900 K St. NW, Suite 509, Washington, DC 20007, tel. 202/265-6653, www.iceland.is/us

Foreign Embassies in Iceland

If you have an emergency while traveling in Iceland and require assistance (for example, if you lose your passport), contact your embassy for help. Embassies in Reykjavík include:

- **Canada:** Túngata 14, tel. 354/575-6500, rkjvk@international.gc.ca
- **United Kingdom:** Laufásvegur 31, tel. 354/550-5100, info@britishembassy.is
- **United States:** Laufásvegur 21, tel. 354/595-2200, reykjavikconsular@state.gov

CUSTOMS

Getting through customs in Iceland is quite easy compared to most other countries in Europe.

Travelers can import duty-free alcoholic beverages and tobacco products as follows: 1 liter of spirits, 1 liter of wine, and 1 carton or 250g of tobacco products; or 1 liter of spirits, 6 liters of beer, and 1 carton or 250g of tobacco products; or 1.5 liters of wine, 6 liters of beer, and 1 carton or 250g of tobacco products; or 3 liters wine and 1 carton or 250g of tobacco products. The minimum age for bringing alcoholic beverages into Iceland is 20 years; for tobacco, it's 18 years.

Iceland has a zero-tolerance policy on drugs, and all meat, raw-egg products, and unpasteurized dairy will be confiscated.

For additional information, visit the official customs website (www.tollur.is).

Recreation

Iceland truly is a nature buff's playground. There is much to do, and locals are thrilled to have you explore their treasured land—safely and responsibly. If you are heading out on a hike or a climb, report your whereabouts. Also, be sure to closely monitor weather conditions, bring all the water and gear you need with you, and be careful. Iceland's rescue team is often called upon to save unprepared tourists in completely avoidable situations. Have fun, but be safe.

HIKING

Hiking is by far the most popular outdoor activity on the island. There are stretches of land in the north, south, Reykjanes Peninsula, west, east, and interior that are begging to be explored. Hikers have their choice of terrain whether they're looking for vast lava fields, steep mountains, or enormous glaciers.

The key is to be well prepared, safe, and smart. Monitor weather conditions, have all the proper equipment with you, and alert authorities about your plans at **www.safetravel.is.** In case something happens during your trip, the search and rescue teams will know where to look for you. While hiking is a beautiful way to explore the island, most emergency calls to the rescue service are due to ill-prepared tourists finding themselves in a predicament on a hiking expedition gone wrong. It cannot be overstated that you must respect Iceland's raw and sometimes treacherous nature.

Detailed maps are available at regional tourist information offices as well as online at the **Ferðafélag Íslands (Icelandic Touring Association)** (www.fi.is).

FISHING

Fishing is how many Icelanders make their living, so who has fishing rights can be political. Your best bet is to sign up for a tour with a local operator who handles the necessary permit as well as bait and gear. A good place to start is through the tour operator **Iceland Fishing Guide** (www.icelandfishingguide.com), which offers fishing tours in Iceland's lakes, rivers, and streams. You have a chance at catching salmon, trout, and arctic char, depending on the tour location.

SWIMMING

Swimming is a big part of Icelandic culture. That may sound strange given the chilly temps compared to say, Spain or Florida, but an Icelander's local swimming pool is part of his or her social scene. If you visit a pool, you will notice groups of Icelanders, friends and family, sitting in hot tubs, sunrooms, or in the children's pool with their little ones. They love the water and they love to socialize. Pools are heated, and many have extensive facilities that include a gym, sauna, and several hot tubs. There are more than 120 swimming pools in Iceland, and they are well used, no matter the weather. Even outdoor pools can be full when there is a light snowfall.

The part about Iceland's swimming culture that frazzles some tourists is the communal showering that takes place before and after your swim. In the gender-divided locker rooms, you will see Icelanders showering stark naked—that's right, sans bathing suit—and you're expected to do the same. You must thoroughly clean yourself before you join the pool. At larger pools, there are often attendants who make sure that visitors shower. Locals are used to shy visitors and find it amusing, but at the end of the day, it just doesn't matter. After a couple of visits to the pool, you get used to it.

Towels and lockers are available at the local pools, and some rent out bathing suits as well. Some pools have fitness centers as well as an area to purchase soft drinks.

Food

TYPICAL FARE

The description of Icelandic food that you get depends on whom you ask, although it can't be disputed that fish and lamb take center stage. Typical fare can range from light to hearty. Local produce means what can survive outdoors (potatoes, rhubarb, moss) and what is grown in greenhouses (tomatoes, cucumbers, broccoli, etc.). Most of Iceland's food is imported, and it isn't cheap.

Local fish includes cod (fresh/salted), salmon, lobster, mussels, halibut, trout, and haddock. A classic Icelandic dish is whitefish cooked in a white sauce with potatoes and onions. A popular snack is hardfish, which is like a whitefish jerky, where the fish is dried and seasoned.

As for meat, lamb is the most prevalent, but there is plenty of beef, pork, and chicken in the Icelandic diet. Some Icelanders also indulge in horse and whale meat as well.

Hot dogs are wildly popular among Icelanders. Called ***pylsur,*** Icelandic hot dogs are done up in a traditional bun with chopped onions, mustard, ketchup, crispy fried onions, and pickled mayonnaise. They're delicious.

Dairy is an important part of Icelanders' diets, including milk, cheese, butter, and the yogurt-like soft cheese called ***skyr,*** which you should try. It's very tasty and chock-full of protein. Icelanders are also known to eat ice cream all year long, despite the weather. There are quite a few popular ice cream shops around Reykjavík, and the ice cream sections in supermarkets offer an astounding number of locally produced choices.

Once a year, Icelanders celebrate the traditional foods of the nation, which sustained their ancestors through the ages. The winter festival, called **Þorrablót,** features *svið* (singed lamb head), blood pudding, lamb intestines and stomach, ram's testicles, fermented shark, seal flippers, hardfish, and rye bread. The food that gets the most attention from foreigners is rotten shark or ***hákarl,*** which is meat from Greenland shark. The flesh is put through an interesting process, where it is buried for at least two months and then is hung for another three or four months to cure. If you dare, *hákarl* is available in small containers for sale. It is an experience you will not forget—if not the taste, then definitely the smell.

FINDING A RESTAURANT

Reykjavík is home to some excellent fine-dining establishments and casual eateries, but eating cheaply in Reykjavík, or on the island as a whole, is not easy. Hours tend to change depending on the season, but for the most part restaurants open their doors for lunch around 11:30am, and kitchens tend to close around 10pm.

Outside of Reykjavík and Akureyri, you will find a lot of fish and lamb restaurants that focus on local cuisine, but inside the two main cities, you have a lot to choose from. You will find sushi, tapas, Indian, hamburger joints, noodle bars, kebab houses, and Italian restaurants to name a few. International cuisine has been growing in popularity over the last 20 years, and new and interesting spots are always cropping up.

DRINKING

The water in Iceland is pure and some of the tastiest in the world. Drinking from the tap is common and safe, and bottled water is frowned upon. Iceland is also a coffee-drinking nation. If you're a tea drinker, you will find some basic choices in coffee shops, but Icelanders are crazy about their coffee.

As for alcohol, Icelanders do have a reputation for indulging, but given the expensive prices, beer is the drink of choice when going out to a bar. And, believe it or not, beer is still relatively new to Iceland. A countrywide alcohol ban went into effect in 1915; the ban was relaxed in phases, with first wine and then strong liquors permitted, and beer eventually became legal to sell in 1989. Outside of bars, alcohol is available only at the government-run shops called Vínbúðin.

Accommodations

HOTELS

Iceland is not known for posh hotels offering every luxury that you desire. However, there is a good mix of "upscale" accommodations, mid-level boutiques, and budget hotels. The "fanciest" options on the island are in Reykjavík, namely 101 Hotel and Hótel Borg, which cater to guests who are willing to pay for top-notch service and amenities. Reykjavík also has midrange boutique or family-run options if you are looking for something a bit more formal than a guesthouse.

Outside of Reykjavík, hotels tend to be of the local chain-hotel ilk in the form of **Fosshotels** (www.fosshotel.is), **Hótel Edda** (www.hoteledda.is), and **Icelandair Hótels** (www.icelandairhotels.is). They are clean, comfortable, and reliable options.

When they compare hotel prices to those in other European countries, some tourists feel that they don't get their money's worth. In fairness, Iceland is a more popular destination than it was 20 years ago, but it's still not meant to be a budget destination. In short, accommodations do cost a lot. Be prepared for slightly shocking rates, especially in the summer months.

GUESTHOUSES

The most prevalent form of accommodations on the island is the guesthouse setup. Guesthouses range from comfortable bed-and-breakfasts that offer shared bathrooms and cooking facilities to more design-conscious options that are chic, modern, and fun. Some guesthouses in Reykjavík can still have "hotel-like" prices, as the competition for scoring a room in the high season has become almost a contact sport. Outside Reykjavík, however, guesthouses could be a good way to save a little money, depending on where you book. Always book a room in advance, as it's not recommended to leave where you will lay your head to chance.

HOSTELS

Hostels are another great option for the budget traveler, but as in guesthouses, beds tend to fill up, so make sure you book far in advance, especially in the summer. Some hostels in Reykjavík, like Kex Hostel and Loft Hostel, cater to young, music-conscious travelers, and beds are almost an afterthought. There is frequently live music in the lounge areas, and the bar is always packed with locals and tourists. Other hostel options cater to a more mature crowd looking to avoid the high hotel rates. Hlemmur Square would be a good option for those travelers. Outside of Reykjavík, hostels are prevalent and it's key to book ahead.

SLEEPING BAG ACCOMMODATIONS

Some guesthouses and hostels around Iceland offer travelers sleeping bag accommodations, which can be great for the budget traveler. For a low price, guests are allowed to sleep in their sleeping bags and have access to shared bathroom facilities.

MOUNTAIN HUTS

Not to be confused with emergency huts, mountain huts are similar to cabin-style accommodation, with many providing a cozy, hostel-like atmosphere with bunk beds. Huts have running water, and there is usually a shared dining hall. As tourism in Iceland has increased, it has become necessary to book in advance to guarantee a place.

For more information, visit the website of **Icelandic Touring Association (Ferðafélag Íslands)** (www.fi.is), which runs several mountain huts around the country.

CAMPING

Camping can be a great option for some travelers, but be prepared. If you're going it alone with a tent, make sure you're ready for any type of weather—it can be unpredictable (even in summer), and you may be on the island during a good week, but maybe not.

There are campsites around the country that allow for tents as well as campers and caravans. Facilities vary; some campsites have top-notch cooking areas and steaming-hot showers, while others have adequate cooking facilities and just toilets.

Be advised that wild camping is strictly prohibited in Iceland, so travelers must stay in campsites. Those that break the law face steep fines.

Most campsites are open mid-May to mid-September. It's not necessary to book a site well in advance. To see a list of campsites, visit www.nat.is/camping/camping_sites.htm.

The main camping information centers in Iceland are:

- **Reykjavík:** info@visitreykjavik.is
- **Leifsstöð** (Keflavík Airport): touristinfo@reykjanesbaer.is
- **Reykjanesbær** (Southwest Iceland): Icelandreykjanes@reykjanesbaer.is
- **Borgarnes** (West Iceland): tourinfo@vesturland.is
- **Ísafjörður** (Westfjords): info@vestfirdir.is
- **Varmahlíð** (Northwest Iceland): upplysingar@skagafjordur.is
- **Akureyri** (North Iceland): tourinfo@est.is
- **Egilsstaðir** (East Iceland): info@east.is
- **Seyðisfjörður** (East Iceland): ferdamenning@sfk.is
- **Höfn** (Southeast Iceland): tourinfo@hornafjordur.is
- **Hveragerði** (South Iceland): tourinfo@hveragerdi.is

Travel Tips

WHAT TO PACK

How you pack depends on where you plan to go and what you're going to do on the island. If you're going for a "city-break" long weekend to Reykjavík, you can afford to pack light; however, if you plan on an extended stay that includes camping, packing light is not an option. Here are some suggestions and tips for your time in Iceland.

Clothing

The key to dressing warm and being comfortable in Iceland is layers. Depending on the weather, it can be cotton T-shirt, fleece or sweater, parka or windbreaker, and perhaps a hat, scarf, and gloves. If it's summer and the sun is shining, it's common to see locals wearing a T-shirt in 15°C (60°F) weather. It's important to keep comfortable and add layers if the temperature warrants it. If you're out hiking, wearing waterproof gear along with proper hiking attire is key. Make sure fabrics are breathable and comfortable and underlayers are cotton. Formal attire in Iceland is reserved for work or funerals, but if you want to bring a nice outfit along for a "fancy" dinner, by all means, pack something, but you won't find stringent dress codes anywhere on this island. Lastly, a bathing suit is necessary. Even if you think you won't take a dip in a pool or hot spring, the temptation might be too great. Pack at least one.

Outerwear

Because the temperature varies so much depending on time of day, season, and where you are in the country, it's a good idea to bring a hat, scarf, and gloves. As for jackets, the best advice is to bring something waterproof; whether it's a windbreaker for summer or a parka for winter, you are likely to encounter rain at some point on your trip. If you need to go shopping for warmer layers in Iceland, expect to pay. Clothes are not cheap in Iceland.

Footwear

Again, if you are staying in Reykjavík for the duration of your trip, and don't plan to climb mountains, you don't need to invest in an expensive pair of hiking boots. That said, if you do plan to be outdoors quite a bit, hiking boots are a great idea. You will need a pair of shoes that can withstand rain, rocks, ice, mud, puddles, sand, and sometimes snow. It's recommended to buy boots in your home country because shoes can be expensive in Iceland, and it's not the best idea to break in a brand-new pair of boots if you plan to do a lot of walking and/or climbing. Comfort is key. Socks are also important to consider. You want socks that are breathable yet thick enough to keep you comfortable in your shoes/boots.

Camping Gear

If camping is in your plan, don't scrimp on the quality of the tent you bring. And, make no mistake, you should bring the tent with you, as quality tents are, you guessed it, expensive in Iceland. You will need something waterproof that can endure punishing winds. A sleeping bag is necessary as well for campers. It's also great to have a sleeping bag on hand because some guesthouses and hostels still offer sleeping bag accommodations at a much lower price. Be sure to call ahead to see if they're available. Because of the likelihood of encountering rain, a sleeping bag made from a synthetic material is the best option, and it should be able to withstand -9°C (15°F) temperatures in the summer and -18°C (0°F) in the winter. If you decide to camp, be sure to monitor weather conditions and be safe.

Holidays in Iceland

Businesses in Iceland close on the following holidays:

- January 1: **New Year's Day**
- March or April: **Maundy Thursday**
- March or April: **Good Friday**
- March or April: **Easter Sunday**
- March or April: **Easter Monday**
- First Thursday after April 18: **First day of summer**
- May 1: **Labor Day**
- May or June: **Ascension Day**
- May or June: **Whitsun**
- May or June: **Whit Monday**
- June 17: **Icelandic National Day** (commemorates achieving independence from Denmark in 1944)
- First Monday in August: **Trading Day**
- December 24: **Christmas Eve**
- December 25: **Christmas Day**
- December 26: **Second day of Christmas**
- December 31: **New Year's Eve**

TIME ZONE

Iceland uses Greenwich mean time (GMT). However, the country does not observe daylight saving time, so Iceland is either four or five hours ahead of New York time, depending on the time of year.

As for the amount of daylight, what you've heard is true. The summers are full of long days, and darkness reigns supreme in the winter. To give you an idea of what that means, here are daylight hours for Reykjavík at different times of year:

- January 1: sunrise 11:20am, sunset 3:45pm
- April 1: sunrise 6:45am, sunset 8:20pm
- July 1: sunrise 3:05am, sunset midnight
- October 1: sunrise 7:30am, sunset 7pm

WEIGHTS AND MEASURES

Iceland uses the metric system. With regard to electricity, the standard voltage is 230 V and the standard frequency is 50 Hz. The power sockets that are used are type F, for plugs with two round pins. If you forget to bring an adapter, they can be purchased in most bookstores and tourist shops.

ACCESS FOR TRAVELERS WITH DISABILITIES

Iceland has taken great strides in making as many tourist-related sites as wheelchair friendly as possible. Visitors in wheelchairs will find that most museums, swimming pools, and restaurants provide access, as do transportation services. For instance, Keflavík International Airport and all domestic airlines can accommodate travelers in wheelchairs, and many buses come with automatic ramps to allow for easy boarding.

For more information on accessible travel, get in touch with the organization **Þekkingarmiðstöð Sjálfsbjargar** (tel. 354/550-0118, www.thekkingarmidstod.is). While the website is almost entirely in Icelandic only, information on traveling in Iceland has been translated into English (www.thekkingarmidstod.is/adgengi/accessible-tourism-in-iceland), and employees are happy to assist in English.

For information on services available to deaf travelers, contact the **Icelandic Association of the Deaf** (www.deaf.is), and for services for the sight-impaired, contact the **Icelandic Association of the Blind** (www.blind.is).

TRAVELING WITH CHILDREN

Children are the center of Icelandic society, and tourists traveling with children will feel right at home, whether in restaurants or museums or on child-appropriate tours. The island is a safe place for children, and many foreign travelers raise an eyebrow at how carefree parents can appear—whether it's a child walking around a shop, or an unaccompanied pram outside a coffeehouse. It's not irresponsible parenting, just a reflection on how safe a society Iceland is. While Iceland is safe, it needs to be said to always take care to watch out for the elements, whether it's high winds, a slippery surface, or cracks in a walking path.

As for attractions and restaurants, there are frequently child rates for museums and tours, and children's options on menus. Discounts can be as great as 50 percent for children under the age of 16.

WOMEN TRAVELING ALONE

Iceland is regularly ranked as being one of the best countries in the world in which to be a woman and a mother. Icelanders are proud to have elected the first woman president in the world as well as the first openly gay prime minister (a woman). However, Iceland is not a utopia. Women are subject to incidents of theft, intimidation, and physical violence. Always keep your wits about you, and if you are a victim of crime, contact the police at the emergency number 112.

GAY AND LESBIAN TRAVELERS

Iceland is a leader in equality, and Reykjavík is one of the most gay-friendly cities in Europe. What many travelers find refreshing is that there is not just tolerance for gay, lesbian, bisexual, and transgendered individuals, but overwhelming love and acceptance of their fellow Icelanders. For instance, the gay pride festival, **Reykjavík Pride,** which takes place every August, attracts approximately 100,000 participants, for a country of just 320,000 people. Think about that. As for laws, the LGBT community is protected from discrimination, gay marriage was legalized in 2010, and hate crimes are few and far between. For such a small population, it's hard to say there's a "gay scene," but there is one gay bar in Reykjavík, Kiki Queer Bar. More information can be found at the **Pink Iceland** website (www.pinkiceland.is).

Information and Services

TOURIST INFORMATION

Visit Iceland (www.visiticeland.com) is the main tourist information website for the country. The website has information on accommodations and activities for each region in Iceland.

MAPS

To properly navigate Iceland, you need maps. That's a given. Lucky for you, they are available all over the island. You can pick up all-inclusive maps for the entire island as well as regional maps, road maps, and hiking maps at tourist information centers, bookstores, and gas stations. If you have the chance to purchase maps before your trip, do so, as they will likely be a lot cheaper in your home country. However, if you plan to stay in Reykjavík for the duration of your trip, it's not necessary to buy a map because quite a few free maps do a nice job detailing downtown Reykjavík.

HEALTH AND SAFETY

Medical Services

The Icelandic health-care system is top-notch, with hospitals in each large town and health clinics in smaller villages and hamlets. Most doctors, nurses, and emergency medical staff speak English. Non-EU citizens must pay for health services provided. If you are having a medical emergency, dial the number 112. Pharmacies (called *apótek*) hold everything from prescription medication to aspirin. Some tourists from North America find it frustrating that cold medicine and aspirin cannot be bought in supermarkets, just at the pharmacy. Pharmacies are typically open 10am-9pm Monday-Friday, 10am-4pm Saturday, and are closed on Sunday and public holidays.

Weather

Weather is the number one safety concern in Iceland, trumping everything from violent crime to volcanic eruptions. The main danger is how fast weather can change. It could be a bright, sunny day when you head out on a trek in the highlands, but there could be a storm brewing that will bring high winds, rain, hail, and snow. And the storm could pass as quickly as it arrived. The joke among locals is that if you don't like the weather in Iceland, wait five minutes. The best defense against inclement weather is to closely monitor weather forecasts and obey advisories. You can check frequently updated forecasts at www.vedur.is. Icelanders deal with the weather by being flexible and never confirming plans far in advance. They learn to adapt after a lifetime of battling gale-force winds.

Temperatures in Iceland can vary, but on average Reykjavík's winter season is warmer than New York City's. That said, always dress for the environment and the activity you are about to embark on. If you are staying within Reykjavík's city limits, dress comfortably with layers and waterproof gear. If you're out in the countryside in the evening, have a hat, scarf, gloves, and warm gear at the ready. It can get chilly and hypothermia can set in quickly.

Emergency Huts

Iceland's emergency huts are strictly for emergencies. Don't even think of staying in one unless you are, in fact, experiencing an emergency. The huts are painted bright orange and are based in isolated areas. Inside the hut, you will find, water, food, bedding, and an emergency radio that will allow you to call for help. The huts can be located on maps, usually depicted as a red house. If you find yourself amid a storm, hunker down in an emergency hut and call for help by dialing the emergency number 112.

Crime

Crime is quite low in Iceland and is mostly limited to theft and vandalism; violent crime is rare. Be vigilant in protecting your possessions (especially bicycles) and trust your instincts. If you're out at night on Laugavegur in downtown Reykjavík on weekends, you might encounter loud and drunk locals or tourists. Don't engage with drunken people; continue about your business. If you are a victim of a crime, contact the police by dialing the emergency number, 112; all police officers are proficient in English.

MONEY

Iceland is not a cheap place to visit. Don't be fooled by the news stories that declared Iceland cut prices to accommodate tourists after its economic crisis of 2008. That period was brief, and Iceland remains an expensive destination. Prices on accommodations, food, gas, and everyday necessities remain high. Here is a list showing prices of common items.

- Milk (1 L): 149ISK
- Loaf of bread: 344ISK
- Dozen eggs: 623ISK
- Apples (1 kg): 323ISK
- Potatoes (1 kg): 278ISK
- Coke/Pepsi: 288ISK
- Meal for two: 12,000ISK
- Domestic beer: 1,100ISK
- Bottle of wine: 2,400ISK
- Pack of cigarettes: 1,300ISK
- Bus ticket (one-way): 440ISK
- Gasoline (1 L): 198ISK

Currency

The official currency of Iceland is the króna (abbreviated kr or ISK). The króna fluctuates often; at the time of writing, the exchange rate was 105ISK to US$1.

There are banknotes in the amount of 500, 1,000, 5,000, and 10,000 and coins in the amount of 1, 5, 10, 50, and 100 kronur. Coins are handy for having exact change for the bus.

Currency exchange is available at the airport and banks as well as tourist information offices. ATMs are available at all banks as well as supermarkets and other shops.

Banks

Banking hours are 9:15am-4pm Monday-Friday, and ATMs are available 24/7. There may be a limit on the amount of cash you can withdraw per your home bank's policy.

Credit Cards

Your best bet to get the most favorable exchange is to use your credit card. Cash overall is not a popular payment method; locals are known to use debit and credit cards for just about every transaction. Using plastic is so common in Iceland that many tourists will not need cash for anything; you can pay for parking, public toilets, and even campsite fees with a credit card. However, you may want to carry a little cash on you if you plan on tipping a guide for an excursion; guides will gladly accept any currency.

Tax-Free Shopping

As tourists encounter high prices for everything from accommodations to food, it only seems fair that you get a break when it comes to shopping.

A refund of local Value-Added Tax (VAT) is available to all visitors in Iceland. The refund will result in a reduction of up to 15 percent of the retail price, provided departure from Iceland is within three months after the date of purchase.

The fine print is that the refund does not apply to food or accommodations and the purchase must exceed 4,000ISK (VAT included) per store. Shops will provide you with a tax-free form (ask the store clerk for a "tax-free check"). Make sure you secure the forms and redeem the rebate at the cash-refund office at Keflavík Airport before your flight. There, you will get an immediate cash refund.

You can also submit the receipts and paperwork by mail for a rebate on your credit card. This, of course, can take considerably longer.

Tipping

Tipping is very new to Iceland. Workers in bars, restaurants, and hotels, as well as taxi drivers, earn a living wage and are not dependent on tips. In recent years, tip jars have cropped up in coffeehouses and bars, but it's just tourists who tend to tip.

COMMUNICATIONS AND MEDIA

Telephone

The country code for Iceland is 354. There are no area codes; if you are calling from within the country, just dial the seven-digit phone number and you will connect.

Icelanders love their mobile phones, and for that reason pay phones became obsolete several years ago. You can purchase international phone cards at local shops (called *sjoppas*) as well as at post offices and gas stations. SIM cards are also available from providers **Vodafone** (www.vodafone.is) and **Siminn** (www.siminn.is) and can be purchased from phone retail shops, gas stations, and the airport.

Cell phone coverage in the countryside is surprisingly strong.

Internet Access

Iceland is wired, with Wi-Fi hot spots all over the country. Hotels typically have free Wi-Fi, as do many coffeehouses.

Media

Given its small population, it's refreshing to see Iceland as such a die-hard newspaper town. Locals have several Icelandic-language print publications and websites to choose from, but publishers haven't forgotten about English-language readers. The ***Reykjavík Grapevine*** (www.grapevine.is) is the unofficial guide to music, museum exhibitions, restaurant reviews, and just about every cultural event in the city. The website is updated daily, and the free print edition comes out every two weeks in the summer and monthly in the winter. ***Iceland Review*** (www.icelandreview.com) is the main English-language glossy magazine on the island. You will find in-depth features on travel, culture, and business issues as well as gorgeous photography.

RUV (www.ruv.is) is Iceland's national public-service broadcasting organization, which consists of one television channel and two radio stations. RUV's television programs include news, dramas, and documentaries, as well as programming from foreign countries, including the United States, Denmark, and Sweden.

Resources

Glossary

austur: east
bær: farm
bíll: car
bíó: movie theater
bjarg: rock, cliff
dalur: valley
ey: island
fjall: mountain
fjörður: fjord
fljót: river
flugvöllur: airport
foss: waterfall
gata: street
geysir: erupting hot spring
gistiheimilið: guesthouse
herbergi: room
hestur: horse
höfn: harbor
hradbanki: ATM
hraun**:** lava field
huldufólk: hidden people
Ísland: Iceland
jökull: glacier
kirkja: church
kort: map
laug: swimming pool
lopapeysa: Icelandic knitted sweater
lundi: puffin
norður: north
safn: museum
sími: telephone
stræti: street
strætó: bus
suður: south
sumar: summer
tjörn: pond
torg: town square
vatn: water
vedur: weather
vestur: west
vetur: winter

Icelandic Phrasebook

Icelandic is not the easiest language to understand. It's a North Germanic language that is related to Norwegian, Danish, and Swedish, but it has the added difficulty of declensions that the other languages lack. Icelandic nouns are declined in four cases, which stumps many people. Fortunately, just about everyone in Iceland speaks English.

PRONUNCIATION

Pronunciation can be very tricky, but Icelanders are thrilled when tourists give their language a shot. Be warned, though; if you attempt to speak an Icelandic phrase, your accent will tell them you're a foreigner, and they most likely will answer you in English.

Vowels

Some vowels in Icelandic have accent marks that modify the sound of each vowel. Vowels can come in long or short forms. In Icelandic, all vowels can be long or short. Vowels are long when they are in single-syllable words or when they form the penultimate syllable in two-syllable words.

A a like the "a" in "land"
Á á like "ow" in "cow"
E e like the "e" in "set"
É é like "ye" in "yet"
I i like "i" in "sit"
Í í like "ee" in "feet"
O o like the "o" in "not"
Ó ó like the "o" in "flow"
U u like the "u" in "put"
Ú ú like the "oo" in "soon"
Y y like the "i" in "sit"
Ý ý like the "ee" in "feet"
Æ æ like the "i" in "file"
Ö ö like the "ur" in "lure"

Consonants

Ð ð like "th" in "this"
J j like "y" in "year"
R r rolled, like Spanish "r"
Þ þ like "th" in "that"

BASIC AND COURTEOUS EXPRESSIONS

Hello *Halló*
Good morning *Góðan dag*
Good evening *Gott kvold*
How are you? *Hvað segir þú?*
Very well, thank you *Mjog gott, takk fyrir*
Good *Allt gott*
Not OK, bad *Ekki okei*
So-so *Bara fint*
OK *Allt í lagí*
And you? *En þú?*
Thank you *Takk fyrir*
Goodbye *Bless*
Nice to see you *Gaman að sjo þig*
See you later *Sjamust*
Please *Takk*
Yes *Ja*
No *Nei*
I don't know. *Ég skil ekki.*
Just a moment. *Augnablik.*
Excuse me. *Afsakið.*
What is your name? *Hvað heiti þu?*
Do you speak English? *Talar þú ensku?*
I don't speak Icelandic well. *Ég tala ekki íslensku vel.*
I don't understand. *Ég skil ekki.*
How do you say ... in Icelandic? *Hvernig segir þú ... á íslensku?*
My name is ... . *Ég heiti ... .*
What's your name? *Hvað heitir þú?*

TERMS OF ADDRESS

I *ég*
you *þú*
he/him *hann*
she/her *hún*
we *við*
they *þeir*
girl *stelpa*
boy *strakur*
man *madur*
woman *kona*
wife *eiginkona*
husband *eiginmaður*
friend *vinur*
son *sonur*
daughter *dóttir*
brother *bróðir*
sister *systir*
father *pabbi*
mother *mamma*
grandfather *afi*
grandmother *amma*

FOOD

I'm hungry. *Ég er svangur.*
menu *matseðil*
May I have ...? *Get ég fengið ...?*
glass *glas*
fork *gaffall*
knife *hnifur*
spoon *skeið*
breakfast *morgunmatur*
lunch *hádegisverður*
dinner *kvöldmatur*
the check *reikninginn*

soda *gos*
coffee *kaffi*
tea *te*
water *vatn*
beer *bjór*
wine *vín*
white wine *hvítvín*
red wine *rauðvín*
milk *mjólk*
juice *safi*
cream *rjómi*
sugar *sykur*
eggs *eggjum*
cheese *osti*
yogurt *jógúrt*
almonds *möndlu*
cake *kaka*
bread *brauð*
butter *smjör*
salt *salt*
pepper *pipar*
garlic *hvítlaukur*
salad *salat*
vegetables *grænmeti*
carrot *gulrót*
corn *korn*
cucumber *agúrka*
lettuce *kál*
mushroom *sveppir*
onion *laukur*
potato *kartöflu*
spinach *spinat*
tomato *tómatar*
fruit *ávöxtum*
apple *epli*
orange *appelsína*
fish *fiski*
meat *kjöti*
lamb *lamb*
beef *nautakjöti*
chicken *kjúklingi*
pork *svínakjöt*
bacon *beikon*
ham *skinka*

ACCOMMODATIONS

hotel *hótel*
guesthouse *gistihúsið*
Is there a room? *Áttu laus herbergi?*
May I see the room first? *Má ég sjá herbergið fyrst?*
What is the rate? *Hvað kostar það?*
Is there something cheaper? *Ódýrara herbergi?*
single room *einsmanns herbergi*
double room *tveggjamanna herbergi*
bathroom *klósetti*
shower *sturtu*
towels *handklæði*
soap *sapa*
toilet paper *salernispappír*
sheets *rúmfötum*
key *lykill*
heater *hitari*
manager *framkvæmdastjóri*

SHOPPING

money *peningar*
What is the exchange rate? *Hvað er gengið á?*
Do you accept credit cards? *Tekur þú greiðslukort?*
How much does it cost? *Hvað kostar það?*
expensive *dýr*
cheap *ódýr*
more *meira*
less *minna*
a little *smá*
too much *of mikið*

HEALTH

Help me! *Hjálp!*
I am ill. *Ég er veikur.*
I need a doctor. *Ég þarf lækni.*
hospital *sjúkrahús*
pharmacy *apótek*
pain *verkir*
fever *hiti*
headache *höfuðverkur*
stomachache *magaverki*
burn *brunablettur*
cramp *krampa*
nausea *ógleði*
vomiting *uppköst*
antibiotic *sýklalyf*
pill *pilla*

aspirin *aspirín*
ointment *smyrsli*
cotton *bómull*
condoms *smokkur*
toothbrush *tannbursta*
toothpaste *tannkrem*
dentist *tannlæknir*

TRANSPORTATION

Where is the ...? *Hvar er ...?*
How do I get to ...? *Hvernig kemst ég til ...?*
the bus station *strætóstöðin*
the bus stop *strætóstopp*
Where is the bus going? *Hvert fer þessi strætó/rúta?*
taxi *taxi*
boat *bátur*
airport *flugvöllurinn*
I'd like a ticket to ... *Einn miða, aðra leiðina til ...*
round-trip to ... *Einn miða, báðar leiðir til ...*
Stop here. *Hætta hér.*
I want to rent a car. *Get ég leigt bil.*
entrance *inngangur*
exit *útgangur*
to the; toward the *til*
right *hægri*
left *vinstri*
straight ahead *beint áfram*
past the ... *framhjá ...*
before the ... *á undan ...*
opposite the ... *á móti ...*
Watch for the ... *Leita að ...*
intersection *gatnamót*
street *stræti*
north; south *norður; suður*
east; west *austur; vestur*

STREET SIGNS

Stop *Stans*
One Way *Einstefna*
Yield *Biðskylda*
No Parking *Engin Bílastæði*
Speed Limit *Hámarkshraði*

AT THE GAS STATION

gas station *bensínstöð*
gasoline (petrol) *bensín*
diesel *disel*
garage *verkstæði*
air *loft*
water *vatn*
oil change *olíu breyting*
tow truck *draga vörubíl*

VERBS

to buy *að kaupa*
to eat *að borða*
to climb *að klifra*
to do or make *að gera*
to go *að fara*
to love *að elska*
to want *að vilja*
to need *að þurfa*
to read *að lesa*
to write *að skrifa*
to stop *að hætta*
to arrive *til koma*
to stay *að vera*
to leave *að fara*
to look for *að leita*
to give *að gefa*
to carry *að bera*
to have *að hafa*

NUMBERS

zero *null*
one *einn*
two *tveir*
three *þrir*
four *fjorir*
five *fimm*
six *sex*
seven *sjo*
eight *atta*
nine *niu*
10 *tiu*
11 *ellefu*
12 *tólf*
13 *þrettán*
14 *fjórtán*
15 *fimmtán*
16 *sextán*
17 *sautján*
18 *átján*

19 *nítján*
20 *tuttugu*
21 *tuttugu og einn*
30 *prjatiu*
40 *fjorutiu*
50 *fimmtiu*
60 *sextiu*
70 *sjotiu*
80 *attatiu*
90 *niutiu*
100 *hundrað*
101 *hundrað og einn*
200 *tvö hundruð*
500 *fimm hundrað*
1,000 *þúsund*
100,000 *hundrað þúsund*
1,000,000 *milljón*

TIME

What time is it? *Hvað er klukkan?*
It's one o'clock. *Klukkan er eitt.*
morning *morgunn*
afternoon *eftir hádegi*
evening *kvöld*
night *nótt*
midnight *miðnætti*

DAYS AND MONTHS

Monday *mánudagur*
Tuesday *þriðjudagur*
Wednesday *miðvikudagur*
Thursday *fimmtudagur*
Friday *föstudagur*
Saturday *laugardagur*
Sunday *sunnudagur*
day *dagur*
today *i dag*
tomorrow *a morgun*
yesterday *í gær*
January *janúar*
February *febrúar*
March *mars*
April *april*
May *mai*
June *juni*
July *juli*
August *ágúst*
September *september*
October *október*
November *nóvember*
December *desember*
early *snemma*
late *seint*
later *seinna*
before *áður en*

Suggested Reading

Guðmundsson, Einar Már. *Angels of the Universe.* 1997. This is a startling tale of a young man struggling with mental illness, set in Iceland in the 1960s. The protagonist, Paul, retreats into his own fantasy world, while friends and family come along for the ride. The book is disturbing at times, funny at others, and almost impossible to put down. It was made into a film in 2000, which was wildly popular in Iceland.

Helgason, Hallgrímur. *101 Reykjavík.* 2007. The protagonist, Hlynur, is a lazy, unemployed twentysomething who lives with his mother, watches a lot of pornography, and hangs out in bars in downtown Reykjavík. His life takes a turn when a former girlfriend announces she is pregnant and Hlynur becomes obsessed with his mother's lesbian lover. It's a fun, unexpected tale that was made into a popular movie in Iceland.

Indriðason, Arnaldur. *Jar City.* 2006. Arnaldur is Iceland's leading mystery author. He pens about one book a year, which is great since his tales are so addicting. *Jar City* was the first of Arnaldur's books to feature detective Erlendur Sveinsson, who is a complicated man with a troubled relationship with his family and an obsession with solving

Reykjavík's violent crimes. Other characters include his partner, Sigurður Óli, and a female colleague, Elínborg.

Kellogg, Robert. *The Sagas of Icelanders.* 2001. This huge volume includes 10 sagas and 7 shorter tales that give a wonderful overview of Iceland's history and literature. If you're looking for a short introduction, this isn't it. It's comprehensive and glorious.

Laxness, Halldór. *Independent People.* 1946. Laxness remains Iceland's sole recipient of the Nobel Prize for Literature for his novel *Independent People.* The tale follows the life of a Bjartur, a sheep farmer, as he grapples with life, loss, and the sacrifices he made to achieve independence. If you're going to read one Icelandic novel, this should be it.

Internet Resources

Discover North Iceland
www.northiceland.is

This is the regional tourism guide for North Iceland, which includes information on towns including Akureyri, Mývatn, and Húsavík. You will find events listings, accommodations information, and a large list of tour operators.

Icelandic Tourist Board
www.visiticeland.com

Iceland's tourist board provides a website with pages and pages of information for travelers. The site offers information on festivals, shopping, national parks, and outdoor activities like hiking, bird-watching, whale-watching, and catching the northern lights in the wintertime. There's also information on accommodations, tour operators, and maps.

Iceland Review
www.icelandreview.com

Iceland's main English-language magazine provides features on everything from culture to travel to politics. The website underwent a revamp in 2014 and is worth checking out for in-depth articles as well as columns written by locals.

Reykjavík Grapevine
www.grapevine.is

Reykjavík's go-to English-language newspaper, which is published every two weeks in the summer and monthly in the winter, also maintains a website. You can bone up on local news as well as check out a listings section that details concerts, art exhibitions, and bars.

Visit East Iceland
www.east.is

Covering everywhere from Egilsstaðir to the Eastfjords, this tourism guide lists camping options, weather advisories, outdoor activities, and tour operators.

Visit South Iceland
www.south.is

Covering the south as well as the Reykjanes Peninsula, this tourism site offers detailed information on driving routes, maps, accommodations options, and tour operators. This region encompasses the Golden Circle as well as the Blue Lagoon.

Visit West Iceland
www.west.is

This is a regional tourism guide for the western section of the country, including Akranes, Borgarnes, Snæfellsnes, and the Westfjords. The site lists upcoming festivals and events, tour operators, and travel information for the region.

Index

A

B

C

D

E

F

G

H

I

JK

L

M

N

O

PQ

R

S

INDEX

T

UV

INDEX

WXYZ

Þ

List of Maps

Photo Credits

Title page photo: © Fyletto | Dreamstime.com

page 4 © rumandawi/123rf.com; page 5 © Gisbal | Dreamstime.com; page 6 (top left) © Bjorn Ludviksson, (top right) © Bjorn Ludviksson, (bottom) © Bjorn Ludviksson; page 7 (top) © Neurobite | Dreamstime.com, (bottom left) © Tatonka | Dreamstime.com, (bottom right) © Bjorn Ludviksson; page 8 © Wasin Pummarin/123rf.com; page 9 (top) © Corepics Vof | Dreamstime.com, (bottom left) © Kristi Mitsuda, (bottom right) © Jenna Gottlieb; page 10 © Biopixel | Dreamstime.com; page 12 (top) © Constantin Stanciu/123rf.com, (bottom) © Derwuth | Dreamstime.com; page 13 (top) © Svobodapavel | Dreamstime.com, (middle) © Alexeys | Dreamstime.com, (bottom) © Jenna Gottlieb; page 14 © Jenna Gottlieb; page 15 (top) © Leonid Andronov | Dreamstime, (middle) © Macsim | Dreamstime.com, (bottom) © Mathiasrhode | Dreamstime.com; page 17 © Filip Fuxa/123rf.com; page 19 © Bjorn Ludviksson; page 21 © Kbphotodesign | Dreamstime.com; page 22 © Dgmate | Dreamstime.com; page 24 © Jenna Gottlieb; page 25 © Paanna | Dreamstime.com; page 27 © Bjorn Ludviksson; page 30 (top) © Hannamariah | Dreamstime.com, (bottom) © Jenna Gottlieb; page 31 © Jenna Gottlieb; page 33 © Jenna Gottlieb; page 37 © Bjorn Ludviksson; page 40 © Bjorn Ludviksson; page 41 © Bjorn Ludviksson; page 42 © Jenna Gottlieb; page 43 © Jenna Gottlieb, *Sun Voyager* © Jón Gunnar Árnason/Myndstef; page 48 © Bjorn Ludviksson; page 52 © Bjorn Ludviksson; page 53 © Bjorn Ludviksson; page 54 © Bjorn Ludviksson; page 55 © Bjorn Ludviksson; page 56 © Bjorn Ludviksson; page 59 © Jenna Gottlieb; page 62 © Bjorn Ludviksson; page 63 © Jenna Gottlieb; page 66 © Bjorn Ludviksson; page 75 © Rudi1976 | Dreamstime.com; page 76 © Alaskagm | Dreamstime.com; page 78 (top) © Tomaz Kunst/123rf.com, (bottom) © Jenna Gottlieb; page 79 © Nazzu | Dreamstime.com; page 87 © Dgmate | Dreamstime.com; page 92 © Jenna Gottlieb; page 95 © Jenna Gottlieb; page 96 © Jenna Gottlieb; page 98 © Stacey Katz; page 102 © Jenna Gottlieb; page 104 © Derwuth | Dreamstime.com; page 106 © Stacey Katz; page 107 © Stacey Katz; page 109 © Sumos | Dreamstime.com; page 110 © Jenna Gottlieb; page 112 © Jenna Gottlieb; page 115 © Stacey Katz; page 117 (top) © Bjorn Ludviksson, (bottom) © Jenna Gottlieb; page 119 © Jenna Gottlieb; page 123 © Jenna Gottlieb; page 127 © Demerzel21 | Dreamstime.com; page 129 © Jenna Gottlieb; page 131 © Bjorn Ludviksson; page 136 © Stacey Katz; page 138 © Stacey Katz; page 140 © Jimmy Wallster/123rf.com; page 143 © Bjorn Ludviksson; page 148 © Stacey Katz; page 149 © Jenna Gottlieb; page 154 (top) © Stacey Katz, (bottom) © Parys | Dreamstime.com; page 155 © Neurobite | Dreamstime.com; page 158 © Santirf | Dreamstime.com; page 162 © Stacey Katz; page 163 © Parys | Dreamstime.com; page 166 © Rudolft | Dreamstime.com; page 173 © Rudolft | Dreamstime.com; page 175 © Deserttrends | Dreamstime.com; page 176 © Jarcosa | Dreamstime.com; page 178 © Jenna Gottlieb; page 179 © Jenna Gottlieb; page 182 © Jenna Gottlieb; page 187 © Dalish | Dreamstime.com; page 188 © Jenna Gottlieb; page 190 © Bjorn Ludvikssn; page 196 © Jenna Gottlieb; page 197 © Tatonka | Dreamstime.com; page 200 © Jenna Gottlieb; page 201 © Macsim | Dreamstime.com; page 203 (top) © Jenna Gottlieb, (bottom) © minnystock | Dreamstime.com; page 205 © Macsim | Dreamstime.com; page 211 © Yggdrasill33 | Dreamstime.com; page 215 © Jenna Gottlieb; page 216 © Sanspek | Dreamstime.com; page 221 © Stacey Katz; page 225 © Leospek | Dreamstime.com; page 229 © Bogdan | Dreamstime.com; page 230 © Bjorn Ludviksson; page 233 © Stacey Katz; page 235 (top) © Luciany | Dreamstime.com, (bottom) © Bjorn Ludviksson; page 237 © Daniloforcellini | Dreamstime.com; page 241 © 36clicks | Dreamstime.com; page 242 © Martinmolcan | Dreamstime.com; page 243 © Fyletto | Dreamstime.com; page 244 © Icerock | Dreamstime.com; page 245 © Icerock | Dreamstime.com; page 246 © Thelastcelt | Dreamstime.com; page 248 (top) © Kunthika Panyawuthikrai | Dreamstime.com, (bottom) © Annemiersch | Dreamstime.com; page 250 © Bjorn Ludviksson; page 251 © Sigurbjorn Ragnarsson | Dreamstime.com; page 252 © Bjorn Ludviksson; page 254 © Ronald Jansen | Dreamstime.com; page 257 © Konstantin Belov | Dreamstime.com; page 261 (top) © Alexeys | Dreamstime.com, (bottom) © Markechristian | Dreamstime.com

MAP SYMBOLS

- Expressway
- Primary Road
- Secondary Road
- Unpaved Road
- Feature Trail
- Other Trail
- Ferry
- Pedestrian Walkway
- Stairs
- City/Town
- State Capital
- National Capital
- Point of Interest
- Accommodation
- Restaurant/Bar
- Other Location
- Campground
- Airport
- Airfield
- Mountain
- Unique Natural Feature
- Waterfall
- Park
- Trailhead
- Skiing Area
- Golf Course
- Parking Area
- Archaeological Site
- Church
- Gas Station
- Glacier
- Mangrove
- Reef
- Swamp

CONVERSION TABLES

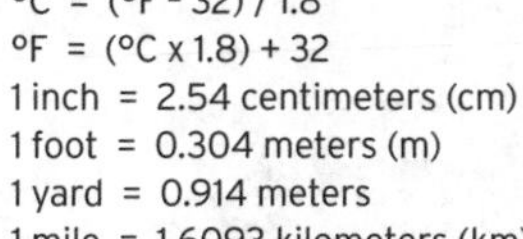

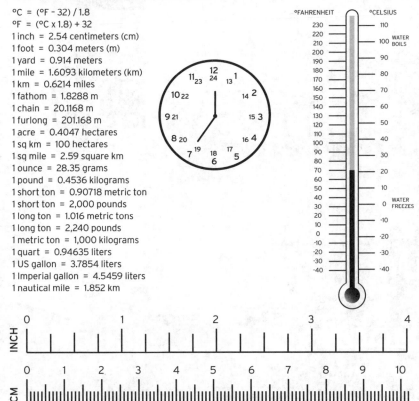

°C = (°F - 32) / 1.8
°F = (°C x 1.8) + 32
1 inch = 2.54 centimeters (cm)
1 foot = 0.304 meters (m)
1 yard = 0.914 meters
1 mile = 1.6093 kilometers (km)
1 km = 0.6214 miles
1 fathom = 1.8288 m
1 chain = 20.1168 m
1 furlong = 201.168 m
1 acre = 0.4047 hectares
1 sq km = 100 hectares
1 sq mile = 2.59 square km
1 ounce = 28.35 grams
1 pound = 0.4536 kilograms
1 short ton = 0.90718 metric ton
1 short ton = 2,000 pounds
1 long ton = 1.016 metric tons
1 long ton = 2,240 pounds
1 metric ton = 1,000 kilograms
1 quart = 0.94635 liters
1 US gallon = 3.7854 liters
1 Imperial gallon = 4.5459 liters
1 nautical mile = 1.852 km

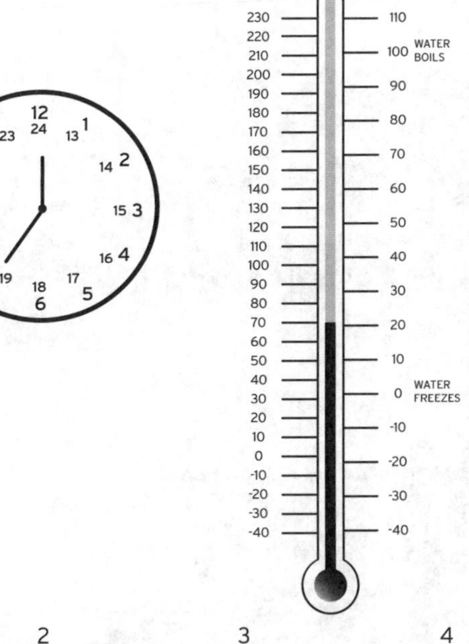

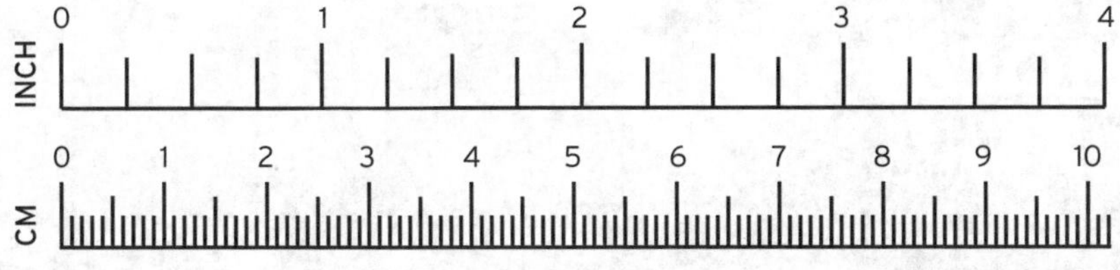

MOON ICELAND
Avalon Travel
Hachette Book Group
1700 Fourth Street
Berkeley, CA 94710, USA
www.moon.com

Editor: Kristi Mitsuda
Series Manager: Kathryn Ettinger
Copy Editor: Brett Keener
Production and Graphics Coordinator: Darren Alessi
Cover Design: Faceout Studios, Charles Brock
Interior Design: Domini Dragoone
Moon Logo: Tim McGrath
Map Editor: Kat Bennett
Cartographers: Lohnes+Wright, Brian Shotwell, Kat Bennett
Indexer: Rachel Kuhn

ISBN-13: 9781640494428

Printing History
1st Edition — 2016
2nd Edition — April 2018
5 4 3 2 1

Front cover photo: Svartifoss waterfall in Skaftafell © SIME / eStock Photo
Back cover photo: view across the scenic harbor of the North iceland town of Húsavík © Rhombur | Dreamstime.com

Printed in Canada by Friesens

Stunning Sights Around the World

Guides for Urban Adventure